THE REAL CAMPAIGN

How the Media
Missed the Story
of the 1980 Campaign

JEFF GREENFIELD

SUMMIT BOOKS
NEW YORK

10   9   8   7   6   5   4   3   2   1
First Edition

Library of Congress Cataloging in Publication Data

Greenfield, Jeff.
  The real campaign.

  Includes index.
  1. Presidents—United States—Election—1980.
2. Campaign debates—United States. I. Title.
JK526 1980.G73   324.9730926   82-3351
ISBN 0-671-41164-0   AACR2

Acknowledgments

The Real Campaign is not a collection of the most titillating gossip about the "media stars" of print and broadcasting. Nor is it a breathless account of the day-by-day efforts at media manipulation by political consultants who have elsewhere been described as "wizards," "czars," or "kingmakers." It is, rather, an attempt to examine the Presidential campaign of 1980 from the perspective of the public record; to assess how the urgent, day-to-day coverage by major print and broadcasting outlets revealed, or obscured, the political choice that was made on November 4, 1980.

My reliance, therefore, has been on what was said, in news accounts, columns, and broadcasts, about the 1980 campaign. Just as I believe the public record of candidates is often more revealing than the breathless "insider" accounts provided to the press during and after campaigns, so I believe that what was actually reported in the media is much more significant than the explanations, rationalizations, defenses, and apologies that are offered to those of us who have made something of a cottage industry out of covering the media as they cover an election.

Nonetheless, many reporters, columnists, and campaign aides were enormously helpful to me in fashioning this account; both through "formal" interviews, and in casual conversations during the campaign. Although I cannot possibly acknowledge each one who helped me—and many would no doubt prefer that I don't—I want to publicly thank some of them.

During the 1980 campaign, I was asked by CBS "Morning" to provide a running account of media issues as they arose in the campaign. Robert Northshield, senior executive producer of "Sunday Morning," first brought me to CBS as a media commentator. His encouragement, enthusiasm, and criticism—each generously and heartily offered—were of inestimable help. Elliott Bernstein, "Morning's" executive producer during most of 1980, was unfailingly helpful in suggesting areas of coverage. Producer John O'Regan spent endless hours helping this print-based novice come to grips with electronic technology.

At the conventions of 1980, Robert Chandler and Roger Coloff made the CBS analysis booth a second home during two hectic weeks. About my colleagues, Bill Moyers and James Jackson Kilpatrick, all I can say is that the often-heard observation of viewers—"you guys really liked each other!"—was one instance where the image and the reality were one.

At Summit Books, Jon Segal and Peggy Tsukahira provided editorial guidance and remarkable patience in the face of my stubborn refusal to adhere to deadlines. And without editor-in-chief Jim Silberman's enthusiasm for the project, *The Real Campaign* would not have been completed.

I owe my biggest debt to Sarah Turner: her research provided the backbone of this book. In a Presidential campaign, words pile up by the millions; her ability to find the most ephemeral quote, the most obscure fact, the most thorough compilation of the broadcast record was the key to getting this book done. My debt to Ms. Turner is immeasurable.

Finally, to Carrie Carmichael and Casey Carmichael Greenfield— my wife and daughter—a note of gratitude and apology. The 1980 campaign meant days away from home, nights buried in a study, and a media history that required work well into 1981. This book is theirs as much as it is mine.

For Janet, Lou, and Marc Elmo

Contents

i   The 1980 Election: Did the Media Make It Happen?

• It happened in the last week of January, just after the Iowa Republican caucuses had given George Bush an upset victory over Ronald Reagan. A CBS correspondent was chatting with former Texas Governor John Connally's news secretary when a Texas politician came up to them. Not recognizing the reporter, the pol anxiously asked the news secretary when the CBS survey would be taken. He explained that he'd brought 150 Texans to New Orleans on a free weekend so they could vote in the survey, thus creating a sense of momentum for Reagan. CBS was taking no such survey.

• It happened in October of 1979 as Florida Democrats were preparing for a statewide series of caucuses six months before the primary at which delegates to the Democratic convention would actually be selected. A "draft-Ted Kennedy" movement had publicly announced its intention to encourage straw votes for Kennedy as a way of demonstrating support for the senator. With Kennedy having all but formally announced his challenge to President Carter, both sides mounted huge "vote pull" operations, spending hundreds of thousands of dollars between them. And on Saturday night, the network news programs all led with front-rank political correspondents reporting to their viewers about an event which, they all explained, didn't mean a thing.

• It happened in November, 1979. Both Connally and President Carter's campaigns had prepared half-hour paid political messages with which to launch their campaigns. The networks, which had been covering every movement of major Presidential possibilities for more than a year, and which had devoted full field coverage to the "meaningless" Florida straw vote, refused to sell the time to Connally or Carter on the ground that the campaign hadn't started yet. "I thought if we could spend a million dollars on TV in the fall, we could cut into Ronald Reagan's lead," Connally commented. "We haven't been able to do that so I'm frustrated." The governor's fundamental political strategy was defeated, not by the public, but by the decision of the television networks.

• It happened in January, 1980. California Governor Jerry Brown, whose challenge to President Carter's renomination had been overshadowed by Kennedy's entry into the race, decided to bypass the Iowa caucuses in order to concentrate on New Hampshire. When the *Des Moines Register* announced its intention to sponsor a debate among Democratic candidates—a debate that would have received national television coverage—Brown was excluded on the ground that he was not campaigning in Iowa. Brown thereupon changed his mind and entered the Iowa campaign solely to be included in the debate. Carter's decision to withdraw from the debate and remain in the White House to supervise American policy toward the Iranian hostage seizure ended any chance Brown had of equaling or besting his better-known rivals.

• It happened at Washington National Press Club on January 27. Less than a week after the Iowa caucuses had given Jimmy Carter a two to one victory over Ted Kennedy, and George Bush a two-point upset victory over Ronald Reagan. Guests at a luncheon were asked who would be elected President in 1980: Carter got 197 votes, George Bush 65, and Ted Kennedy and John Connally 19 each. Ronald Reagan's total was too insignificant to report. Who, they were asked, would be the Republican nominee? George Bush, said 185 respondents. Twenty-nine chose Ronald Reagan, the same number as chose John Connally.

• It happened in July, at the Republican National Convention, on the Wednesday evening after Gerald Ford, in an interview with Walter Cronkite, strongly hinted that he was considering accepting a place on the ticket as Ronald Reagan's running mate. As Ford left the CBS anchor booth above Joe Louis arena, a swarm of reporters, photographers, and cameramen surrounded the former President. In the lead was a hysterical Barbara Walters; at the point of tears, she begged and pleaded with Ford over and over again to accompany her to ABC's booth for a separate interview. After several moments, Ford joined her and acknowledged on a second network the possibility of his running for vice-president. Some two hours later, Cronkite was reporting that the deal had been made, and that Ford and Reagan would come to the arena that night to appear before the delegates; that report was hitting the airwaves at about the time negotiations between the Reagan and Ford camps were breaking down.

• It happened that same night. When Reagan decided to choose George Bush as his running mate, operatives were sent streaming across the floor to pass the word to state leaders. NBC's Chris Wallace and CBS's Lesley Stahl both heard the news and scrambled for air time. Wallace's audio report was broadcast approximately thirty seconds before Stahl's video report. At the postsession grouping of NBC floor reporters, veteran correspondent Garrick Utley acknowledged Wallace, saying proudly, "The kid did it."

• It happened on September 19, two days before Reagan and independent candidate John Anderson met in debate in Baltimore—a debate President Carter refused to join, insisting that he would debate Anderson only after he had met Reagan one-on-one. ABC, which had chosen to run the hit movie *Midnight Express* instead of covering the debate, joined the other two networks in carrying Carter's press conference live; a conference that was kicked off when Carter read what amounted to a five-minute speech extolling his Administration. The Reagan campaign angrily demanded equal time, and critics pointed to the press conference as yet another example of the power of an incumbent President. As it turned out, virtually the entire conference was given over to sharp questioning of Carter about his charges against Ronald Reagan; and it kicked off the entire spate of "mean Jimmy Carter" stories that climaxed with Carter apologizing—not to the American people, but to Barbara Walters on the ABC evening news.

• It happened in August of 1980, when Ronald Reagan traveled to Dallas to address the public affairs briefing of the Religious Roundtable, a gathering at which many of the most prominent and well-financed conservative "electronic preachers" would appear. Reagan, asked about the movement by many conservative ministers to provide "equal time" for the creationist theory of human origin, replied that evolution was something less than a proven scientific fact. This was, the news stories had it, the most telling and damaging evidence yet that Reagan was ill-informed, a shoot-from-the-hip speaker likely to destroy his credibility with his off-the-cuff remarks. On Election Day, Reagan carried white Bible Belt districts overwhelmingly, and in the white South generally turnout was up—in sharp contrast to the national patterns.

• It happened in October, when independent John Anderson visited the *New York Times*. A former high school teacher of a part-time network commentator wrote him, angrily assailing Anderson's media advisor David Garth for destroying Anderson in New York State. How? By permitting him to be photographed in front of a painting in the *Times* offices featuring the face of Jesus Christ, thus insuring the loss of the Jewish vote.

The year 1980 was the one in which the American electorate, and the media itself, began to look at television and the press almost as intensely as they looked at the candidates and the election. Never before, it seemed, had so many reporters, correspondents, editors, executives, candidates, consultants, and just plain citizens been so conscious of the power of the press, and of television in particular. After twenty years of exposure to the fact that the impressions of candidates and campaigns could be as significant (if not more so) than the character and positions of the candidates, the 1980 campaign took place in an atmosphere that at times suggested a fun house mirror, with participants watching how they performed as they were performing. A generation ago, one imagines, a local pol might have rushed up to a candidate's advisor after a debate complaining about a misstatement of fact or the slighting of a constituency. Nineteen eighty was the year when a Baltimore Republican ran up to Reagan campaign manager William Casey and complained in agony, "My God, Bill—he was wearing *a white shirt!*"

And 1980 was also the year when many of the most treasured myths about the all-encompassing power of the media were buried under an avalanche of reality. From the primary season through the general election, the political events of 1980 were powered by factors far more fundamental and far more consequential than the images and daily data of television and the political press.

Without in any way debating the clearly *consequential* nature of mass media—to deliver information, impressions, and images about candidates and the country—1980 demonstrated clearly and convincingly that the shaping influences of American political life are still embedded in political realities that media coverage affects only marginally, *if at all*. To a remarkable extent, the successes and failures of candidates as they battled for the White House *cannot* be explained by how they were covered, by their commercials, by the efforts of their media advisors, or by the way in which network news and the major organs of the print press covered the campaigns.

Across the political spectrum, and up and down the list of "basic rules" of political media coverage, myth after myth was shattered by what happened in 1980:

• The early triumphs of a candidate are supposed to create irresistible momentum; but 1980 demonstrated that momentum means nothing if an opponent has a long-standing political base.

• Charisma is the key ingredient of the age of television; but 1980 demonstrated that a charismatic candidate who cannot explain what he means to do with the power of the Presidency faces an enormous obstacle.

• The gaffe and the blunder are, in a mass-media age, supposed to be fatal to a candidate's chances; but 1980 demonstrated that a candidate with a firm political base can commit at least as many disastrous gaffes and blunders as any other candidate and it will not matter at all.

• Television gives the President enormous power, as an incumbent, to shape the news and to command national attention; but 1980 demonstrated that a President whose underlying record is unappealing may actually hurt himself by commanding so much media attention.

• The dark skills of media manipulators are supposed to be able to bend the passive viewer's sense of reality; but 1980 demonstrated that some fundamental issues *cannot* be appreciably moved by image-making, and that image makers themselves risk great damage in attempting to move beyond what voters believe deeply to be real.

• Television is supposed to have ended the power of the political parties; but 1980 demonstrated that party financial, organizational, and ideological strength can still have an enormous impact over the results.

At root, the 1980 campaign was a demonstration of a thesis almost unspeakable in a time when American citizens have become aware of the capacity of television to influence the way they perceive the world, and when the "politics is all marketing" outlook has become a central conviction of politicians and journalists alike. "The media *is* the campaign," Theodore H. White wrote in *Life* magazine this year, and that view has come to dominate the way American politics is perceived.

But the thesis of this book is that *television and the media made almost no difference in the outcome of the 1980 Presidential campaign.* The victory of Ronald Reagan was a political victory, a party victory, a victory of more coherent—not necessarily correct, but more coherent—ideas, better expressed, more connected with the reality of their lives, as Americans saw it, than those of Reagan's principal opponent, a victory vastly aided by a better-funded, better-organized, more confident and united party.

Allied with this thesis is a second basic notion: the failure of the mainstream press, and especially television, to recognize the nature of this campaign stemmed in large measure from the media's fascination with itself as a political force, and from its fundamental view that politics is more image than substance; that ideas, policies, positions, and intentions are simply the wrappings in which a power struggle takes place. The failure to recognize the enduring political terrain of American politics by the media, and its obsession with the mechanics, both distorted the nature of the 1980 elections and deprived citizens of a sense of connection to the campaign.

Do these twin arguments mean the media was unfair or biased? No; a detailed look at press coverage suggests that the accusations of *ideological* bias are misplaced. Every major candidate was covered critically and admiringly; every one was the subject of adulation and attack depending upon the nature of his campaign. There were, to be sure, instances of unfairness toward different candidates at different times, but to confuse discrete instances with a general approach is a distortion. Yes, Ted Kennedy probably suffered the most from the media—an irony considering his long-standing reputation on the Right as the "liberal media darling"—but his troubles stemmed less from a bloodthirsty media and more from his own fundamental political failures, and from an accident of timing. Yes, John Anderson probably benefited the most from his media coverage, but his fate demonstrates how sharply limited the impact of media coverage can be, absent a more fundamental political strength.

It would take a book—this one—to explore the details of how media coverage provides less of a clue to the fortunes of candidates than other, more "prosaic" matters, such as a candidate's record. What needs to be understood at the outset is how the political community became so convinced that mass media—and television in particular—came to dominate the electoral process. As with most myths, it contains enough seeds of truth to seem highly plausible.

At regular intervals during the last two decades, politicians seemed to be using television to create new ways of reaching the electorate, surprising, and usually dismaying, those who practiced politics and those who wrote about it.

● In 1952, a besieged Republican Vice-Presidential candidate bought a half hour of television time to answer charges of malfeasance in office. From the perspective of twenty-eight years, and with the hindsight of the shabby end to his public life, Richard Nixon's "Checkers" speech seems a blend of the hilariously maudlin and the repellently insincere. But the speech was a stunning political triumph when it was delivered. The dollar-by-dollar recitation of income and expenses, the detailing of Senator Nixon's modest circumstances, and the relentlessly personal recounting of his fortunes triggered an outpouring of support for Nixon and almost certainly kept him from being bounced from the ticket. In that same election—the first in which television played a significant role—Eisenhower's campaign unveiled a series of sixty-second commercials. Run under the title, "The Man From Abilene," the ads, produced by Batten, Barton, Durstine & Osborn, used newsreel footage and an apocalyptic narration to introduce the larger-than-life war hero, following which Eisenhower "answered the nation" with three- or four-sentence answers to questions posed by an "ordinary citizen." This first use of spot advertising replaced the more traditional device of buying half-hour chunks of broadcast time.

● In 1960, the first debate between the two major party candidates for President produced what is now widely regarded as a major cosmetic triumph, when a tanned and assured Senator John Kennedy appeared more physically attractive than his nervous, tense, and lined rival, Vice-President Nixon. Volumes have since been devoted to the impact on the election of Nixon's makeup and shirt-collar size, the relative appearance of Nixon's face on black-and-white, as opposed to color cameras, and the surveys that suggested that those who heard the debate on radio believed Nixon had won, whereas those who saw the first debate believed Kennedy had won.

But well before the election, Kennedy had taken the lesson of

Richard Nixon's "Checkers" speech and extended it into a years-long demonstration of television's power to transmit personality. As early as 1953, the newly elected Massachusetts senator had invited the cameras of Edward R. Murrow's "Person to Person" into his home to meet his beautiful bride Jacqueline and to show off mementoes of his, and his dead brother Joe's, war heroism. The impact of Kennedy's personality was captured brilliantly in a novel by Ward Just called *A Family Trust*. In one scene, the members of an old Midwest Republican family watch Kennedy on a 1960 edition of "Person to Person." As moderator Charles Collingwood coos over the antics of little Caroline, the more political members of the family groan with frustration, while the younger members are dazzled by the quasi-royal family's personality.

• In 1964, a desultory Presidential campaign was enlivened by a controversial piece of advertising: a piece in which a little girl counts the petals on a daisy, then looks up as a doomsday voice counts down toward a nuclear explosion that fills the screen; then President Johnson tells us that "we must love one another or die" as an announcer urges a vote for Johnson because "the stakes are too high for you to stay home." The commercial never mentioned the name of Johnson's opponent, Barry Goldwater, and the ad ran exactly one time as an ad (although the furor over it caused it to be shown several times in the context of news). What the ad's creator, Tony Schwartz, had done was to demonstrate a power of television never applied to political commercials until then: the power to make implied arguments through the use of voice and image, without the need to argue those positions.

The commercial's effectiveness rested not on a series of premises leading to a conclusion; instead, it rested on the argument which had been raised all through the Republican nominating process, that Barry Goldwater's views on foreign policy and the use of nuclear power were too imprudent to put him into the White House. This argument had been made by Goldwater's two key opponents, first Nelson Rockefeller and then William Scranton, and was a key reason why a bloc of moderate and liberal Republicans had refused to support Goldwater, even after he had won the nomination. The "daisy" commercial used these facts to trigger these doubts among the ad's viewers without mentioning a single word about Goldwater's foreign policy, views on the deployment of nuclear weapons, or Goldwater himself.

• In 1968, two distinct controversies over television's use or misuse dominated the political atmosphere of that chaotic, violence-filled year. The coverage of the antiwar demonstrations at the Democratic Convention in Chicago raised new questions about media bias and selectivity. Chicago Mayor Richard Daley, among others, charged that TV coverage showed acts of police violence without showing provocations on the part of the demonstrators; later, it was found that, because of the delay in getting film on the air of some street confrontations, it appeared as if the police were assaulting demonstrators at the very moment Vice-President Hubert Humphrey was winning the Democratic Presidential nomination. Moreover, the networks ran some of the footage over and over again, giving an impression that there were many more acts of violence than was actually the case. In any event, the belief that television had overplayed and distorted the story helped to fuel the resentment over TV news coverage that would surface a year later in the celebrated attack on TV news by Vice-President Spiro Agnew, even though this distortion (if that be what it was) may have accounted for the election of the Republican ticket.

It was also in 1968 that criticism of the marketing approach to Presidential politics grew significantly. A young Philadelphia writer named Joe McGinnis gained entry into the inner circle of Richard Nixon's media advisors. In a celebrated best-seller, *The Selling of the President, 1968,* McGinnis detailed the cynical, manipulative approach to the use of television on Richard Nixon's behalf, and the tailoring of style and substance to fit research surveys that suggested the kind of President America wanted. It is probable that both McGinnis and the public drew the wrong lessons from Richard Nixon's 1968 media campaign. The most demonstrable result was that, with a fifteen-point lead after the two conventions, and with twice as much money for broadcast commercials as Hubert Humphrey, Richard Nixon's campaign managed to lose virtually all of that lead by Election Day, winning by barely 500,000 votes out of the 72,960,802 cast. But the lesson that was, in fact, drawn from McGinnis's account was that television had produced a new kind of politics, in which the packaging and marketing of candidates could overwhelm more traditional political devices.

• By 1976, the power of television to rewrite the rules of politics seemed to take on new force. An unknown former governor of Georgia, Jimmy Carter, had embarked on a four-year-long effort to win the Democratic nomination, guided by a memo from strategist Hamilton Jordan which subordinated programs and policies almost entirely to strategic calculations, in which the power of the press, and of television in particular, was emphasized. Especially significant was Jordan's assertion, drawn from the campaigns of 1968 and 1972, that victories very early in the nominating process would win a disproportionate share of media attention, and catapult any winner into sudden national prominence. Thus, the Iowa political caucuses, all but ignored in every other election, took on great importance as the political press looked for the earliest possible clues to the eventual winner of the nomination.

Jordan's view was prescient; as early as October 27 of 1975, *New York Times* reporter R. W. Apple, Jr., filed a story, based on a straw poll taken at an Iowa Democratic dinner, suggesting that Carter had unexpected strength in that state. The fact that Carter's supporters, knowing of Apple's intention, had packed the dinner did not detract from the fact that this was the first consequential national attention paid to Carter's campaign. And on the night of the caucus, Carter did not travel to Iowa. He was in New York, with ready access to the late-night specials and the next morning's network news shows, where his "victory" (he came in second to an uncommitted slate) put him into national attention and onto the covers of the national news magazines. A 5,000-vote plurality in New Hampshire against a field of divided liberals, with both of the better-known and politically potent possibilities, Hubert Humphrey and Ted Kennedy, on the sidelines, made Carter the front-runner, and from that position, despite the late challenge of California Governor Jerry Brown, he went on to win the nomination.

Moreover, the impact of television in the 1976 campaign was not confined to Carter's shrewd use of early victories to gain national recognition, nor to his uniquely personal campaign, which argued that after Watergate the key to an effective Presidency was a moral, personally humble, unpretentious President. It also marked the first time that an incumbent President had debated his rival; an event dictated by Gerald Ford's narrow nomination victory over Ronald Reagan and by Carter's underdog status as the general election campaign opened.

And here, as in 1968 and 1972, another apparent consequence of television's coverage emerged: the enormous significance of the gaffe, the blunder. Shortly before the opening of the 1968 campaign, Michigan Governor George Romney—considered a major contender for the nomination—observed on a Detroit interview show that he had been "brainwashed" on a trip to Vietnam. The wide dissemination of that quote effectively destroyed Romney's bid for the Republican nomination. In 1972, Senator Edmund Muskie denounced *New Hampshire Union-Leader* publisher William Loeb in front of the newspaper's offices; newsfilm caught the emotionally affected senator with what appeared to be tears on his cheeks. This incident was widely blamed for Muskie's "disappointing" showing in New Hampshire's primary, which he won with less than 50 percent of the vote, thus losing the sense of "momentum." And in the second 1976 debate, President Ford declared that Poland, among other East European nations, did not consider itself under Soviet domination. The storm of criticism—some of it bordering on ridicule—that greeted Ford's misstatement was the key impression left by that debate and stalled what had been a steady gain by the President in his catch-up campaign against Carter. The heavy political consequences of what was apparently a slip of the tongue pointed to television's capacity to turn a single statement into a matter of overwhelming weight.

However oversimplified the view that television has made the "gaffe" into an unprecedentedly influential matter,* that view helped to form a final part of a conventional wisdom about television's impact on the political process that had, by the 1980 election, become a starting point for analyses of how Presidential politics works. That conventional wisdom went something like this:

Largely through the influence of television, the American political landscape had been remade. The political parties had become irrelevant, as politicians made their appeals directly through the voters, in primary campaigns that took delegate selection out of the hands of the experienced party professionals and put it into the hands of the voters themselves. The older route to Presidential nominations, building political alliances with representatives from state and local party bases, has been jettisoned. Now the key is to attract national attention and enthusiasm through the press, and especially television, by winning, or by doing unexpectedly well, in very early primaries, caucuses, or unofficial preference polls.

This process has wreaked havoc on the political system. First, the demand for early success means that it is necessary to begin running for office years before the Presidential election is to take place. This has meant that qualified potential presidents who hold responsible office, and who cannot devote months on end to slogging through Iowa or New Hampshire, are virtually barred from campaigning effectively for the Presidency. By the time Senate minority leader Howard Baker, 1980s favorite moderate, credentialed candidate, really began running for the Republican Presidential nomination, he had been all but foreclosed as the moderate alternative to Ronald Reagan by the year-long head start of nonoffice-holding George Bush.

Second, it made the process interminably long, wearying the candidates and boring the American voter so thoroughly that by Election Day the turnout was inevitably lower than in the previous election. Illinois Congressman Philip Crane, the first candidate of either party to declare officially for the Presidency, announced his candidacy on August 2, 1978, *twenty-seven months* before the voters would choose a President. This, combined with the impotence of party officials to control large blocs of uncommitted delegates, made it impossible to wait until the nominating convention to choose a qualified candidate with broad party appeal; no candidate starting so late could possibly gather enough delegates to win.

* From the "Rum, Romanism, and Rebellion" quote, which sank James G. Blaine in 1884, to Charles Evans Hughes's accidental slighting of a political ally, which cost him California and the Presidency in 1916, to Thomas Dewey's flippant insult of a railroad engineer in 1948, the "blunder" has been a constant throughout modern politics, not an invention of the television age. I deal with this at some length in *Playing to Win* (Simon and Schuster, 1980).

Most serious, the charge went, was that television had gutted politics of any semblance of substance, turning the battle for the Presidency into a test of marketing: thirty-second television commercials devoid of subtlety but long on symbolism and flash; candidates crisscrossing the country to hit three or four media markets in key electoral states, offering dollops of rhetoric tailored for the evening news, dressing, speaking, thinking according to the dictates of media image makers and pollsters reading the pulse of the citizenry as a fever chart. In such a campaign environment, the candidate was a prescription drug, designed almost completely to alleviate the symptoms of unhappiness and discontent among the voters. The skills needed to be nominated and elected had become divorced from the skills needed to govern the nation effectively.

Throughout the 1980 campaign, this pessimistic—almost despairing—view of television was a dominant note in the coverage of the election, including coverage by the most prominent journalists themselves.

Wrote the *Washington Post*'s Haynes Johnson on September 21, 1980, "citizens now view the press with far more appreciation for its vital role in society than in the recent past. But, they say, at a time when they're looking toward the press for more serious information, the press is letting them down. And they are right. They expect better —and they're not getting it." Pulitzer-Prize journalist David Halberstam wrote in January, 1981, "In an important year when grave questions confronted the nation on how it would retool itself to face a changing world and deal with a changing economy, we had a trivial process trivially covered, a shallow campaign made even more shallow by the media's participation. . . . Much of the nation was frustrated with the campaign and the coverage of it."

Warned by *The Selling of the President* not to be taken in by media manipulation, the press put itself in the awkward position of analyzing attempts at such manipulation even in the process of covering an event. Thus, CBS's Lesley Stahl, at the White House celebration for the victorious U.S. Olympic hockey team, held the day before the New Hampshire primary, reported, "With the economy gloomy and the hostage situation in Teheran tenuous, what better for the President on the eve of the New Hampshire primary than to be seen on television surrounded by a group of young, happy and victorious American heroes?"

Thus the *New York Times* coverage of independent John Anderson's visit to Chicago just after the Reagan-Anderson debate, "Anderson aides had said they would try to build up big crowds today and tomorrow in an effort to make it appear that the debate had enhanced the candidate's support."

Media coverage itself became an increasingly familiar subject for exploration in the press, from academics, and even on television. The *Washington Post*'s Robert Kaiser did weekly reports on how the candidates were doing on TV and in the print press; Adam Clymer's pieces in the *New York Times* focused heavily on media coverage as a means of analyzing who had good and bad weeks during the campaign; NBC's Linda Ellerbee regularly explored the advertising strategies of the candidates; I appeared once a week on CBS "Morning" talking about the media and politics (although as the campaign progressed I found myself repeatedly arguing that media coverage was an inadequate explanation of campaign fortunes); at M.I.T., Ed Diamond headed the News Study Group, which developed content analyses of newspaper, magazine, and broadcast coverage; Michael Robinson's Media Analysis Project at George Washington University did the same.

But is the underlying premise of all this attention and self-examination correct? Given that media coverage of a Presidential campaign is a necessary aspect of campaign analysis, did the media, *in any sense,* determine the outcome of the 1980 election?

The central argument of this book is that the answer to this question is no. Rather, the 1980 campaign is a textbook illustration of what, in my view, is the fundamental misapprehension about the influence of the media, especially television, over the fortunes of political battles: if you try to understand politics by focusing on the media, you will miss the point. It is the equivalent of trying to plot the course of a star by looking through the wrong end of the telescope.

Rather, by looking beyond the scramble to dominate the headlines and the nightly network news programs, by looking beneath the tactical and strategic considerations of the candidates, we will discover that all through 1980—and indeed, for years before—*a real campaign* had been taking place. And it was this real campaign that accounted for the results of the 1980 battle.

The real campaign, which led to the election of Ronald Reagan and the Republican sweep of 1980 was a *political* election, even— within the limits of the American system—an ideological election. While no one fact explains the outcome, the central facts about the campaign—which were apparently so obvious that they could almost be discussed glancingly in the midst of the frantic chase after today's headlines—go a long way toward explaining the outcome, *even if it had taken place long before the invention of television.*

Among these central facts of the real campaign:

• An incumbent Democrat has never had to run for reelection in the middle of a recession, much less a recession in part deliberately triggered by policy decisions of his Administration and publicly welcomed as a cure for inflation.

• A party united behind a candidate and a fundamental policy stands a far better chance of winning than a party bitterly divided over who shall run for President and what his program shall be.

• In the years 1979 and 1980, the Republican Party fund-raising apparatuses for congressional, senatorial and national campaigns raised more than $100 million, using the most sophisticated techniques of direct-mail and computer-organized fund raising. In those same two years, the equivalent Democratic committees, at a time when that party controlled the White House and both houses of Congress, raised $18.8 million. The party with five times the money of its opposition tends to be in a superior tactical position.

• The voting patterns of the post-World War II years had produced a Republican advantage that, for all of the enormous resources of the major media, went unnoticed until Texas political consultant Horace Busby examined it in his newsletter in the closing weeks of the campaign. In states with almost half of the electoral votes needed to win the Presidency, the Republicans had established something approaching an "electoral lock"; while the old Democratic Solid South had been shattered since 1944, a new Republican Solid West had emerged. From 1948 to 1976, Republicans had won 2,421 electoral votes to the Democrats' 1,759—and fully 486 of those Democratic votes had come in the Johnson-Goldwater race of 1964. This meant that the Republican nominee could almost surely count on 120 to 140 electoral votes (the West, plus Virginia and Indiana), concentrating his energy and resources on the Northeast and South. To use the kind of sports analogy so favored in politics, it is as if a football team began every series of offensive plays on the fifty-yard line.

• Ronald Reagan had come to the Presidential nomination after sixteen years of national political recognition, based on his ability to speak compellingly out of a clear ideological position. In those years, his party had come to accept his premises overwhelmingly; four years earlier, Republicans had almost rejected an incumbent President of great personal charm in order to nominate Reagan. He had conquered his party from within. Jimmy Carter had won the White House in 1976 as a self-proclaimed outsider; one who had boasted in his acceptance speech that he "had never met a Democratic President." He had never won the hearts of his fellow Democrats during his term of office, seeming too conservative and too distant from the assumptions of liberals, urbanites, and intellectuals; but in his efforts to appeal to the fundamental Democratic constituencies, he had effectively foreclosed any appeal to more conservative voters. In a national sense, Jimmy Carter had no base.

These facts underlying the real campaign cannot be filmed or taped, and they make for very poor drama. They lack the dazzle of colorful balloons ascending from a crowd, the whiff of grapeshot accompanying angry charges from candidate to candidate, the compelling soundtrack provided by a brass band. And since they do not change from day to day, they cannot be touched on day after day on the evening news programs without running the risk of repetition. If news is what happened today that is different from what happened yesterday, then overriding political realities are not news—even if they determine the outcome of a campaign far more than how a candidate looked and sounded on a week's worth of broadcasts.

Moreover, the twenty-year progression away from covering politics at face value, and instead examining a campaign as a behind-the-scenes tactical struggle—the so-called "Teddy White syndrome"—had made it something of a heresy to suggest that what the candidates were saying was actually of overriding importance. Political reporters knew full well that when a candidate made a proposal, it was to be taken as a bid for votes *and as nothing else*. In a minute-and-a-half news report, not even the most gifted correspondent could analyze a proposal for its substantive content and its political appeal; in the context of 1980, the choice was clear.

Thus, in covering Ronald Reagan's speech in August to the National Urban League—a detailed attempt to argue that the liberal ideology had failed black Americans and that economic justice was fully compatible with conservatism—CBS took forty-five seconds of Reagan's thirty-five minute speech, and then explained it this way: "Reagan's strategists hope the governor's speech . . . will finally lay to rest the idea he's insensitive to the problems of blacks. They also hope that translates into much-needed black votes in November." And in what may have been the most extreme example of the obsession with mechanics over ideas, CBS's Phil Jones, covering Ted Kennedy's attempt to redefine his candidacy, noted that "Kennedy looked at the TelePrompTer" in giving his speech—as if the use of a TelePrompTer demonstrated the manipulative nature of everything he said.

This preference for the mechanical, strategic kind of coverage is also rooted in a tension between a reporter's sense of skepticism about the political process and a sense of fairness and self-restraint about what he is supposed to be reporting. As former chief strategist John Sears has noted, the press of the pretelevision era was much more of a conduit of a candidate's views than it is today. No decent political reporter would file a story offering nothing but undigested chunks of a speech or position paper, because no reporter believes that is what the real political story is. *Why* did the candidate stand in front of the abandoned factory? *Who* selected the dignitaries who would sit on the platform with him? What poll results determined that the candidate would speak about foreign policy to a group of Catholic bankers in Cleveland? Given the track record of the last twenty years, it is understandable that reporters bring to the political arena a sense that the participants have an agenda separate from that which appears in the public discourse.

But it is equally true that very few reporters really believe that it is their job to tell the audience what to think about ideas.

On September 8, 1980, for example, the *Washington Post*'s David Broder—as widely read and thoughtful as any of the first-rank political writers in America—told Phil Donahue, "I am totally unqualified to judge the MX missile system. . . . That's not false modesty. It takes a certain amount of expertise to talk seriously about a weapons system. I ain't got it. . . . There are a lot of things, even with a University of Chicago education, that I don't feel professionally qualified to judge." Even if the men and women who covered campaigns felt themselves fully qualified to pass such judgments, it would be completely alien to any notion of objective journalism.

It is unthinkable, for example, that a campaign story on CBS would have begun with Bill Plante standing in front of the Reagan campaign plane, saying, "Good evening. In one of the most ridiculous and crass attempts to secure the backing of his wealthy big-business supporters, Ronald Reagan today proposed to cut the heart out of government auto safety regulations which some estimate have saved 5,000 to 10,000 lives a year."

Such a report may be true or false, but it is not reporting. The only appropriate way for a network news piece to dissect a proposal on auto safety would be to sketch the background of the dispute, quote Reagan and/or his advisors at some length, find a Carter and Anderson representative to reply, go to outside sources for an attempt at evaluation, and then put the story together—a story that would take up, at a bare minimum, a third to a half of an entire half-hour (for which read twenty-two-minute) newscast.

In contrast, a correspondent can be relatively free in expressing skepticism about the purpose of a candidate's visit to a state fair; he or she can report with a strong sense of fairness a candidate's slip in the polls which are, after all, objective, quantifiable numbers requiring nothing at all like an opinion; and he or she can assert that advisors are hopeful or pessimistic without much of a background in the substance of a debate over social issues, defense spending, or the meaning of distributive justice.

What these trends produced in 1980 was a series of paradoxes in the coverage of the Presidential campaign:

• Convinced that the "real" story was behind the scene, the press as a rule spent tens of millions of dollars covering events that were supposed to provide Delphic clues to the unseeable future ("who's going to win?"), while giving short shrift to the flow of ideas and the underlying political terrain that—as it turned out—provided important clues about the nature of campaign '80.

● Convinced that speeches and issues are the tinsel behind which the real campaign happens, the press in general seemed barely to consider the notion that millions of Americans were weighing the policy records and intentions of the candidates and the constituencies they honored.

● Convinced that political parties were irrelevant to the political process, the press—except for comments during the national conventions—seemed to ignore the fact that most Americans still think of parties as well as of individual candidates, and that the relative health and illness of the two parties—in organization, money, and ideological confidence—might have something to do with the outcome; thus accounting for the astonishing fact that not a single major pollster came close to predicting the national Republican sweep.

● Thus—and herewith the paradox that envelops what has so far been said—the press's insistence that the struggle for power and position is all that matters, and that the "who's ahead" question is far more important than boring questions of ideas helped mislead the press about the one question it cares most about—who is going to win? A deeper respect for the power of words and thought in an election might have had the effect, not only of better informing the public about the choice at hand, but of coming closer to analyzing what was going to happen.

But this neglect is far more than a matter of professional frustration. For while Campaign '80 in general put the lie to the idea of an ideologically skewed press, the nature of campaign coverage, especially on television, was a major disservice to the American voter. The failure to cover consistently and conscientiously the struggle among competing views about the nature of government—which was at the heart of the real campaign—effectively helped disenfranchise the voter *by stripping him of a reason to care about the outcome*.

Consider the favorite sports analogies of political journalists and critics. The "horserace" is shorthand for the kind of coverage that reports who's ahead, who has momentum, who's fading as the finish line nears, and similar fare. But in a real horserace, there is intense interest in the outcome, at least among those who have wagers on the race. The track announcer at Aqueduct does not have to remind the fans why they care so much about who is going to win. Their money is on the line.

But a political horserace is very different. In a direct sense, very few people have anything on the outcome of a Presidential race. Unless a voter has a job or government contract to be gained or lost, nothing is riding on the outcome.

The point, of course, is that there is a good deal riding on the outcome of an election, *provided the voter has a chance to understand the link between himself and the policies of the government*. However much polls over the last decade have shown that most Americans believe the government is not listening to them, there is always, in the nature of a Presidential election, a series of links between the voter and the government, and these links are relatively easy to explore.

Among the major Presidential contenders in 1980, there were clear differences of both specific programs and general philosophies of government. President Carter argued throughout the campaign that a victory for him was essential to preserve the social welfare programs of the last forty years; that his reelection would insure no lessening of federal intervention on behalf of the aged, lower-income groups, and a constellation of middle-class professionals who depended on federal programs for jobs. Edward Kennedy represented—in the last six months of his campaign—the one voice of unrepentant liberalism, arguing for more federal spending directed toward the have-nots, for greater federal intervention in the economy through wage-price controls and gasoline rationing, and stepped-up regulatory attacks on corporate predators. Ronald Reagan said clearly that he intended to reverse the fundamental governing philosophy of the last forty-five years; that the federal government had grown too large, spent too much, intruded into the economy, harassed the business sector, and at the same time helped to fund movements at war with traditional American notions of morality.

The division was equally clear in the foreign policy area, with President Carter simultaneously arguing for higher defense spending and sanctions against the Soviet Union, while warning against the danger of nuclear war if negotiations with the Soviet Union were abandoned. His Democratic rival, Kennedy, argued that too often the United States had found itself allied with unrepresentative anti-Communist regimes around the world, and that new policies, such as draft registration and the grain embargo, were neither equitable nor effective. Ronald Reagan had been identified for fifteen years as an unbending foe of Soviet expansionism and ideology, going so far as to tell the *Wall Street Journal,* "if it weren't for the Soviet Union, there wouldn't be any hot spots in the world." The very clarity of his foreign policy views enabled him to oppose the grain embargo and draft registration, and even to flirt with the idea of opposing the boycott of the Moscow Olympics, while retaining the support of those who believed the United States had weakened itself in its defense and foreign policies against the Soviet Union. All of Reagan's Republican rivals shared this view of foreign policy, with the single exception of John Anderson, who remained throughout the campaign a clear advocate of the SALT II treaty and an opponent of most of the big-ticket defense spending increases, such as the MX missile system and the B-1 bomber.

It is, I think, a reasonable conclusion from the 1980 list of characters that no careful observer could fairly argue that "there wasn't any difference" among the candidates. Whether there was enough difference to satisfy a citizen who believed in a radical reordering of the American government and economy is another question; whether any of these candidates was even worthy of the job of President was a fair—and frequently raised—question. But to argue that these major candidates were in any sense indistinguishable required a deliberate refusal to consider the evidence.

● The election of Edward Kennedy or John Anderson would have meant a President committed to federal funding of abortions for poor women. The reelection of Jimmy Carter would have meant a President against federal funding, but also against a Constitutional ban on abortions. The election of Ronald Reagan meant a President who supports such a ban.

● The election of John Anderson or Edward Kennedy would have meant a President who would have sought either gasoline rationing or a fifty-cent-a-gallon gasoline tax to discourage consumption, combined with strict federal controls on oil company profits. The election of Ronald Reagan meant immediate decontrol of all oil prices and a clear effort to cut back on environmental regulations, which, he argued, discouraged the search for new sources.

● The election of Kennedy, Anderson, Carter, or one of Reagan's Republican rivals would have meant a continued encouragement of federal funds for "public-interest" legal and community work. The election of Ronald Reagan will almost certainly mean an administration committed to the sharp reduction, if not complete elimination, of such programs.

Draw up whatever list you choose and the meaning is clear. Whether in the areas of taxes, business regulations, the regulation of morality, the approach to poverty, the way to revise the American economy, the purpose and exercise of American foreign policy, the attack on inflation, the choice of a President makes a difference in the lives of most Americans.

But the voter would only know that to the extent that the media coverage of the candidates kept a consistent focus on that fact. The less successful the major media were in linking the choice of a President to something more than the mere winning or losing of power, the less connected a voter was likely to feel to the exercise of an election. Particularly in an era when sharp, personal identification with parties had long since been diluted, the press had to serve the function of explaining not simply who was gaining or weakening, but what the stakes were. In another time, voters would pour into the streets for torchlight parades at the behest of tightly organized political machines, or vote to protect home and farm from the ravages of big-city corruptions. The label "Republican" or "Democrat" was enough to explain what was at stake. In 1948, when Harry Truman upset Thomas Dewey, the atmosphere was one of wholesale celebration in the major auto plants around Detroit, with cheers and applause for the upset "their" side had won; and the identification of Truman as a New Deal-Fair Deal Democrat was enough to make it clear what "their" side meant.

By 1980, neither party labels nor party bosses were clear guides to voter interest. In this limited sense, political practitioners were correct when they observed that the media had filled a vacuum formed by the collapse of strong party structures. John Sears, who managed Ronald Reagan's campaigns in 1976 and in 1980 until the New Hampshire primary, argued that "Presently, the bosses of our political system are the combined news media, the press, radio, and television. Now that is not because they decided they wanted that power. That is because the politicians have given it to them. This really started at the presidential level because of the reforms that were made in the Democratic Party after the 1968 presidential race. Those reforms took the control of selecting a presidential nominee out of the hands of the party leaders and gave it to the primary voters. . . . The only way [those voters] can make any kind of judgment is to look at the press."

David Keene, who helped direct George Bush's 1980 drive, echoed Sears's point. "The people who make the decisions," Keene said, "are different from those who made it a few years ago. It used to be the professional pros, but today somebody has to say, 'This fella's serious and this fella isn't.' A lot of the weight of this decision has fallen on the press." As a description of who comes to the attention of the public, this perception was overstated; as John Anderson demonstrated, it is possible for a candidate to get massive press attention even though the press does not regard that candidate as a likely winner. But in another sense, the press is for most voters the only source for information about what a candidate's election will mean to *them*. Coherent *political* coverage can serve as a bridge between citizen and candidate. Absent that coverage, the press becomes not a bridge, but merely a plate-glass window, offering endless pictures of candidates, but no link between the passive citizen and the frenetic campaigners. To a substantial extent, the press in 1980 provided the window, but not the bridge.

It is too much, I think, to argue that media coverage by itself explains the steady fall-off in voting in American elections. Enfranchisement of groups less likely to vote—blacks, non-English-reading citizens, and eighteen to twenty-one year olds over the last fifteen years—is one likely source of lowered voting turnouts. We know that in the early twentieth century, the spread of the franchise to women, immigrants with limited literacy in English, and non-property-owning classes saw a dramatic drop in the turnout of eligible voters.

Nor is there anything inherent in the medium of television that explains the fall-off in voting. In 1952—the first year television was really involved in electoral coverage—the voting turnout jumped dramatically over 1948, from 51.4 percent to 62.6 percent, and contemporary studies of the convention and election coverage suggested that the viewing public was captivated by such coverage. In 1980, the massive coverage of early primaries and caucuses showed moderate to enormous increases in voter turnout—in the Iowa and Maine caucuses and in the New Hampshire and Florida primaries, for example. Only in the late primaries, where the identity of the two major party nominees was clear, was voter turnout down.

If, however, we look to the nature of media coverage—to the overwhelming dominance of the horserace perspective over the political perspective—we can see one likely element of voter apathy. If a voter sees no connection between himself and the candidate, then what is the reason to vote? To a major extent, the voter who did not come to the 1980 election with a clear political agenda found little guidance from the mainstream media coverage in answering the question "why should I care?"

It is, or should be, obvious that in examining how "television" covered the 1980 election, or looking at "the press," we are dealing with a broad brush. The viewer who watched "The MacNeil-Lehrer Report" and "Bill Moyers' Journal," and the weekly CBS late-night specials, and ABC News' "Nightline" or who, through cable, had access to Cable News Network and to the Cable Satellite Public Affairs Network, who watched "The Advocates' " six-weeks-long examination of the candidates' proposals, or who spent his weekends with "Issues and Answers," "Face the Nation," and "Meet the Press," found television to be a rich source of political information.

But this is not how the Presidential campaign comes to most Americans. The network evening news broadcasts and prime-time television are the sources of information and escape for the American citizen. And in 1980, the competitive pressures of commercial television made prime-time a virtual wasteland of information. Except for the nominating conventions, two debates, and Election Night, the *only* prime-time information about the election came either through a handful of pieces on "60 Minutes" and "20/20" or through paid political advertising on behalf of the candidates. An observer looking only at prime-time network programs in 1980 could be forgiven if he concluded that there *was* no Presidential election. It is, thus, the network evening news broadcasts—and the morning news programs which despite their low ratings are avidly followed by the political press—that form the only consistent political coverage. And, as network executives and correspondents freely recognize, these programs cannot begin to provide anything more than, in Walter Cronkite's phrase, "a headline service."

But is it true given the limits of time—twenty-two minutes of nonadvertising time in a half-hour broadcast—that coverage could not be different? The news programs themselves frequently demonstrated that many of the limits on television political coverage are *self-imposed,* based on a formula whose time has long since past. Each of the networks demonstrated on occasion how a Presidential campaign can be covered—succinctly and without sacrificing visual appeal—so as to suggest, and at times illuminate, the choices at stake among candidates and policies. What these efforts had in common was, first of all, *time* to prepare them, and a solid grounding by correspondent and producer in the *substance* of the report. Significantly, *none* of them were produced while traveling on a campaign swing with the candidate; almost without exception, these campaign-day reports— which dominated network news coverage—proved the least worthwhile and informative accounts of the election. And this was so not because of lack of skill on the part of the correspondents, who were often the same people involved in the more venturesome sorts of coverage, but because there was no time to prepare a substantive account, or *because there was nothing of any importance that happened that day.*

Richard Salant, NBC vice-chairman and former President of CBS News, is fond of saying that "just once, I wish we had the guts to say that 'Today, Candidate X campaigned at six stops and didn't say a goddamn thing.' " The realities of broadcasting make this more a fantasy than a reality, if only because networks and outsiders chart the allocation of news broadcasts rigorously, and a candidate who chose to campaign on generalities would find himself getting far less air time than a candidate who campaigned on a specific platform. But the 1980 campaign did demonstrate that at the least, two-tier coverage is necessary. If the press is going to cover the day-by-day journeyings and statements of major Presidential candidates—and they will—then there must be a systematic attempt to minimize such coverage when nothing of consequence happens, and to expand the kind of stories that offer insight into the intentions of the candidates and the underlying issues that, in fact, have so much to do with the outcome of the election—and, incidentally, with the future of the country.

Two other points require noting. First, this "revisionist" look at the impact of media on the Presidential campaign of 1980 is not an attempt to argue away the importance of media or the necessity for rigorous examination of the nature and competence of its performance. One of the premises of this account is that the coverage of our political process can make a difference, not in affecting the outcome of a campaign, but in connecting the citizenry with the process; better coverage, I believe, will lead to a healthier public climate. My intention is not to challenge the proposition that the press plays a role in our political life, but to challenge the idea that the press has remade our political life, divorcing electoral struggles from more enduring realities. The frantic energy of mass media has, I believe, too often been confused with a kind of power and influence which is at the least greatly overstated.

Second, there is a limit to what better media coverage of campaigns can establish. It is, I think, missing the point for the press to argue that they are not covering the issues because the candidates are not speaking to issues. Even if this were always the case—and it was to a fair extent in 1976 and to a much smaller extent in 1980—it will still make a difference who wins the Presidency and the Congress, and the press cannot be excused from laying out those differences whether the candidates want to or not. But it is certainly true that the press can be no more than a tool; if great portions of the public choose not to become informed, that cannot be blamed on the press. For example, *some* of the reason for the steady decline in viewing nominating conventions can be laid to the kind of coverage those conventions receive, the smothering scramble for every piece of trivia, even when a convention has nothing to decide. But the primary system has *thus far* resulted in conventions which do not deliberate, and which ratify primary choices, rather than choose on their own. The most ennobling, brilliant coverage imaginable cannot make a convention interesting if nothing is happening.

Moreover, Election Night is always a bonanza for those independent stations that show blockbuster movies, for millions of viewers simply do not care that much about political campaigns. Once they know who has been elected, they have learned enough; they want neither exit polls analyzing how the votes broke down, nor thoughtful commentary about the nature of the new Congress, nor anything else. Similarly, in a nation half of whose people have no idea where El Salvador is, it is clear that a significant number of citizens do not choose to involve themselves in matters of public policy.

I concede a "Jeffersonian" bias that more thoughtful political coverage of the real campaigns of the future will find a more thoughtful audience; that a rediscovery of "the public discourse" in the mass media will improve the level of political understanding and interest. But there is no guarantee of such an improvement, and the mass media cannot be charged with this responsibility. Voters can choose to vote on impulse, on rumor, on prejudice, on blind fears, and they can choose not to vote at all. But I believe the results of the 1980 campaign demonstrate that voters do try to discover where their interests lie, and do make choices based on the level of information made available to them. In any event, that is the premise on which political coverage must rest. Anything else represents surrender to the belief—already spread far too pervasively among Americans—that the process by which the governed choose the governor has nothing to do with our lives and the lives of our children.

ii   George Bush's Strategy: The Politics of Momentum

No candidate in 1980 based his campaign on the power of the mass media more securely than George Bush. No candidate executed more skillfully the "politics of momentum" than George Bush. No candidate demonstrated more convincingly the limits of momentum than George Bush.

There was no secret to Bush's strategy; he had taken not a leaf from Jimmy Carter's 1976 run for the Presidency, he had taken the entire book. Like Carter, Bush was a relative unknown nationally. As Walter Cronkite said in November of 1979, "In Campaign '76, the question was 'Jimmy Who?' For Campaign '80, it might well be 'George Who?' " Bush had been a two-term congressman from Texas, chairman of the Republican National Committee, director of the Central Intelligence Agency, and envoy to China—credentials that gave him, in his own words, "a splendid resume." But his lack of public recognition placed him in the ranks of "Others" among those Republicans trying to challenge Ronald Reagan for the nomination. Polls early in 1980 showed that Reagan's most formidable challenger would be former President Gerald Ford, who had chosen not to compete in early caucus and primary states. Senate Minority Leader Howard Baker and former Texas Governor John Connally, both better known than Bush, were next in line. As two key polls demonstrated, Bush was far behind:

GALLUP (JAN 4–6)		ROPER (JAN 5–19)	
Reagan	33	Reagan	25
Ford	27	Ford	27
Baker	9	Baker	14
Connally	9	Connally	13
Bush	9	Bush	8

Nonetheless, there were signs that Bush had understood exactly how his 1980 campaign would duplicate that of Carter in 1976, in using the power of the mass media to turn small early successes into nationally publicized signs of strength. He had announced for the office back in 1978. He had hit early voting states over and over again, spending twenty-seven days in Iowa and fifty-four days in New Hampshire. And the Bush campaign recognized that the political press, like generals throughout history, always tend to be prepared for the last war. Having missed the political appeal of Eugene McCarthy in 1968, George McGovern in 1972, and Jimmy Carter in 1976, they were on the lookout for any sign of unexpected strength, no matter how insignificant and meaningless. The press would not miss any Ames County, Iowa straw polls in 1980.

Thus, on November 3, 1979, Bush received widespread attention when he upset Senator Baker in a straw vote taken at a Maine Republican convention. Baker had expected to win the straw vote, and had even brought his press entourage along to celebrate the victory. Instead, Bush, with the help of a highly effective speech, won the poll by 20 votes out of 1,336 votes cast. The next day's *New York Times* used the upset as its front-page lead story, with a page-one subhead declaring "Bush Gaining in Stature as '80 Contender."

As CBS reporter Richard Roth reported on November 12, "the way George Bush hopes to build recognition is by following up his surprise win in Maine's straw vote with strong showings in the early contests that count, Iowa and New Hampshire, developing enough momentum to force Howard Baker out of the race in Alabama and Florida, and eventually rolling over Ronald Reagan."

This was, after all, the way political campaigns were now conducted—at least that was the assumption of much of the press. A *Wall Street Journal* report on November 27, 1979, noting that "political experts say there is a good chance [Bush] can upset Ronald Reagan in the January 21st caucuses," argued that a successful Presidential campaign apparently required "a candidate who is willing to start early and spend hundreds of hours meeting with people in their living rooms and answering questions at endless Rotary lunches and Chamber of Commerce dinners." In fact, the *Journal* found one grass-roots Republican who had made his choice of a candidate based on precisely these standards. Ralph Brown had chosen Bush over Baker because Baker was "the minority leader [of the Senate]. Holding down jobs like that may not be good Presidential politics these days, because to win, you've got to get out early and full-time."

In one key area, however, Bush faced a very different challenge from that which had faced Carter in 1976. In that year, neither of the two Democrats with strong, long-standing national followings had contested the Democratic primaries. Former Vice-President Hubert Humphrey had stayed on the sidelines, waiting for a deadlocked party to turn to him. There had been hints throughout the primary campaign that Humphrey would enter the race; and in the late primaries, Carter had lost more contests than he had won, especially in states such as Maryland, New Jersey, and California, where Jerry Brown had won the support of those seeking to find some other alternative to Carter. But Humphrey ultimately chose to stay out, and Ted Kennedy never came in. Thus, Carter faced a divided opposition—George Wallace and Henry Jackson appealed respectively to social conservatives and neoconservatives; Birch Bayh, Morris Udall, and Fred Harris appealed to liberals. There was no "Mr. Democrat" to stand between Carter and the nomination.

For Bush, however, there was a very different challenge. Ronald Reagan *was* "Mr. Republican." In 1976, he had won more primary votes than had Gerald Ford; and he had narrowly missed taking the nomination away from a sitting President. A stronger presence in the Ohio primary, a handful of delegates from the Northeast, a stronger appeal to the bloc-voting Mississippi delegation, and the nomination might well have been Reagan's four years earlier. Reagan was the spokesman for a brand of conservatism that no longer was one wing of the Republican Party, but was rather its core, its heart and soul.

Confronting this challenge, Bush—like every other Republican candidate save John Anderson—chose not to challenge the Reagan philosophy, but to attempt to capture it.

(Indeed, at the outset of his campaign, Bush was so much a long shot that he had to confront the more "serious" candidacies of John Connally and Howard Baker—especially the moderate appeal of Baker—before taking on the nominee-apparent. Said media advisor Robert Goodman, "we were probably running against Baker at the beginning more than Ronald Reagan.") He argued for tax cuts to spur business and investment; he decried the "decline in America's stature overseas"; he attacked excessive government regulation; and his essential effort was to win the Reagan constituency, not to argue against the philosophy. The premise of his campaign was to present himself as an experienced, youthful, energetic, electable version of Reagan—and to rely on momentum to defeat the opposition.

Thus, Bush's campaign pointedly offered network camera crews photo opportunities of the candidate jogging in the early morning hours with his youthful supporters, as a way of reminding voters about Reagan's age without directly raising the issue. He proclaimed in every interview, "I'm *up* for the '80s." He persistently refused to debate issues with any specificity, telling CBS's Diane Sawyer in early February, "if they can show me how it will get me more votes someplace, I'll be glad to do it."

The Bush advertising campaign was keyed directly to the philosophy of creating a sense of personal excitement, rather than a following based on a philosophy. Created by Baltimore media advisor Robert

Goodman, who declared often that "voting is an emotional experience, not an intellectual one," the ads were fast-moving, newsfilmlike portraits of an energetic, dynamic Bush creating excitement and moving through crowds, with an upbeat musical track playing behind him. Each of the advertisements used a slogan that attempted to capitalize on Bush's experience, while hitting Carter's on-the-job performance and Ronald Reagan's inexperience on the national scene: "George Bush," the announcer said—"a President we won't have to train."

Nothing in any of the commercials raised an issue remotely criticizing Reagan's philosophy; they were instead designed to create the sense that George Bush was a winner. One ad, shot at an airport in Lebanon, New Hampshire, showed the exuberant candidate climbing out of a private plane, surrounded by supporters wearing straw hats and waving placards. "We're going all the way!" Bush yelled, as the crowd cheered and the music played.

(The response to this ad among the press showed how deeply ingrained the suspicion had grown about media manipulation by 1980. The Lebanon airport was closed by bad weather on the day the spot was to be shot, so Bush drove to the airport and boarded the plane, which taxied a short distance to the gate so that Bush could disembark and greet his supporters. A "60 Minutes" camera crew happened to be shooting Bush for a forthcoming piece, and caught an angry press corps furiously protesting the dishonesty at work in Bush's pretending to have flown into the airport. Given the fact that Bush probably made a thousand airplane flights in his two-year campaign, the staged landing seemed more a venial than a mortal sin, but it demonstrated that the press was in no mood for a "Selling of the President, 1980.")

Other commercials showed Bush talking generally about inflation in front of approving factory workers inside a plant, or put together short pictures of his "splendid resume." In one outstanding piece of luck, Goodman found a home movie film made by a sailor on a ship when Bush, then a World War II fighter pilot, had been shot down over the South China Sea. In the grainy black-and-white footage, Bush climbs aboard an aircraft carrier as the announcer explains that Bush "is the man America turns to when a tough job has to be done."

All of the ads reflected Goodman's notion that "people tend to vote on honesty, competence, and charisma in that order. We try to show a candidate—he's sensitive, he's attractive, he's nice. The musical background is very important. The Bush ads are very newsreel, very rough, the way he might be covered. I've tried to counterpoint this with music, Presidential music, George Bush music. I hope it's subliminal. It's really the wallpaper of the thing."

In his essential strategy of winning momentum, Bush benefited enormously from the Reagan strategy, insisted upon by campaign manager John Sears, of not making more than a token effort in Iowa. It was Sears's notion that Reagan was in effect an incumbent, and that given his need to run a fifty-state campaign, it would be self-defeating to become "an ordinary man like the rest of us" and slug it out in every farmhouse and Holiday Inn meeting room in Iowa. But he benefited as well from the press's fascination with its own role in making the winner of an early battleground a major national figure. It was almost as if, in an attempt to explain the importance of perception, the commentators were adding fuel to the fire.

In a discussion on the morning of the Iowa caucuses on January 21 on CBS "Morning," Roger Mudd observed that "any election is as much a matter of perception and how people perceive they're going to do and how the press perceived they're going to do. . . . If Reagan doesn't finish first, then he's damaged."

"The thing about being a front-runner," Bruce Morton commented, "is that you have to win them all. And I think if [Reagan] loses one, then maybe it's very easy to lose another one. If anybody comes very close—if it's, you know, Reagan 29, Bush 27, or Baker, or whatever—then I think that person gains."

In their recognition of the importance of perception, Mudd and Morton were, of course, correct. But there was another inference from their discussion, almost a totemic sense that a front-runner who lost one early race was like a sovereign who had been shown to be mortal; that once momentum had shifted, it was as if some symbol of power had rendered that figure no longer invulnerable, but impotent.

That was certainly how the press played the loss of Reagan to Bush in the caucuses. From the time that Monday night when it became clear that Bush would far exceed his expectation of a strong second-place finish, and would, in fact, win more votes than Reagan, the politics of momentum became the dominant story in the Republican race. Having fully absorbed the idea that media images themselves were critically important, if not decisive, in Presidential campaigns, Bush's two-point margin over Reagan in Iowa the press covered almost wholly as a question of perception. It is useful to look in some detail at the breadth of this coverage, to see how fully the politics of momentum was assumed to be the critical factor in a modern Presidential campaign.

CBS's special 11:30 report on caucus night began with Walter Cronkite declaring "George Bush has apparently done what he hoped to do, coming out of the back as the principal challenger to frontrunner Ronald Reagan." In an interview that night with Richard Roth and with Cronkite, Bush spoke of his victory in purely organizational and strategic terms; if there was a hint of a policy or an idea for which he stood, it was not apparent in any of his comments, either to the CBS team or to any other journalist.

"Clearly," Bush said, "we're going to come out of here with

momentum. . . . We appear to have beaten both Connally and Baker very, very badly. The numbers look substantial. And they are going to have to get some momentum going, and I'm coming out of here with momentum. . . . You know, and I know, and all you listeners know that four months ago on everybody's polls I was a little star, an asterisk, and today we've done well."

"Will your victory flush Ronald Reagan out?" Cronkite asked. "Who knows," Bush replied. "It may be a little late. There's a lot of momentum going on now."

In his analysis, Bruce Morton harked back to his observations earlier that morning. "The Bush scenario, as you know, was always really the Jimmy Carter scenario of four years ago," he said. "Well, it seems to me he's done that. . . . He did well in terms of this test. It will be written that way, I think; it will be played that way.

"A lot of people in the politics business have said for a long time that if Ronald Reagan loses once, or maybe even just gets tested once, then the magic is gone, and all of a sudden he's an elderly candidate instead of a sure winner. We don't know yet that that's going to happen, but it's something to watch in New Hampshire."

Those two stories—Bush's momentum and Reagan's surprising, perhaps fatal, vulnerability—dominated coverage of the Republican campaign for the next two weeks. On the next "Today" show on NBC, anchor Tom Brokaw called Bush's victory "a major upset," and said of Reagan, "I guess we now refer to him as the *former* frontrunner." Reagan campaign chief John Sears acknowledged that "what we have now, Tom, is what appears to be a two-man race." As part of a round table of commentators, which included columnists Jack Germond of the *Washington Star* and David Broder of the *Washington Post,* NBC correspondent Tom Pettit carried the fervor to its logical extreme, when he said, "I would like to suggest that Ronald Reagan is politically dead."

On ABC's "Good Morning, America," matched photos of Reagan and Bush appeared behind correspondent Steve Bell; visually symbolizing the two-man race of which John Sears had spoken. In their footage, ABC cut from George Bush addressing a cheering throng to footage of a weary, old-looking Ronald Reagan, dressed in a distinctly non-Presidential turtleneck and sports jacket, emerging from a supporter's home in Los Angeles. And Bell's interview with the victorious Bush again avoided any hint of a substantive issue that might affect the voters' choice. It was again an analysis and perception.

"Do you have to win in New Hampshire?" Bell asked. "No," Bush replied, "because I'll start poor-mouthing that. I've gotta do better than I would have if I hadn't won Iowa."

And on CBS "Morning," Bush coined a new version of the 1980 obsession.

Speaking of the New Hampshire primary, Bush noted that "what we'll have, you see, is momentum. We will have forward 'Big Mo' on our side, as they say in athletics."

" 'Big Mo'?" interviewer Bob Schieffer asked.

"Yeah," Bush said. " 'Mo,' momentum."

The accuracy of Bush's claim to "Big Mo" was demonstrated in the days following Iowa. The Bush campaign took in $150,000 in two days, and the requests for press seats on the Bush campaign tripled within twenty-four hours. "We've proved it," Bush's Iowa director, Richard Bond, exulted. "The emperor has no clothes." The *Wall Street Journal* argued two days after the caucuses that Reagan was in the same position as Edward Kennedy, who had been defeated 2–1 by President Carter. Both, the *Journal* said, "really need to win the February 26th New Hampshire primary to remain credible candidates for their parties' nomination." "Reagan," the *Boston Globe* reported the next day, "faces the real possibility that Bush can lick him four times in a row, and that could be fatal to the hopes of the former California Governor." Even among Reagan staffers, according to CBS background reports, there was talk that should Reagan lose in New Hampshire he should pull out of the race. Such talk would have been unimaginable twenty-five years earlier, when candidates were expected to have areas of geographic strengths and weaknesses; and it was in the West and South that Reagan had his committed support, not in New England. But so thoroughly had mass media converted every vote, no matter how small or insignificant, into a kind of national primary, that Reagan's own people understood what a devastating *perception* of political weakness a New Hampshire loss would be to his hopes.

Two other reflections of the politics of momentum appeared in the week after the Iowa caucus. *Time* and *Newsweek,* with combined circulations of 7,431,603 and a powerful reach into the better-educated, higher-income, active-voting communities covered the Bush victory with full flourish. *Newsweek* put Bush on the cover as he happily jogged with supporters. "Bush Breaks Out of the Pack," the cover line read. On the inside, a huge picture of Bush dominated the page, with smaller pictures of a disappointed Baker with hands on hips, and a Reagan with lips pursed in front of microphones, reflecting the agony of defeat. *Newsweek* placed heavy emphasis on Bush's emulation of President Carter's campaign, calling it "a replay of Jimmy Carter's 1976 script" and stating that Bush's win "raised the serious possibility that he could accomplish on the Republican side this year what Carter did in 1976—parlay a well-tuned personal appetite for on-the-ground campaigning into a Long March to his party's Presidential nomination."

Time, featuring similar contrasting photographs of a huge, grinning Bush and a smaller, distressed Reagan, proclaimed "Bush Soars," although it laid somewhat more emphasis on the fact that Reagan spent only forty-five hours in the state, compared with ten full days for Bush in January alone.

But the more astonishing impact of Bush's Iowa victory came in the polls, which had shown him (in his own words) as an asterisk at the end of 1979 and placed him behind Reagan, Ford, Connally, and Baker in the days just before the Iowa caucus vote. Now, with network exposure and news magazine covers, the sense of Bush as a possible winner seemed to be making headway. Where Bush had trailed Reagan by margins of 3–1 and 4–1 just before Iowa, polls a few days after the caucuses showed that Bush had caught, and in some cases passed Reagan. *Time* had Bush ahead of Reagan 35–31; *Newsweek* had it Reagan 33, Bush 27. The ABC-Lou Harris poll had Reagan leading Bush ten days before Iowa 32–6; within a day after the caucuses, Bush had tied Reagan in a national sampling 27–27. And these numbers, in turn, were affecting the judgments of political professionals. At a Republican regional meeting in New Orleans at the end of January, Harry Dent, a long-time Republican operative in South Carolina, disclosed he was taking over Bush's campaign in his state, having been persuaded by the caucuses and the national surge of support for Bush that he was electable.

Such judgments were not confined to one region or a handful of political professionals. In their column of February 22, columnists Jack Germond and Jules Witcover wrote that "A rough consensus is taking shape among moderate Republican politicians that George Bush may achieve a commanding position within the next three weeks in the contest for the 1980 Republican nomination. And those with unresolved reservations about Bush are beginning to wonder privately if it is even possible to keep an alternative politically alive for the late primaries."

The *Boston Globe*'s Robert Healy went even further on the same day, predicting that "even though he is still called the leading candidate in some places, Reagan does not look like he'll be on the Presidential stage much longer." It is possible, Healy wrote, that Bush "will go through 1980 . . . without losing an important Presidential primary."

Even some of Reagan's outspoken press supporters reflected the doubts spawned by Bush's Iowa win. *New York Times* conservative columnist William Safire reported on February 11 that his conversations with Republican veterans around the country produced "a growing suspicion that Reagan may once again be bypassed for the historic role . . . a general feeling that he may be a man whose cause may triumph, but whose own time may never come."

What was operating here was, in microcosm, the kind of closed circuit that seems to crystallize politics in the mass media age. Having observed that one or two early victories (or defeats) could propel a candidate into serious consideration (or knock him off the pedestal of the front-runner), the media began explaining this phenomenon to the voters. But instead of "demystifying" the impact of early straw votes or caucus decisions or primaries from small, unrepresentative states, the venting of the momentum issue seemed, curiously, to elevate its importance. The press justified its full-press coverage of an event—a Florida straw poll, an Iowa caucus—because of its impact on a candidate's momentum. The candidates themselves were then forced to examine such an event from that point of view; to celebrate their momentum or to justify their lack of it. The citizenry, being polled about its choice of candidates ten months before a general election and six or seven months before a nominating convention, responded not to any sense of what a candidate stood for, but to that candidate's performance. In the specific context of the Republican race, for example, the only fact that a reasonable Republican voter could have learned from the seventy-two hours of coverage surrounding the Iowa caucus vote was that George Bush had won, and that all of the television networks and all of the print press were reporting that he had gained critically important momentum. That fact is the only possible explanation for Bush's gains—in a matter of days—of twenty and thirty points in Republican preference polls. But professional politicians, now reading these polls and listening to the reports of momentum, were basing judgments about which candidate would win and which candidate they would support on information about momentum. In the case of George Bush, it all appeared to be another validation of the politics of momentum.

There was only one small flaw in this analysis. George Bush did not win the Republican Presidential nomination. And at least part of the explanation for this outcome lies in a simple fact of modern campaign life: the politics of momentum is a highly incomplete account of how Presidential politics works. It is an accurate account of a pattern that emerges with some frequency in an age of mass-media politics; but that pattern is by no means dominant, and is fully capable of being overwhelmed by other, more enduring political patterns. To put it most simply: there was never any reason to vote for George Bush for President. In premising his campaign on the factor of momentum, George Bush stripped his effort of any substantive or ideological rationale; and a campaign lacking such a rationale is almost impossible to sustain against a candidate who has labored long and hard to build a *political,* as opposed to a *strategic* case for his candidacy; which is what Ronald Reagan had been doing within the Republican Party for sixteen years.

While it can be argued that George Bush was simply the victim of a countervailing "media event"—the Nashua, New Hampshire, debate three days before that state's February 26 primary, in which an angry Ronald Reagan demanded his right to be heard through a microphone he had paid for, and cast Bush in the role of an arrogant, spoiled rich kid—that account of Bush's troubles is, at best, inadequate and superficial. The obstacles between Bush after Iowa and the Republican nomination ran far deeper than a poor performance in a small New Hampshire town.

First, even given the full equation of 1980 with 1976, Bush's campaign had misread the nature of a campaign based on momentum. As soon as Jimmy Carter emerged as the man to beat in the Democratic Party, both his challengers and the press began focusing more attention on him, and that attention was not simply a gasp of admiration for his strategy. What, they wanted to know, did Jimmy Carter really stand for? When was he going to overcome his "fuzziness"? Carter never really shook that impression, which accounts in fair measure for the string of losses he suffered during the last third of the primary season in 1976 and for his near-loss to Gerald Ford in the general election campaign—a campaign he entered with a thirty-point lead in the polls. As Michael Robinson and his colleagues noted in a media evaluation piece midway through the 1980 campaign, the stories about candidates "treated the front-runners more critically than the challengers." This kind of treatment, they noted, may well be warranted since "with media playing a large role in establishing 'momentum' for candidates in the early primaries, the system probably needs a counterbalance, something which calls into question the candidates who emerge as most likely to be elected."

A campaign that had studied more closely the Carter 1976 campaign would have recognized that momentum is a two-edged sword; that with higher visibility comes a higher standard. Now the press is not looking for a glimmer of excitement surrounding a candidate; now they are looking with more critical and skeptical eyes at a figure who may well hold the power of life and death over the world.

Thus, in another demonstration of how the press's recognition of the previous campaign's patterns accelerates its response to those apparent patterns in the next, questions began being raised about Bush as soon as his stature rose to that of Reagan's principal challenger—and sometimes at the same time. Thus, the same *Newsweek* piece that detailed his victory noted that "already, Bush is being pressed about his somewhat vague solutions to economic and foreign policy problems." The *Washington Post* reported on February 1 that Bush "has been ill-prepared to respond to simple questions about basic issues as they arise. When he was asked about President Carter's new budget this week, his replies were vague and contradictory." A *Wall Street Journal* account on February 13 commented that "his positions are short on detail. In economics his spending and tax priorities remain fuzzy. In foreign policy, he hasn't made it at all clear how he envisions using American military power to advance economic and political interests."

At times, Bush's reluctance to land firmly on a policy stand reached proportions bordering on the absurd. Once, asked whether he would support an embargo on the importing of Russian-made Stolichnaya vodka, Bush said, "I've got to be careful. I'd have to know where it's bottled, and if it's bottled in the United States, how many people are employed doing it."

Further, Bush's early visibility attracted the opposition of his opponents, both electoral and ideological. Until Iowa, all of the candidates seemed to be following Ronald Reagan's old "Eleventh Commandment: Thou Shalt Not Attack Fellow Republicans." But on February 14, on CBS, Senator Howard Baker, battling to survive as a possible alternative to Reagan in the face of Bush's new visibility, charged that Bush's notion of reduced revenue sharing would cost the state of New Hampshire $25 million, raising the possibility of local tax increases. The charge was less than explosive—it seems to have been designed to duplicate Ford's 1976 success in arguing that a Reagan idea of transferring powers back to the states would force New Hampshire to enact a state income tax—but it did reflect a chipping away of the "eleventh commandment."

There were no such bounds of propriety when it came to the *Manchester Union-Leader,* New Hampshire's only statewide paper and the personal fiefdom of publisher William Loeb. Every four years the national press rediscovers this unique blend of far-right-wing philosophy and an accompanying journalistic philosophy of "take no prisoners." It was Loeb whose paper precipitated Senator Edmund Muskie's "crying" incident in the 1972 New Hampshire primary. It was Loeb who in 1976 called President Ford "Jerry the Jerk" in backing Ronald Reagan. In 1980, Loeb's candidate was again Ronald Reagan. Under other circumstances, Loeb might have had to scatter his fire against several of Reagan's opponents. Thanks to Iowa, the enemy was clear, and it was George Bush.

To the readers of the *Union-Leader,* Bush emerged as a closet internationalist-liberal tool of Eastern bankers who were wired in with a shadowy intelligence operation designed to undermine the country. In a February front-page editorial, the paper described Bush's Iowa victory this way: "The Bush operation in Iowa had all the smell of a CIA covert operation. . . . Strange aspects of the Iowa operation [included] a long, slow count and then the computers broke down at a very convenient point, with Bush having a six percent bulge over Reagan. . . . Will the elite nominate their man, or will we nominate Reagan?"

Over and over again, Bush's membership in the Tri-Lateral Commission—a David Rockefeller-founded association of political and financial leaders from the non-Communist world—was cited as evidence of his ties to this "elite." "George Bush is a Liberal," a page-one commentary stated the day before the primary, and Loeb's editorial described him as a "spoiled little rich kid who has been wet-nursed to succeed and now, packaged by David Rockefeller's Tri-Lateral Commission, thinks he is entitled to the White House as his latest toy." Its view of Ronald Reagan was summed up in another front-page article two days earlier, headlined, "God Has Chosen Ronald Reagan to Lead Us."

But all through New Hampshire, Bush continued to campaign on strategic rather than policy grounds. He told *Time* magazine the week before the primary, "If somebody comes out with something that shows me way out front, I'll be poor-mouthing it. I'll say, 'this is ridiculous. God, how could you expect that from a little guy like me?' "

Bush, in sum, was inviting the media to judge him by one standard: winnability. In this context, it is not surprising that Bush and his aides saw the famous February 23 debate in Nashua as the Waterloo of his efforts, the single moment when Bush's campaign collapsed. But a closer look suggests that we pause before inscribing that moment into the history of overriding campaign events.

To review the case briefly: Bush and Reagan had been invited by the *Nashua Press* to appear jointly—without the other Republican Presidential candidates—at a Saturday night debate at the Nashua High School. A few days before the debate, the Federal Election Commission ruled that the newspaper could not pay for the costs of the debate since, by excluding the other candidates, the $3,500 cost amounted to an illegal campaign contribution to Reagan and Bush. The Bush campaign declined to cofinance the debate because its spending was so close to the FEC-decreed limits that the money might have pushed them over the limit, exposing them to a fine and to embarrassing publicity. (Ironically, the FEC found after Reagan was elected to the Presidency that his campaign had exceeded the spending limits for New Hampshire.) The Reagan campaign then agreed to put up the funds for the debate. And, unbeknown to the Bush campaign, Reagan strategist John Sears invited the other candidates to the hall, and in a series of last-minute conferences, agreement was reached to bring the other candidates onto the stage for brief remarks before the Reagan-Bush debate began.

Looking back on the event months later, Bush media advisor Robert Goodman said wistfully, "Even at the last minute, if Bush had said, 'look—this thing's gone too far. I can't see my brother Republicans being ushered off the stage with such indignity. Either they're here or we might as well call this thing off'—if he'd said something like that, we win the whole election. But George does not have a sense of theater." Instead, Bush said simply that he was abiding by the rules set down by the press. And when Reagan began explaining his position, with Dole, Anderson, Baker, and Crane standing behind him, moderator Jon Breen ordered the technicians to turn off Reagan's microphone.

"I am paying for this microphone, Mr. Breen!" Reagan snapped, and with that the audience broke out into cheers, as did the four excluded Republican candidates, who then filed off the stage and laced into Bush as soon as the debate ended. The debate was not carried in any form outside New Hampshire, but all through the weekend and on Monday night's news programs, the confrontation dominated political coverage. All three networks showed the four excluded Republicans applauding and cheering as Bush sat glumly and silently. They quoted the angry attacks on Bush ("He refused to even come back here and talk," said John Anderson. "He didn't want us to debate; he can't provide leadership for the Republican Party with that attitude," said Robert Dole. ". . . the punkest political device I ever saw," said Howard Baker), and the more-in-sorrow attitude of Reagan ("I'm puzzled and I—I just don't understand it at all."). The heavy, almost incessant play by the press was a predictable response to the old axiom that in a political campaign, conflict and controversy is the stuff of network news and front-page headlines; in a battle where no one had anything unpleasant to say about any of their rivals, the shattering of the "eleventh commandment" was heady stuff.

Bush's advisors quickly recognized the potential for disaster. Last-minute radio commercials covered New Hampshire, as an announcer explained that "at no time did George Bush object to a full candidate forum. This accusation by the other candidates is without foundation whatsoever. . . . " From his home in Texas, Bush was interviewed on the telephone by Walter Cronkite and complained that "I wanted to do what I agreed to do. I wanted to debate with Ronald Reagan . . . the paper has publicly confirmed that we would be willing to debate with the others if that was the decision of the paper [but] I didn't go back on my word with that newspaper." And on reflection, Phil Crane acknowledged that "maybe we were sandbagged"—a feeling buttressed by the remark of one Reagan aide who said, "We opened it up hoping Bush would make a mistake—and he did."

But the explanations did not work. Bush had invited voters and the press alike to judge him as a winner, as a campaigner; having chosen to live by the sword of electability, he had committed a blunder which went to the heart of his own claimed strength. In a postprimary assessment, the *Washington Post*'s Haynes Johnson—echoing some of the imagery of William Loeb—wrote that "It was Bush's own personal response to the controversy that destroyed him. The self-portrait of George Bush drawn these last few days before the balloting was singularly unattractive.

"Bush came over as a petulant politician, lacking grace and dignity, and complaining peevishly about being 'sandbagged' and 'ambushed' by all the other nasty politicians. He resembled nothing more than a spoiled child whose toy has been taken away."

Conversely, Reagan was seen by the press as having liberated himself from the confines of Sears's "incumbency" campaign. NBC's Don Oliver reported on primary day, "There has been a new spring in Reagan's step since the mixed-up debate of last Saturday night, a new upbeat mood among the campaign staff. You'd think the performance in Nashua has given Reagan the edge in today's election. The debate is all the people of New Hampshire are talking about."

Tom Pettit echoed this view. "Reagan," he reported, "had not looked so animated since 1976, so dynamic. Bush in a bind, play by the original rules and look bad, or play by the new rules and look bad."

New Hampshire's primary turned out even worse for Bush than his gloomiest expectations. Reagan won 50 percent of the votes, beating Bush's 23 percent by better than two-to-one. While Bush won a clear second place—Baker winning 13 percent and Anderson gaining a "surprising" 10 percent, the expectations of a close Reagan-Bush contest proved devastating to Bush, as we shall see.

But was the Nashua debate the real source of Bush's decline? A CBS poll showed that Bush and Reagan were even on the Friday before the primary (and the day before the New Hampshire debate), that Reagan surged into the lead over the weekend, and that Bush was falling fast on Sunday. According to Bruce Morton's March 1 report, "On Saturday . . . Reagan was slightly ahead. But on Sunday, Reagan's margin widened dramatically to better than two-to-one . . . the number of people with an unfavorable impression of Bush jumped sharply on Sunday. So did the number with a favorable impression of Reagan."

The CBS poll also showed that of Bush's preelection supporters, only 55 percent actually voted for him, and more than half of the undecided or not-likely-to-vote Republicans ended up voting for Reagan.

This finding, however, runs into two other polls that showed a substantially different picture. Richard Wirthlin, whose Decision Marketing Information was the Reagan polling operation throughout the campaign, found a major surge for Reagan beginning *five days before the Nashua debate,* after a low-key, friendly debate among all of the candidates in Manchester, sponsored by the League of Women Voters and seen nationally on public television and on a delayed CBS broadcast.

According to Wirthlin's figures, Bush held an eight-point lead eight days before the primary. Among those who saw the Manchester debate, Reagan was judged the winner by fully fifteen points over Bush —a remarkable spread considering that nothing of any drama occurred during the debate, and considering also that no major policy divisions broke out. Further, Wirthlin said, by Sunday evening only 12 percent of those polled even knew of the Nashua debate, but Reagan already held a twenty-one-point lead. Dick Bennett, who was polling New Hampshire for Reagan, also pointed to the Manchester debate, rather than the Nashua debate, as the turning point of the primary.

It is possible to point to another "media event" as an explanation for the margin of Reagan's victory. Following the advice of his state chairman, former governor Hugh Gregg, Bush had left New Hampshire for Texas forty-eight hours before the primary; New Hampshire voters thus saw Bush jogging in his shirtsleeves in the Texas sun in the two days before the vote, while Reagan was slogging through the snows of New Hampshire.

But if the Manchester debate was the key, it may have been because of a ridiculously simple fact: that once Reagan *showed up,* once he demonstrated that he had the energy and the stomach to fight for the nomination, the Republicans of New Hampshire remembered just who "Mr. Republican" was. Reagan had, by the start of the 1980 campaign, long since reached into the less-affluent core of the Republican constituency. In a highly perceptive piece of reporting in the *Washington Post,* reflecting a political awareness that was never captured in the television reporting, *Post* writer Mark Shields, a long-time political operative, contrasted the working-class background of Reagan campaign leader Gerry Carmen with the tweedy, liberal Republican past of State Senator Susan McLane. The race, Shields argued, was "between Schlitz and sherry, between citizenship papers and collected papers, between night school and graduate school."

In the end, Reagan took the hard-core conservative issues constituency almost without a struggle. He won the votes of gun-control opponents, ERA opponents, abortion opponents, and he also took the votes of those with no more than a high school education and those with lower incomes. Bush, in contrast, did better among college graduates and the more affluent. But in New Hampshire, the Reagan constituency far outnumbered the Bush constituency.

What the voters saw in the undramatic Manchester debate, then, was that the candidate who had for so long spoken their views was, in fact, up to the job; that he had, in pollster Wirthlin's words, the "mental agility" to compete with any of his opponents. A draw in the

Manchester debate for Reagan was much more than a draw; since he spoke to the political issues Republicans embraced, and since he had gone unchallenged on those views by all save Anderson, *there were no reasons not to vote for Reagan except for strategic ones*. These, indeed, had emerged as his problems in a *Wall Street Journal*-sponsored "focus group" held in Keene shortly before the election. The *Journal* had reported that of fourteen participants, six had voted for Reagan four years earlier, but *none* were planning to do so now, largely because he was too old, too arrogant (he had ducked Iowa), and couldn't win. Analyst Bill Hamilton, who had run the group, noted that Bush "could still lose it if he made a big mistake. But the anti-Reagan comments seem solid. Even if Bush lost ground, I doubt if many of his people would drift back to Reagan."

The impact of Reagan's appearance at the Manchester debate suggests that Republicans did not so much "drift back" to Reagan, but that they had never drifted away in any fundamental sense. Throughout the primary campaign, the questions raised about Reagan never touched the core reasons for his political strength.

"He's too old," Bush's slogan implied, but Bush's fifty-four days in New Hampshire compared with Reagan's twenty did not demonstrate Reagan's weariness.

"Vote for me and I'll win," Bush had implied. But by the end of the campaign in New Hampshire, the obvious response was, "but if we vote for Reagan, *he'll* win."

Instead of building a base of supporters that was drawn to Bush out of a sense of what he might *do* as President, Bush had built—most effectively, it must be said—a following based on the idea that he could *become* President. With his first bad stumble, the politics of momentum became Bush's millstone. As the *Boston Globe*'s Marty Nolan wrote, "after a long campaign of hard work, Bush discovered that it is not possible to survive as an ideological chameleon, at least not in New Hampshire."

Now Bush told CBS's Richard Roth, "I thought we were going to do better. Reagan did a good job. I think there was an adverse effect on my candidacy by the debate incident." And Roth then asked Bush, "Does this mean, do you think, that Ronald Reagan cannot be stopped?" He told NBC's "Today" show and CBS "Morning" the next day that "if you had said to me four months ago, this is going to be a two-man race between you and Reagan early on—say, by Massachusetts—I would have said, 'Wow, this is very good.' But I don't want to look like I'm making excuses, because I did less well than I thought I would." And CBS's Diane Sawyer cited anonymous Bush aides who said, "After Iowa, Bush's support ballooned artificially . . . and he made the mistake of failing to give them anything substantive and ideological to cling to, once he had their attention early on."

On the "Today" show, Tom Pettit resurrected Reagan from the ranks of the "politically dead," noting that "we shouldn't underestimate the fact that there was an enormous sleeping giant of Reagan sentiment in New Hampshire from four years ago," while David Broder argued that "Bush still has some assets, if he can pull himself together and figure out something to say to the voters, other than the fact that 'I've got momentum.' " And later that night, on the "Mac-Neil-Lehrer Report" on public television, columnist Jack Germond— who had discovered the "Bush is unstoppable" sentiment seven days earlier—now argued that "the first question for the Republican Party is whether George Bush is a salvageable political commodity." And Germond reflected the emerging theme of the press, arguing that "Bush had no issues foundation for his campaign . . . the foundation of his campaign was that he was a winner. He has now lost, so he is no longer a winner." *New York Times* columnist Anthony Lewis wrote the next day that "Bush has come across so far as a man campaigning primarily on his ability to campaign."

The frustration of campaigning on momentum was heightened for Bush the week after New Hampshire, when Massachusetts and Vermont staged their primaries. Looking back on those primaries now, it is possible to argue that Bush should have been credited with a strong comeback from his New Hampshire debacle, narrowly winning the Massachusetts primary and running within 5,494 votes of Vermont victor Ronald Reagan. But the coverage of the March 4 vote produced a very different result; thanks to the close second-place finishes in both states of Illinois Republican Congressman John Anderson.

The Tuesday night and next-day stories were dominated by the Anderson story, as the press focused once again on the "momentum" phenomenon, and on the emergence of a surprisingly strong candidate. It would prove to be the only time in 1980 that the "expectation game" surfaced, at least in the Republican primary struggle, the only time that a candidate was credited with "winning" races he did not actually win. But it was enough to throw the Bush campaign off-stride once again.

"The surprise here," Walter Cronkite reported Tuesday night, "is the strong surge by Congressman Anderson." And a few minutes later he said, "It's another night of surprises for New England . . . we'll see how John Anderson has created a three-man Republican race by running even with Ronald Reagan and George Bush in Massachusetts and Vermont . . . a little-noticed candidate came out of nowhere to become a factor in the race for the Republican Presidential nomination. John Anderson, the congressman from Illinois, well regarded by his colleagues but little known to the public at large, emerged as one of the front-runners, jolting both Ronald Reagan and George Bush." Anderson's credibility was further established by his appearance, on a split screen with Walter Cronkite, in a discussion of his "strong show-ing." (Future political historians may choose to note that by 1980, the chief benefit of a strong, early primary showing was not the number of delegates won, but the number of minutes accorded that candidate in face-to-face discussions with Cronkite.) And the CBS anchor noted that "George Bush's performance in Massachusetts and Vermont fur-ther slowed the bandwagon he had rolling in the campaign." ("I think I did pretty damn well," Bush said.)

On Wednesday's "Today" show, Tom Brokaw said, "We've got quite a political story to tell you this morning. John Anderson is very happy indeed." That same day's *New York Times* observed that "Mr. Anderson's unexpectedly strong showing in both states established him as a more serious contender in the crowded field of Republican candidates." By Thursday, the *Times* had it that Anderson "estab-lished himself as a major candidate."

It must be said that for much of the press, the Anderson victory was kept in reasonable perspective. Bruce Morton on CBS "Morn-ing," recognizing Anderson's "spectacular showing," commented that "if you look ahead to the South and Illinois, it's kind of hard to know what other state he's going to do this well in. The future looks very good for Reagan, it seems to me. . . . Looking ahead, I think he's going to be very hard to stop." And the *Los Angeles Times*'s Robert Shogan said, "I don't even know that John Anderson can win another primary . . . [but] Bush was hurt even worse than Reagan; he could only get half of moderate and liberal Republicans. I think it has to be a big disappointment for him."

The impact of Anderson on the Bush campaign was indeed a blow of telling proportions. First, Bush was no longer the big story, no longer the Jimmy Carter of 1980, coming out of nowhere to establish momentum. Now it was John Anderson who could claim to share the surging outsider category. More important, Anderson's insistence on being explicit, even provocative, on the issues produced a contrast with Bush that colored the remainder of his primary campaign. The press had already begun to scorn him as a loser; one typical report on CBS on April 12 began with Bush asking, "What are we doing?" and had Richard Roth answering, "What George Bush is doing in Pennsyl-vania is trying hard to keep alive his faltering drive for the Republican Presidential nomination. . . . He went to a factory gate to greet steel-workers, but spent most of his time waiting in the rain." Now they had, in substantial measure, begun to treat him as an *unworthy* loser.

Liberal *Washington Star* columnist Mary McGrory wrote just after the Massachusetts primary, "no one told [Bush] that one cam-paign is never exactly like another, and that while Jimmy Carter got along without discussing any issues in the primaries, the 1980 voters are unaccountably interested in them. . . . The voters seem to be saying that you can be as conservative as Ronald Reagan, or as liberal as John Anderson, but you've got to be the real thing.''

The *Washington Post* weighed in editorially on March 14, responding to Bush's self-analysis that ''I've got to get off dead center now.''

''What Mr. Bush has to get off of is this compulsion to bore the country to tears with endless, minute-to-minute readings of his campaign health. [He] seems to have become absolutely mired in concern with the tactics and superficialities of the contest. He is squandering chance after chance to say something useful or instructive to the electorate, invariably coming on instead with yet another hospital-chart style account of his condition.''

Said David Broder in mid-April, ''Neither Bush nor his managers had the confidence when the year began to take on Reagan directly. [They feared debate] would simply antagonize the core conservatives in the party, and thereby jeopardize his chances in the general election. Bush said nothing to differentiate himself from Reagan.'' Bush's chances, Broder argued, lay in ''talking seriously and effectively about the hard policy choices the country faces.''

But Bush was trapped. He began declaring that ''I'm the issues candidate now,'' refusing again and again to discuss campaign strategy; but his basis for doing so seemed itself to be strategic, as he argued with the press that ''what I want to do is talk about issues; and if I said each time and discussed, you know, win lose or draw, I'd find that people focus on—I'm talking strategy and politics.'' After the New York primary, he promised, ''I'll keep focusing on these issues, and stay with that plan of not going into the mechanics of campaigning. . . .''

His advisors considered an advertising campaign more directly aimed at Ronald Reagan's vulnerabilities. They shot footage of senior citizens talking dubiously about Reagan's age; they drafted commercials in which Bush would talk about ''Iran—Afghanistan—the world as it is, not as we wish it to be,'' hoping to remind people of Reagan's inexperience on foreign policy. One commercial actually showed a huge photograph of Jimmy Carter. As the announcer spoke somberly of the dangers of an inexperienced President in the White House, the picture slowly but surely changed into a photograph of Ronald Reagan. In what Goodman later called ''the 'Dorian Gray' spot,'' the announcer reminds the viewers of ''promises that sounded good, but never worked for our country. Today the picture changes only slightly. Promises about a budget—that will end up robbing retirees, widows, and veterans of government benefits. Promises from Governor Reagan that, if heeded, will result in the worst inflation this country's ever seen. The kind of promises that tell us—we're not going to make the same mistake again. This country needs ability. This country needs

George Bush. This country needs a future." But Bush campaign chief Jim Baker quickly vetoed the commercial; it would simply alienate the Reagan constituency, he argued, and it would damage the fall campaign if Reagan turned out to be the nominee.

There was, in other words, nothing left to say. Bush's personal appeal, his campaign style, his effective speechmaking were indeed potent political tools; and even when the Illinois primary all but ended the battle for the nomination, Bush kept a cadre of supporters. With the help of a million dollars in advertising, he won the Pennsylvania primary; he ran Reagan a close second in Texas; and with another $300,000 in unopposed advertising in Michigan, he won that primary. Given the Reagan campaign's total lack of funds at the end of the primary season, stronger Bush showings in the middle primaries might well have made a real fight of it for the nomination. But by putting all his chips on the "momentum" strategy, there was no argument left to be made once Bush's own vulnerability was established, beginning in New Hampshire. As Baker put it after Illinois had apparently clinched the nomination for Reagan, "We established the George 'Who?' but we never established the George 'What?' " Jimmy Carter got away with that approach in 1976 because there never was another "What?" in the race. With Ronald Reagan and John Anderson both standing for a clear set of choices, the politics of momentum could not succeed.

iii Edward Kennedy and the Media, I: A Self-Inflicted Wound

If media coverage of a candidate is decisive to his fortunes, then the Presidential campaign of Senator Edward Kennedy in 1980 has an obvious turning point: the one-hour "CBS Reports: Teddy," broadcast to a nationwide audience on the evening of November 4, 1979. The documentary, narrated by Roger Mudd and featuring extended interviews with a rambling, uncertain, almost incoherent Kennedy, triggered a spate of columns and broadcast reports that set the tone for Kennedy's first ten weeks of campaigning, and, along with a spurt of support-the-President sentiment that followed Iran's seizure of American hostages on November 4, created a climate around Kennedy and his campaign that he was not able to shake until it was too late.

Without question, the Mudd interview played an important part in the decline and fall of Edward Kennedy, and it is especially important in revealing the interplay among the different media, which can crystallize an impression of a candidate into an unyielding mass. But it is important to put the Mudd interview and the whole question of the media's coverage of Ted Kennedy into a broader perspective. Among the points worth remembering:

● Media reaction to Kennedy was no more a function of preexisting hostility than their positive coverage of him was of ideological sympathy. The press is not only obsessed by the horserace, its coverage tends to reflect a sense of discretion about a probable winner. The hostile response to Kennedy after the Mudd interview was a consequence of Kennedy's political ineptitude in his conduct of that interview and the scent of blood in the water, which always galvanizes the political press.

● The accusations of unfair treatment of Kennedy should be looked at with several grains of salt; as we shall see, the principal fear of the media in the late summer of 1979 was that Ted Kennedy might get a free ride from the press.

54

• Kennedy's political wounds inflicted by the Chappaquiddick issue were not created by "CBS Reports," or by the flood of newspaper and broadcast questions about the 1969 accident at the dike bridge. The wounds were a result of the incident itself and of the impression given by Ted Kennedy's conduct, which no amount of media manipulation or political rhetoric could erase. If anything, the precampaign judgment that Chappaquiddick would not harm Kennedy's Presidential chances reflected a myopia about voter concerns which in some cases are beyond the power of media to eradicate. As I will argue in this chapter, the question of Chappaquiddick was simply misread by the polls, because polls cannot measure the difference between a hypothetical question about a hypothetical President, and a yes-or-no question that a voter must face when a candidate suddenly stands within reach of the White House.

• The inarticulate Ted Kennedy of "CBS Reports," unable to talk sensibly or convincingly about Chappaquiddick, unable to deliver himself of a clear English sentence about why he wanted to be President, was not the creation of Roger Mudd or of CBS producers and executives. In fact, that was very much the real Ted Kennedy of the summer of 1979, and of his campaign then taking shape: a campaign that assumed that Kennedy's presence and charisma would be all that was needed to topple President Carter. The Kennedy of the early campaign could not explain why he was running for President because the campaign itself never bothered to figure it out. In this sense, the press's obsession with Kennedy's gaffes and slips of the tongue was, in a clumsy way, an accurate portrayal of a candidate without a theme.

• The voters' doubts about Ted Kennedy's fitness for the Presidency did *not* begin with the Mudd interview and the critical press that followed, and those doubts did *not* begin when the Iranians seized the American hostages. They were in full flower well before those two events, as the polls at that time showed. Those doubts stemmed, I will argue, not from any portrait painted in the press, but from real questions about Kennedy's character, and about the policies he had espoused throughout his Senate career.

These points cannot erase the fact that the media played an important role in the demise of the Kennedy candidacy. They are to be taken as a kind of corrective, a reminder that the media do not create political impressions out of whole cloth. Rather, the shaping role of the media is one that is sharply limited by reality—in this case, the reality of Ted Kennedy's vulnerability to doubts about character and policy. Kennedy was wounded badly by the media coverage he received in the first two and a half months of his campaign; but it was, in substantial measure, a self-inflicted wound.

It is almost impossible to reconstruct the political atmosphere of the autumn of 1979. Carter's "crisis of confidence" speech of July 15 had been met with cautious approval, which had vanished overnight when he had demanded the resignations of all of his cabinet members, and had fired four of them. An ABC-Harris poll of early October gave Kennedy a 63–32 margin over Jimmy Carter nationally, and in the early-delegate-selection states of Iowa and New Hampshire, Kennedy's lead over Carter was between 2–1 and 3–1. A *New York Post* of October bannered, "They're All Crazy for Kennedy. 'Draft Teddy' fever sweeps the nation. Tip O'Neill and Labor say: he's a cinch. They just love him in New Hampshire."

A series of "CBS Evening News" reports in late August of 1979 concluded that Carter faced an all but unstoppable obstacle to renomination if Ted Kennedy decided to run. It showed former Iowa State Democratic Chairman Tom Whitney stating flatly, "The heart of the Democratic Party in Iowa belongs to Ted Kennedy. It's his for the asking." Two days later, looking at Carter's support in the South, CBS showed a poll of Southern Democrats, showing Ted Kennedy with a 47–30 lead over Carter in that region. On September 7, CBS's Bruce Morton, citing a July CBS poll giving Kennedy an incredible 53–16 lead over Carter, reported "the consensus among political professionals here, is that Edward Kennedy can have the Democratic Presidential nomination anytime he wants it." On October 10, Lesley Stahl quoted House Speaker Tip O'Neill as saying, "I don't think he can be denied the nomination if he runs."

Much of the concern of the press over Kennedy concerned the question of whether the senator was getting something of a free ride from the Fourth Estate. ABC's Av Westin said as much when he mused, "We don't want to end up giving him a free ride." Dennis Britton, national editor of the *Los Angeles Times,* conceded in early October, "The media have not been as vigorous on Kennedy as on some other people." *Time* wondered in late July that "perhaps because readers are inured to his indiscretions, the impact is blurred. His growth as a Senator, his devotion to important national issues, his overcoming of wrenching sorrow, are more likely to create the image of a sympathetic, decisive, if all too human leader." *Newsweek* reprinted a letter to the *Quincy* (Mass.) *Patriot Leader* which asked sarcastically, "How much does the Kennedy family pay the American press for continuous publicity?" Columnist Richard Reeves wrote in *Esquire* that "we did it. The press drafted Teddy Kennedy."

The idea that the American press, as an institution, would roll over and play dead in the wake of a Ted Kennedy campaign was never a reality. The tenth anniversary of Chappaquiddick in July, 1979, had produced a spate of television and print reports, in which Kennedy himself had participated to show his lack of fear over the issue.

"I bear full responsibility for that accident," he told CBS on July

17. "I acknowledge that many of the actions I was involved in on that night were irresponsible."

That same CBS news report quoted Reagan aide Lyn Nofziger as saying, "it was a matter of not only a girl—a girl dying, but a man who wants to be President panicking in—in the clutch." But the CBS-*New York Times* poll seemed to suggest that Chappaquiddick would not stop Democrats from tossing out Jimmy Carter in favor of a potential Kennedy challenge. While 80 percent of those polled knew of the accident, those polled gave Kennedy higher marks for being "good under pressure" than they did Carter by a 55–40 margin.

The more conservative press commentators, for whom Kennedy was the ultimate potential liberal President, were hardly disposed to give Kennedy a "free ride." William Safire, in his October 29 *New York Times* column, recounted a 1958 speeding arrest of Kennedy, then a University of Virginia law student. Noting that Kennedy had turned out his lights and was found lying across the front seat when the police officer approached his car, Safire constructed a case for the incident being "a psychological prelude to Chappaquiddick . . . a trait in his character, leading him to run from reality in a crisis." Citing this incident, his expulsion from Harvard for cheating on an examination, and Chappaquiddick, Safire wrote "when in big trouble, the repeated history has been to run, to hide, to get caught, and to get away with it."

In fact, as Kennedy's September 6 "leak" to major newspaper outlets—that his family had given their permission should he decide to run—marked him as an all-but-certain candidate, other critical accounts of Kennedy's character began to appear. The sensitive topic of Kennedy's strained marriage, with wife Joan living in Boston and repeated rumors of marital infidelity, surfaced when the *Washington Monthly*'s December, 1979, issue, appearing on the stands in late October, ran an article by Suzannah Lessard called "Kennedy's Woman Problem; Women's Kennedy Problem."

The article detailed—without naming any names or sources—Kennedy's alleged pattern of affairs, in which an aide or friend would invite a woman to lunch with Kennedy, from which would follow casual "dalliance." This pattern, Lessard wrote, "suggests a severe case of arrested development, a kind of narcissistic intemperance, a large, babyish ego that must constantly be fed. . . . I don't believe men who really like women carry on in this way."

Because the piece was rejected by *The New Republic* it received major attention, including a mention in *Time* magazine's November 2, 1979, issue—again, *before* the Mudd interview—under the heading "Sex and the Senior Senator." The article in turn quoted writer Henry Fairlie as commenting that during a Washington dinner party, "for a full hour and a half, 14 talented and interesting men and women talked of nothing but the sexual activities of Edward Kennedy.''

All of this suggests that, even before CBS ran its November 4 documentary, "Teddy," there was nothing like a "free-ride" mentality at work in the press. As we shall see, such outlets as the *Washington Star,* the *Reader's Digest,* the *Wall Street Journal,* and the *New York Times* all were preparing major examinations of Chappaquiddick, because Kennedy's impending announcement for the Presidency had *made the issue legitimate once again.* Since the question of Ted Kennedy's fitness for the Presidency was moving beyond some hypothetical poll question into the realm of real possibility, the subject—indeed, any subject about Kennedy or any other candidate—was fair game for the most rigorous possible scrutiny. And questions about a potential President's compulsive infidelities and his possible association with negligent manslaughter would not, it would become clear, stand on the same plane as questions about his soundness on agricultural policy.

Why, then, this notion that Ted Kennedy, with the aid of a complaisant press, would sweep into the White House the moment he consented to run? First, political observers are frequently trapped in the wisdom of the moment. The heady mixture of neutral, "objective" polls, with their "possible error" of plus or minus 3 percent, along with the pronouncements of political insiders, creates a conventional wisdom very difficult to challenge. The 2–1 lead Kennedy had over Carter in the polls, the evident pleading of worried Democratic senators and congressmen for Kennedy to salvage the party from a rout at the hands of Carter suggested that the public had already come to terms with the question of Kennedy's character and had decided those questions would not prevent a vote for Kennedy. The notion that minds can be changed during the actual conduct of a Presidential race, and that questions can be raised with new force *because* the hypothetical race had become a real one, was very little in evidence in media coverage of Ted Kennedy.

Moreover, the judgment was—as so often happens in the way political races are now covered—focused almost exclusively on the fact that Kennedy was likely to win a race. What he was running *to do,* whether his policies or character had *earned* him the White House, were questions unworthy of asking in the context of huge leads in the polls and a "Teddy Can't Lose" certainty within the press. Kennedy himself suggested that policy questions did not lie at the heart of his challenge to Carter; as a front page *New York Times* interview with Kennedy in mid-September had it, "Kennedy Says That Leadership, Not Economic Policy, Is At Issue." According to Adam Clymer, Kennedy "did not differ substantially with President Carter's economic policies," but said that "leadership" was needed "to make them work." As Blair Clark noted in the *Columbia Journalism Review* after the 1980 primaries ended, "by stressing 'leadership' Kennedy gave the press an excuse to explore a subject reporters and editors had treated gingerly: the character issue. Inevitably, that led to Chappaquiddick."

Two television programs that dealt with Kennedy in the days before the Mudd interview aired suggested that the senator's "free ride" from the media had become something very different. On ABC's "20/20" magazine show on November 1, Tom Jarriel began his interview with Kennedy this way:

"Senator, you cheated in college, you panicked at Chappaquiddick. Do you have what it takes to be President?"

And NBC's irreverent "Saturday Night Live" on November 3 opened with an excited crowd waiting for Ted Kennedy's Presidential announcement. Suddenly, a dripping wet Ted Kennedy (played by Bill Murray) appeared, covered with seaweed, unable to explain what had happened to him.

But it was "Teddy" that drew a clear line between the media image of "Teddy the winner," and the "Teddy the klutz" view that dominated the next few weeks. It was, according to "CBS Reports" Executive Producer Howard Stringer, originally designed as a series of reports on the major Presidential contenders, designed to go beyond the severe time constraints of the "Evening News." (As it turned out, the pressures of the prime-time ratings race and the limits of the equal-time provision of the Federal Communications Act proved equally constraining. The equal-time rule—section 315 of the nation's basic broadcasting law—permits exemptions only for *regularly scheduled* news and public affairs shows. Since "CBS Reports" was not a regularly scheduled program, but instead appeared occasionally on the prime-time schedule, it was governed by the equal-time rule—a rule that affected *formally announced* candidates. By November 4, 1979, every Republican candidate for President except Ronald Reagan had officially announced for President; that meant that any profile of any Republican would require an hour of prime time for every Republican. By contrast, *none* of the Democratic candidates had announced by early November; when CBS learned Kennedy was planning to announce on November 6, they moved up the documentary to Sunday, November 4. "If we'd known how bad it was going to be," one Kennedy staffer said much later, "we could have sprung a surprise announcement three days earlier and the damn program would never have run.")

CBS correspondent Roger Mudd interviewed Kennedy at length on two separate occasions: at Hyannisport in mid-September, then at the senator's McLean, Virginia, home in early October. Some Kennedy staffers charged after the show that the program had been unfair because the program aired when Kennedy had all but formally announced for the Presidency, but had been shot well before the senator had decided to run, and thus caught Kennedy in an ambiguous frame of mind. Given Kennedy's leak to the press about his family's changed attitude toward a Presidential campaign, which occurred on September 7, this complaint seems misplaced.

What may account for the tone of the "Teddy" documentary is the possibility that Kennedy's staff assumed that Roger Mudd's friendliness with the Kennedy family would produce an hour of cozy chit-chat. Mudd is, in fact, a McLean neighbor of the Kennedys; he was in Los Angeles when Robert Kennedy was shot and guided Ethel Kennedy through the crowd to her fatally wounded husband; he is—was—a regular participant in the Robert F. Kennedy Pro-Celebrity Tennis Tournament. This could be why Kennedy Press Secretary Tom Southwick urged Ted Kennedy to participate in the interview sessions, and why no one bothered to brief Kennedy about the possible range of questions. Kennedy himself was neither much experienced nor especially skilled at the art of the political interview. In the decade of the 1970s, he appeared on network Sunday interview shows perhaps a half-dozen times. And his less-than-firm command of the English language was commonly known among Washington journalists, who ascribed it to choice rather than ineptitude. He was often stumbling in his ad lib remarks, Richard Reeves wrote in July of 1979, and David Broder had said, "the front half and back half of his sentences match up less frequently than most politicians. . . . I think it is a technique for slowing himself down and not saying what he doesn't want to say."

A *Time* magazine cover piece on Kennedy, which went to press before the Mudd interview was aired, called him "one of the most effective stump speakers in the country," but also described a Senate hearing where "he lapsed into the stammering, wandering style that sometimes makes his questions or unrehearsed remarks seem relatively incoherent."

(*Time* quoted Kennedy thus: "The case we, uh, that has to be made, and I'd like to see what each of you has to say on this, is, uh, why should we do it for Mexico, and why not others?")

And a Judy Bachrach feature piece in the October 15 *Washington Star* had the reporter asking Kennedy, "Why do you talk so oddly? Why can't you complete a sentence?" (Kennedy attributed it to growing up as the last child in a big family.)

"It never seems to get in any article," she quoted a Kennedy friend as saying, "but journalists, because they use words, assume that anyone who cannot make a complete sentence is not bright. But Teddy is like Eisenhower that way—you had to watch him to understand what he said." But in the context of a friendly interview by a friendly correspondent, how much harm could it do?

The answer came with the opening moments of the documentary; Kennedy, his children, and his mother Rose gathered outside his

Hyannisport home ready to leave on a camping trip. Then came Mudd's voice:

"This is probably the way a mother whose son is running for the Presidency would like a documentary about him to begin," he said. "A nice walking shot of the two of them as he sets off with her grandchildren on a summer camping trip." As the picture shifted to Kennedy and his children at an amusement park, Mudd commented, "This is the raw material for magazine cover stories. Less than an hour in an amusement park near Springfield gives the press plenty of time to watch and compare notes."

What made this political profile immediately different was not that Mudd's view was especially harsh, but that it it so uncommon for a network television correspondent to describe the pictures the audience is seeing from the perspective of a politician's *hopes* about those pictures. It was, however, not the opening shot that made the "Teddy" documentary so significant, but three different sets of questions posed by Mudd to Kennedy.

Sitting with a casually dressed, overweight, and uneasy-looking Kennedy, Mudd first asked the senator, "How fair has the American press been to you and your family?" and "What sort of separatism should the press maintain between your public life and your private life, or any public official's?"

"Well," said Kennedy, "I think there's a natural inquisitiveness of people about all aspects of—of people's lives. I—I mean, I sort of understand that."

"What—what's the present state of your marriage, Senator?"

It was a clean shot; having gotten Kennedy's "understanding" of the press's curiosity, he asked, as Executive Producer Stringer said later, "the question the viewer wanted to ask Kennedy himself."

It was, to be sure, exactly the kind of question that an intense briefing by political advisors would have anticipated; over the course of a day's hard work, shaping such an answer over and over, something like this would have evolved: *

"We've had a rough time of it. We're apart now. I want us to be together soon, because I love her very much."

The answer Kennedy gave began in that spirit, but quickly veered into the rhetoric of a congressional committee report.

"Well, I think it's a—we've had some difficult times, but I think we've—have—we've I think been able to make some very good progress, and it's—I would say that it's—it's—it's—I'm delighted that we're able to share the time and the relationship that we—that we do

* This is *not* an attempt at post facto second-guessing, since, as a former political consultant, I had frequently played the role of hypothetical Kennedy advisor with colleagues and friends. With remarkably little variation, this was the response they all came up with long before the Mudd interview.

share.'' When asked whether he and Joan were separated, Kennedy said, ''I don't know whether there's a single word that should—have for a description of it,'' and expressed his pride in her conquest of alcoholism.

After a commercial break, the documentary resumed with an account of Chappaquiddick; here the picture showed a car, at night, driving along Chappaquiddick's main road, from the point of view of the driver. The picture lent devastating evidence to Mudd's account.

''After a minute or two of driving,'' Mudd said, and we saw, ''the reflector sign, the yellow line and the hard surface of the road all indicated that the main street to the ferry bore sharply to the left, but Kennedy turned sharply to the right. . . . only an unpaved bumpy road leading to the Dike Bridge''—and here the camera shook as the car headed down the bumpy road. There was, the camera clearly suggested, no way to believe that a sober, reasonable driver could have made that turn by mistake. Then the interview resumed. Four times, Kennedy said he would be absolutely candid in his responses.

''I'd respond to any particular question that you'd have,'' he said. ''I'll answer any question that—that you have or that you have right now. . . . I'll answer any question that you want to ask me, and I'll answer any question that is asked me during the course of a—a campaign. . . . I'm glad to answer any question that you have right now on any of the aspects of it.''

As Mudd described Kennedy's attitude, ''no matter which questions are asked of him, he still does not seem at ease with the answers. And he still talks about Chappaquiddick in a rather bloodless third-person way, referring to his own conduct that night, for instance, as 'the conduct.' '' Kennedy's most coherent summary of the issue as it affected his fitness for the Presidency was this answer:

''. . . the circumstances at that—that particular eve—evening did involve physical trauma, did involve an accident, did involve enormous sense of—of—of loss in terms of the—the life of an individual, and did involve the—what I have recog—what I've recognized basically as an irresponsible behavior in not reporting the accident earlier. Now, I think that that is—I have served in the United States Senate for a position of seventeen years, I've taken positions, I've spoken out on issues, I've spoken on questions, and there have been other factors which have impacted on my life, and people will have to make that judgment.''

In summing up the section of ''Teddy'' dealing with Chappaquiddick, Mudd offered these possible choices for the American voter:

''One, that Kennedy's account of a tragic accident is believable, and is therefore of no political consequence. Two, that Kennedy's account is not believable, but that knowing any other account could have ruined a career which, since Chappaquiddick has become substantial, makes it an acceptable defeat. Three, that Kennedy's own account not only is a fabrication, but is also a major flaw that disqualifies him for the Presidency.''

The documentary's own camera seemed to suggest that the first choice was impossible to accept; and although Mudd is said to have been dissatisfied with his questioning of Kennedy on the issue, feeling that he never managed to frame the questions so as to force Kennedy to confront the inconsistencies, the Chappaquiddick section was powerful enough to unsettle some of his most ardent supporters.

But the single most devastating section of the interview was yet to come. After a section dealing with Kennedy's dizzying pace in the United States Senate and in his personal appearances, Mudd said over footage of Kennedy campaigning, "On the stump, Kennedy can be dominating, imposing, and masterful. But off the stump, in personal interviews, he can become stilted, elliptical, and at times appear as if he really doesn't want America to get to know him."

Then the picture switched to Mudd and Kennedy talking in the yard of Kennedy's Virginia home—and Mudd posed this question:

"Why do you want to be President?"

In journalistic terms, this is a "softball." It is not Mike Wallace confronting a reluctant politician with hotel registers signed "Mr. and Mrs. Smith," or with check disbursements from Abscam Enterprises. It is an open invitation to a politician who has been a presumptive Presidential candidate for twelve years to explain why he wants the job. Here, in full, is what Kennedy said:

"Well, I'm—were I to—to make the—the announcement and—to run, the reasons that I would run is because I have a great belief in this country, that it is—has more natural resources than any nation in the world, has the greatest educated population in the world, the greatest capacity for innovation in the world, and the greatest political system in the world. And yet, I see at the current time that most of the industrial nations of the world are exceeding us in terms of productivity, are doing better than us in terms of meeting the problems of inflation, that they're dealing with their problems of energy and their problems of unemployment. And it just seems to me that this nation can cope and deal with its problems in a way that it has in the past. We're facing complex issues and problems in this nation at this time, but we have faced similar challenges at other times. And the energies and the resourcefulness of this nation, I think, should be focused on these problems in a way that brings a sense of restoration in this country by its people to—in dealing with the problems that we face—primarily the issues on the economy, the problems of inflation, and the problems of energy. And I would basically feel that—that it's imperative for this country to either move forward, that it can't stand still, or otherwise it moves back.''

Was America startled or dismayed by what it saw of Ted Kennedy? The question cannot be answered in those terms, for most Americans weren't watching. That night, ABC was running the first network television showing of *Jaws,* one of the biggest movies in history; and the film took 57 percent of the audience then watching television. As is true of most documentaries, "Teddy" drew a low audience share, about 16 percent. In his comments on the program, *New York Times* columnist Tom Wicker wrote that, "Since 'Jaws' took 57 percent of the available audience, the damage was probably limited."

Which, of course, missed the point. While the audience's numbers were small, it is fair to say that every political writer, every political and campaign official, every "opinion maker" watched "Teddy." And the impact of such a program is hardly confined to the original audience. As with many political events on television, most especially debates and speeches, the press—print and broadcast—acts as a mediator, explaining to the country at large what it is they have seen. And the unanimous verdict, among Kennedy's staunchest friends and most unremitting foes, was that his performance was a disaster.

Mary McGrory, the *Washington Star*'s liberal columnist, wrote that the program "reveals that the Senator, even when invited to expand on the themes of his own choosing, like leadership, is not articulate or even coherent." Jimmy Breslin, whose attitude toward Robert Kennedy was almost worshipful, wrote that "as I watched this Kennedy, the third Kennedy, on television on Sunday night, I suddenly found him to be annoying, wanting, and disturbing. . . . I think people will think [about Chappaquiddick]: 'if this guy doesn't care about what happened to the girl, why is he going to care about me and my kids?' " Tom Wicker, after doubting the enormity of the damage, noted that "even when he sought to say why he wanted to be President, he wandered away into platitudes couched in incomplete sentences." Anthony Lewis, the other *New York Times* liberal columnist, described Kennedy as "stumbling, inarticulate, unconvincing . . . a man unsure of the why's and where's in his life—unsure who he was. . . . He has some difficult convincing to do, about his policy and person." *Newsweek* referred to Kennedy's "faltering responses to questions about Chappaquiddick" and the differences he had with Carter.

The impression of Kennedy's inadequacy was reinforced by Mudd's reputation as a fair-minded reporter without a killer-instinct public personality.

"Mudd is too decent a reporter to set out to do a job on anyone," the *Washington Post*'s Colman McCarthy wrote. "As it turned out, Teddy did a job on himself." (Mudd was also, a colleague observed wryly, one celebrity journalist who could ask a question such as

onduct
g over
tergate
g Ken-
d to the
tured a
he case

ce came
azine in
ny piece
Kennedy
mportant
—which
t-clad re-
' expose,
. This is

which to
as that the
ad created
which cov-
and over
gn, former
blackbirds.
away, they
seen a well-
on the part
y wanted to
ombudsman
cious of the
edentials for
Seib said, is
t where it is

ennedy as he
Faneuil Hall.
his side, ner-
im, was duly

egan investigat-
e article, which
ituted an illegal
aises significant

ur marriage?" without having it thrown back in

cumentary did, then, was to help shape a cli-
s most powerful claim to the Democratic Pres-
leadership skill and his political ability to lead
lace of a faltering incumbent—was severely
his most likely ideological allies were embar-
e. That this interview aired on the very day
zed American hostages at the embassy in
but the perception of Kennedy's ineptitude
s problems in dealing with that politically
oincided with another aspect of the media
no amount of interviewing skill could have
appaquiddick and the character issue.
nmer and early autumn had suggested that
k would not have an impact on the votes
y challenge Carter. Longtime Democratic
was not so sure. "Nobody has measured
it the time Kennedy announced. "All of
ery straightforward questions. To really
appaquiddick, it is necessary to ask a
h more oblique." Kennedy's campaign
t all, largely because—incredible as it
all until well after Kennedy had an-
e factor that a static view of polling
ble will change their minds about an
re subjected to new information or
hey had forgotten. And the press, far
ate life of public figures than it had
pened in 1969, and determined to
le for the "liberal media darling,"
days and weeks surrounding Ken-

ovember 6, the day Kennedy for-
ran an editorial with a photograph
ge, an event all but unheard of in
d "even though the Chappaquid-
e the conduct of public office, it
uestions it raises about credibil-
' William Safire dubbed the in-
ears-long effort to demonstrate
as President Nixon had done.
vell. A *New York Times* edito-
"used his enormous influence

to protect himself and his career by leading a cover-up of misc[
—and the known facts lead to that suspicion—there will han
him not just a cloud of tragedy, but one of corruption, of the Wa
kind." Cartoonist Oliphant portrayed Richard Nixon watchin
nedy, and saying, "so once upon a time he went on TV and lie
people; so what's wrong with that?" The *Washington Post* fea
two-part series on the incident in which Martin Schram called
"politically, a ticking time bomb."

Perhaps the most aggressive example of the issue's presen
from the *Reader's Digest,* the second biggest-selling mag
America, which published in its February, 1980, issue a lengt
on Chappaquiddick, using computer studies to prove that
had to have been driving at an excessive rate of speed. As i
as the article was a *Reader's Digest* television commercia
never mentioned Kennedy by name—featuring a trenchcoa
porter looking as if he had just stepped out of a "60 Minutes]
talking about an event "which may have changed history
Chappaquiddick," he said. "And this—is the bridge." *

This was, to say the least, an unpleasant atmosphere in
begin a campaign for the Presidency. What made it worse w
Mudd interview, and the coverage of that television show, h
an impression of Kennedy as something of a stumblebum,
erage of his early weeks of campaigning reinforced ove
again. In a famous remark after his 1968 Presidential campa
Senator Eugene McCarthy had characterized the press as "
One flies onto a telephone wire, they all fly on. One flies
all fly away." Everyone in the world of political media had
regarded reporter discover a heretofore unseen weakness
of a major political figure. Now, no one covering Kenned
miss that story, especially since, as *Washington Post*
Charles Seib noted in mid-November, the press "is con
charge of softness, and it is determined to establish its cr
tough, unbiased political coverage." (The question,
whether the press is "leaning over backward to the poi
now unfair to the man it was accused of pampering?")

"Pampering" was hardly what the press did to K
launched his campaign on November 6 from Boston's
The presence of Kennedy's estranged wife, Joan, by
vously, but graciously, promising to campaign with

* After the 1980 election, the Federal Election Commission b
ing *Reader's Digest* to determine whether tapes promoting th
were distributed to broadcasters throughout the nation, cons
campaign contribution. As of this writing the case, which
First Amendment questions, has not been resolved.

noted; and so was the contrast between his effective announcement speech and his appearance when confronted by Mudd. David Broder called Kennedy "a magnificent orator in full cry, who has yet to prove that he can communicate much more than his name when addressing the American people at less than a shout." "Action verbs will not do," the *Washington Post* editorialized, and an analysis in the *Boston Globe,* perhaps the most pro-Kennedy publication in the country, noted that "for the two months during which his campaign has been taking shape, Kennedy has yet to give an indication of how he would apply his activist concept of the White House to a specific problem."

But these criticisms were gentle compared with the impression of Kennedy on the television screen, an impression clearly shaped by the Mudd interview. The hesitancies and rhetorical sloppiness which had always been a part of Ted Kennedy's makeup now were moved to center stage on the network news programs, which in turn made them grist for the print press and analyses.

On the "CBS Evening News" of November 17, Phil Jones reported that "the candidate has exhibited some early campaign sloppiness. . . . Twice in one day [Kennedy] talked about the Wabash Railroad. The problem: the Wabash doesn't exist in Iowa." Kennedy, Jones said, has become "increasingly strident in his attacks on President Carter's leadership. . . . But when it comes to questions of his own policies, he often appears to be a man without a plan . . . he appeared uncertain." And the report showed Kennedy stumbling through an answer. "I will speak to it and outline—I mean, I mentioned that—and—but I mean—that, I think is the best example." When Kennedy on November 19 turned his pledge to help "every farm family" into the Spoonerism "every fam farmily," all three networks used the clip in their evening news reports. Two network reports pointed out Kennedy's mid-December remark to the Rochester, New Hampshire, Chamber of Commerce in which he talked of "weatherization" of his energy conservation program, rather than "weatherizing" homes.

Newsweek's December 10 issue joined the "Kennedy-as-klutz" coverage, reporting that at the University of Iowa, "Kennedy read a prepared speech as if he had never seen it before, seldom looking up to make eye contact with his audience. [In questions and answers] Kennedy began to ramble and students began slipping out of the hall or reading textbooks." David Broder, on December 26, wrote that "professional monitors in the press corps noted that Kennedy once again was the victim of tangle-tongue disease, helplessly snarled in his effort to convey to a man in a wheelchair his support of a program to procure special buses for the handicapped."

The press was looking for Kennedy to reinforce the impression of a stumbling, incoherent candidate not fully in command of the facts. And it was this perception that made his remarks about the deposed Shah of Iran so damaging.

On December 2, Kennedy was in San Francisco, where he gave an interview to Rollin Post, a longtime Bay Area political analyst, on KRON-TV. In the course of that interview, Post asked Kennedy what he thought of Ronald Reagan's suggestion that the Shah be granted permanent political asylum in the United States. With one eye apparently on the large California Hispanic vote, Kennedy geared his answer to the question of entry into the United States. The Shah, he said, "ran one of the most violent regimes in the history of mankind. How —how do we justify, in the—the United States on the one hand accepting that individual because he would like to come here and stay here with his umpteen billions dollars that he's stolen from Iran, and at the same time say to the Hispanics who are here legally that they have to wait nine years to bring their wife and their children to this country?"

That part of the interview was not aired in the KRON-TV broadcast. But when the *San Francisco Chronicle* saw the complete text of the interview, it made the remark page-one news.* The "CBS Evening News" report on December 3 moved directly away from the point of Kennedy's statement to its political ramifications, as Susan Spencer described "distracted aides and speechwriters [who] clustered near telephones to review his statements," and predicted that "the uproar over Kennedy's comments today may prompt him to return to his former vow of silence on Iran." That report was followed by a Lesley Stahl piece from the White House, which noted that "top aides at the White House are convinced that Kennedy blundered . . . and decided to draw attention to it."

So they did. Carter campaign chairman Robert Strauss deplored any remarks "that could in any way endanger the lives of the people over there . . ." and Secretary of State Cyrus Vance said "anything that tends to undermine (national consensus) is clearly unhelpful." Robert Dole and Jerry Brown similarly jumped on Kennedy, with Brown opposing any remarks that could "jeopardize the lives of American citizens in Iran." To compound Kennedy's troubles, one Teheran newspaper headlined the story, "American Public Opinion is Shifting in Favor of Iran," and a prominent Iranian banker appeared on CBS the next day to say that Kennedy's statements proved "we are winning in our campaign to convince American people." In the context of the

---

* The accidental nature of the uproar recalled an earlier incident; when Michigan Governor George Romney made his famous "brainwashing" statement about his Vietnam views on a Lou Gordon interview show, the program failed even to make the remark a featured element of its show. It was secondary press interest that turned the remark into a political disaster for Romney.

anger raging over the Iranian seizure of American diplomats, this was roughly equivalent to winning the endorsement of the Central Committee of the Soviet Communist Party.

Most revealing about the press's attitude toward Kennedy's remarks, however, was how widely they were analyzed strategically, rather than substantively. Columnist George Will did attack them on their merits, arguing that Kennedy's words lent "bogus legitimacy to Iran's agenda." But the dominant theme was that Kennedy had stumbled again, that he had committed a gaffe. He hadn't hurt himself because he was wrong, the argument implicitly ran; he was wrong because he had hurt himself.

"A classic political blunder," Germond and Witcover wrote, comparing it to Romney's brainwashing remark and Ford's mistaken "liberation" of Eastern Europe in the second 1976 debate. Indeed, they wrote, "Kennedy's gaffe has little or nothing to do with the substance of what he said about the Shah. [Rather] it was the wrong time." And, they said, "a candidate who gets a reputation for political ineptitude can be compromised beyond recall." Wrote Evans and Novak, "in portraying Ted Kennedy in yet another stumblebum guise, it is politically disastrous. . . . Some politicians are now asking each other: is it possible that Ted Kennedy really is a stumblebum?" *Time* magazine's headline summed up the press reaction: "Kennedy Makes a Goof." (The *Des Moines Register and Tribune* was one of the very few press organs to come to Kennedy's defense, noting that Henry Kissinger and Ronald Reagan had both urged the granting of asylum to the Shah—a course of action that might have placed the lives of the hostages in imminent danger. Kennedy, the paper said, "created the least danger for the hostages. Yet, Kennedy's statement was more bitterly denounced . . . a large measure of politics figured in the reaction. The politicians had a field day at Kennedy's expense—and possibly at the expense of the hostages.")

By the middle of December, barely a month after announcing and with more than a month to go before the Iowa caucuses, President Carter had overcome the 2–1 lead with which Kennedy had entered the fall season, and actually passed Kennedy among Democrats 48–46, according to an ABC-Lou Harris poll. The apparent combination of doubts about Kennedy's ability, doubts about his character, doubts about Chappaquiddick, and support for a President under siege had turned the expected Kennedy rout around. Clearly, the view of Kennedy in the press in the first month of his campaign—from Mudd to the Shah, so to speak—had played a part in Kennedy's misfortunes. But to point to the press as the active player in Kennedy's fall from grace is, I think, to misunderstand the relationship between political events and the media. Important as the climate was surrounding Kennedy's entrance into the race, it is important to remember that a climate is not *created* by the media; their role is much more passive, and the role of the candidate and of the preexisting political climate much more active than a media-based interpretation of events might suggest.

First, Kennedy's declining fortunes did not begin with the airing of the Roger Mudd interview, the consequent storm of press criticism, or even the seizure of the hostages in Iran. Two polls, taken *before* any of these incidents, suggest that Kennedy had already begun to lose a huge chunk of his lead over Carter simply by moving toward an active declaration of candidacy. A *Time* magazine poll taken by Daniel Yankelovich, and published in *Time*'s November 5, 1979, issue, reported that Kennedy's thirty-point lead over Carter of the previous summer had shrunk to ten points—a loss of two-thirds of his margin *before* his media-related troubles. An earlier *New York Times* poll is consistent with that finding; it showed Kennedy dropping from a thirty-point lead to a sixteen-point lead over Carter in the months of August and September. On ABC News, a poll of Democratic state chairmen showed that the huge surge of support to the President occurred *before* either the Mudd interview or the hostage seizure.

Two factors might account for this drop in Kennedy's support: First, Chappaquiddick had, as I argued earlier, been examined by voters in a hypothetical context involving a hypothetical candidate; between summer and midfall Kennedy had moved much closer to declaring his candidacy, and now voters were confronted with the real possibility of electing a President who (a) had a reputation for marital infidelity and (b) had been involved with the reckless, perhaps criminal, death of a young girl. The nature of the Presidential office, its stature as a place of moral as well as political leadership in American life, argues that the more the prospect becomes that of electing a "morally unfit" President, the quicker such concerns rise to the surface.

Second, Kennedy was an unregenerate liberal, a propoor, pro-black, progovernment-spending politician running in a time when the portents were not favorable to such a candidacy. Indeed, Kennedy had said at the 1978 midterm Democratic convention that "sometimes a party must sail against the wind," in resisting the drift toward conservatism. However noble a sentiment, it is not necessarily a guarantee of electoral success, if the wind against which you are sailing is blown by public discontent. Carter himself was the most conservative Democratic nominee since John W. Davis; Kennedy's own liberal colleagues in the Senate had suffered a near-rout in the 1978 congressional elections. And he was the exemplar of the faith, what conservative James Jackson Kilpatrick called "a curly-haired McGovern."

In the summer of discontent that surrounded Jimmy Carter in 1979, Kennedy's popularity was less a sign of agreement with his philosophy than it was a way to say, in the broad-brush stroke that political choice requires, "We don't want Carter." That helps account, for example, for the CBS poll of that time showing Kennedy running far ahead of Carter in the South. But as Kennedy became less a way of saying "not Carter," and more a candidate with an intention of actually seeking the Presidency, that philosophy became a source of discontent to substantial parts of the electorate. (One poll taken in New Hampshire and reported in the *Boston Globe* before the Mudd interview suggests the potency of the discontent with Kennedy's liberalism. When New Hampshire voters were asked whom they would vote for in the primary, Kennedy received 58 percent. When voters were reminded of Chappaquiddick, Kennedy dropped five points. When voters were reminded of Kennedy's record, his support dropped *twelve* points.)

Kennedy's initial strategy, in fact, suggests that his campaign regarded his record as his biggest vulnerability. In stressing leadership, rather than specific policy differences with President Carter, Kennedy hoped to focus attention on his high ratings in the polls for forceful leadership, rather than alienating more moderate and conservative Democrats. Instead, it made his own inarticulateness a devastating campaign setback, because it undermined his own core argument for his candidacy. (In contrast, Ronald Reagan experienced more than his fair share of blunders and misstatements. But Reagan's commitment to a program and a philosophy helped protect him from the damaging political consequences of such mistakes.)

By the time the Iowa caucuses drew near, Kennedy's image had become the opposite of that with which he first moved toward the Presidency. The polls that had argued away the importance of Chappaquiddick now told a totally different story. A Gallup poll for *Newsweek* in mid-January showed that 57 percent of Democrats and Independents said that they were not very likely to vote for Kennedy in November if he were nominated; the comparable number for Carter was 27 percent. That same poll, which showed Carter leading Kennedy 39–21, showed that of those who said they had seen Kennedy on television, 19 percent felt more sympathetic to him, but 31 percent felt less sympathetic to him. (This does not necessarily prove that television was unfair to Kennedy; it may be, as one advisor said before the campaign had even begun, "the problem with Chappaquiddick isn't that people haven't *heard* Teddy's answers—they just don't *believe* those answers.") Another indication of the Chappaquiddick issue's power was that 68 percent of those asked said the issue wouldn't be very important; but later in the poll, 56 percent thought it would bother people.

More generally, Teddy was firmly seen in the press as a hopeless loser. When Iowa delivered a 2–1 margin for President Carter, the deathwatch began. With 110,000 Iowa Democrats turning out—twice the number that participated in the 1976 caucuses—the vote was, in Tom Brokaw's description on the January 22 "Today" show, "a stunning landslide victory . . . a major blow for Senator Kennedy." Said ABC's Cassie Mackin on "Good Morning, America," "no one in the Kennedy campaign was prepared for a defeat like this one." On CBS's special report on caucus night, Roger Mudd said, "after the defeat [Kennedy] took here tonight, if he does not come out of Maine and New Hampshire really blazing, I think it will be all over for him."

In his appearance after the Iowa defeat, Kennedy resorted to a kind of humor that seemed forced.

"Well," he said with a smile, "we could have done a *little better* in Iowa." And he gave a distinctly unhearty laugh. But he canceled campaign appearances for a series of meetings in Washington with his staff amid rumors he would pull out of the race—stark testimony to the way in which a single vote in a state with 50 of the 3,383 delegates to the Democratic National Convention could wield outsize power in a campaign which, it was supposed six weeks earlier, had a wide, national base of support.

"Can Kennedy Hang On?" *Newsweek* asked in its follow-up to the Iowa vote, showing a picture of a forlorn Kennedy looking for his seat at President Carter's State of the Union address. "Not even his own people were immune to the spreading suggestion that his candidacy may be beyond repair," the magazine wrote. " 'It's almost terminal,' said one old Kennedy hand. 'The country isn't in love with Jimmy Carter—but people really don't want Ted.' Money-grubbing and penny-pinching became sudden obsessions for a campaign that began with the air of a royal progress," *Newsweek* added, referring to the abandonment of the chartered jet and the cutting of the paid staff and media budget. Ellen Goodman, the *Boston Globe* syndicated columnist, suggested the ultimate heresy for a Kennedy.

"Watching him go through the motions," she wrote on January 26, "I feel embarrassed . . . I want to change the channel. His voice is strained, his timing is off, his eyes are glazed. . . . Everything is wrong. [But] one sentence keeps recurring in my brain: the guy doesn't want it."

Such was the post-Iowa media atmosphere surrounding the Kennedy campaign. It was not, however, the whole story. For a combination of events—including the "thermostatic" nature of press coverage and a key decision by the Kennedy campaign to change the nature of the campaign in midflight—produced a second chapter in the story of Kennedy and the media which, whatever its effect on the 1980 campaign, may have resurrected Ted Kennedy for a future run at the Presidency. For it turned Kennedy from "Teddy the klutz" into "Teddy the classy loser."

iv   Teddy and the Media, II: From Klutz to Class

In the wake of the Iowa caucus disaster, the Kennedy campaign was dead in the water. The polls, which had beckoned Kennedy into the race four months ago, had turned completely around. The ABC-Harris poll just after Iowa showed Carter with a 60–28 lead over Kennedy; *Time*'s post-Iowa poll had it 62–28. A *Boston Globe* poll just after Iowa of New Hampshire Democrats—Kennedy's neighboring state which had given him a 2.5–1 lead in the fall—now gave Carter a 54–36 advantage. Reporters responded to Kennedy's tortured post-Iowa metaphor—"it's a 15 inning fight and we're maybe in the first round"—with a starkly simple question, put by CBS and every other news organization, "Do you have to win in Maine and New Hampshire now, sir?"

"Yes," Kennedy said.

The Iowa disaster, however, brought with it two events, separate in origin, but linked in consequence. First, the press, with that increased self-consciousness that has come to be a permanent part of Presidential campaigns, began asking whether it had been too tough on the candidate once seen as the possible beneficiary of the free ride. Second, the Kennedy campaign made as the centerpiece of its post-Iowa strategy a conscious decision to redefine the basis for Kennedy's campaign. This basis—geared now to a frontal assault on the economy and an all-out championing of the liberal agenda—revived both the candidate and the campaign. As a corollary, whether intended or not, it seemed to offer the press a reason to reassess the Kennedy campaign, and to praise it even as it was planning to cover the funeral services. The transformation of "Teddy the klutz" into "Teddy the classy loser" is a splendid illustration of the relationship between a campaign's themes, and the press's institutional tendency to counter the general impressions it forms, much as a thermostat automatically kicks on and off when the temperature moves beyond a set range. The press had responded to the concern over its adulation of Kennedy with a determination to be tough on the front-running challenger; it responded now to concern over excessive hostility with a solicitous hand to the man on the canvas.

Shortly after the Mudd interview had turned loose a torrent of critical comments about Kennedy's performance, conservative columnist James Kilpatrick gave credit to "a new breed of journalists [which] has emerged, harder and hungrier than the reporters who once functioned as troubadors at court." By the time of the Iowa caucuses, the critical treatment of Kennedy had become so dominant a part of the coverage that *Time* magazine felt compelled to point out that "out in Iowa, Ted Kennedy is not so bad a performer as his Eastern drama critics make out." A few other journalists noted that Kennedy's initially weak campaign style had gotten better, and that the press was perhaps still reacting to his earlier style. The *Washington Post* noted on January 22 that "Kennedy on the stump today is markedly different from the Kennedy of two months ago. Today, he delivers a superb political speech crisply and confidently, handles questions adroitly. . . . There's no faltering, no fumbling, no vague wandering from issue to issue." In her campaign diary covering the last ten days of the Iowa campaign, *New Yorker* writer Elizabeth Drew wrote of the media portrayal of Kennedy on the campaign.

"People," she said, "seem to be more aware that he said 'fam farmily' last fall, and that he can stumble around when he speaks—which he has essentially stopped doing in his public appearances—than of anything else about the campaign he is conducting. And there is a time lag: two of the networks ran stories about his verbal stumbling after it had greatly diminished. . . . Kennedy, who can be both inarticulate and articulate, is still being portrayed as essentially inarticulate on the trail, when that is no longer the case."

The press, in other words, had begun to check its portrait of Ted Kennedy at the very time the Kennedy campaign had begun to recognize the enormous damage it had done to its cause by launching a candidate without a message. The campaign's decision to redefine its purpose, coming at a time when the press was beginning to look for the redeeming qualities in the man, produced a key milestone in the press coverage of Kennedy: the Georgetown speech of January 28.

In the mechanistic view of Presidential politics, ideas do not count for much; they are, at best, the tinsel behind which the real—that is, strategic—business of the campaign goes on. But a speech still remains the one forum in which a candidate can define, on his own terms, the purpose of the campaign exercise. What Kennedy did at Georgetown was, in essence, to scrap the "leadership" premise—that he could better guide America to goals he and Jimmy Carter shared—and challenge the goals of the Carter Administration. His indictment was wholesale: from charging that the admission of the Shah, based on "dubious medical advice," had triggered the hostage crisis, to a charge of weakness in the face of Soviet adventurism, to a charge that draft registration was "moving toward the brink of sending another generation of the young to die for the failures of the old," to specific calls for gas rationing and across-the-board controls on the entire American economy.

Out of this speech emerged a curious distinction between the broadcast and print press. With restricted limits of time and television's demand for drama, television reporters as a rule are much more imprisoned by the mechanistic analysis of politics than their print brethren. Whereas the print reporters—and analysts and columnists especially—seemed to focus on the content of Kennedy's challenge, television approached it almost solely from the strategic point of view.

CBS's Phil Jones, in what was perhaps the single worst example of unfairness toward an individual candidate in the entire 1980 campaign, followed Kennedy's challenge to Carter to a debate with this line:

"And with that, Kennedy looked into the TelePrompTers and read a speech filled with attacks on President Carter and controversial proposals of his own."

The implication was clear: this was another political device on the part of a candidate who could neither write his own words nor even deliver a speech without the aid of a mechanical crutch. The CBS report then went from excerpted highlights of the speech to White House and Carter campaign reaction, which was, in the main, a charge that Kennedy was being driven to the Left out of political desperation.

Among the print press, whose analytical freedom tends to appear later, in diluted form, in broadcast reports, the reaction was very different. Possibly because of a bias against the strategic reporting that dominates campaign coverage, possibly to compensate for the words hurled at Kennedy after the Mudd interview, they hailed the speech without regard to political preferences.

Germond and Witcover said it "provided a much stronger justification for his candidacy than he had been able to offer until now." Anthony Lewis in the *New York Times* said "he gave some real reasons for running, based on issues. And he sounded like a man who wanted to run." Joseph Kraft remarked that Kennedy "can now go down honorably, as the keeper of a certain conscience." "Yesterday," the *Boston Globe* said, "Senator Edward M. Kennedy recovered his political voice."

Conservatives seemed to welcome the speech just as enthusiastically. Vermont Royster in the *Wall Street Journal* said, "He has done the country a service by offering the Presidential campaign a choice, not an echo. . . . A clear alternative to the policies, foreign and domestic, of the other candidates, including President Carter."

William Safire, whose love of language is stronger than his ideology, was almost euphoric.

"What a . . . pleasure it is," he wrote, "to see the chastened man shake his head clear, get up off the floor, and—by dint of the intellectual and emotional effort of a powerful speech—give his presidential campaign life and give his political life meaning." He praised Kennedy for "espousing a point of view that exists in the US electorate and has —in this crisis—gone unarticulated. The trend in wolf pack journalism is to savage Mr. Kennedy while treating Mr. Carter's Rose Garden campaign with awe and reverence. As one who has kicked Mr. Kennedy when he was up, I want to salute his first performance as an underdog. He showed class, even character, though I'm not sure yet."

And while criticizing some of his specific proposals, the *Washington Post* editorialized, "the Senator has managed at last to suggest what he is doing in the race."

The Georgetown speech marked the beginning of the transformation from klutz to class. Now, it was clear, Kennedy had a political argument to make. But it was equally clear that the campaign was hopeless. Through the next two months, the press coverage of Kennedy moved along two different roads—charting the absolute certainty of his defeat at the hands of President Carter, while treating the candidate and his campaign with more respect.

Kennedy received a slight "reprieve" when he came within four points of beating President Carter. (The Maine caucus vote also produced a small preview of the Election Night controversy over early projections. At 4:38 P.M. on Sunday afternoon, CBS went on the air with a report that "President Carter is the winner" in the Maine caucuses, although the voting in the caucuses was not to end until 10:00 P.M. According to Kennedy delegate chief Rick Stearns, "as soon as the Kennedy people heard the report, they said, 'what's the use?' and didn't bother to turn out." Without that projection, Stearns argued, Kennedy might well have beaten Carter. CBS polling chief Warren Mitofsky argued that local Maine stations were, in fact, reporting big Carter margins all afternoon, but Ernest Leiser, director of Special Reports for CBS, acknowledged that the phrase, "President Carter is the winner," should not have been used.)

But with the vote in New Hampshire, the Kennedy campaign as a political Titanic was the dominant motif of the coverage. *Newsweek* reported on the "Sinking Feeling in Camelot," describing Kennedy's campaign—before the first primary of 1980 had been held, and after two caucus states with 72 of the 3,383 convention delegates had held their first skirmishes—as "fighting the sinking feeling that [New Hampshire] could be the last for him and for the twenty-year legend of Camelot," and sketched a campaign where "pamphlets are stacked up for want of postage. Expense money has dried up to the trickle needed to buy gasoline for staffers. . . ." Network reporters, having committed to memory the "expectations" strategies of past primary campaigns, where "doing better than expected" was the key to victory, covered every nuance of the game. "Top Presidential aides [are] working the bars where the press hangs out," NBC's Ken Bode reported the night before the primary, February 25, "shaping expectations, promoting the notion that really it's closer than the polls say," while CBS's Jed Duvall reported that same night "the last-minute Kennedy tactic is to poormouth his chances in New Hampshire, to complain that Carter is far ahead, and therefore to look good if the results are closer."

Lesley Stahl reported the next night on CBS the Carter aides as "nervous, because say the aides, he will not win by the twenty-point margin forecast by recent polls, and therefore the poll may describe the showing as something less than a clear victory."

On primary day, NBC's Tom Brokaw and Kennedy, on the "Today" show, engaged in a classic media duel—Brokaw demanding that Kennedy talk honestly about his nonexistent chances, Kennedy insisting that the issues were the key.

"If you lose in New Hampshire, how can you possibly survive as a candidate?" Brokaw asked.

"Well," said Kennedy, "I'm very hopeful that we'll do well," and began talking about fuel prices and inflation.

"Can you survive?" asked Brokaw. Well, said Kennedy, the Maine caucuses were closer than the polls indicated.

"Can you run second in New Hampshire and go on?" Brokaw wanted to know.

". . . I believe we're doing increasingly well in the issues that we're raising," Kennedy retorted, adding that New Hampshire voters "don't want to really rubber-stamp the policies that have not worked."

"If you run second twenty-four hours from now . . ." Brokaw began.

"Maybe we can talk at that time," snapped an exasperated Kennedy, "but the important point now is that people can make a difference up here. They can vote for change. They can reject high rates of inflation, high fuel bills, high costs of living at the supermarket . . ."

That night, after Carter beat Kennedy 47 percent–37 percent, 52,692–41,745, Kennedy attempted to play the "expectation game," saying to his supporters with that exaggerated Rooseveltian parody of campaign rhetoric that increasingly became his trademark, "four years ago Jimmy Carter got 28 percent of the vote and he claimed victory, and we're claiming victory tonight! Heh-heh-heh-heh." But the press wasn't playing the "expectation game." On the CBS special report Tuesday night, Walter Cronkite went out of his way to remind viewers that Lyndon Johnson had, in fact, beaten Eugene McCarthy in 1968, and that Edmund Muskie had, in fact, beaten George McGovern in 1972. Worse for Kennedy, polls and commentaries were beginning to make the "loser" image more specific and damning. The CBS exit poll, for example, showed that Kennedy's new-found issues campaign was cutting. Among people who said the economy had worsened for them personally in the last year, Kennedy was a 2–1 winner; and the more people heard Kennedy on the economy, the more they tended to vote for him. But four in ten Democrats said they would *never* vote for Kennedy, even if he won the Democratic nomination. And, in a remarkable foreshadowing of Jimmy Carter's later media campaigns against both Kennedy and Reagan, NBC's Ken Bode gathered anti-Kennedy comments focusing on his personality ("I don't trust him," "I don't think he's too dependable," "I don't like him. Period.").

As Kennedy's losses mounted—except for the expected Massachusetts victory, he lost every primary or caucus from Iowa through New York, on March 25—the loser coverage remained constant; but slowly a new tone of respect began to permeate press reports of Kennedy's campaigning. It is impossible to indicate precisely when this began, although the January 28 Georgetown speech clearly marked the first burst of positive coverage Kennedy had received since the Mudd interview. But somewhere after it became clear to the press that, after New Hampshire, Kennedy was virtually certain to lose the struggle for the nomination, the coverage shifted dramatically.

T. R. Reid, who covered Kennedy brilliantly for the *Washington Post,* wrote on March 2, "Kennedy today is a forceful campaigner who has positioned himself on the popular side of the central economic issue, who clearly has his opponent on the defensive on pocketbook questions.

"The press," he added, "now consider Kennedy's slips to be an old story. . . . Many reporters have decided it is unfair to zap Kennedy for the kind of mistakes that every candidate makes now and then." His observation was validated by the stream of complimentary newspaper and television reports that accompanied Kennedy through his string of losses.

Some came from liberal columnists who had been unsparing in their denunciations of Kennedy's entry into the race. *New York Times*-man Anthony Lewis wrote in mid-March that "in adversity, Edward Kennedy is uncomplaining . . . he is good-humored, patient, never irritable with the press or unfriendly members of the public . . . this difficult campaign has shown Edward Kennedy performing well under stress." Tom Wicker wrote in the *Times* that "there is something gallant in the way he has accepted his devastating political decline and continued his campaign—lonely now and perhaps hopeless—so that his simple persistence in it speaks to a strength of character that the public overlooks." The *Washington Post*'s Mark Shields said on

March 28 that "Kennedy . . . has developed into a confident, forceful and, yes, articulate presidential candidate. Neither defeat nor diatribes have diminished his good humor. He is the unwhining professional who communicates a conviction that he is doing what he believes is important to do and to do well."

But the "classy Teddy" theme also appeared in less friendly surroundings. The *Wall Street Journal*'s Norman Miller extolled Kennedy in mid-March, calling him "relaxed, cheerful. Senator Kennedy's resilience and perseverance are demonstrating an admirable aspect of his character. . . . In personal terms, he is giving a gutsy performance under very trying conditions. Those who question Ted Kennedy's character should, in fairness, consider that in their judgment." And George Will, while noting that "Kennedy is almost perfectly wrong on most matters of public policy," said, "he is a cheerful, passionate, believing professional. He is, in a word, a politician. He likes the business. He likes the people in it."

In a sense, the "classy Teddy" theme of press coverage mirrored —and perhaps influenced—a shift in the voting pattern within the Democratic Party after the March 18 Illinois primary, which saw Kennedy suffer a 2–1 defeat at the hands of Carter, and made Carter the all-but-certain Democratic nominee. Just as the press seems to have eased up on Kennedy once his defeat was a near-certainty, so the Democratic voters seemed to regard Kennedy as an acceptable vehicle for registering their discontent with Carter—so long as it was clear Teddy would not be the nominee. There are, of course, other explanations for the dramatic change in the vote from the New York primary of March 25 through the remaining weeks of the primary season: Kennedy's hammering of the economic issue, validated by continuing bad economic news; the coherence of Kennedy's campaign themes; the waning of the hostage issue as a patriotic spur to voting for the incumbent among them. But the certainty of Kennedy's inability to capture the nomination may well have made his campaign a focus for a protest vote that would not come out for Kennedy as long as he was seen as a potential nominee.

For even as the "classy Teddy" theme emerged as a full-blown press perception of Kennedy, it was never separated from the "gallant loser" view of the senator. Judy Bachrach's March 25 *Washington Star* piece exemplified this linkage when she observed, "he knows it's all over for him. It is in that knowledge that he now finds a certain strength, a peculiar sense of relief." On March 21, the *Washington Post*'s Haynes Johnson praised Kennedy's "rare grace and gallantry" in a column that described itself as "an anatomy of his failure, perhaps the greatest fall in U.S. political annals."

True, Senator Kennedy's March 25 victories in the New York and Connecticut primaries—a New York win of eighteen points one week after a Lou Harris poll had put Carter more than twenty points ahead —did trigger some of the traditional "momentum coverage." NBC's John Chancellor described Kennedy as "a born-again candidate for the Presidency" on the March 26 "Nightly News," stating that "he was revitalized," and Mark Shields argued on the "MacNeil-Lehrer Report" that if Kennedy could continue to make the incumbent the issue "then we could have a turnaround." But most of the press coverage, reflecting the skepticism over "momentum" and "expectation" coverage that had surrounded George Bush earlier in the season, accepted the view that Kennedy could not win. As *Time* magazine's John Stacks observed, "Kennedy has to win over ⅔ of the remaining delegates to be chosen, which would mean a rather consistent set of landslides to overtake Carter." And—in what proved to be a perceptive account of the difficulties that would confront any Democrat—Stacks called the contest "a sack race for cripples, if you will," with "negative votes going both ways."

The emergence of Kennedy as what Safire called "a safe vehicle for a protest vote" meant that both campaigns had become mirror images of each other. Carter, recognizing the impossibility of campaigning on his record, had structured his entire campaign on a single premise: *I am not Ted Kennedy*. Kennedy, after a disastrous attempt at establishing himself as a more effective and competent leader than Carter, turned his campaign around by arguing, in effect, *I am not Carter*. It was the shift in Kennedy's campaign—vastly aided by the press reports of his gallantry, good-humor, and new-found articulateness, that enabled Kennedy to make a real contest out of what appeared to be a rout.

From New York and Connecticut on March 25 to the end of the primary battle on June 3—"Super Tuesday"—Kennedy and Carter battled in twenty-five primaries and caucuses. In these later primaries, Carter won 6.6 million votes and 912½ delegates; Kennedy won 4.9 million votes and 775½ delegates. Given the steady decline in the President's political fortunes from the Iranian rescue failure in April through the August convention, it is a distinct possibility that had the entire primary campaign been as close as the New York-to-California run, the move to an open convention in New York would have succeeded, and Carter would have been denied renomination.

This shift, however, cannot be understood as a "media-dictated" shift. As with so much else in the 1980 Presidential campaign, it was much more a matter of the interplay between the media and underlying political factors. The press certainly reported Kennedy's stumbling entry into the 1980 race; but the press did not create his unfocused candidacy, or his attempt to subordinate ideological differences and emphasize his personal leadership qualities. Such reporting was sharply critical; but it is the fate of *any* serious Presidential candidate to be subjected to harsh scrutiny. Indeed, as Michael Robinson's Media Analysis Project discovered after the end of the primary season, front-runners in general are subject to more critical press scrutiny than are underdogs or also-rans. When Ted Kennedy entered the Presidential contest in the fall of 1979, having never run for national office, and with all the polls and pols indicating a certain nomination, he was treated as a presumptive front-runner; and, as his own performance made clear, he was simply unprepared to deal with the kind of critical press that he and his campaign should have expected. When he found himself—because of his own performance and because of the hostage issue—thrown into the role of a likely loser, he responded by redefining his campaign. In so doing, he remade himself into a candidate capable of stating a coherent *political* argument against a sitting President—and both his press coverage and his political fortunes improved. To the extent that the fundamental issue of character was not resolved in the minds of voters, that is a circumstance with which media coverage had almost nothing to do. It was for Kennedy, as the candidate, to recognize that the issue of his character was, in a sense, "unmanageable." It could be answered only by arguing, in effect, that Chappaquiddick was a flaw that did not bar Kennedy from becoming an effective President, able to cope with the pressing issues of the economy and foreign policy better than the incumbent. To the extent Kennedy demonstrated his determination to remain in the race as the candidate of "true" Democratic Party principles, he gained credibility and admiration, *even though* the Chappaquiddick questions remained as serious as they had been when the campaign began.

In sum, neither "Teddy the klutz" nor "classy Teddy" was a media creation. They did reflect certain tendencies of press coverage in Presidential campaigns: to scrutinize the front-runners, to praise the underdogs. But it was Kennedy's fundamental campaign posture and arguments that produced both the negative press that haunted his early days, and the more positive press that greeted his long-distance attempt to win the nomination.

Ronald Reagan and the Republican Nomination: Media Disaster, Political Triumph

What better proof could anyone offer for the argument that the mass media determine the outcome of our key elections than the elevation of Ronald Reagan to the Presidency of the United States? This one-time motion picture actor whose life's work was the speaking of other people's words and the portrayal of fictive emotions, this novice who could exclaim to his 1966 gubernatorial media advisor, "politics is just like show business!" this figure whose profession was the manipulation of images, in all these things Ronald Reagan seemed the embodiment of the Age of Television Politics, where reality is swept aside by the manipulation of images and symbols.

The only problem with this proof is that it requires a willful refusal to examine the 1980 campaign with open eyes and a clear head. True, Ronald Reagan demonstrated superb skills at "communicating" with the American electorate; he delivered speeches and jokes alike with zest and flair. (So did John Kennedy and Franklin D. Roosevelt, and so did generations of politicians from Orville Faubus to Hubert Humphrey. In an age when we were too unsophisticated to understand the omnipotence of imagery, we used to call this a political skill.) True, on several occasions, ranging from the Nashua debate to the Republican Convention to the Anderson and Carter debates of the fall, Reagan stood in the spotlight of national attention and "performed" with exceptional skill (so did JFK in his speech to the Houston ministers in 1960, and in that fall's debates against Richard Nixon; so did Richard Nixon in his "silent majority" speech of 1969).

To assume from these facts that Ronald Reagan's 1980 victory was a consequence of his media skills is to miss the point almost entirely. With respect to his nomination, Reagan won principally because after thirty years of preaching conservative gospel, after sixteen years as a key figure in the conservative Republican movement that seized control of the party in 1964 and never let go, after a decade and a half during which the once-dominant Eastern moderate-liberal Republican wing all but disappeared as a force within the party, and during which conservatism became the overwhelming consensus belief of that party, the Republicans nominated the figure who had spoken the beliefs of that party, and whose political base had been gathering strength for sixteen years.

Indeed, an analysis that attempts to demonstrate Reagan's nominating victory as a consequence of either his media skills or his coverage by the media would fail at almost every turn. For the fact is that Ronald Reagan made his full share of those gaffes, blunders, and mistakes that are supposed to derail the campaigns of potential presidents. Both the candidate and the campaign completely misread the formula of contemporary campaign lore, ignoring the psychological importance of first tests and ceding to George Bush a weeks-long head start that made him the candidate of momentum and saw Reagan's campaign consigned for an early burial by major elements of the national press, and by many of his long-time supporters within the Republican Party. And for a candidate supposedly trained in every nuance and gesture that Hollywood could impose on an eager, attractive young man almost half a century ago, Ronald Reagan frequently seemed as unsure of himself in front of a camera as a politician resurrected from a 1938 courthouse in rural Louisiana. The aspects of a genuine "media" candidate—carefully controlled, measured answers to questions, an ability to project calm, unruffled emotions in the presence of difficulties or hostile questions, doling out responses to questions with computerlike regularity, avoiding controversy and trouble—these were not the skills of Ronald Reagan as he campaigned for the Republican nomination, nor when he battled Jimmy Carter for the Presidency.

Rather, it was the ability of Reagan to convey a clear, coherent sense of what he was seeking to do that accounted in substantial measure for his nomination—remembering that in American politics we are almost never talking about a set of defined, specific policies the way a European opposition party would define such a program in day-to-day parliamentary battle with a governing party. We are talking, instead, about a set of principles and broad policies generally understood by adherents and opponents alike. In Reagan's case, those principles and policies had been defined by years of political battles, public speaking, radio commentaries, and newspaper columns; and, to a degree not often found in American politics, Reagan was on the record on a vast number of political arguments, and his positions in the 1980 campaign were not substantially different from those he had been struggling for since he became a convert to conservatism.

By 1980, that philosophy—scaling down the size and scope of the federal government; easing the regulation of business and industry by federal agencies; greatly increasing defense spending and stiffening our behavior toward the Soviet Union; ending the hectoring of friendly nations whose treatment of citizens was repressive; opposing many of the "cultural revolutions" of the last twenty years from feminism to gay rights to abortion rights to the "secularization" of schools—had become the dominant philosophy within the Republican Party, and there were signs stretching back fifteen years that such a philosophy would find allies across a broad regional and economic base within the Democratic Party as well.

And in 1980, no Republican candidate with the single exception of John Anderson chose to challenge Reagan's philosophy; they fought, instead, over the issue of whether Reagan was the strongest candidate to take that philosophy into the battle for the White House. There was, at root, *no argument at all* over what the Republican Party should be standing for in 1980, no attempt whatsoever to argue over direction. In fact, so convinced were Reagan's opponents that he had the loyalty of the great mass of Republicans that little effort was made to attack Reagan even within the boundaries of normal intraparty strife; an odd development considering that four years earlier, Reagan had mounted the first real challenge to an incumbent Republican President since 1912, and had divided the party so thoroughly that it may very well have cost Gerald Ford the White House. Even though Reagan had smashed the famous "eleventh commandment" in 1976, his hold on the party was considered too strong to shake by a frontal assault. And this firm hold on the base of the party was to prove the key to his nomination.

In the conventional scorecards of contemporary Presidential campaigns, Reagan and his much-advertised "media skills" proved more sizzle than steak. From the moment he entered the campaign, Reagan proved himself every bit as capable of mishandling the media side of campaigning as a politician whose only relationship with a camera stopped with an Insta-matic.

Consider his entrance into the race. On November 13, 1979, Reagan formally announced for the Presidency with a $500-a-plate dinner in New York City—a site picked for its symbolic demonstration that Reagan was not writing off the industrial Northeast and the remnants of the Republican establishment, and a site enabling Reagan to appear on all three network morning television news programs. This entry was to be trumpeted with a videotaped version of the speech on network television, but none of the networks would sell Reagan the thirty minutes he wanted, telling him, as they had told John Connally and Jimmy Carter, that the Presidential campaign had not yet begun. Instead, Reagan's speech, introduced by actor Michael Landon, was seen on ninety stations around the country, with the time bought on a station-by-station basis.

In appearing on ABC's "Good Morning, America," NBC's "Today" show, and CBS "Morning," Reagan was breaking a months-long moratorium on network news interviews, a policy in keeping with campaign manager John Sears's "above the battle" posture. But his lack of practice may have caused him to stumble badly during his first appearance "on stage."

Anticipating the age issue which the press and Reagan's opponents had singled out as the most likely area of vulnerability, Reagan and his campaign had developed a stock answer or two. One was to joke that the Japanese worried about his age, too. "They think I'm too *young,*" he would say. Another was to cite the ages of European heads of state and government, something he did, almost word for word, in his interviews with all three morning newsmen.

"If I become President," Reagan said, "other than perhaps Margaret Thatcher I will probably be younger than almost all the heads of state I will have to do business with."

NBC's Tom Brokaw, alone among the newsmen, followed up.

"Giscard d'Estaing of France is younger than you," Brokaw said.

"Who?" said Ronald Reagan.

"Giscard d'Estaing of France," Brokaw repeated.

"Yes, possibly," Reagan said. "Not an awful lot more."

Apart from the fact that Giscard was fifteen years younger than Reagan, the answer went to the heart of not one, but *two* separate Reagan vulnerabilities. The one-word answer "Who?" to the name of the President of France suggested two possibilities—first, that Reagan could not hear Brokaw, which would have reflected badly on a campaign trying to soft-pedal the question of whether a sixty-eight-and-a-half-year-old man would be fit for a Presidential campaign and the burdens of that office; second, perhaps Reagan did not know who the President of France was, which would have reflected badly on a campaign worried about the lack of foreign policy experience and intellectual depth of its candidate.

That gaffe, seized on by the *New York Times*'s editorial writers, by the *Washington Post*'s chief Reagan-watcher, Lou Cannon, and by other writers, soon gained national circulation. But it was only one of several critical themes that soon enveloped the Republican front-runner.

One of them involved the early Reagan strategy of soft-pedaling his sharp ideological views in favor of a less confrontational campaign. John Sears well remembered the 1976 campaign against Gerald Ford, when a complicated proposal to transfer $90 billion worth of federal programs and revenues back to the states had caused enormous problems in New Hampshire and Florida, and he was determined not to give critics a similar target in 1980. The consequence early on was that both conservative allies and campaign reporters found Reagan's campaign very short on ideas.

Even before his announcement, Jack Germond and Jules Witcover had observed—in early October, 1979—that "no politician of recent memory has [a basic speech] that is so limited in content and makes such a virtue of offering no solutions to any of the ills that it identifies." Without addressing complicated questions and ideas, they added, "the question of his age inevitably will be raised in the most damaging way." And with his announcement—a speech whose only concrete idea was a suggestion for a North American accord—Reagan drew the same kind of critical comment that linked the lack of tough-minded ideas to the age question. In a stinging editorial on November 15 entitled "Ritual Reagan," the *Wall Street Journal,* the sternest of conservative national publications, thundered:

". . . perhaps Mr. Reagan will offer more, as time goes by. For his sake, he will have to; for political packaging, we do not need to turn to a 68 year old man. . . . There was no general theme, no sense of priorities—none of the sense of direction that can come not from staff directors or writers or public opinion polls, but only from the candidate himself. . . . If we are not picking someone with a vision, but merely choosing from a list of politicians, the age issue does become a serious liability."

Allied with this view of Reagan was the common perception—well grounded in reality—that he was running a highly controlled, cautious campaign, the kind that has historically been dangerous to a front-runner. From Thomas Dewey in 1948 to Edmund Muskie in 1972, to countless senatorial and gubernatorial campaigns, front-runners have attempted to run out the clock, holding the lead by taking as few risks as possible, and have found it does not work. But with Reagan so dominating the polls and early delegate tallies, the campaign, in effect, adopted a Rose Garden strategy. It is a strategy even incumbent presidents have difficulty carrying out, because the political press has a natural bias toward the aggressive campaigner, criss-crossing the country and rallying voters to his cause. (It also makes for a much more exciting campaign to cover, which may account for the press's bias as much as its deep dedication to robust, free-wheeling democracy.) But Reagan was not running that kind of campaign, and—especially given the possible link between a nine to five campaign and questions about a sixty-eight-year-old President—the press coverage was skeptical.

"Ronald Reagan's campaign calendar has slowed to two events a day," wrote the *Washington Post*'s Lou Cannon on December 17, 1979. The strategy, he wrote, is "to limit the candidate's appearances and as much as possible to restrict their content to well-rehearsed generalities, reducing the possibility of mishaps . . . Reagan already is behaving as if he were the Republican presidential nominee," spending only thirteen of fifty-five days campaigning. In contrast to the all-out Bush campaign in Iowa, Reagan's above-the-battle posture, which played perfectly into Bush's attempt to paint himself as the more vigorous, energetic, electable alternative, gave the press a legitimate reason to focus on the age issue, much as Ted Kennedy's refusal to spell out his ideas legitimated the "Chappaquiddick and character" issues in his campaign.

Haynes Johnson, in the February 4 *Washington Post,* summed up the prevailing view of the early Reagan this way:

"In that pitiless eye of the TV camera closeups his age shows through—the lines around his eyes, the jowls, the so-called 'turkey-neck' of those approaching their 70's.

". . . Something else comes through. There is a certain hesitancy, a stumble here and there, that one doesn't recall from other Reagan campaigns. He blows his lines now and then, says boycott when he means blockade, mentions turning over surplus funds to his gubernatorial predecessor instead of successor, refers to dismounting from an aircraft instead of disembarking, and displays at times an embarrassing unawareness of events. (Reagan, for example, did not know that American diplomats had escaped from Iran for eight hours during a recent campaign day.)"

Indeed, Reagan was steadily embarrassed during his first weeks of campaigning by gaffes and slips of the tongue. He talked about supplying arms to Afghanistan freedom fighters—sometimes confusing Afghanistan and Pakistan—without knowing that what he was suggesting was specifically barred by federal law. His attempts to reconcile his traditional free-market positions with federal help for New York City and the Chrysler Corporation caught him flatfooted at times. He was spared a potential political disaster when he called in December for permanent asylum for the Shah of Iran only because the press was focusing on Ted Kennedy's gaffes and seized on Kennedy's attack on the Shah as that day's "Teddy screws up" story; otherwise, Reagan would have been caught advocating a policy that could have threatened directly the safety of the American hostages. And when he avoided the January 5 Iowa Republican debate, Reagan made himself the one clear loser of that high-level, effective exchange of ideas. A week before his loss to Bush in the Iowa caucuses, Evans and Novak reported that Reagan's twenty-four-point drop in Iowa was angering his local supporters.

"This is what we've been complaining about for months," an Iowa campaign aide said. "There is no visible Reagan campaign." And the *Wall Street Journal*'s Norman Miller noted three days later that a possible Reagan loss would "shake the cool confidence of his entourage, hearten some of his rivals, and throw all the predictions of the political pundits into a state of marvelous confusion."

This is, of course, largely what happened after Bush scored a slim victory over Reagan in Iowa. When the heralded momentum swung to

Bush, Reagan was forced to alter his "incumbency" strategy, campaigning for twenty days in New Hampshire and joining in debates. While this proved to be the best possible tonic for Reagan's campaign, it did *not* turn the press coverage into a triumph. All through the spring, television and newspaper reporters began focusing on another question—did Reagan know what he was talking about?

The question of Reagan's intelligence and grasp of the issues had dogged him throughout his political career—a natural enough question given his past as an actor and the understandable (if unfair) notion that a professional speaker of other people's words was unlikely to have any of his own. In his first campaign for governor of California in 1966, California Democrats had pieced together a commercial using old Reagan movie clips, implying that his race for the governor's chair was just another role. In battling to hold the White House in 1976, Gerald Ford used a line about Reagan in the primaries that raised the same issue: "There are no retakes in the Oval Office." Now in 1980, with his New Hampshire victory once again establishing him as the odds-on favorite for the nomination, the press turned to the question of substance and found much to criticize.

Just a week after his New Hampshire win, the *Washington Star*'s John J. Fialka wrote that "a number of serious discrepancies" emerged from a detailed examination of Reagan's basic speech. "The factual underpinnings of many of the detailed anecdotes and descriptions of issues Reagan is raising are either missing, distorted, or misquoted."

The story cited such examples as:

● Reagan's claim to have rebated $5.7 billion in taxes as governor of California, without mentioning the tax increases he had signed into law amounting to more than double that amount;

● Reagan's claim of reducing welfare costs in California, which, Fialka wrote, were directly linked to liberalized abortions;

● His statement that there was more oil in Alaska than in Saudi Arabia;

● A GAO study which "found" $11 billion in identifiable federal waste (it was actually a Republican study);

● His claim that 23,000 General Motors employees were employed to fill out government forms; the real number was closer to 5,000. The *Post*'s Lou Cannon picked up this theme later that month, writing that the issue of Reagan's conservatism "has largely been replaced by another: does Reagan know what he's talking about?"

But the most influential and ambitious undertaking in the challenge to Reagan's factual arguments came from an unlikely source—television. For weeks, "CBS Evening News" producer Tom Bettag and correspondent Bill Plante had been piecing together a detailed examination of Reagan's claims. On Thursday, April 3, the "Evening

News" devoted more than six minutes to the piece—a highly unusual length for any political story in a twenty-two-minute evening newscast, and one characterized by a remarkable willingness to challenge a ranking politician on flat-out factual grounds.

After noting that "Reagan's campaign rhetoric is loaded with facts and figures," Bill Plante began dissecting the claims with the assistance of a mechanical device called a Qantel, which can animate graphics. Reagan was seen claiming that "it costs HEW three dollars in overhead to deliver one dollar to a needy person in this country"— and viewers saw three dollars next to a dollar bill.

Then, Plante said flatly, "Reagan is wrong. It doesn't cost three dollars to deliver a dollar of welfare, but twelve cents"—and the three dollars disappeared, to be replaced on the screen by a dime and two pennies.

On and on the piece ran, with animated graphics demonstrating the gap between Reagan's numbers and the real numbers—not 23,000 GM paper-pushers, but 5,000; not a JFK tax cut of 30 percent or 27 percent, but 19 percent. There was no Bellingham, Washington, school district threatened with an HEW fund cutoff for "spanking boys and girls in unequal numbers," but another town in Washington involved in a dispute with Washington over discrimination in vocational and athletic programs, and there was no threatened cutoff.

At the end of the piece, Plante raised this perceptive point: "Does it really matter? To some, it's a sign that Reagan isn't smart enough for the job he seeks. But to others, it's simply a matter of style. They point out that, right or wrong, all of those facts and figures help Reagan make his point, which is that in government, less is usually better."

The "Reagan-is-wrong" coverage did not start with the Plante piece, even confining the arena to television. On ABC's "Issues and Answers" of March 16, correspondent John Laurence forced Reagan to acknowledge that he did not know what was in his own commercial —using his own statements with his own face and voice—about John Kennedy's tax cuts, which, Laurence noted, "raises the question of whether you're aware of what you're saying in your own commercials." But the CBS piece triggered a wave of similar reporting and criticism.

The *New York Times*'s James Reston argued on April 5 that Reagan "has a backside-foremost way of saying things first and thinking about them later. . . . He blunders cheerily along, dramatizing the disaster of the Democrats, and the Republicans seem determined to gamble on him anyway." Evans and Novak raised the danger two days later that Reagan's slips will enable Carter to "come closer to switching the spotlight from Jimmy Carter's competence to Ronald Reagan's brains." On April 10, the "CBS Evening News" reported that Reagan was "expressing embarrassment over a stump speech blooper made in

Grand Island, Nebraska, last night, where he claimed Vietnam veterans were not eligible for the GI Bill of Rights with regard to education . . ." Reagan explained that his mistake came from information provided him by two four-star generals and said smilingly, "having only gotten to two bars myself in the military, when four stars told me something, I figured it was right." * And in one of his few public blasts at the media, Reagan added that "what we're seeing with some of the papers and what's going on now is a little journalistic incest."

The criticism continued. The April 14 *Time* magazine, in an article titled "Where Did He Get Those Figures," reviewed some of the misstatements detailed elsewhere and said, "Quite apart from the substantive merits of his views, Reagan consistently discounts them by misusing and misstating facts—a fact that disturbs many of those in his entourage. . . . The misstatements have proved effective; the crowds have cheered, and the voters have pulled the Reagan levers. The big question: do the facts, after all, really matter?" A week later, *Newsweek* asked "How's That Again, Ronnie?" in examining "*a continuous* media inquest into whether he knows or cares what he is talking about in his rote political speeches? . . . Is he shallow? 'It depends,' said Michigan representative Vander Jagt, 'on how you define shallow?' " On May 6, "NBC Nightly News" examined "The Fact Factor," which John Chancellor described as "a report on Reagan's imprecision with some of the facts he is using." Don Oliver, questioning Reagan on his notion that tax cuts could produce more government revenue, asked Reagan, "What if you're wrong?"

"What?" Reagan responded.

"What if you're wrong?" Oliver repeated.

"Well," said Reagan, "could it be worse than it is now?"

After examining some of Reagan's statements on the amount of documented government fraud, the amount of American oil reserves, and other matters, Oliver concluded, "If the facts are wrong, the solutions don't exist."

Throughout the spring, then, the press had given wide circulation to facts supporting the premise that Ronald Reagan did not know what he was talking about. And Reagan himself had provided ample evidence that he could fumble in front of a national audience as regularly as any other candidate. The question is: why didn't these slips and fumbles undermine, or at least severely cripple his campaign for the nomination?

One answer lies in the observations of Bill Plante and *Time* magazine: for Reagan's supporters, the mistakes were about issues where

---

* Few reporters chose to follow-up on the potentially devastating implication of this off-hand remark: namely, would he "assume" that the military had correct information about matters such as a future Bay of Pigs or Vietnam.

their agreement with Reagan was almost total. Suppose there were "only" 5,000 General Motors employees filling out government forms, instead of 23,000—were they going to change their belief that government imposed a massive amount of red tape on business and industry? Suppose HEW did not threaten to cut off school funds to a district spanking boys and girls in unequal numbers? Did that mean that federal bureaucrats were not imposing an ever-more complicated set of rules and regulations on local school boards, universities, and other public enterprises? Suppose there was no General Accounting Office report detailing billions of dollars in easily identifiable fraud and waste? Did that mean the federal government was an efficiently operating collector and disburser of public funds?

For Reagan's supporters, even those who did not hold to a Nixon-Agnew view of the press as a liberal thought police attacking conservatives, these kinds of criticism had little impact. A *Wall Street Journal* editorial of April 18 treated the scrutiny as a seasonal political event, rather than as a serious blow to Reagan's outlook, saying that Reagan "has been welcomed to the game. The press has been piling up accounts of his flubs, his mistakes, his tendency to 'pluck facts from the air.' " And it then asked, "Does anyone doubt that the federal government is growing? . . . If there isn't a lot of overhead in making payments to the poor, how come the Census Bureau shows little or no reduction in poverty despite the explosion in transfer payments?" The *Journal* concluded by arguing that, as a strategic matter, "Mr. Reagan and his staff need to spend some time getting themselves up to speed."

The more remarkable aspect of the critical press scrutiny of Reagan's ideas, however, lies in the behavior of his Republican opponents. Like Sherlock Holmes's dog that barked in the night—important because the dog did *not* bark when it was supposed to—these kinds of attacks on a front-running candidate might logically have been expected from Reagan's rivals for the nomination. But nowhere in the late winter and early spring did this potentially attractive vulnerability make its way into the arguments of Reagan's opponents.

George Bush did call Reagan's supply-side tax theories "voodoo economics"; John Connally did argue that "I really don't know where he stands" on issues in his January 5 comments during the Iowa caucuses; and Senator Baker repeatedly talked about his ability to draw independent and Democratic votes in his senatorial races as a way of arguing that Reagan's political support was too narrow. But none of them ever tried to make the case that Reagan's lack of accurate knowledge about the government made him a dangerous candidate for the Presidency, both as a target for the Democrats and as a potentially disastrous chief executive.

This absence is especially puzzling, given the nature of a political campaign. Attacking the ideas of an opponent is as much a part of a run for office as a kiss on a baby's cheek. It is, in fact, a necessary part of campaigning, even though it is generally described as "mud-slinging" and "dirty tricks." Because politics is an adversarial business, a voter is like a juror, weighing the character of the candidates and the credibility of the evidence. And a candidate should no more present an objective view of himself and his ideas than a lawyer for a party in a law case should seek total objectivity. It is in the clash of claims and arguments that the judgments are supposed to emerge. Thus, every political campaign staff has a staff member supervising what is euphemistically called "negative research," looking through all of an opponent's speeches, suggestions, and actions in his public— and sometimes private—life. If a candidate proposes a defense cut that appears to weaken America's protection, then his opponent is likely to subject that proposal to a devastating critique, as Hubert Humphrey did to George McGovern in 1972. If a candidate's tax proposals suggest that property owners may lose a tax shelter through the repeal of mortgage interest deductions, an opponent will push that candidate hard on the issue, as Henry Jackson did to Jimmy Carter in 1976,

And if a candidate whose vulnerability is supposed to be old age and lack of national government experience repeatedly blunders his way through a critique of federal policies, his opponents can be expected to point these mistakes out, as a way of demonstrating that candidate's unfitness for office. But that is precisely what did not happen to Reagan in 1980. And the reason, once again, lies in a recognition of the political high ground, which Reagan had seized long before the campaign began.

Which Republican—Anderson excepted—wanted to be the candidate arguing *against* the core beliefs of the essential Republican constituency? Who wanted to be the defender of an efficient, well-run federal establishment? Who wanted to argue that the Department of Health, Education, and Welfare was a smooth-running operation? Even Jimmy Carter, the incumbent Democratic President, had not come to office as an enthusiastic advocate of wide-ranging federal programs; his biggest boast in 1976 had been that he had cut hundreds of separate agencies out of the Georgia government when he was governor of that state. For conservative Republicans, a wholesale assault on Ronald Reagan's evidence would have been a confession that they did not share his commitment to attacking the overgrown, secular, permissive, redistributionist federal monster in Washington, sending out food stamps to long-haired, dope-smoking college students, high-living black welfare recipients, or laboring folks who ate steak while on strike, courtesy of the federal government. And the basic argument of Reagan's rivals was not that they disagreed with his world view, but that they could get elected to do the job Reagan had been advocating for years.

Moreover, the line between winning over Reagan's constituency and alienating it was a fine one, and neither in their campaigns nor in their advertising did any of his rivals want to cross it. Implying that Ronald Reagan was ignorant of basic facts—something that rivals in past campaigns had cheerfully charged—was simply too dangerous a way to win over people who liked and admired Reagan.

Thus, the basic questions with which the press plagued Reagan did not begin to surface until *after* the New Hampshire primary had restored Reagan to clear front-runner status, which he never lost. To the extent that the press raised these questions, they were raised in a potential vacuum, with none of Reagan's opponents turning his mistakes into capital, on the stump or on the airwaves. Just as his supporters discounted his flubs because they concerned matters about which they were convinced, so his rivals could not use those mistakes, because attacking Reagan's mistakes would inevitably have been seen as an attack on the conservative critique of America.

There is another point worth noting about Reagan's gaffes, a point which once again throws into doubt some of the generally accepted propositions about politics in an age of mass media. In past years, gaffes and mistakes had usually wounded politicians whose positions and policies were not all that well known—politicians who had indeed been raised to national prominence through the mass media's capacity to make people instantly—but shallowly—known.

When Governor George Romney made his "brainwashing" remark about his trip to Vietnam in the fall of 1967, he was just beginning his campaign for the Presidency, and it was for that—his intention to seek the Presidency—that he was best known. Where he stood on Vietnam, what he thought should be done about it, was not very clear. Similarly, Ed Muskie's "tears in New Hampshire" performance in 1972 was the act of a man who was known for his "decency" in his 1968 Vice-Presidential campaign, and who was running for the White House as a centrist seeking as little definition of his positions as possible.

But Reagan was more like a Harry Truman—at least in this respect. People felt they knew where he stood, that he said what he had in mind clearly, if clumsily. A Reagan gaffe was more like a mistake that came from a family friend, or a well-known colleague of a voter— and people are much less likely to change their opinion of a well-known figure than they are to draw sweeping conclusions based on what amount to "first impressions."

The single most important decision of the Reagan campaign was made after the Iowa caucus loss—and that was to begin campaigning, to remind people that Ronald Reagan was alive, well, vigorous, and actively seeking the nomination. Once he really entered the campaign, the coverage about his slips, gaffes, blunders, and misstatements all became irrelevant. He was the candidate the Republican Party's conservatives had been dreaming of for decades—an articulate exponent of a clear point of view, and one who had the promise of electability. Since he had long ago captured that political base, the fact that Reagan's nominating campaign was replete with media blunders simply did not matter.

vi   John Anderson
and the Media, I:
Only So Far...

The independent candidacy of John Anderson was fundamentally different from any independent Presidential campaign of the twentieth century. It was not characterized by a regional political base, as was Robert LaFollette's in 1924, or Strom Thurmond's in 1948, or George Wallace's in 1968. It lacked a passionate ideological base for its energy, such as Eugene V. Debs had in the first part of the century, or Theodore Roosevelt in 1912, or Henry Wallace in 1948.

The Anderson campaign, both in its first phase as an unlikely bid from the left for the Republican nomination and as an independent drive in the summer and fall, was made possible by mass media; *not* because television and the print press were ideologically biased toward Anderson, but because the media make possible national attention and recognition outside the traditional political machinery of the past. It enabled a candidate to move from the obscurity of the Congress to a national stage in a matter of weeks, and enabled that candidate to reach millions of sympathetic voters who otherwise might never have considered John Anderson as a possible choice for the Presidency.

In this sense, the Anderson campaign does show the most significant way in which the mass media have changed the political process. Such a run for the Presidency would have been unimaginable in an age when candidates had to fuse local and statewide organizations together in a short-lived, loose-fitting coalition to win convention delegates and then electoral votes.

Indeed, in a limited and curious way, the Anderson campaign had had a precursor four years earlier: the campaign of Jimmy Carter. In both cases, a relative unknown had emerged into national prominence through the force of character rather than through the force of ideas. In both cases, he spoke a language outside the mainstream of his political party. In both cases, a certain degree of romantic heroism characterized the media coverage of his campaign. And in both cases, the spotlight of the mass media elevated small political victories into

95

national triumphs: Carter in the 1976 Iowa caucuses, Anderson in the Massachusetts and Vermont Republican primaries in 1980. Neither campaign would even have been conceivable in a political process characterized solely by regional and interest group alliances. Both depended on a way to convey the central message of character directly to the voter.

To look at the Anderson campaign as a validation of the power of mass media, however, is to look at the wrong end of the telescope. Fully granting the ability of media to supply a new route toward swift national recognition, Anderson's campaign shows that this power is of a distinctly limited and largely passive kind. For example, the Carter campaign in 1976 did not succeed simply because Carter won an early contest that was magnified into a national victory by the media. Carter had a solid regional base—the South—which provided him with an unchallengeable field of delegates (once George Wallace left the primary field after Florida) matched by no other candidates. Carter was facing the second tier of Democrats, with neither Hubert Humphrey nor Ted Kennedy competing in the primaries. And Carter was speaking the language of honesty and goodness with the memory of America's worst national political scandal very much in the recent memory of the American voter. In other words, his political message was well suited to the times. Anderson—a Midwesterner barely known in his own state, competing against the most powerful Republican candidate of his time, speaking the language of social liberalism at a time of growing conservatism—had none of those advantages.

Moreover, the triumphs John Anderson did achieve in the late winter and early spring of 1980 were not "media-created." They were victories of his own making, carried to the voters by an essentially passive media. They were triumphs that were as open to Philip Crane and Robert Dole and John Connally and Howard Baker as they were to John Anderson—the triumph of impressing a constituency on a nationally televised debate, the triumph of performing unexpectedly well in an early primary test. Why John Anderson achieved these triumphs, and why he seemed by June of 1980 to be in a position to run the strongest independent Presidential campaign in history is only in part a media story. It is a story about the illusion that media can replace real political support as the underpinning of a campaign. For as the campaign progressed into the fall, it was the absence of the most old-fashioned of political weapons that turned Anderson from a historical milestone in American history into an asterisk. The elements Anderson never gained in his campaign—adequate money, strong ideological or regional support, and a clear and coherent set of ideas —prevented the potential strength shown by his media attention from being converted into real political strength.

It is true that John Anderson was an unknown when he entered the contest for the Republican nomination, if we are measuring recognition on the basis of national polls. He had been in Congress since 1961, a leader of the House Republican Conference since 1969, and had gained some attention in 1973 by being the first Republican in either house of Congress to call for the resignation of Richard Nixon. But for a variety of reasons, congressmen are far less well known than senators. There are 435 of them, as opposed to 100 senators, and ever since the days of Sam Rayburn, live coverage of House committee meetings has been forbidden; so the kind of national attention that went to the Army-McCarthy hearings, the Kefauver hearings, the labor hearings, and the Watergate hearings were not available to members of the House of Representatives. (The one exception—the House impeachment hearings of 1974—produced a flood of publicity for the representatives involved.)

But even in the first days of his campaign, Anderson was at least distinguishable from his Republican rivals: he was the closest thing to a liberal in the race. The importance of this fact to the media needs a historical step back.

From the time of the New Deal through the 1960 election, there was, in fact, a substantial power bloc within the Republican Party composed of Eastern, internationalist-minded publishers. *Time* and *Life,* controlled by Henry Luce, the Whitney family's *New York Herald Tribune,* the Scripps-Howard papers did, in fact, reflect a broad unity of outlook that characterized the Eastern wing of the Republican Party.

It was their conscious publicizing of a Midwest utility executive that led to Wendell Willkie's nomination for the Presidency in 1940. It was their opposition to isolationism that helped keep Robert Taft from the Republican Presidential nomination he sought from 1940 to 1952; their enthusiasm for an alternative to Taft that helped lure Eisenhower into the Presidential campaign in 1960. (It was also their opposition to Taft and isolationism that planted the seeds of media hostility among generations of conservative Republicans, even as Democrats throughout this era condemned the "one-party" press that backed the GOP candidate, election after election, in overwhelming numbers.)

But beginning in 1964, the dominance of the Eastern liberal Republican press began to wane, and the power of liberal Republicanism began to disappear. In 1964, the living symbol of moneyed liberal Republicanism, Nelson Rockefeller, not only lost the Presidential nomination but was booed lustily when he spoke from the podium in San Francisco's Cow Palace. In 1968, the chief rival to Richard Nixon was neither Michigan Governor George Romney—anointed by liberal Republicans—nor the late-running Nelson Rockefeller, but California Governor Ronald Reagan. Only the support for Nixon from conservative stalwarts such as Barry Goldwater and conservative Southerners such as Strom Thurmond kept Reagan from mounting a serious challenge to Nixon's first ballot nomination. In 1972, the liberal "insurgency" against Richard Nixon's nomination mounted by California Representative Paul McCloskey never reached 10 percent of the vote in any primary state. So devastated were liberal Republicans that by 1976 they rallied to the side of conservative Gerald Ford to prevent the Presidential nomination from going to Ronald Reagan.

By 1980, then, the Anderson candidacy seemed almost like a science-fiction story, in which a candidate from 1944 emerges thirty-six years later to run for the nomination of a party that has completely changed. Anderson was a liberal Republican in a time when there weren't supposed to *be* any more liberal Republicans. But in fact, this early attention to his ideas and his political stance proved to be John Anderson's most important media asset. For while Baker, Bush, Dole, Crane, and Connally all had to run as potential heirs to Ronald Reagan's political base, Anderson could run without limiting himself to polite answers about his energy or electability. It was not, of course, a way of winning over Reagan supporters, but it did make Anderson a noticeable, recognizable candidate. And this early, free-wheeling quality of Anderson's would soon become his stock-in-trade.

A "CBS Evening News" profile of Anderson—one of a series done on the nominees late in 1979—is a good example of how Anderson's political profile was sketched. As it ran on November 23, 1979, the interview began with Cronkite calling Anderson "the most liberal —he would say 'progressive.' In twenty years as a congressman from Rockford, Illinois, he supported open housing, opposed the Vietnam War, and called for the resignation of Richard Nixon, and yet was consistently reelected by his colleagues to the third-ranking post in the House Republican leadership." After quoting a newspaper article praising Anderson's intelligence and courage, the profile moved to a series of questions and answers with Anderson, in which Anderson opposed the MX missile system, favored the SALT II arms control treaty with the Soviet Union, supported abortion, the Equal Rights Amendment, gun control and school busing, opposed school prayers, and declared that "I'm not going to go in and try to balance the budget on the backs of the poor." He also opposed the Kemp-Roth across-the-board tax cut proposal, advocated his 50-cents-a-gallon tax on fuel —compensated for by a Social Security payroll tax deduction—and agreed with his mainstream Republican rivals only in his support for decontrolled fuel prices and his opposition to inflation.

Perhaps because Anderson's positions made him so unlikely to win, the praise of his personal qualities characterized by CBS's quote of a complimentary newspaper article became one of the two inevitable aspects of media coverage—the other being the fruitlessness of his quest. A *Washington Post* piece on November 17, 1979, was headlined

"Anderson Climbs Uphill Toting Heavyweight Issues." It noted that "back in Washington, Anderson is very well known. Handsome, bright, articulate, known around town as honest and outspoken, John Anderson has made news in the capital for years. Reporters, in fact, love him."

The *Post* quoted Anderson's own view of his early lack of media attention. Said Anderson, "I really think it is fair that I don't get written about unless I can manage in the course of my campaign to say something distinctive. Otherwise I'm a Bush or Baker. But if I'm saying something that is truly unique, if I project a different Republican voice, then that's news."

"The Lonely Liberal" was *Newsweek*'s December 24 notion of Anderson, again combining the hopelessness of the quest with heavy praise for the candidate. "Anderson," *Newsweek* reported, "barely registers in the public consciousness. And yet, within the comfortable bounds of political Washington, he is regarded as a thoughtful legislator with a considerable gift for oratory . . ." The magazine described the 50-cents-a-gallon fuel tax proposal and his calls for sacrifice "hopeful, little-to-lose candor."

"He's Hopeful Despite Odds," the January 4 *Boston Globe* said. "As he campaigns in New Hampshire, there is none of the swarm of Secret Service agents and media agents that follows other, better-publicized candidates. He has won accolades in the press and from his peers in Washington for his intelligence and competence, yet his campaign is still floundering in anonymity."

Said a *New York Times* "News of the Week in Review" analysis on December 23, 1979, "So far he has won the respect of other politicians and commentators—a rival called him 'the brightest man in the race,' the *Wall Street Journal* described him as 'a thinker and probably the best orator in Congress'—but not the support needed for the nomination." The *Times* piece quoted liberal Republican McCloskey as saying, "I'm closer to Anderson ideologically than to Bush or Baker, but I've chosen to help Bush because I feel that if we're going to move the Republican Party away from the right, we've got to do it gradually."

This kind of early coverage of Anderson was not taking place in a political vacuum. It was happening at a time when the candidacy of Senator Edward Kennedy was floundering badly because of the self-inflicted wounds of his entry into the Presidential campaign. For liberals, the rapid decline of Kennedy meant that there was no appealing candidate in the race in either party. To learn of a fiscally conservative Republican who was for all of the causes seemingly in retreat—from the Equal Rights Amendment to gun control to abortion to negotiations with the Soviet Union to opposition to big defense increases to social programs for the poor—was an encouraging sign.

And it was given much more encouragement by Anderson's performance in the Iowa Republican debate on January 5—almost certainly the single most important boost to his candidacy of the entire campaign year.

With President Carter's refusal to participate in a Democratic debate in Iowa, and the subsequent collapse of that debate, the Republican contest was the first and only early direct clash among contenders for the Presidency. None of the commercial networks carried the debate live—public television did, and CBS carried the debate in its entirety at 11:30 P.M. But, as with many debates, the combination of the close attention paid to it by politically interested voters, and the heavy coverage on network newscasts and in the print press in the days following the debate, made it an important political event. As it turned out, it significantly affected *two* campaigns. Ronald Reagan's absence offended Iowans, reinforced the impression that Reagan was running a Rose Garden above-the-battle campaign, and almost certainly contributed to his narrow loss at the hands of George Bush in the Republican caucuses.

For Anderson, his performance in the debate marked the real start of his campaign. And it happened with his answers to two specific questions. At an early stage in the debate, interrogator Mary McGrory of the *Washington Star* asked the participants what specific public position or decision they most regretted. Most of the candidates chose to tap-dance around the question: Senator Dole, for example, "regretted" that he had called Jimmy Carter a "Southern-fried McGovern" because he'd come to respect McGovern. Senator Baker declaimed that whatever he might have done wrong, he always acted in good faith. John Anderson, in contrast, pointed to his vote on the Gulf of Tonkin resolution "which started America down the road to war in Vietnam," and ended up costing more than 50,000 American lives.

Later in the debate, the candidates were asked how it would be possible to balance the federal budget, increase defense spending, and lower taxes. While the other candidates talked of eliminating waste in government, Anderson responded this way: "You do it with mirrors, because it can't be done."

Combined with his defense of the grain embargo in a farm state—which Anderson described as politically unpopular—and his insistence on reaching out to moderates and liberals as the only way to win the election in the fall—Anderson managed to ignite a spark of interest, not among Iowa Republicans, but among voters around the country—especially of the big-city and campus-liberal variety—who found themselves cut adrift from the politics of 1980 by the character and strategic defects of Ted Kennedy. Anderson had suddenly become a story in the press, a more visible extension of the "lonely courageous Republican liberal" that had characterized the early coverage. Now there was a real, if still small, element of "momentum" in his campaign.

Before the debate, Anderson's biggest network exposure in 1980 had come on NBC's late-night, irreverent "Saturday Night Live" in which a skit set in a typical Iowa home featured a single household surrounded by candidates. Anderson was the "missing man," although the skit ended with Anderson being "elected" President of the United States as the cameras moved in on Anderson himself—in person—smiling and waving from the audience. Now the debate had "legitimated" him. On January 10, "CBS Evening News" featured a report that Anderson's debate performance "rang up a 50 percent increase in headquarters phone calls across the country, brought in more mail and contributions of money, increased new campaign volunteers from ten to fifty a day, and triggered a sudden renewed interest on the part of national news organizations."

David Broder, in a prescient column on January 9, wrote that "for sheer eloquence there was no one in the Republican presidential candidates' debate the other night who bested Rep. John B. Anderson of Illinois." Linking the Anderson performance with the clear disaffection of conservative Democrats with Carter, Jerry Brown, and Kennedy, Broder saw Anderson as a possible candidate who could draw these disaffected Democrats behind a moderate Republican. (Broder had the right idea, but the wrong formula; as it turned out, the disaffected conservative Democrats such as the *Commentary* magazine intellectuals Norman Podhoretz, Irving Kristol, and Jeane Kirkpatrick went en masse to Ronald Reagan, while disaffected *liberal* Democrats moved to Anderson's support.)

A *New York Times* January 13 editorial specifically declined to endorse Anderson, but its title—"Why Not the Best?"—accurately captured the flavor of its argument. "If a candidate is really that appealing," the editorial asked, "why shouldn't he have a chance. . . . He deserves at least the chance to show more. We hope voters in New Hampshire and other early primary states give it to him." *

This kind of support, however, was not enough to sustain an Anderson campaign. Even though press coverage was so favorable that Anderson was able to put together a full-page fund-raising ad com-

---

* Perhaps unintentionally, the *Times* editorial showed the curious role of early primary states. So thoroughly had these states become nationally significant that the *Times* was, in effect, urging New Hampshire voters to give other states the chance to vote for Anderson by giving him enough support to enable Anderson to remain in the race. The idea that a candidate might have no support in early small states, but great support in later-voting, bigger states had become an antiquated notion, a throwback to the days when the mass media had not yet turned every state primary into another round of a nationally waged battle.

posed almost solely of favorable press clips, he would still be everybody's favorite loser unless there was a political victory somewhere early in the battle. Without it, Anderson would still be the candidate of the Doonesbury comic strip, addressing halls of empty chairs as a lone listener explains that the low turnout was caused by "an Annette Funicello Film Festival," or driving his staff crazy by announcing—with name and address—who would be out of work in defense industries hurt by Anderson's opposition to big military spending increases. Through New Hampshire, Anderson was still the "lonely loser" candidate, overshadowed by the Bush-Reagan battle—although one significant incident did serve to demonstrate how a mass-media campaign enables a candidate to campaign on two levels at once.

On February 18, candidates or their representatives appeared before a forum of the New Hampshire Gun Owners' Association. For those who favored gun control, it was largely an unappetizing spectacle.

The candidates and their surrogates regaled the crowd with expressions of undying affection for their weapons of choice:

"I grew up in South Texas with a gun in my hand as long as I can remember," John Connally said.

"My fellow hunters," George Bush began, pointing to his ownership of a .22 rifle. Howard Baker reminisced about hunting in the Tennessee woodlands, and called gun control "inimical to the best interests of the United States."

"My father really knows how to shoot," said President Carter's son Jack, declaring that the President had shot his first quail as a small boy. And Ronald Reagan thanked "my fellow members of the N.R.A." for their warm welcome. Senator Kennedy, targeted for political action by the gun owners, who distributed bumper stickers saying "If Kennedy wins, you lose," chose not to share his gun-related memories with the group.

John Anderson, in contrast, spoke in favor of licensing gun owners, and was roundly booed for his trouble. But his audience was not the assembled gun owners—it was, rather, a national political audience. And on the "CBS Evening News" the next night, Walter Cronkite, reporting the event, said, ". . . all opposed controls save one. It was not surprising. John Anderson often has found himself standing apart from the crowd in this Campaign '80."

The tape showed Anderson saying, "What is so wrong about telling the law-abiding public of this country we will license gun owners? We will tell them . . ." and boos drowned out his conclusion. Reporter Bob McNamara tagged the piece this way, "Even though many voters see him as the most articulate, honest, and best candidate, Anderson has been labeled the man who can't win because he's too liberal."

Seen as a test of whether John Anderson had won the hearts and minds of the gun owners of New Hampshire, the appearance was a disaster. But in an age of television coverage, as I wrote in an earlier political work, "every speech by a reasonably prominent figure has two audiences: the one he is speaking to, and the audience that hears about the speech. The very fact that you have shown yourself willing to confront an angry audience will almost surely benefit you in the wider community . . . a reporter who can be persuaded to begin his story, 'Confronting an angry audience . . .' has already done your campaign an enormous favor." The widespread coverage of this face-down reinforced two impressions of Anderson: that he was indeed willing to embrace the liberal verities that were going all but unspoken in 1980, and that he was a man of courage, of character—given the fact that the most prominent liberal in the race, Edward Kennedy, could hardly be embraced even by liberal zealots as a paragon of virtue, Anderson's courage under fire was an attractive commodity.

New Hampshire, however, was no victory for Anderson. As Ronald Reagan swamped the field with 50 percent of the vote, and Bush collapsed from a neck-and-neck rival to a sorry second with 23 percent of the vote, Howard Baker won 13 percent and withdrew from the race almost immediately—proof, it was said, that even for a well-established and well-regarded political figure, weak showings in the first stages of the campaign were fatal to any chance of success. But Anderson, who finished fourth with 10 percent of the vote, was not treated as a candidate who had come to the end of an unpromising line, principally because his "lonely liberal" posture had so deflated expectations. For most of the candidates, 1980 was a year when the press ceased playing the "expectation game," assigning "weak victories" and "better than expected" defeats to different candidates at different stages in the primary race.* Anderson was the exception.

The *New York Times* analysis of the New Hampshire vote reported that "the one Republican gainer besides Mr. Reagan was Rep. Anderson, the outspoken Illinois liberal. . . . He picked up nearly twice his vote in Iowa, but was still far behind . . ." Since Anderson was not seen as a potentially "serious" candidate, there was no negative effect from a 10 percent showing. What was clear was that, barring some genuine surprise from the Anderson camp, there was no way his campaign could become anything but the semiofficial Don Quixote effort of 1980.

A week later, it all changed.

On March 4, the Massachusetts and Vermont primaries were held,

---

* This may have been due to the press's recognition of past campaign practices, but the more likely explanation is that none of the primaries broke that way; had Bush run a close second in Iowa's caucuses, rather than winning them, and had then placed a close second to Reagan in New Hampshire, it is likely the "expectation game" would have been played to the hilt.

a direct consequence of the Carter White House's concern about Ted Kennedy. Realizing in the fall of 1979 that Kennedy was a certain opponent, and worried about the potential impact of early primary votes on the momentum within the Democratic Party, Carter officials persuaded Vermont's officials to move their primary date to coincide with Massachusetts', reasoning that a possible Carter victory in Vermont might offset press coverage of the expected Kennedy win in Massachusetts. By March 4, of course, Carter was the odds-on favorite for renomination. But the twin primaries did produce a major publicity advantage for John Anderson.

With Bush in eclipse, with Baker out of the race, liberal and moderate Republicans began casting about for a possible alternative to Reagan. At the same time, independents and Democrats—who realized Ted Kennedy would certainly win in Massachusetts—were looking to that state's open primary as a way of sending a different sort of message. The result was that on Tuesday night, voters saw a nip-and-tuck three-candidate race evolving in both Massachusetts and Vermont—and the lonely liberal, John Anderson, was battling for the lead in both states. For the network late-night specials, and for the next day's press coverage, the only story that night was John Anderson.

CBS's Walter Cronkite said that "John Anderson has created a three-man Republican race . . ." and has "emerged as one of the front-runners . . ." raising "the idea of a viable candidate who can appeal to independents." (Bruce Morton's analysis did raise a cautionary flag later that evening, when he said, "it's kind of hard to know what other state he's going to do this well in.") The three morning network news shows on Wednesday all featured Anderson's "victory" statement as a lead item, although Anderson won neither primary, finishing a close second to Bush in Massachusetts, and a close second to Reagan in Vermont, and Anderson was interviewed both on the late-night specials and the morning news shows—the principal political victory sought by candidates in the early primaries.

(Interestingly, when Anderson was asked by Tom Brokaw about a possible independent bid for the White House, he called it "highly premature . . . I'm absolutely convinced that the way to win the Presidency is to win it within the two-party system at this point . . .")

The evening news shows featured Anderson surrounded by reporters, camera crews, and press planes; indeed, the surge of the press to a newly successful candidate was treated as the surest sign that Anderson was now a "serious" candidate, just as the crush of the press surrounding George Bush after Iowa was his "official" entry into serious coverage. Anderson, said CBS's Bob McNamara, "was suddenly cloaked in the trappings of a Presidential contender, and he liked the attention." "Today," said NBC's Tom Pettit, "he was on

NBC, CBS, and ABC. Now, when Anderson talks, big-time journalists listen.''

Perhaps the most curious aspect of Anderson's press treatment after his March 4 showing was the gap between the political coverage and the "expectation" coverage. In assessing Anderson's prospects in the remaining Republican primaries, the press almost universally showed a clear sense of realism and restraint; in examining Anderson as a "phenomenon," however, the press seemed to accept the notion that attention and coverage was itself a key to success in the battle for the Republican nomination.

For example, all of the post-March 4 analyses showed that Anderson did well because of his ability to attract independent and Democratic votes. Among regular Republicans, NBC's Pettit noted, "he was slaughtered." On that night's "MacNeil-Lehrer Report," Robert Shayan of the *Los Angeles Times* said, "I don't even know that John Anderson can win another primary." With most of the later primaries excluding independents and Democrats from voting, with Anderson not even entered in many of the Southern states, the reporters explained to the public that Anderson's chances to contest seriously for the Republican nomination were almost nonexistent.

But the focus on the one-day good showing, the press's attention paid to the fact that the press was now covering Anderson, seemed to reflect a different kind of understanding—one rooted in the "media-is-everything" school of politics, which holds that the achievement of momentum, of personal interviews by Cronkite, Chancellor, and Company, can somehow substitute for delegates in the battle for the nomination. In this limited sense, Anderson's sudden elevation to national stature in the face of the clear political facts of life was an example of the press's "doublethink." A traditional, "unsophisticated" analysis of the Republican Party in 1980 showed that John Anderson was far outside the party's mainstream; that his support came from constituencies outside the party; that his well-earned success on March 4 could not be duplicated anywhere else in the country. A "sophisticated" analysis held that Anderson would now be on the covers of national news weeklies, and accorded a prominent place on network political coverage, and that somehow *that* factor would override "conventional" politics. Out of March 4 emerged two buzzwords of the campaign: "surprise" and "volatility." Each week we would be "surprised" by a new political development; each week voters would lurch from candidate to candidate in a display of "volatility."

In fact, there was "volatility" only if each state's primary was regarded as a "national" event. Since each primary was played out on national media, it was understandable that these contests should be examined, week after week, as if the entire nation was taking part in them. After all, the entire nation saw George Bush claim victory one week, Reagan the next, Anderson the next. All of us saw the same network newscasts reporting the results to an entire country. In that sense, of course, what happened in Iowa or New Hampshire did have clear national implications. But a state primary or caucus is still taking place in only one state, whose politics may well be very different from the state holding a primary a week later. To assume that the votes in an Eastern, liberal state with open voting could be replicated in a conservative Southern state with a Republicans-only primary was to be willfully blind to the way politics works. But so prevalent was the idea that media attention conquers all that Anderson was elevated even beyond the press's own understanding of the political terrain.

As events demonstrated, the "traditional, old-fashioned, unsophisticated" analysis of the press turned out to be correct. John Anderson did not win a single primary throughout his campaign as a Republican. In his home state of Illinois, where he had the endorsement of both Chicago papers, he finished second to Ronald Reagan, who won a 49–38 victory, with Bush finishing a distant third, with 11 percent of the vote. His liberalism, so attractive to some independents and Democrats, made him anathema to conservatives and to mainstream Republicans. Two days after his March 4 showings, columnist George Will, apologizing for his earlier praise of Anderson, labeled him an "opportunist," and cited his fund-raising letter on behalf of proabortion candidates for the Congress. In a March 13 Republican debate in Chicago, Anderson's rivals virtually read him out of the Republican Party, with Congressman Philip Crane saying, "You're in the wrong party, John. . . . He's the classiest Democrat in the race." Anderson and Bush clashed angrily in a finger-pointing exchange, with Bush saying, "I did not interrupt you. Would you just keep calm, just calm down," and Anderson replying, "I have to interrupt you when you don't tell the truth." Reagan, the principal beneficiary of this dispute among his rivals, skewered Anderson with humor, saying at one point with mock incredulity "John, you really—you really would find Teddy Kennedy preferable to me?"

In both Illinois and Wisconsin, moreover, Ronald Reagan demonstrated what had been evident in his gubernatorial campaigns and in his 1976 run for the Presidency: that *he* was capable of drawing large numbers of disaffected Democrats; more, both in Illinois and Wisconsin, than Anderson drew. In Wisconsin, for example, Reagan went to Milwaukee's Serb Hall, where Democratic candidates had traditionally campaigned, and where no Republican had been since the days of the flood, to address hundreds of enthusiastic "lunch-bucket" Democrats, largely of Eastern European stock. These Democrats, and millions of others, had been drifting away from liberalism for more than fifteen years, since the first emergence on the national scene of George Wallace. They were repelled first by the social agenda—permissive sex, rioting, crime—then by the economic agenda, as inflation and taxes seemed to turn government from a friend into a foe. Reagan had shown a capacity to attract these votes from his first foray into politics in 1966.

Among some elements of the press, however, it was Anderson who was seen as the one Republican with real appeal to Democrats and independents. The *New York Times*'s Russell Baker wrote ironically in early March that "professional Republicans [complain that Anderson] is spoiling their primaries, they say, by getting independents and Democrats to vote on the Republican side of the line." Mary McGrory was one of many who noted that Anderson, in appealing to large numbers of college students, had "awakened the campuses from their long sleep." *Newsweek* wrote that Anderson's "idealism endears him particularly to a cohort of student supporters unrivaled since the antiwar crusade of Eugene McCarthy." John Oakes described Anderson in the *New York Times* on March 20 as "the only Republican who could probably defeat President Carter—if he could only first defeat the G.O.P.'s ingrained death wish that the Reagan candidacy represents."

It is almost certainly wrong to argue that John Anderson's good press was the key to his decision to abandon the Republican race and move toward an independent drive for the Presidency. Yes, Anderson's liberalism made him an appealing figure to liberal columnists and editorial writers; but it was more the "what's new?" element that gave Anderson his visibility; the prospect of a Republican becoming steadily more liberal at a time when the party itself was becoming steadily more conservative made Anderson a "man bites dog" story. It was because of the *exposure* given Anderson that the possibility of an independent run was strengthened. After all, it can hardly be said that the national press was in sympathy with the rise of Alabama Governor George Wallace in the early 1960s, or that his Democratic primary battle of 1964 against Lyndon Johnson's stand-ins inspired a good national press. What counted was that those Americans who agreed with Wallace were given ample exposure to his views; that exposure, rather than its content, gave Wallace the basis on which to build a third-party movement that won 10 million votes in 1968.

Anderson's exposure performed the same function. But it must be understood in the context of two other factors, one political, one much more "media"-related. The first is that by the middle of March—after the March 18 Illinois primary, to be exact—it had become clear that the major party contests were over. Ronald Reagan and Jimmy Carter would be fighting for the Presidency in November, and there would be no "real" liberal in the race. With President Carter having long since lost any true appeal for liberals, it left a vacuum on the left side of the political spectrum.

Second, by early spring the press had already begun to sound what was to become the dominant note of its 1980 campaign coverage: discontent. All through the last three months of the primaries, press coverage was stressing the faults of the primary system: its length, its expense, the unfair weight given to early results, the lack of quality in the apparent choices. To what extent this discontent was a product of press boredom with the certain major party outcomes cannot be quantified, but clearly Anderson's movement toward independent status qualified as a "man-bites-dog" story, a possibly major alteration of the Presidential line-up. More important, the discontent expressed by the press had by the spring also begun appearing in the opinions of the citizenry. Anderson himself in talking about the potential of an independent campaign on the April 11 "Today" show began by saying that "recent polls have indicated that 58 percent, I think, to be exact, have expressed themselves as unhappy, literally disconsolate at the prospect of being forced to choose only between two men in November of 1980." Similar measurements of discontent by the CBS-*New York Times* poll provided the underlying basis for Anderson's flirtation with an independent run, as did other polls showing that, in a three-way race, Anderson could get somewhere between 17 and 22 percent of the vote.

When Anderson announced on April 23 that he would "pursue an independent course toward the Presidency of the United States," he was in a position unthinkable for an unsuccessful major party candidate in a pretelevision era. Polls showed that he would get 18 percent of the vote, as against 35 percent for President Carter, and 24 percent for Ronald Reagan. Stated another way, these mid-April numbers indicated that, if John Anderson could hold his level of support, and persuade just one out of every seven Carter and Reagan voters to switch their allegiance to him, there would be a three-way battle for the Presidency in November.

It was a remarkable demonstration of the power of the media to provide the opportunity for an unknown political entity to achieve genuine national stature. It had been barely a hundred days from Anderson's appearance at the Iowa Republican debate to his declaration of the pursuit of an independent path to the Presidency (his actual declaration did not come until July 1). He had had no primary victories, and barely 10 percent of the Republican delegates needed for a nomination. There was no party, no structure, nothing but a public perception of an intelligent, outspoken, honest liberal who would provide an alternative for voters who—out of their own discontent or the press's coverage of the 1980 campaign—were looking for an outlet for their unhappiness.

The modern campaign process had given John Anderson a chance to make a real run for the White House without any of the traditional sources of political strength in America. But as we shall see, it was precisely the lack of these traditional tools of politics—party, structure, money, and regional and ideological constituencies—that took John Anderson from a position of potential victory to 6 percent of the 1980 vote and a shutout in the Electoral College. What Anderson had done was to achieve as high a level of strength as a media-based candidacy could imaginably achieve; what happened through the summer and fall was to show just how crucial the "obsolete" aspects of Presidential politics were.

vii Jimmy Carter's Renomination: The Media Held Hostage

Ever since television came to dominate thinking about national politics, one of the major concerns has been the power that the medium confers on the President. Access to millions of dollars worth of free time, all but irresistible power to command the attention of the American people, the capacity to improve image through carefully staged media events, the very setting of the national agenda by control of the public discourse—all of these elements have suggested that television would be an ominous tool for the unhealthy growth of Presidential power. As a 1973 book, *Presidential Television* (ed: Newton Minow *et al.*), put the case:

> An intricate set of constitutional balances limiting the power of each of the three government branches added force to the separation of government functions. These political and constitutional relationships served the country well for many years. Television's impact, however, threatens to tilt the delicately balanced system in the direction of the President.

Given the results of the last two elections, and the fate of the last four Presidents, it seems just as logical to stand the argument completely on its head. Both Gerald Ford and Jimmy Carter were defeated in their bids to retain the White House—the first time two incumbents have successively lost the White House since Benjamin Harrison and Grover Cleveland evicted each other in 1888 and 1892. Three of the last four Presidents have been seriously challenged for renomination, and the only incumbent to escape that fate—Richard Nixon in 1972—was driven out of office two years later. Given the fact that television and the mass media in general have assumed far more power than political party organizations, incumbent Presidents have found themselves unable to use the party as a protective shield from the shifting public moods; intraparty rivals with wide public recognition can and

110

have used the media to provide their alternative ideas and their personalities to an electorate which can then use the primaries to challenge incumbent Presidents. And the sharpening of the adversary relationship between press and President, which began during the Johnson Administration and has never subsided, has stripped a cloak of protection from the chief executive, who could once share secrets over an evening of poker and whiskey. Instead of turning the President into a superman, this intimate medium has made the chief executive much more mortal.

The problem with either of these theories, as with so many other notions about politics and the media, is that they do not match up with the facts—or, rather, they each match up with some facts, but not with others. Incumbent Presidents have tried to bend the media to their wills ever since the era of popular Presidential politics began: Andrew Jackson installed a newspaperman, Amos Kendall, in an obscure Treasury post to help him deal with the press; Abraham Lincoln visited Civil War battlefields in 1864 to prove his concern for the Union soldiers; Theodore Roosevelt curried favor with the White House press corps on a daily basis; Calvin Coolidge gave up his summer vacation in 1924 to project the image of the hard-working chief executive. And with every innovation in technology, presidents have changed the techniques of manipulation: from Coolidge posing for motion-picture newsreels, to FDR using highly personal, folksy metaphors to reach the radio audience, to Richard Nixon's embrace of local television station and newspaper executives to go over the heads of hostile national news organizations.

And just as consistently, the press has been at odds with the President of the United States. New York newspapers published cartoons of Abraham Lincoln cracking jokes upon hearing the latest Civil War death toll; the *Chicago Tribune* published "mug shots" of civilians wearing dogtags to show the totalitarian implications of FDR's Social Security plans; Truman denounced the "one-party" press which overwhelmingly backed Republican candidates; and the hostility between Richard Nixon and the media is legendary. Gerald Ford's public image never fully recovered from the photos of his recurring head-bumping and other acts of physical gracelessness on the part of the most athletic chief executive in history.

Moreover, presidents are rarely covered monolithically. The same attempts to manipulate the press, to use incumbency as a tool for reelection, can succeed brilliantly or fail dismally, depending upon factors completely outside the President's control. The same personality trait that is described as a breath of fresh air, untainted by corrupt Washington, may be seen as shocking evidence of Presidential naivete if it follows two years of congressional inaction. The same public relations posture that is hailed as a prudent response to a crisis may be viewed as blatant media manipulation if it goes on for too long. In sum, neither Presidential attempts to use the media, nor media coverage of a President, is static. And the year between August of 1979, when President Carter seemed a defeated chief executive without the hope of renomination, and August of 1980 when he was renominated by the Democrats with what appeared an even chance of winning reelection, illustrates this point clearly. Looking at the way President Carter was covered in these twelve months shows:

● Two complete turnabouts in the general press perception of Carter: from a well-meaning boob sure to be denied renomination, to stern-visaged leader of a nation in crisis, to a cynical manipulator of images, blatantly using the White House for his political advantage;

● A growing determination by the press to explain its own role as an unwilling transmitter of Presidential messages; a determination which had little, if any, political effect on President Carter's renomination, but which may well have had serious consequences in the fall campaign;

● A use of incumbency that appears to have had as much direct impact on President Carter's renomination as his entire media strategy, using the most traditional political devices—from the timing of government grants and announcements to the marshaling of specific interest groups that had received special attention from the Carter Administration—all of which was covered by the press, none of which had any measurable impact on voter attitudes;

● A relatively short, but critically important, shift in the coverage of President Carter, from critical to favorable, stemming from the seizure of American diplomats in Iran and, secondarily, the Soviet invasion of Afghanistan, both of which gave President Carter the opportunity to act as the determined leader of a nation in crisis. While the "national unity" atmosphere was neither universal nor long-term, it was strong enough and just long enough—lasting from November, 1979, through the spring of 1980—to provide Jimmy Carter with enough of a protective umbrella to enable him to build up a big enough lead in delegates to assure his renomination without campaigning for the nomination in any visible or "official" way.

● Paradoxically, this "success" of President Carter in gaining renomination may have been one cause of his ultimate failure to win reelection, since it prevented the President from testing his fundamental themes until it was too late. Having been propelled by crisis, by the failure of his opposition, and by his effective mobilization of traditional, bedrock constituent Democratic *leaders,* the President and his campaign may well have been misled into believing that such a posture would inevitably lead to success in November; that the sense of crisis leadership, unacceptable opposition, and mobilization of traditional Democratic *voters* would lead to victory over Ronald Reagan.

Looking at Jimmy Carter in the summer of 1979, the press saw failure—a nice guy who was simply not up to the job of President of the United States. In mid-July, Carter had taken the biggest gamble of his Presidency: postponing a conventional speech on energy for a two-week retreat to Camp David, much-ballyhooed consultations with public officials, journalists, and philosophers, surprise visits to "ordinary citizens" in Pennsylvania and Maryland communities, climaxed by a July 15 speech in which Carter proclaimed that "a crisis of confidence . . . strikes at the very heart and soul and spirit of our national will . . . threatening to destroy the social and political fabric of America." He quoted findings of his pollster Pat Caddell to warn that "for the first time in the history of our country, a majority of our people believe that the next five years will be worse than the last five years"—a finding of national "malaise" that Caddell had been detecting in the national spirit for almost the entire decade of the 1970s.

It was an ardently delivered speech, complete with fist-clenching and desk-pounding as suggested by Carter media advisor Gerald Rafshoon. Its mixture of Churchillian firmness ("beginning this moment," Carter declared, "this nation will never use more foreign oil than we did in 1977—never!" which happened to be a level the United States would likely never approach for at least a decade), self-criticism, and patriotism ("whenever you have a chance, say something good about our country") seemed to have made some impact. While CBS's Bruce Morton was dubious about whether "he can convince people that . . . he can run this enormously complex country," and while the *New York Times* editorialized that "he might be judged timid in his response" to the energy crisis, polls showed a jump in Carter's approval ratings from a disastrous 26 percent to a merely terrible 37 percent, and 40 percent of those surveyed by CBS said they had more faith in Carter than they had felt before his speech.

But two days after the speech, while the gist of Carter's complex energy proposal was still being digested, the White House announced that the President had asked for the resignation of the entire cabinet and White House senior staff. The reaction was more hostile to a sitting President than any since Watergate. When the dust had cleared, when Joseph Califano of Health, Education, and Welfare, Brock Adams of Transportation, Mike Blumenthal of Treasury, James Schlesinger of Energy had been given their walking papers, when newly appointed Chief of Staff Hamilton Jordan began to demand report cards to judge the loyalty and competence of administration staffers, the Carter White House was enveloped in ridicule.

"They're serving Kool-Aid at the White House mess" was a joke making frequent appearances in press accounts—a morbid reference to the Jonestown massacre. CBS reported on July 20 that "House aides ridiculed the proposal by circulating 'report cards' evaluating

Carter insiders and his family." And Republican Senator Stevens suggested publicly that the President "might be having a breakdown" and needed a rest. *Time*'s Hugh Sidey, whose White House column provided an unerring clue to the conventional Washington wisdom, wrote, "There is a deep sadness in Washington this week. Concern about Jimmy Carter and his Administration has gone beyond anger . . . doubts about the President will grow even larger and seep out across the world." Said the *New York Times,* "Now Jimmy Carter has decided whom he wants to run against—himself."

The attempt to resurrect his Administration with a bold stroke had backfired; instead, Carter was being skewered as a kind of Richard Nixon without the efficiency. And the political implications of this disaster were summarized in CBS's four-part examination of Carter's strength, which aired in late August. Every region of the nation was reported in rebellion, with former Democratic Party Carter loyalists alternately angry and regretful. Bob Faw's report from the Midwest told of a view that Carter "hasn't delivered the goods, doesn't seem to be in control. The consensus, in short, that he's a good man who's in over his head." From the West, Carter's weakest 1976 region, Bernard Goldberg found Carter "in trouble" in a bellwether Oregon county, and featured black California Assembly Speaker Willie Brown calling Carter "dull . . . uninteresting. He's perceived as somebody whom you would not invite to dinner. You might want him to come by for cocktails and leave early." In the South, Ed Rabel found two former Carter organizers building a draft-Teddy movement in Florida, and showed a poll that had Kennedy leading Carter 47–30 among Southern Democrats. "Competence and ability to lead," Bruce Morton summarized, "are the key areas bothering voters."

With Ted Kennedy's all-but-formal announcement of his Presidential intentions—leaked to key print and broadcast reporters on September 7, 1979, in the form of a report that his family was no longer raising objections to a White House bid—the Carter Administration began a strategy of what Jack Germond and Jules Witcover called "rich-mouthing." Instead of adopting the traditional campaign posture of downplaying expectations, the White House began reminding the country—specifically the media—that Jimmy Carter was still the President, and that the potency of Ted Kennedy as a national candidate was still theoretical.

Some of the actions seemed questionable at best. Even before Kennedy's full-tilt, public "assessment" of his candidacy, President Carter made his own assessment clear. In a White House meeting with Democratic congressmen on October 5, 1979, Carter said, "If Kennedy runs, I'll whip his ass." Asked to repeat his comment by an incredulous congressman, the President did so, and White House aides took pains to insure that the comment received widespread publicity.

If the intention was to show Carter's determination, the effect was more ludicrous than macho.

Carter ran into more trouble on two other occasions where the White House seemed to have forgotten that Jimmy Carter was the President—that it was not necessary to stage events in a desperate attempt to get his picture in the newspapers. After the Pittsburgh Pirates defeated the Baltimore Orioles in an exciting seven-game World Series, the cameras switched to the victorious Pirates' dressing room, where Baseball Commissioner Bowie Kuhn was presenting the trophy to the Pirates. Suddenly, on the tiny raised platform appeared a halting, slight figure—the President of the United States—who murmured a few remarks of congratulation, and then found himself ignored by Willie Stargell, Bowie Kuhn, and ABC commentators alike. A few minutes later, the President simply shuffled off the platform and melted into the crowd.

And on September 15, Jimmy Carter entered an outdoor run through the Catoctin Mountains of Maryland. "If you start," Press Secretary Jody Powell had told the President, "just be sure you finish." But the heat and the terrain proved too much for the jogger, who had to be helped from the course by Secret Service agents; photos of the sweat-drenched, exhausted Carter ran in newspapers and television stations across the country.

Other events, however, demonstrated a far shrewder appreciation of "media perceptions"—a perception to be expected from a campaign whose chief strategist, Hamilton Jordan, had helped guide an obscure governor into Presidential contention four years earlier by laying out a detailed plan for building press credibility. All through the summer of 1979, two former Carter workers had been trying to build support for a "draft Teddy" movement by mobilizing Kennedy sentiment for the October 20 caucuses of Florida's Democratic Party. These nonbinding county meetings would simply record a straw poll of candidate preferences; the actual delegates would be chosen in the March, 1980, primary. But once Kennedy signaled his intention to enter the race, the event became a first battleground between the contenders. With Kennedy far ahead in public opinion polls, the Carter forces saw the Florida straw vote as a chance to puncture the sense of invincibility. ("If Kennedy loses, it'll have a very large major impact, because right now Kennedy is perceived as the front-runner," said *Newsweek* chief political correspondent James Doyle.) Kennedy's unofficial announcement, in turn, put pressure on him to make a respectable showing. And the press—remembering that an October, 1975, straw vote in Ames, Iowa, was the first recorded sign of Carter strength—was determined not to miss any straw votes in the wind this time. Besides, the Florida vote meant that there was *something* tangible to be covered three full months before the Iowa caucuses.

The result was a splendid—sometimes hilarious—example of the press and politicians chasing each other, each explaining how the other guys had made the event important. For three days, the network news programs of ABC, CBS, and NBC devoted major space to the Florida caucuses, with all of the correspondents standing in the Florida sunshine, solemnly explaining that this caucus vote was a meaningless exercise—a media event. (It was reminiscent of the old formula for turning lead into gold: dunk a pound of lead in water, and *don't* think about elephants. If the event was unimportant, what were they doing down there?) Columnists Jack Germond and Jules Witcover called criticism of the press rush "horsefeathers," arguing that the event was important because "the reelection strategists for President Carter decided to make a major effort to give Senator Ted Kennedy a black eye . . . [and second] the caucuses came along shortly after Kennedy conspicuously started sending out signals that he would run. . . . The stakes are name recognition, a perception of forward movement . . . and, of course, mass media attention."

Trying to figure out whether the press descended on Florida because the candidates were making major efforts, or whether the candidates were making major efforts because the press was covering the event was, as *Washington Post* writer Nicholas Lemann noted, a classic chicken-and-egg case. But the fact is that Carter spent more than $250,000 to dispatch surrogates, from Mother Lillian and Wife Rosalynn to Andrew Young and Vice-President Mondale, and the Kennedy forces spent more than $175,000 to dispatch Julian Bond and Allard Lowenstein across the state. And President Carter did win some 60 percent of the vote—"about ten buses more than we had," a Kennedy aide said, and it was probably in a good cause. The defeat of an incumbent President in any contest with so much press attention could have undermined the key first element of Carter's renomination strategy.

Even as an unpopular underdog, facing a strong challenge from within his own party, Jimmy Carter was still the President of the United States. And for the governors, mayors, congressmen, and senators around the country—most of them Democrats—Jimmy Carter still controlled the flow of government grants and programs, and would for fifteen more months no matter what his political prospects. This decidedly old-fashioned political reality was the key to the support that began flowing toward the beleaguered President in the autumn of his discontent. From Los Angeles's Tom Bradley to Detroit's Coleman Young to New York's Ed Koch, big-city Democratic mayors lined up behind Carter—Chicago's Jane Byrne, a major exception, proved so unpopular as the campaign year began that her endorsement of Kennedy became a major political liability. While summer reports had Democratic senators urging Ted Kennedy to run to save the party from a 1980 debacle, *Newsday* reported in late October that twenty of twenty-two Democratic senators *denied* urging Kennedy to run—a story given wide circulation by the White House. And Carter aides were further building the case for Democratic Party support by pointing to Kennedy's voting record of more than 80 percent support for the Carter program, arguing that Kennedy had "difficulty in developing a rationale for his candidacy . . . a President he has supported and with whom he has had no overriding differences." And, in what would be a major Chappaquiddick-related campaign theme, the internal memo advised supporters to stress the point that "Mr. Carter *has told people the truth.*"

Much of the Carter campaign's work was done for it by Kennedy's disastrous entry into the race. In his inability to explain why he was in the race at all, in his failure to define sharp disagreements with the President because of his unwillingness to run on a clearly liberal record, in his inability to defuse the Chappaquiddick issue, the Kennedy campaign made it comparatively easy for Carter to move the battleground away from his record, and onto the question of whether Democrats really wanted to put Ted Kennedy into the White House. As the press turned toward a highly critical scrutiny of Kennedy's character and competence, the Carter campaign was largely spared the need to defend its candidate's record as President. But accompanying this advantage was the sudden appearance of the most overriding event of the primary season: the seizure of the American embassy in Teheran, Iran, on November 4, 1979. The nature of the press coverage of this event, and the Carter Administration's use of the crisis, was as critical an advantage for President Carter as anything that happened during the primary campaign of 1980. And while the Carter Administration obviously did not seek this crisis, its response was a perfect demonstration of the media's essential passivity in dealing with a President determined to frame the terms of crisis coverage.

Twelve years earlier, in December, 1968, North Korean naval forces had seized the American intelligence ship *Pueblo*, taken its crew prisoner, and held the crew and the ship for eleven months. Even though that seizure took place on the eve of a Presidential campaign, the *Pueblo* incident played almost no role in the election debate. This was so in part because the *Pueblo* was clearly a military vessel engaged in spying and may well have entered into North Korean waters, and in part because there were no Western newsmen in Pyongyang, North Korea. Without cameras, without a satellite beaming pictures back to the United States, and without a clear sense that international law had been violated by American adversaries, there was little sense of outrage to be stirred up by incessant coverage. In fact, so mild was the American response that Robert Kennedy essayed a small jest about the matter in the course of his 1968 Presidential campaign. Asked after a speech how he felt about the *Pueblo* seizure, Kennedy said "badly."

But the 1979 seizure was a very different matter. First, the taking of American embassy personnel was in clear violation of international law, which treats an embassy as sovereign soil of the nation whose embassy it is. Second, and much more significant, the seizure itself, and the daily mass demonstrations of Iranian militants, was beamed back to the United States every day by satellite. Outraged Americans saw mobs of chanting, shouting, fist-waving foreigners (from the American perspective) parading past the seized embassy, and at times displaying bound and blindfolded Americans in front of mobs chanting, "Death to the spies" and "Death to America." The films were not, in a technical sense, staged; but in a political sense, they were films high in pictorial drama and human emotions. They seemed to confirm a growing feeling that the United States had demonstrated irresolution and weakness in matters abroad, and that hostile forces had come to believe, in the words of one slogan prominently displayed in television coverage, that "the U.S. can do nothing," because President Carter, as Ayatollah Khomeini said, "does not have the guts to engage in a military operation."

In the face of this crisis, the President cancelled political forays into Florida, a trip to Canada, a Camp David weekend, and Thanksgiving at Plains, Georgia. The White House became a crisis center, and President Carter became the besieged commander-in-chief, denouncing Iran for "terrorism" and declaring that "The United States of America will not yield to international terrorism or blackmail." And the element most lacking in Carter's first thirty-four months—the sense of strength and resolution—was suddenly thrust upon him by an outside force. In this press, Carter suddenly emerged as a master of prudent, wise strength.

Barely five days after the seizure, the *New York Times*'s James Reston wrote that Carter "has been leading us through the latest Iranian crisis with admirable restraint, and deserves the patience and support of the nation." He praised him for rejecting the "politically popular" path of military support, and called for "a little more support than he has been getting." The *Times* editorial pages, which had ridiculed his Administration three months earlier, now said that "President Carter is being both wise and firm in his contest against Ayatollah Khomeini. . . . The President has skirted the twin dangers of inaction and overreaction. He deserves admiration and support." CBS's Bruce Morton commented on November 23, "There's no military option that does the hostages any good. . . . Second, there's a national tendency, a tradition almost, among politicians, when American lives are at hazard, that you say, 'well, I'm not going to rock the boat.' "

Indeed, the almost unanimously favorable press was premised on both of these points. The argument that the United States was somehow to blame in part for this crisis, through its support of the Shah's regime for decades, and for admitting the Shah to the United States, was impossible to make in the context of a clearly illegal act in violation of basic international law. Ted Kennedy found that out when his critical comments about the Shah blew up in his face. In contrast, the argument that the hostages were, in effect, prisoners of war, and that strong action had to be taken, even if the hostages were placed at risk, suggested a kind of casual recklessness that neither the press nor rival candidates cared to risk. Moreover, the hostages were not faceless abstractions. Thanks to television, we had seen them "face to face," courtesy of Iranian propaganda footage. We had come into the homes of their families, met their wives and parents and children. Even without the intense personal identification between Americans and the hostages and their families, the hesitancy to invoke direct military action that was a remnant of the Vietnam War reaction meant that Carter's restraint could not be assailed as inaction without invoking the specter of large-scale loss of American life. Thus, the *Times*'s summary of Carter's position—which might have seemed critical in another time —was actually meant as a compliment: "get tough, America, not with someone else's son in the 82nd Airborne, but by driving less, shivering a little, and thus dispelling the impression that the nation is so hooked on oil it can be held up for any price."

The President and his aides clearly understood the proper stance for Carter to take: the leader, above the battle, appealing for national unity, solemnly warning against criticism, not to protect his political posture, but because it might endanger innocent American lives. In a nationally televised prime-time press conference on November 28, Carter delivered a statement neatly embracing these themes.

"I want to thank all Americans for their prayers," he said, "their courage, their persistence, their strong support and patience. During these past days our national will, our courage, and our maturity have all been severely tested, and history will show that the people of the United States have met every test. . . . One thing tonight is clear: we stand together. We stand as a nation united, a people determined to protect the life and honor of every American." And, in a powerful demonstration of the advantage of running for the White House from the White House, Carter said, "We have encouraged all of those who have become announced candidates for President to restrain their comments, which might be misinterpreted overseas, and to have a maximum degree of harmony among those who might be spokesmen for our country. . . . I will have to continue to restrict my own political activities, and call on those who might be opposing me in the future for President to support my positions as President, and to provide unity for our country and for our nation in the eyes of those who might be looking for some sign of weakness or division in order to perpetuate their abuse of our hostages."

It was a remarkable use of the White House to rule commentary out-of-bounds: to criticize the Carter Administration, the President was arguing, was to subject hostages to potential torture or mistreatment, and, in effect, the President was arguing for a suspension of the ebb and flow of campaign-year rhetoric as a matter of patriotism. And the press seemed to accept this formulation. Although columnists such as George Will and Joseph Kraft argued that the very willingness to negotiate was a kind of capitulation to blackmail, the mainstream press continued to paint Carter as a commander-in-chief pursuing the only possible course.

"Contenders like Ted Kennedy," said *Time* magazine in late November, "have yet to assert—much less agree—where and exactly how the United States should throw its weight around." And Haynes Johnson wrote on December 2, under the headline, "If the Sabre Doesn't Rattle It's Because the Hand is Firm," that Carter's press conference exemplified "restraint, measured and strong. . . . The present national response to the agonizing crisis in Iran should bring a renewed pride in the country."

Carter's own reelection announcement continued the policy of "subordinating" politics to the national crisis. Having cancelled trips and vacations, the President continued to insist that he would remain in the White House until the American hostages were freed. On December 4, Carter declared for reelection, comparing himself with a President fighting a major war:

> At the height of the Civil War, President Abraham Lincoln said, "I have but one task that is to save the Union." Now I must devote my considered efforts to resolving the Iranian crisis. The overriding fact is that fifty of our fellow Americans have been unjustifiably thrust into agony and danger, and I have a personal responsibility to get them out of that danger as fast as possible.

Carter even apologized for declaring his candidacy for reelection, noting that "election laws in certain states" required the formal announcement. It was made from the East Room of the White House, and the President declined to attend the $500-a-person reception later that evening. It would prove to be a harbinger of the entire renomination strategy: Rosalynn Carter and Vice-President Mondale stood in for the President, who, it was assumed, was directing some kind of diplomatic-military-political pattern from deep within the bowels of the White House. There was, however, a hint in Carter's announcement of the approach planned against Ted Kennedy.

"There is no such thing as cheap energy," Carter said in his speech. "That is a truth. We cannot wish our way out of inflation.

That is a truth. We cannot spend our way out of every problem. That is a truth." Given the suspicions surrounding Kennedy's character, and the subsequent use of paid media to attack Kennedy's "truthfulness," it was apparent—as network correspondents such as CBS's Robert Pierpoint noted, that this constant reference to "truth" was at least an attack on Teddy by "subtle indirection."

Within a few weeks of Carter's reelection declaration, the Soviet Union provided a significant, if unintentional, boost to the President's "commander-in-crisis" image by invading its insufficiently loyal client state, Afghanistan. As television showed Soviet tanks rumbling through the streets of Kabul, Carter announced a series of steps: embargoing grain to the Soviet Union, contemplating a boycott of the coming Summer Olympics in Moscow, dispatching National Security Advisor Zbigniew Brzezinski to the Pakistan border where he brandished an automatic rifle, asking the Senate to hold up debate on the already troubled SALT II nuclear-arms treaty with Russia.

It does not require a conspiratorial mind-set to understand that the political benefit to Carter from the combined Iran and Afghanistan crises was enormous. Campaign Director Robert Strauss described the atmosphere as "good leadership being good politics. It's a quiet, firm, responsible leader type of leadership." And Robert Squier, who prepared a half-hour "documentary" commercial about the President,* said that "it's a kind of uncovering of something about this man as President that not many people have seen." As *Time* magazine described the change in Carter's image at the end of 1979, "this was Jimmy Carter, President, leading the U.S. in a way that, until the Iranian crisis erupted in November, the former Governor of Georgia had not managed in his three years in the White House. . . . Riding a wave of patriotic fervor and a degree of unity unseen in this country since the Cuban Missile Crisis of 1962, Jimmy Carter has suddenly become the solid choice to be renominated and reelected to a second term in the White House."

The polls documented the astonishing change—a shift in the Kennedy-Carter race of sixty-three points in four months. Kennedy's 58–25 August, 1979, lead had become a Carter lead of 53–22, accord-

* The documentary produced a landmark legal decision about the relationship between a campaign and the television networks. Carter sought a half hour of network time on December 4 to air the paid commercial announcing his re-election. All three networks declined to sell him the time—CBS offered Carter a five-minute spot—on the ground that "the campaign had not started." This raised the question of what armies of correspondents and camera crews had been doing for the previous several months covering every straw poll and county political dinner. At any rate, the FCC, and finally the Supreme Court, decided that networks could not flatly rule out such a "right of access" on the part of Presidential candidates. This may mean that the first 1984 commercials will be airing before this book goes to press.

ing to *Time*'s Gallup Poll. The ABC-Lou Harris poll showed Carter leading likely Republican rival Ronald Reagan by twenty points. In Tom Wicker's shrewd January 6 observation, the twin crises had "galvanized the elites," turning opinion makers toward a more respectful attitude for a President clearly grappling with major dilemmas. Hugh Sidey, in his January 28 *Time* column, seemed to detect a sense of physical grandeur.

"President Carter now has the body and face of a far younger man," he wrote. "His muscles and bones have adjusted to the new physical challenge. The corners show. . . . He is coiled physical vitality behind the desk in the Oval Office or sitting in an overstuffed chair in the family quarters."

All through the first two months of 1980, President Carter was able to enhance the "President in crisis" image. This was *not* because the press was ignoring the political implications of his posture; far from it. It was, rather, that the nature of press coverage precluded any possibility of balancing the dominant images of a President grappling with world affairs inside the White House with an explanation of the political agenda. For example, the Presidential lighting of the White House Christmas tree on December 13, carried by all three networks, showed Carter lighting only the star atop the tree. "The other lights will be turned on," the President said, "when the hostages come home." It was a genuinely solemn moment; and it would have taken a leap far beyond the bounds of journalistic objectivity for a White House correspondent to interject a skeptical appraisal of the political benefits of the gesture. Even more clearly political decisions had to be treated gingerly. On December 28, one day after the Soviet move into Afghanistan, Carter pulled out of the three-way Iowa debate with Kennedy and Jerry Brown. White House Press Secretary Jody Powell fed a memo to the press, in which he and other political advisors had warned Carter of the political costs of not debating.

In a handwritten scrawl, Carter had replied "Jody—I can't disagree with any of this but I cannot break away from my duties here which are extraordinary now and ones which only I can fulfill. We will just have to take the adverse political consequences and make the best of it. Right now both Iran and Afghanistan look bad and will need my constant attention." To a jaundiced eye, this memo, the reply, and the leak to the press seemed to suggest at least a hint of manipulation— something White House advisors conceded months later. But once again, the limits of objectivity forbade a correspondent from raising sharp questions about this event, particularly given the undeniable fact that there *were* two authentic crises.

To be sure, the press faithfully reported the political moves of the Carter reelection campaign. Evans and Novak reported in early February that the President was making twenty to forty calls a night to supporters in Maine and New Hampshire, as he had to Iowans during that caucus. Newspapers such as the *Washington Star* recounted Carter's "Running in Place from the Rose Garden." *Newsweek* headlined its story "See Jimmy Run—In Place," as it ticked off the uses of incumbency: $1 billion in grants to Florida just before the October straw poll, $75 million to Maine in one month—just before the Democratic caucuses—and the refusal to close an air force base. A $500,000 housing project in Nashua, New Hampshire, and the "coincidental" switch of support by that town's mayor from Kennedy to Carter. One hundred million in grants to San Francisco, whose mayor had backed Carter, and warnings by Transportation Secretary Neil Goldschmidt that Chicago—whose mayor, Jane Byrne, had endorsed Ted Kennedy —would have its grants proposals carefully scrutinized.

In those first two months, the Carter campaign was clearly able to use the White House as a staging area with little negative fallout. Perhaps the best illustration of the gap between the power of the image and the attempt of the press to put that image in context occurred on February 25—not so coincidentally, the night before the New Hampshire Presidential primary. On the preceding Friday night, at Lake Placid, New York, the underdog American Olympic hockey team had scored an astonishing upset over the Soviet team. A victory over Finland two days later—with Vice-President Mondale in attendance—had clinched the gold medal for the team, and President Carter congratulated the young Olympians by telephone in their locker room. Now, on Monday, the entire hockey team and such premier American performers as gold medalist skater Eric Heiden were invited to the White House for an elaborate reception.

NBC's David Brinkley noted on the "Nightly News" that "at a time when the American people must have felt a need to win something, the Olympic athletes did; and this pleased and excited this country as it has not been for a long time. Today, President Carter invited the whole pack of them to the White House for lunch, and sent airplanes to get them." After the cameras showed the President embracing Heiden and members of the hockey team, John Palmer noted ". . . the mood today was one of joy and celebration. Some felt there were political overtones on the day before the New Hampshire primary. . . . Whether politics was involved or not, it was the candidate's dream to be surrounded by Olympic medal winners on the day before an important primary."

CBS's Lesley Stahl declared that it was "hard to remember a time when the entire country was so united in its excitement and happiness over anything. . . . It almost seemed that the President was awarding the medals to men and women who were coming home from fighting a war." After exploring the controversy over the proposed summer Olympic boycott, Stahl ended her piece much as Palmer had his:

"With the economy gloomy and the hostage situation in Teheran tenuous, what better for the President on the eve of the New Hampshire primary than to be seen on television surrounded by a group of young, happy, and victorious American heroes? Lesley Stahl, CBS News, with the Carter campaign at the White House."

That sign off, an echo of Dan Rather's 1972 attempt to point to the political impact of Richard Nixon's Rose Garden campaign, was, in the eyes of Stahl and her network superiors, a tough-minded attempt to signal viewers that President Carter was using the White House for political purposes. The impact of that closing, of course, could not begin to compare with the favorable publicity generated by the reception for the Olympic heroes and heroines.

But this was not a case of the press failing to do its job. It was instead another example of the relative passivity, the inherent passivity, in the press's relations with a politically active President. The only way for a network correspondent to have *really* balanced the pictures with an account of the political calculation inherent in the reception would have been to turn into an editorialist, to say again and again that "what you are watching is a patriotic tableau dripping with political manipulation." No fair-minded broadcast organization would have permitted such editorializing, and, indeed, it might not even have been fair, assuming that an incumbent President can mix patriotic feelings with political decisions. In this context, there was no way to override the impact of the event itself, and countless others like it, which the President—any President—indulged in during the primary season.

What could happen, and what did happen, was the kind of thermostatic change in the climate of press coverage of politicians, which characterizes both campaign seasons and Presidential administrations. As a general proposition, the general approach to a political figure is one of initial skepticism, followed by the kind of "gee whiz" journalism surrounding political success, followed by the "who-is-he-*really?*" scrutiny that some politicians can survive (Jimmy Carter, 1976) and some cannot (George Bush, 1980). During a typical Presidential reign —if there is any such thing anymore—the excitement of a new face is generally followed by the first crisis or screw-up, followed by the "he's-in-big-trouble" coverage, which then changes places with the "growth-in-office" portrayal. For Jimmy Carter, the press coverage after the first six months of his Administration had been almost uniformly bad, save for the brief high of the Camp David accord with Israel and Egypt in the spring of 1979. In January and February of 1980, Carter was finally receiving the kind of press which cast him as somewhat larger than life. It was not to last long; but it lasted just long enough for Carter to build an insurmountable lead for the Democratic renomination. But just as reporters covering a President will, sooner or later, start wondering if they have been too harsh, the inevitable tendency of incumbents to use the White House for political gain will sooner or later trigger critical responses from the political press.

One of the first signs of this coming shift in the coverage of Carter came from David Broder of the *Washington Post*, who is both a key political reporter and a nationally syndicated columnist. He is not only read by virtually every political journalist and practitioner in America, but is usually considered to be a man without ideological or personal axes to grind. On February 3, Broder wrote, "I am getting a queasy feeling. It is the same feeling I had in 1972, when the incumbent president of the United States treated his reelection campaign as a matter too unimportant for his notice." Noting Carter's refusal to meet his Democratic rivals, his failure to hold public meetings with reporters for more than two months, save for his "Meet the Press" appearance the day before the Iowa caucuses, Broder accused Carter of denying the country a debate on critical policy choices. "Let him," Broder said of Carter, "cast aside his protective cloak and face his duties as a politician seeking office in a democracy."

Two weeks later, Broder continued the criticism. "His self-isolation," said Broder, "is damaging to him and to his Presidency." Referring to Carter's February 13 nationally televised assault on Ted Kennedy—during a press conference he said that Kennedy's criticisms "have not been accurate . . . and they've not helped our country"—Broder said, "to unleash such a counterattack from a presidential forum, carried live on all networks, when there can be no comparable opportunity for reply, is really to use the White House as a protected base from which the president 'carpetbombs' his political challengers."

As a columnist, Broder was not bound by the restraints of reportorial journalism that would have forbidden a network correspondent from launching such an attack. But whether because of Broder's own importance, or because of a slowly spreading sense that Carter had indeed immunized himself from appropriate criticism as a President seeking reelection, the signs of disaffection with Carter's Rose Garden strategy began to spread. Tom Wicker wrote on February 26 that "Mr. Carter has wrapped himself in the flag since the day the hostages were taken," and predicted that Carter was bound to fall from his temporary popularity "too late to rescue Edward Kennedy, but [perhaps] just in time to help the Republicans next fall." Hugh Sidey wrote in *Time* in mid-March that "after more than three years on the job, [Carter] still expends as much or more energy shaping his image and protecting his political flanks as he does ordering government personnel into action . . ."

As long as President Carter was winning every test against Edward Kennedy, the press criticism would be of limited *political* impact. Victors tend to write their own scripts in Presidential politics. Thus, if

Press Secretary Jody Powell claimed the day after New Hampshire that President Carter's victory was proof that "the people want the Congress to give the President a national energy policy," the press was likely to let such an absurdity slide, in its rush to decide how severely Kennedy had been wounded by his loss. When Carter demolished Kennedy in the March 18 Illinois primary, beating him 2–1 in the popular vote and 10–1 in the delegate count, the critical comments that were building over the Rose Garden strategy could almost be classified as grudgingly admiring: Carter was using the White House for political gain, but it was *working*. Campaign chief Strauss, a master of the proper postelection comments, could casually note that "Senator Kennedy would have to probably get 62,3,4 percent of the delegates from here on in to stop the President. . . . The senator is a wise man, and he's surrounded with good people, and they'll make up their own minds about what this does to this candidacy." The press was in unanimous agreement: Carter and Reagan, CBS's Bob Schieffer reported the morning after Illinois, "seem on the verge, at least, of locking up their party's nominations." *Time* and *Newsweek,* covering the Illinois primary in issues that would hit the stands on the day of the New York and Connecticut primaries on March 25, both declared that Carter and Reagan were all but unstoppable.

But on March 25 something curious happened to Jimmy Carter. Despite polls showing him as much as twenty-seven points ahead of Kennedy in New York a week before the primary, he actually lost to Kennedy by sixteen points. Whether it was the result of a United Nations vote against Israel, followed by a clumsy attempt to explain the vote as a "communications failure," or by the continuing slump in the economy, or by Kennedy's better press treatment and political performance, there was now another dimension, perhaps a critically important one, to Carter's Rose Garden campaign—it had, at least for a week, failed. This failure had to be *explained,* especially given the polls and predictions that had proven Kennedy would again lose decisively to Carter and be forced to withdraw (David Broder had written a piece for the *Washington Post* praising Kennedy's class, from the perspective of Carter victories in both New York and Connecticut, which ran the day of the primaries). The Kennedy campaign sought to do to the New York results what the Carter campaign had tried to do with its earlier primary triumphs: explain the votes as a triumph for their political arguments.

Thus, Kennedy told CBS's Susan Spencer that New York and Connecticut voters had sent a "very clear, powerful, strong message to this Administration and across the country that the economic policies of this Administration are inadequate for the working families of this nation." And Kennedy aide Paul Kirk told the "MacNeil-Lehrer Report" that "the problems we're faced with, of 18 percent inflation and no hope in sight, plus a rather stutter-step foreign policy, has been one of the things against which people will now really focus and protest."

The Carter campaign sought to picture the loss as an inevitable political consequence of the President's willingness to make unpopular decisions.

"There will probably be other decisions, both in the anti-inflation fight, and in the attempt to keep the Middle East Camp David peace process alive that may be politically difficult," White House Press Secretary Jody Powell explained. "The President's prepared to make those decisions and to accept the consequences." And campaign chief Robert Strauss, in a remark that was to run throughout the rest of the primary season, tried to discount the press reaction to the loss, saying on NBC's "Today" show, "you know, the pundits write this and they write that. I suspect the people listening to this know better than anyone what happened. [There's been] a lot of bad news, and now I think people will put it in perspective."

The most important consequence for President Carter's campaign was that the losses demonstrated his vulnerability, the sharp limits to both the effectiveness of the Rose Garden strategy, and the larger-than-life commander-in-chief presence he had established from the time in November when Iran seized the American embassy personnel. As with most other primary results in the 1980 campaign, the press did *not* exaggerate the impact of Kennedy's victories in New York and Connecticut. The message of Strauss and company after the Illinois primary—that Kennedy would need about a 2–1 margin of victory from New York through California to overtake Carter—was both vivid and accurate. Rather, as John Chancellor of NBC said, the victory made Kennedy "a born-again candidate"; it "breathed new life into [his] ailing candidacy," in Cronkite's words. In other words, it kept the Kennedy campaign alive, which would have been impossible with one more loss. (Less than a week before the New York primary, Kennedy and Carter aides had come together to attend the funeral of Allard Lowenstein, a political activist who, for more than twenty years, had brought young men and women into the world of liberal causes and campaigns, and who had been murdered by a former associate. Inevitably, the funeral became a clearinghouse of political gossip, and Kennedy aides were anticipating a loss in New York and the certain end to the Kennedy campaign.)

Carter, the results showed, had just about come to the end of his above-the-battle phase; in Jack Germond's words, "Carter became the subject of a referendum yesterday, rather than Kennedy." John Stacks of *Time* magazine argued that the results showed the startling weakness of both Democratic candidates, calling the battle "a sack race for cripples, if you will, and there are negative votes going both ways."

For the Kennedy campaign, the attempt to keep the attention focused on Carter meant a sudden, one-week attempt to blitz the Wisconsin primary of April 1. And this, in turn, would lead to the most widely noted Rose Garden gambit of the entire primary campaign, one which was to have serious consequences for Carter in the fall.

All through the primary campaign, the Carter White House was issuing a steady stream of announcements and decisions with obvious political overtones. To some extent, the press analyses of the "political timing" of the events was misleading, for almost every week between January and June there would be at least one primary or caucus; the only way for the White House to have avoided all political timing in its announcements would have been to shut down. Moreover, even an event such as the U.S. Olympic team reception the day before the New Hampshire primary was one of those mixtures of politics and Presidential pomp that had to be covered, to some extent, at face value. But on Tuesday, April 1, the Carter White House appeared to overstep the line between a skillful use of incumbency and outright manipulation.

In the predawn hours of that Tuesday—primary day in Wisconsin and Kansas—the Iranian government appeared to be taking the first real step toward ending the hostage crisis. President Bani-Sadr had apparently won the agreement of the Revolutionary Council to get the hostages turned over from the militants at the embassy to the government; since Bani-Sadr was known to want the hostage crisis resolved, that almost certainly meant the swift removal of the hostages to another country, or to the jurisdiction of a special United Nations commission.

President Carter called a "news conference" to hail the decision as a "positive step," and to say, in answer to a question about the actual release, that "we do not know the exact time scheduled at this moment";—a statement which, at the least, implied that the release was only a matter of timing.

At 7:15 A.M., of course, all three networks are broadcasting their morning news shows, and the press conference was carried live; for the majority of Americans who listen to the radio at that hour, either at home or in their cars, the press conference was also the key news item of the morning. It was hardly the first time an event had been timed for the cameras; earlier in the spring, when President Carter had left the White House to attend the economic summit in Venice, the entire departure had been timed for the morning news shows. But holding a press conference at the very moment polls were opening in a crucial primary state crystallized the argument that the President was milking the hostage crisis for political gain. And when the transfer of the hostages fell through, the Rose Garden campaign became the focus of sharp press criticism.

David Broder, who had been among the first to express skepticism over Carter's incumbency campaign, detailed what he called Carter's "good news" strategy in an April 6 column. It was, he said, "a textbook case in the manipulation of public opinion by a White House politician." The *New York Times*'s Hedrick Smith wrote on April 12 of the "April 1 press conference which his aides conceded was designed for maximum impact in the primary states. . . . the President's handling of the five-month-old crisis has finally emerged as a full-fledged issue in this campaign." William Safire wrote on April 7 that the press conference "demonstrated a willingness to manipulate news of the hostages for his political profit."

As often happens when the print press establishes a political perspective, television followed. On April 18, "CBS Evening News" presented a long, unusually sharp look at the Rose Garden strategy.

"Ostensibly," Walter Cronkite said, "it is dictated by concern about the hostages in Iran. But has it been above the fray of politics?"

In her report, Lesley Stahl referred to the "timing of the President's policy decisions and announcements [which] raised a suspicion that a number of them" were made "for practical political considerations." After showing President Carter's flat denial of any political timing, the CBS report took viewers back almost three months—from a pre-Iowa "Meet the Press" appearance, to a pre-Maine caucus announcement about a possible Iran hostage breakthrough, through the Olympic reception just before New Hampshire, to special pre-New York interviews with local TV reporters, to the April 1 "positive step announcement," to "exclusive" interviews with local Pennsylvania TV reporters. "In four days," Stahl notes, "he faces a tough contest in the Pennsylvania primary."

Although a narrow Kennedy win in Pennsylvania did not seriously threaten Carter's renomination, the late stages of the primary campaign had turned Carter into the very thing his Rose Garden campaign had avoided in its early stages: he had become a *politician;* it was as if viewers and readers of the news could now see out in the open the telephone calls, structuring of the flow of public money, the promises and threats that had been well-hidden in January and February by the patriotic bunting that had been hung from the White House in the first weeks of the Iran-Afghanistan crises.

Ironically, the full impact of the press's unveiling of the Rose Garden campaign was never fully felt by the Carter campaign in the primary season because of a clear-cut disaster—the failure of the attempt by American armed forces to rescue the hostages from Iran. Early on the morning of April 25, the President again went on television to talk to the American people. But this time the news was horrible: eight helicopters filled with American arms and men had headed for the Iranian desert in the first stage of a rescue operation. Only five had remained workable, and the mission was aborted. In the attempt to leave the staging area, a helicopter had collided with a transport plane, and eight American soldiers had died. As always happens when a full-fledged disaster in military policy occurs, criticism from Presidential opponents, both Republican and Democratic, stopped. Although Carter aide Hamilton Jordan was to write after the election that the rescue failure may have cost Carter the 1980 election, by reinforcing the impression of weakness, its short-run impact may have been positive, in muting political criticism of the President and in softening the attacks on Carter's political manipulation. The solemnity of the death of the American servicemen, the resignation of Secretary of State Vance, the knowledge that there were indeed fifty-two Americans whose safety was very much at risk helped maintain what the *Washington Post*'s Haynes Johnson called "the politics of sympathy." Even Carter's decision to leave the White House for active campaigning received only muted criticism, although it was surrounded by the kind of Orwellian language for which Carter had been justly criticized. At a White House meeting of supporters in late April, Carter aides asked a supporter to ask Carter publicly if he thought the time had come to leave the White House for limited campaigning. Yes, he said, because the Iranian problem had become "more manageable." And he referred to the rescue operation as a "limited success." Here again, it would have taken a sharp breach in the conventions of journalistic reporting for a television correspondent to have noted the remarkably dishonest use of such a phrase—comparable to writing of a coast-to-coast plane flight which crashed in Nevada as an "incomplete nonstop flight."

As the primary season ended—with a Carter victory in Ohio on "Super Tuesday" offsetting Kennedy victories in New Jersey and California and giving the President more than enough delegates to gain renomination—most of the luster gained in the first weeks of the Iran crisis had worn off. Following the failure of the hostage rescue, the entire Iran issue seemed suddenly to disappear from the American landscape. What had been an obsession from November to April became overnight a fading memory. This was so in part because of logistics: the Iranian government had expelled all American reporters and was no longer feeding first-grade footage of events in Iran to the United States via satellite. In the eyes of the American television networks, film and tape that was two or three days old was "old news"—even if it had never been seen on American television, and even if it was arriving at the same time as it would have in the pre-COMSAT area of instant access to foreign events.

Moreover, as Adam Clymer wrote in the *New York Times* at the end of June, "Carter has been almost totally silent" about Iran since the rescue failed. One political pollster, Houston Republican V. Lance Torrance, reported his finding that with the lack of attention the entire Iran issue "has nearly faded out" as an element of opposition to Carter. What perhaps remained was the same question that had plagued Carter in the summer of 1979: the question of *competence*. In a grim sense, the pictures of American corpses and gutted aircraft in the desert of Iran were like the photos of Carter collapsing in the middle of a marathon run in suburban Maryland in the fall of 1979. They suggested impotence, incompetence, a failure of will against foreign enemies that had been the theme of all of Carter's Republican rivals or his conservative critics in the press, such as William Safire, James Jackson Kilpatrick, and George Will, and of the neoconservative Democrats, such as Senator Daniel Moynihan and Senator Henry Jackson, and the group of former liberals and social Democrats loosely grouped around the *Commentary* magazine philosophy, who saw Carter as a kind of warmed-over McGovern.

And with the hostage issue no longer the subject of nightly late-night specials on ABC, with only Walter Cronkite's day-by-day count of the number of days "of captivity for the American hostages in Iran," the fact of potential blue-collar Democratic desertions to Ronald Reagan was once again becoming part of the press's focus. Even as Carter was insuring his renomination on "Super Tuesday," press coverage was paying close attention to his vulnerability. NBC's Ken Bode noted on the eve of the last primaries that "Kennedy's strength among blue-collar workers, and their sour view of the economy, could spell trouble for November. The recession is already very deep in the old industrial cities" of states Carter had to win, and "Ronald Reagan has showed some pulling power among workers in early primaries . . ." In CBS's late-night special on June 3—primary night—Bruce Morton, in charge of reporting poll data, noted that "there's not much really good news in the good news" for Jimmy Carter. He was receiving negative ratings on the economy, and Reagan actually got more votes in New Jersey, Ohio, and California than Carter did, even though the Republican nomination had long since been decided.

Said Morton, "There's a sense of theme and direction to the Republicans this year. There's no split, no great division, and they're pretty much in agreement on some ideas. . . . If President Carter is leading [Democrats] off in a direction that arouses much fervor, I've missed it, I guess."

The *New York Times,* in its exegesis of the CBS-*Times* poll, noted the next day that the economy "could produce serious defections among Democratic voters next fall" and found that fewer than half of Democratic voters said they would stick with the President in the fall. David Broder argued that "it is a sign of weakness that [Carter] ran no better this time around when he was the incumbent President of the United States than he did four years ago when he began as Jimmy Who?''

This perception of Carter is especially noteworthy when contrasted with the view of the campaign that developed once the general election began. Remarkably, the press's view of the contest turned out to be much more accurate from a distance of five months than from a distance of five days. Once the general election began, the mixture of polls, frenetic campaign travel, dope stories, flubs, gaffes, slips, and fumbles turned attention away from the broader sweep of the 1980 campaign into the day-to-day scramble that passes for political journalism. As a result, *even given* that the primary job of a political journalist is to predict the outcome, the press could have done a far better job by ignoring the campaign, and going back to the perceptions formed months before the fall battle began.

For Carter, the successful battle for renomination probably turned out to be fatal. The combination of Kennedy's inadequacies as a campaigner, and the sudden atmosphere of crisis which had elevated his Presidency had carried Carter through the early, critical phase of the primary season without the need for him or his campaign to develop any coherent account of his successes or failures. With the exception of the Camp David peace accords, there was no dramatic triumph that could be used to symbolize the President's achievements over four years; and events of the primary season had removed from Carter's campaign the need to develop such a rationale. From the beginning of Kennedy's insurgency, Carter aides had predicted that the President would gain once the voters stopped treating Carter in a vacuum, and started comparing him to the alternative. Kennedy's own campaign had fully validated that.

Carter's own presence in the campaign had received a huge boost from the international crises. He had gained in majesty, not by any deeds or from a conscious act of political definition, but by the Iran and Afghanistan events *themselves*. The capacity of those events to ''force'' the press into a more somber, inevitably respectful portrayal of the President did not last long; by the time of the New York primary defeat and the April 1 press conference, the bloom had clearly faded from the Rose Garden. But it was long enough to win the nomination for Carter, and probably long enough for the White House to believe that the same combination would work again in the fall; that Ronald Reagan's extremism and simplistic, often inaccurate notions would make him a laughingstock in the press, and in the country at large, and that President Carter would come to be seen as the same prudent, sensible alternative he had become to primary voters. Democrats may not have voted for Carter enthusiastically, but they clearly preferred him to Kennedy. That was bound to happen again in the fall.

As for the evident failure of Carter to develop a case for a second term, the potential appeal to traditional Democrats that Reagan had shown throughout his political career, the disparate disaffections visible in Democratic bases such as Catholics, Jews, labor union members, and Southerners, these could be met by the simple contrast of candidates. Carter had had no theme, save that of personal probity and high moral character, when he ran in 1976, and he had won then. He had had no theme, save that of president-in-crisis and alternative to Teddy, when he gained renomination this time. The press had effectively transmitted those themes in 1976 and again in the 1980 primaries. There was no reason for the Carter campaign to assume that anything would be different in the fall; unless, that is, they had entertained the silly notion that the coherence of a candidate's ideas and the credibility of his record have something to do with how people vote. And such a notion was clearly out of fashion with sophisticated technocrats of the modern political age.

viii Advertising
in the Primaries:
The Futility of Manipulation

Every four years, political writers discover that candidates for the Presidency employ media consultants, advertising specialists, music writers, film editors, and graphic designers who create television commercials for the candidates. Since the candidates pay for the production and airing of these ads, the commercials are not objective statements of the candidates' strengths and weaknesses. They are designed to make the candidates as attractive as possible: to "sell" them to the American voters.

From this practice comes the conclusion that political advertising has degraded the American political process. In 1980, an advertising executive wrote a book designed to argue that political ads were *more* deceptive than product ads, since, in his words, "you can't regulate political speech and of course product commercials are probably the most highly regulated thing around." Theodore H. White, the best-known chronicler of Presidential campaigns, has argued that voters are "swayed and brainwashed" by this new technique which has "torn down the old structures of American politics." Malcolm MacDougall, who was President Ford's media consultant, called political advertising "snake oil politics." And every political writer short of a column topic appears to have devoted at least one day to a stirring denunciation of the "media wizards" who were "selling candidates like soap."

Putting aside the question of how candidates for high office were presented to America in the days before the mass media,* what did the political advertising during the 1980 Presidential campaign do to this prevailing view of politics and paid media? In brief, it knocked this theory into a cocked hat.

Both in the primary campaigns and in the general election, the

* For an account of the "selling of candidates" throughout American political history, see chapter 9 of my book on politics, *Playing to Win* (New York, Simon and Schuster, 1980).

advertising efforts of the candidates were more constrained by political reality than ever before in modern Presidential history. A combination of increasing voter sophistication, persistent and highly skeptical press scrutiny, and the dominance of serious issues throughout the Presidential campaign left the treasured theories of media manipulation and packaging-is-everything as laughably inadequate explanations for political success. As a general proposition, the 1980 political ads succeeded in direct proportion to their link to reality. Those commercials that seemed best to exemplify the state of the art in packaging, but that did not reflect credible political arguments, were almost totally ineffective in winning voter support. The 1980 election demonstrated that political advertising is not some shockingly new phenomenon of politics. Advertising is an extension of political speech, with the same strengths and weaknesses as other forms of political speech. It is not some form of brainwashing inflicted on a passive, credulous electorate, but competes in a marketplace of ideas with competitors and with other data from the candidate. In addition, the press by 1980 had absorbed the lesson that advertising had to be covered as an integral part of the campaign. There would be no "Selling of the President, 1980," where the "real" Presidential campaign would take place all but unnoticed on prime-time television spots, while the press covered the surface campaign of the candidates. Every network and every major print journal watched the commercials, reported—in detail—on possible hints of deception or inaccuracy, and held the campaigns to far *higher* standards of precision than ever before. As a consequence, the 1980 battles for the nomination probably gave viewers a clearer sense of the candidates' basic messages than any other set of campaign ads had ever done.

Consider, for example, the single most notable commercial of the Republican primary campaign—the "Iran" commercial of Senator Howard Baker. On December 4, a month after the hostage seizure, Baker was speaking at the University of Iowa. The advertising firm of Bailey-Deardourff was filming Baker's speech and question-and-answer session for possible use as a television commercial—without informing the audience. At one point, an Iranian student asked Baker why, "when the Shah was killing Iranian people with U.S. weapons," the senator didn't raise his voice to denounce the regime. An angry Baker snapped back, "because, my friend, I'm interested in *fifty Americans,* and when they're released . . ." The rest of the sentence was drowned out by the sound of tumultuous applause and a standing ovation. An upbeat jingle filled the soundtrack as the graphics popped onto the screen: "Baker—Republican—President—Now."

It was, to be sure, an attempt at "media manipulation" in the sense that the Baker campaign was seeking to appeal to the patriotic sentiments of Republican voters, to make Baker appear tougher and more martial than his "moderate" image as Senate minority leader had thus far permitted him, and to overcome some of the antipathy on the part of conservatives toward Baker for his support of the Panama Canal treaties.

But the ad did not run in a vacuum. CBS's Betsy Aaron tracked down the student, looked at the outtakes of the footage—that is, the film not actually used in the commercial—and presented a five-minute report on the "CBS Evening News" of February 8 that revealed some surprising facts. Baker, in a "Face the Nation" interview in January, had called his remarks "determination not to let that student take over the meeting." But the student was not part of a group of "forty to fifty" Iranians, as Baker had asserted; he was not a supporter of the Iranian embassy takeover, and the burst of applause and the standing ovation, according to Baker's ad specialists, actually came nine minutes *after* the exchange and was edited in. Three days after the news report, Baker's campaign announced that the commercial was being dropped because it had served its purpose.

Or consider a Ronald Reagan primary commercial, in which Reagan compared his supply-side tax cut plan to President Kennedy's "30 percent" tax cut proposals. On ABC's "Issues and Answers" on March 16, correspondent John Laurence challenged Reagan's figures about the Kennedy tax plan.

"I don't remember saying that," Reagan replied, "because I honestly don't know what the rate of tax cut was."

"Well," said Laurence, "perhaps someone else wrote them for you and . . ."

"I'm sure, and I don't even remember reading that," Reagan cut in.

"Well," said Laurence, "that raises the question of whether you know what you're saying in your commercials."

Given this kind of scrutiny by the press, the temptation to cross the boundaries of factual accuracy was severely constrained; no campaign wants to see itself held up to suspicion or ridicule on national news programs or in the national print media. Instead, to a remarkable degree, the primary campaign commercials became extensions of the fundamental premises of the campaigns. They worked or failed less because of outright artifice than because of the potency of the messages.

Senator Baker's campaign, for example, featured the senator in New England settings for the New Hampshire and Massachusetts primaries. He stood in a living room in front of a fireplace with a rifle mounted on it—"I thought for a minute it might be a Pepperidge Farm commercial," commented media critic Ron Powers—and called for a national program to build an automobile that did not burn gasoline. Other spots showed Baker calling for a "First Brigade," a military unit capable of responding instantly to international crises. The ads clearly demonstrated a candidate in command of the facts, able to address a wide variety of issues. But the ads did not, *could* not, answer the fundamental question about Senator Baker's campaign: what is there about his record that makes him preferable to Ronald Reagan, other than his claim to be more electable? And if that is the key issue, why did Baker's election to the Senate from Tennessee make him more electable than Reagan's record of two landslide elections to the chief executive's office in the biggest state in the country? Baker was best known for his scholarly, pipe-smoking appearances during the 1973 Senate Watergate hearings (''what did the President know, and when did he know it''), but this was seven years after the hearings, when the country had already elected a President on the honesty question and had begun to question not his honesty but his competence. Thus, the Baker commercials effectively did a job that did not have to be done by demonstrating the presence of a well-informed, articulate senator. And they did not do the job of turning that image into votes, because there was no political reason to abandon Reagan. In fact, not a word of criticism about Ronald Reagan was ever uttered in Baker's commercials.

This was also the case in John Connally's ad campaign, fueled by privately raised funds that by the end of his campaign totaled more than $12 million. (Connally had rejected public financing for his campaign, preferring to rely on his reputation in the financial big-business community as a strong-willed exponent of probusiness philosophy and an enthusiastic proponent of a more forceful foreign policy.) In his short-lived campaign, Connally tried every kind of commercial. There was a ''bio'' spot, detailing his long record of public service, which referred only to President John Kennedy by name—Kennedy had named Connally Secretary of the Navy in 1961—and alluding to Lyndon Johnson and Richard Nixon only obliquely. There were live call-in shows; martial commercials showing Connally in a business suit talking about trade battles with the Japanese; five-minute speeches about encouraging business and investment; folksy spots for Iowa where Connally, clad in jeans and a Western jacket, perched in front of a huge fireplace and talked about acreage yields and his understanding of the farmers' problems.

How did any of these appeals deal with Connally's fundamental problem: that he was simply not trusted by a significant percentage of Republican voters? The short answer is, they didn't. Connally came into the Presidential race with higher ''negatives'' than any other Republican candidate; that is, basic attitude polls showed a far higher level of active disapproval toward Connally than toward Reagan, Bush, Baker, or anybody else. It may have been a result of Connally's trial on bribery charges in 1974; in the public perception, an acquittal does not erase the fact of an indictment and a trial. It may have been Connally's long history as a prominent Democratic political figure, a protege of Lyndon Johnson. Reagan had been a Republican since 1962 and a prominently conservative figure for a decade before that. But as late as 1972, Connally was a nominal Democrat. It may have been these factors and others: his identification with the wheeler-dealer financial world of Texas and oil, the vaguely shady aura of that whole world conjured up by the success of the "Dallas" television series, or simply that the cut of Connally's jib did not fit the Republican constituency. Much as the Republican Party is labeled the "big-business" party, the fact is that bedrock conservatives have always been suspicious of the centers of financial power. Robert Taft's backers were Midwesterners, bitterly resentful of Eastern bankers and financiers who jammed internationalist candidates down their throats. Goldwater's backers had much the same philosophy, and Reagan's campaign said over and over again that "Reagan is the candidate of Main Street, not Wall Street." But Connally was indeed the candidate of Wall Street, of the Fortune 500. It was never Connally's competence or strength that was at issue, but his trustworthiness. And as Ted Kennedy was to find out in the course of his campaign, trustworthiness cannot be summoned into being in a political advertisement. The only possible media strategy is to put that issue aside and hope that the rest of the campaign can compensate for the doubts. That was never the case in Connally's campaign, which ended with a grand total of one delegate.

Perhaps the best "fit" of candidate and media was the Bush campaign. In what was to be one of the splendid—and virtually unnoticed —ironies of the 1980 primaries, Bush ran as the candidate of experience while mounting the most "image-oriented" of all media campaigns, whereas ex-actor Ronald Reagan ran the least elaborate, least gimmicked-up, most issue-oriented ads of the entire campaign.* The Bush campaign, as described elsewhere, was premised almost entirely on the media-and-momentum principles of Jimmy Carter's 1976 campaign. It was directed by Robert Goodman, a James Coburn look-alike based in suburban Baltimore, whose basic principle of media is that "voters do not vote on issues, they vote on images, impressions." And Bush's media campaign was designed, *as was his campaign schedule* and his basic stump speech, to convey an impression of highly experienced, energetic, *successful* candidate. A "bio" spot showed Bush as "the man America turns to when there's a tough job to be done"; after reviewing his life as Yale baseball captain and World War II pilot, the spot showed Bush as a congressman, director of the

---

* Since I made this point on the CBS "Morning" news broadcast of March 20, 1980, I trust this observation will not be chalked up to 20–20 hindsight.

Central Intelligence Agency, and envoy to China in the preambassadorial days. But the predominant kind of commercials were less resumes than "newsy"-looking quick cuts of Bush campaigning, in an atmosphere of excitement, cheers, placards, balloons, and music.

As the patriotic theme swelled, and the light glinted off the camera, Bush's voice was heard over shots of the campaigning candidate saying, "I've seen this country up close. I hear what Americans are saying. Yes, they want change. Yes, they want solutions. But they don't want yesterday's ideas, promising everything to everybody. Americans today are ready to roll up their sleeves and rededicate this country to excellence in principle and to leadership from strength. And that's why I'm optimistic about our future."

To accompanying cheers and a final *fortissimo,* the announcer proclaimed: "George Bush—A President We Won't Have to Train." It was a clever slogan, indicting Jimmy Carter for coming unprepared to the White House, while implicitly raising the "credentials" issue of another ex-governor with no national experience, Ronald Reagan. Other commercials showed Bush, in shirtsleeves, talking to factory workers about the menace of inflation, or handshaking his way through supporters while the announcer spoke of his "great personal energy."

But in the whole of the initial phase of Bush's media campaign— as in his whole campaign posture—there was no mention of a policy position Bush thought should be adopted as national policy; there was no attack on the record of Ronald Reagan as governor of California, or on his challenge to an incumbent President in 1976, or on any of Reagan's factual mistakes that would soon become press fodder in the 1980 campaign. Bush could have argued that Reagan raised taxes in California by $12 billion during his tenure as governor, and signed what was then the most liberal abortion bill in the United States; or argued that Reagan was directly responsible for putting Jimmy Carter in the White House in 1976 by challenging President Ford for the nomination and then refusing to campaign for Ford; or argued that Reagan's persistent refusal to be accurate demonstrated his lack of fitness for the Presidency. But he didn't; and the reason he didn't is because those tactics flew in the face of the central problem facing a contentless campaign: how do you woo Reagan's voters without alienating them? There was no alternative vision of the nation and the world to Reagan's, because it wasn't part of Bush's basic message. The whole point of his effort was, as he told CBS's Bob Schieffer in early 1980, "I'm up for the 80s; I'm the most up. I'm the uppest. I'm in the best shape." The object was to inherit Reagan's supporters, who would be alienated by Reagan's age and conservatism, rather than building an alternative base of support among moderates and liberals. To have assailed Reagan directly would have made Bush the target of the core Republican constituency.

It may be that this fundamental strategy was wrong. Given the facts that at least one Republican, Gerald Ford, consistently ran ahead of Reagan in the spring polls, and that Reagan overall won less than half of the Republican primary vote, it is arguable that a more confrontational approach would have worked. It is even more arguable that, since campaigns can change people's minds, a hard-hitting campaign and media attack on Reagan's *competence* and *loyalty,* as opposed to his ideology, could have been more successful than the media-and-momentum campaign that was waged. But apart from the uncertainty of this approach, what absolutely would *not* have worked was a media campaign at odds with the substance and style of the candidate.

Instead, Bush cut a new series of ads in front of the White House, in which he attacked President Carter for inflation, foreign policy losses, and a ruinous economic policy. As with the earlier ads, only the slogan attacked Reagan and then by indirection. "George Bush," the announcer intoned. "The one candidate Carter hopes he *never* has to run against." The statement was true as far as it went; the White House was all but publicly celebrating the apparent nomination of Ronald Reagan as the easiest candidate to beat. But as with the earlier ads, there was no explication of this theme, not even a direct statement to Republicans that they were likely to nominate the Democrats' favorite target.

There was, however, one lesson to be learned from the Bush media campaign: in a battle where one contestant uses media and the chief rival does not, paid media can make a big difference. Because the Reagan campaign had spent $12 million of its $18 million preconvention limit *before* the first primary took place in 1980, the media budgets of the Reagan campaign were severely constrained. In more than a dozen states, there was no Reagan advertising *at all*. Since most of these battles came after the Reagan nomination was a near-certainty, it did not have an effect on the outcome. But in Connecticut, Pennsylvania, and Michigan, Bush put on major advertising drives against nonexistent efforts on the part of the cash-strapped Reagan campaign. In all three states, Bush won the primaries. This is not to argue that media made all the difference. Connecticut is one of Bush's "home" states by upbringing and education, and all three states have large numbers of that vanishing species, the liberal Republican. In Michigan, popular Governor William Milliken actively campaigned for Bush.* But it does suggest that when paid media is not met by coun-

* Michigan provided an interesting sidelight into the nature of campaign coverage in 1980. Although Bush won a big victory in the Michigan primary, beating Reagan 341,998 to 189,184, Reagan's share of the delegates, plus victories in Oregon and Idaho, put him over the top for the nomination according to ABC and CBS delegate polls. Both networks led their late-night reports with this story, which shocked the Bush camp, savoring its victory. There was

tervailing media, the advantage can indeed be almost as powerful as the mythological power ascribed to all political commercials. It also raises an intriguing question: what would have happened had Bush stayed more or less even with Reagan in the early contests and then moved into the last six weeks of primaries with millions of extra dollars for the media campaign? Since the Bush campaign never defined itself as a crucially necessary alternative to Reagan, the question did not arise. Bush's commercials, in sum, faithfully reflected what the candidate and the campaign wanted Republicans to know about him— which was simply not persuasive enough to win enough votes.

The Reagan media campaign in the primaries was almost a direct contrast to the Bush commercials. They were "artless," in the sense that they had almost no "production values." They were simple statements of fact or opinion about foreign policy, welfare, and taxes, with a few sentences from Reagan summarizing his intentions or beliefs. They did not vary from New Hampshire through the rest of the primary campaign, and they were so unpolished as to draw criticism, both from the campaign and from outsiders. What they achieved was to state, quickly, simply, and forcefully what Ronald Reagan was all about.

The commercials were shot by a thirty-three-year-old Philadelphia-based advertising man named Elliott Curson after the first flight of spots had proven ineffective. These first commercials, by New York's Clyne Company, showed Reagan in a classroom with young children as he talked of inflation, which "could cost Joan and Billy here seventy-five thousand dollars to go to college," or showed Reagan holding heating bills that were rising because of "restrictive controls" and foreign "blackmail." All of these commercials began with Reagan saying, "This is a great country, but it's not being run like a great country." All of them ended with a freeze frame of Reagan, and the slogan, "Let's Make America Great Again," as an announcer said, "Only one man has the proven experience we need."

Since Bush outspent Reagan in Iowa by about 3.5–1, it may be too much to say the spots had been "proven ineffective." But just as a baseball team fires the manager after a slump, so the Reagan campaign brought in Curson. Given the growing sophistication of political advertising, it may be surprising to find that Curson took no polls, held no "focus groups" with typical citizens, and wired no viewers up to measure galvanic skin responses. Instead, he researched old speeches, and hooked up with thirty-nine-year-old Jeffrey Bell, a New Jersey

---

no "momentum" or "expectation" story, for by now, the networks were counting delegates, not emanations of mood. After a brief period when Bush protested the coverage, saying that soon the networks could just "put Howard Cosell on at halftime" to say who'd won, he and his campaign bowed to the inevitable and ended formal campaigning.

Republican and ardent supply-side enthusiast who had unseated Senator Clifford Case in the 1978 New Jersey Republican primary, and then ran a respectable race in losing to Bill Bradley in the general election.

Working with Reagan's public record (and cribbing from some of Bell's 1978 Senate campaign speeches), the Reagan primary campaign was mapped out quickly, and was shot by Curson in a single day in a southern California TV studio. Apart from taking care with the lighting to underplay Reagan's "turkey neck," there was no special attention paid to Reagan's wrinkles or hair. "You can't look at the guy and possibly think he's too old to be President," Curson said later. "So why bother?" It was also a matter of clear policy within the campaign to downplay any connection between Reagan and his former acting career. Thus, the simpler the commercial, the better.

And simple they were. About the most elaborate commercial was one showing Soviet troops parading through Red Square as an announcer said that "Ronald Reagan spoke out on the danger of the Soviet arms buildup long before it was fashionable. . . . He has a comprehensive program to rebuild our military power." Reagan then came on camera saying, "We've learned by now that it isn't weakness that keeps the peace. It's strength. Our foreign policy has been based on the fear of not being liked. Well, it's nice to be liked. But it's more important to be respected."

Another commercial—the one over which Reagan stumbled in his "Issues and Answers" appearance—was a concise distillation of supply-side economics, coupled with a skillful political move toward the ideological center. "Ronald Reagan believes that when you tax something, you get less of it," the announcer said. "We're taxing work, savings, and investment like never before. As a result, we have less work, less savings, and less invested."

Then Reagan said, "I didn't always agree with President Kennedy. But when his 30 percent federal tax cut became law, the economy did so well that every group in the country came out ahead. Even the government gained $54 billion in unexpected revenues." Then, with a chuckle, Reagan concluded, "if I become President, we're going to try that again."

Other commercials in this package included the claim that Reagan cut welfare costs as California governor while increasing "benefits for the truly needy [by] 43 percent"; a pledge of some kind of metallic backing for the dollar; and a so-called "good Samaritan ad" (which greatly annoyed some of Reagan's more rigorously conservative aides), which argued that the poor were hurt most by a weak economy. "We've got to move ahead," Reagan concluded, "but we can't leave anyone behind."

The style of the commercials would have brought a blush of shame to the more style-oriented "media wizards." There were no symbols, just newsreel photos or newspaper headlines over the announcer's words, and just Reagan himself talking into the camera. So simple was the package that, in reviewing the ads on a February 21 "Bill Moyers' Journal," Moyers and media critic Ron Powers expressed amazement at the poor quality of the delivery.

"His eyes are dropping down to the cue cards," Powers observed.

"How do you explain that?" Moyers asked.

"I don't explain it, it's an astonishing lapse," Powers said, adding that it would hurt Reagan because "we all remember and associate the classic shifty-eyed problems of Richard Nixon." Moyers said that "it could well suggest what a lot of pundits have been saying, that there's trouble within the Reagan organization." These ads were contrasted with Bush's campaign, called by Moyers "probably the most effective being run in New Hampshire."

Judging on the basis of production values, Powers and Moyers were probably right. But the Iowa caucuses seemed to show that what hurt Reagan most was the absence from the fray; that in the Republican Party at least, a clear reminder of what Ronald Reagan stood for would produce votes for Reagan. In this sense, the commercials fit an old-fashioned, turn-out-the-vote strategy: if enough people can be reminded of where Reagan stands on the issues, they will remember his long fight for conservative principles, and they will vote for him. Thus, the Reagan commercials were limited in reach because they did not have to accomplish a major leap of faith; they simply had to reinforce the inclination on the part of Republicans to support the most venerable and eloquent exponent of the conservative philosophy. Whether the ads were dazzling enough to win an industry award is dubious. It is even doubtful that the commercials were a major factor in Reagan's sweep toward the nomination. Rather, the commercials can best be measured by a more modest-sounding set of goals. They were consistent with the view of the candidate coming from the "free" media— news reports, debates, interview programs. They accurately reflected where the candidate stood on broad issues. They delivered oversimplified, but truthful, accounts of Ronald Reagan's themes.

If most of those voting in the Republican primaries had disagreed with Reagan's philosophy, then the commercials would not have persuaded Republicans to vote for him. This can be demonstrated by analogy: the John Anderson commercials, which showed all of the other candidates agreeing with each other and then referred to "the Anderson difference," also accurately reflected the position of the candidate. But most Republicans did not agree with the different philosophy Anderson espoused; and except in Massachusetts and Vermont, the maverick Republican never came close to achieving victory. In Reagan's case, the "media wizard" came to the remarkable conclusion that the best vote-getting tool would be to let the voters know the general intentions of the candidate. And it worked.

In the Democratic battle for the nomination, the terrain was very different. That contest was, in every sense, more dramatic. Apart from the quixotic effort of California Governor Jerry Brown, it was a two-candidate battle, and, in effect, it was a battle of two incumbents. Jimmy Carter was the first elected Democrat to campaign for reelection since Franklin D. Roosevelt; Ted Kennedy was the best-known figure in the Democratic Party, a man of presumptive Presidential ambitions for more than a decade. One candidate was vulnerable on the record of his three years in office; the other was vulnerable on the basis of character and morality.

Ted Kennedy's advertising effort was characterized by the same kind of confusion that characterized his campaign: there was no clear message about what the campaign was about. In his initial feint toward candidacy, Kennedy had declared that leadership, rather than specific policy differences, was at the heart of his decision to seek the Presidency. The hasty decision to run for the Presidency meant that there was no campaign organization, no comprehensive strategy, no one figure in charge of media. (There wasn't even any polling through the first month of the campaign effort, on the ground that it was too expensive, and that Kennedy was so well known and so clearly on the record because of his years in the Senate that it would be superfluous.) At one point, former Civil Aeronautics Board chairman Philip Baker was supervising the media. And long-time Kennedy colleague Herb Schmertz took a six-week leave of absence from his job to help coordinate the media effort. Since Schmertz was a vice-president and director of Mobil Oil, one who had designed an extremely aggressive and effective campaign against almost all of the energy policies endorsed by Kennedy in the Senate, this suggested that specific liberal programs would not be a major part of the Kennedy media effort. In addition, media experts such as Tony Schwartz, Joe Napolitan, and David Garth were swiftly considered, and then rejected, as possible directors of media.

The result was that the early advertising—called by Napolitan "the worst television ever produced for a Presidential candidate in American history"—was, in fact, an accurate reflection of the campaign's confusion. In what can only be considered an act of blind faith in the power of images to erase voters' strong perceptions of reality, the Kennedy commercials tried to "sell" the senator as a family man to overcome character issues about his alleged infidelity and marital difficulties. One early ad showed Kennedy on the beach with his wife and children as an announcer said, "The kinds of things he has suffered have made him a strong, more mature man." When it became clear that the character issue was cutting deeply, Charles Guggenheim, a veteran Kennedy filmmaker who specialized in "documentary" commercials, shot members of the family talking about Kennedy's inner strength. Ethel Kennedy appeared in a tennis dress to praise her brother-in-law for "holding the family together" after Robert Kennedy's assassination.

The problem, of course, was that these ads only reminded voters of Kennedy's problems: seeing the candidate on a beach could only trigger memories of the waters off Chappaquiddick; listening to a Kennedy relative talking about the senator "holding the family together" had to stir questions about what Kennedy's wife had been doing living apart from the family in Boston. These matters were not subtle questions of tax policy or agricultural economics or the nature of the Western alliance; they had for eleven years been the stuff of tabloid journalism, gossip magazines, underground jokes, and (to use a usually unreliable phrase) "common knowledge." They were not about to be erased by a sentimental, thirty-second television commercial.

The failure of these Kennedy "character" commercials did not lie in the execution of the theme, but in the theme itself. Contrary to the mixture of awe and fear with which some observers regard political commercials, the fact is that in the context of a Presidential election, where information fills the airwaves and newspapers, commercials have only a marginal impact on perceptions. For most Americans, Chappaquiddick was, *at best* (and in Kennedy's own words), an example of "indefensible" conduct. At worst, it was a criminal act in which a wealthy, powerful, well-connected individual had escaped the consequences of his acts because of his position. *That* was the reality that faced the Kennedy campaign, and it was the failure to recognize that reality that made the early ads so terrible. It wasn't that the commercials sent the wrong message about Chappaquiddick, but that *no message at all* could or should have been sent.*

Until January 28, however, there was no other message that Kennedy's advertising could have sent because there was no campaign theme, other than the "leadership" chestnut. But when Kennedy redefined his candidacy in his January 28 speech at Georgetown, the commercials began to reflect that change.

In New Hampshire, for example, Kennedy turned his attention to Carter's "report card." Sitting in a "Presidential" office, clad in a "Presidential" blue suit, Kennedy offered this shorthand speech:

---

* At almost every speaking engagement I had during the 1980 campaign I was asked, "As a former media consultant, what would you have said about Chappaquiddick, what ad would you have put on?" My answer was always the same: none. I offered a challenge in return, "Assuming you had unlimited resources, what commercial would *you* have prepared to deal with Chappaquiddick?" There may have been a better answer than mine, but I did not hear it.

Everybody remembers the candidate who said in 1976, "I'll never mislead you and you can depend on it." But do you remember what else he said? He said he would reduce inflation and unemployment to 4 percent by the end of his first term, that he would never use high interest rates to fight inflation, that he would never decontrol the price of oil and natural gas, that nuclear power is the resource of last resort, that he would get the Equal Rights Amendment passed during his first year in office, that he would balance the budget and reduce the size of government. But now he's secluded in the White House, telling us to rally around his failure overseas. He refuses to discuss the issues . . .

Beginning in New Hampshire, and extending through the rest of the campaign, Kennedy's media never stopped attacking Carter's record. As with most "negative" campaigns, there was balance. Shots of John and Robert Kennedy, banished in early ads because of fear that Kennedy would be exploiting his dead brothers, began reappearing. An Apollo rocket headed toward the moon as an announcer said, "This country landed a man on the moon, and yet we're told we can't meet the challenges we face today. Ted Kennedy says we can. He knows the American spirit." Basic "bio" spots detailing Kennedy's record in the Senate were aired. But fundamentally, Kennedy's advertising, starting in New Hampshire, recognized that the strongest factor in persuading people to vote for Ted Kennedy was not Kennedy at all, but, rather, the fact that he was not Jimmy Carter.

Shortly before the New York primary, Boston media advisor David Sawyer was put in charge of Kennedy's radio and television campaign. And the attack on Carter grew sharper. A smiling President Carter was shown in a softball game, with his bat on his shoulder, as his record was detailed in the form of called strikes. Actor Carroll O'Connor, television's Archie Bunker, compared Jimmy Carter to Herbert Hoover and predicted that "Jimmy would lead us into a depression." And in one of the few references back to Chappaquiddick, O'Connor said of Kennedy, "Folks, I trust him. In every way." In New York, the fiasco of the anti-Israel UN vote, which Carter explained as a failure in communications, was hammered home on radio and television ads. In sum, the Kennedy campaign had found its theme and pursued it relentlessly in making Carter, rather than Kennedy, the issue for Democratic voters.

In its first assessment of the battle for renomination, the Carter campaign understood its own vulnerability clearly: most voters, in the words of media consultant Bob Squier, "liked Carter personally, but thought he wasn't competent." The Jimmy Stewart-outsider, who came to Washington early in 1977 with a "close, intimate, personal" relationship with the people of America, had more or less kept their affection, but it was overlaid with an emotion somewhere between sympathy and pity: ole' Jeb from up the road had gone to the big city, and the big city had eaten him alive.

The initial decision, then, was to convince the voters of something Carter had been unable to demonstrate in three years: that Jimmy Carter was, in fact, the President of the United States. At the request of Carter media chief Gerald Rafshoon, Squier produced a half-hour documentary—the one the networks originally refused to air on the night of December 4, thus triggering the Supreme Court case over candidates' rights to access—called simply "The President." Out of this single production came most of the "positive" Carter commercials for the primary: and it was all geared to the transformation of Carter from "friendly outsider" to "tough-minded President."

As the announcer put it, "for a few days last October, cameras were permitted inside the White House" to show the President at work; a comment designed to leave the implication that the President had accommodated himself to a skeptical press, rather than to his campaign organization. Viewers saw the President talking with rural health advocates, farmers (jokingly telling a farmer from Iowa, the first caucus state, that the folks back in Iowa were probably a lot smarter than Washington experts), and members of his own staff and cabinet, as well as his family. To show Carter's capacity to make tough decisions, the commercial showed Carter facing down Stansfield Turner, director of the Central Intelligence Agency, answering his request for a lower budget by asking Turner if he wanted the cut to come out of his own agency.

"You certainly know how to put a fellow on the spot," Turner chuckled.

"Well," Carter said, "I'll make a decision on it tomorrow." *

In what was to become a much-aired excerpt from the commercial, Carter was shown helping his daughter Amy with her homework and spending time with Rosalynn. Speaking over the footage, Carter said, "I don't think there's any way you can separate the responsibilities of being a husband or father and a basic human being from that of being a good President. What I do in the White House is to maintain a good family life, *which I consider crucial to being a good President.*"

In the spot commercial, the announcer concluded, "Husband . . . Father . . . President . . . He's done these jobs with distinction."

(One journalist—Robert L. Turner of the *Boston Globe*—on February 28, assailed this argument as "cynical stuff and nonsense . . . domestic bliss has absolutely nothing to do with outstanding Presiden-

* The commercial drew some criticism for using a holder of such a sensitive job as CIA chief in a paid political commercial. Defense Secretary Harold Brown and Deputy Secretary of State Warren Christopher also appeared in the ad.

tial performance. If anything, history indicates the reverse,'' citing John Kennedy and Franklin D. Roosevelt as philanderers who were good Presidents, and Richard Nixon as a monogamous disaster. Candidates are used to "wrapping themselves in motherhood,'' Turner wrote, "but Carter may be the first Presidential candidate to wrap his campaign in fatherhood.'')

The Carter media campaign also displayed a clear sense of how to exploit Ted Kennedy's character vulnerability without directly raising the issue. A tape of President Carter at a town meeting was shown, and for a few seconds viewers heard Carter talking, although the subject matter was unclear and, as it turned out, irrelevant. The announcer began, "You may not always agree with President Carter, but you'll never find him wondering if he's telling you the truth. It's hard to think of a more useful quality in any person who becomes President than telling the simple truth. . . . President Carter—for the Truth.''

As a political matter, this observation may be debatable. FDR is not known as "The lion and the fox'' for his probity. But as a weapon against Ted Kennedy, the commercial was effective *because it reflected a sentiment of the voters, rather than trying to create one out of whole cloth.* Most Americans, even the most ardent of Kennedy supporters, did not believe his explanation of Chappaquiddick and did indeed wonder if he was telling the truth. It was, in this regard, an updated "Daisy spot.'' Just as in 1964 the Johnson campaign had implied that Barry Goldwater would incinerate the world, in an ad that never mentioned his name—but just showed a nuclear holocaust wiping out a little girl and let the voter fill in his own fears—so this "truth'' spot simply talked of Carter's own virtue and let the voter fill in his doubts about Kennedy.

As we have seen, a prime goal of the Carter commercials was to make the President more "Presidential,'' to show him less as a warmhearted Gomer Pyle, and more as a strong-willed leader of the Free World. Whether the Carter ads would have accomplished this goal by themselves is pure conjecture, for with the emergence of the Iran and Afghanistan crises, the Presidency of Jimmy Carter *in fact* became a crisis Presidency, and the news programs carried torrents of words and pictures of the chief executive in action. By any comparative measurement, the advertising was a marginal part of this effort, although in Iowa and New Hampshire and Maine the patriotic theme was not neglected. In Iowa, Carter was shown in the Oval Office poring over papers as an announcer demanded, "Do we or do we not support the President as he makes the hard decisions in response to the challenges from Iran and Soviet aggression in Afghanistan?'' The grain embargo, which had been attacked by Kennedy as unfair to farmers, was defended in radio commercials as an important signal against Soviet militarism. "Stand up for Maine and America by supporting Jimmy Carter," Democratic voters in the Maine caucuses were told. To allay fears of Democratic liberals that Carter might be turning into too much of a "born-again hawk," later commercials ran footage of the Camp David peace conference, with Prime Minister Menachem Begin saying jokingly, "It should be called the Jimmy Carter conference."

As long as Carter was riding the crest of the crisis Presidency, and as long as Kennedy's character was dragging him down to defeat after defeat, Carter's advertising campaign could afford to refer to Kennedy only obliquely. But with the New York and Connecticut results showing that Carter had become the question to an increasing number of Democratic voters, Carter's advertising strategy changed direction. When Pat Caddell's polls showed the potential for a New York-style loss in the April 22 Pennsylvania primary, Caddell urged Rafshoon to remind voters that this was, in fact, a Presidential election. From the days when George Wallace won huge chunks of Northern Democratic votes in the 1964 primaries, voters have used primaries to signal dissatisfaction without really meaning to *elect* the candidate they vote for.

Democrats, then, had to be reminded that if they did not like Jimmy Carter, they liked Ted Kennedy even less—especially if he had any chance of being elected President. Taking a cue from Gerald Ford's 1976 campaign, when Georgians were interviewed about why they were not supporting Carter, the 1980 Carter commercials featured Democrats talking bluntly about why they did not like Ted Kennedy: "I don't like Senator Kennedy's philosophy," one said. "I trust Carter more than Kennedy," said another. "I don't think he can deal with a crisis," said another. "I don't trust him."

The ads may have been nasty, but they went to the heart of voter dissatisfaction with Kennedy; in fact, the ad was in some sense a word-for-word replay of an NBC news report at the time of New Hampshire, in which Democrats expressed their dislike for Kennedy in much the same terms. Whether because of the ads or not, Kennedy won Pennsylvania by less than a percentage point, and he and Carter split the 185 delegate votes almost evenly. (It should also be noted that Kennedy's advertising campaign, which had been openly attacking Carter since February, had grown even more hard-hitting, with his own people in the street saying, "I think the nation is embarrassed by the leadership we have"; "I think the job's a little too big for him"; "I voted for him last time, but never again.")

Perhaps the most important aspect of the Carter *and* Kennedy media campaigns was the lack of a political focus beyond the battle for power. When James Baker, George Bush's campaign chief, rejected the "Carter-turns-into-Ronald-Reagan" ad of Robert Goodman, part of his thinking was that it would damage the Republican Party, which had a good chance of victory. This was a common philosophy in the days when political parties battled for nominations at a convention with the clear understanding that wounds would be healed once the battle was over. But in primary battles, where individual candidates rather than parties direct the tactics, the broader focus is sometimes lost. In the case of Carter and Kennedy, the struggle was so bitter that the commercials might as well have been used in November by the Republicans against whoever the Democratic nominee turned out to be.* None of the Carter or Kennedy ads ever mentioned the flaws in the philosophy or intentions of Ronald Reagan. None ever mentioned that in the fall, voters would be choosing between a Democratic and Republican candidate, and that the issue of electability was important to Democrats. There was almost no attempt in the primary—except for Kennedy's late identification with his brothers—of a political tradition that was in grave jeopardy at the hands of the Republicans.

Here again, the media campaign was a reflection of the two campaigns themselves. Locked in a passionate struggle for renomination, both candidates seemed to forget that a difficult campaign against a united, enthusiastic, rich Republican Party would be difficult for either candidate to win. Neither Carter nor Kennedy spent any time defending the Democratic record or warning against the perils of conservative Republicanism (although Kennedy did refer to "twelve long years of Republican rule"—meaning that Carter was a closet Republican—and at one point implied that Carter was a "clone" of Ronald Reagan).

This failure to define the terms of the general election battle becomes especially significant, given one more media campaign that began in February of 1980 and continued intermittently throughout the election year. It was not a campaign for any one candidate, but rather for the Republican Party. And it may have been the most successful media campaign of all in the 1980 year for reasons that go directly to the heart of the Democratic Party's dilemma that year.

The ads were produced for the Republican National Committee by Malcolm MacDougall of the Boston firm of Humphrey, Browning, and MacDougall (this is the same MacDougall who referred to political advertising as "snake oil politics" shortly before the campaign year began).

The $8 million campaign was not aimed at heartland Taft-Goldwater-Reagan Republicans. Instead, it was aimed at the younger voters, twenty-five to forty, who were just starting to raise a family, or were in the midst of building families and career, and who were feeling the full crunch of the faltering economy. "If you want to know who's

---

* For a brief period in the fall, the Reagan campaign got an uncopyrighted Kennedy primary ad and ran it as a paid political announcement in New England. After protests from Kennedy, the ad was dropped.

responsible," the ads in effect said, "look who's been running the Congress for the last twenty-five years."

One ad showed a "Democrat commemorative dollar" shrinking to thirty-seven cents of its former worth in the quarter-century that the Democrats had controlled Congress. Another showed hands trying to count out "a million dollars a minute"—the spending rate of the federal budget. A third showed a young man and woman, growing from childhood to adulthood over the twenty-five years of Democratic congressional control, facing a bleak economic future. (Intriguingly, these young people were shown passing through the 1960s with distinctly long hair and countercultural garb: a shrewd calculation on the part of the admakers that not all Republicans favored Marine crew cuts and white plastic belts.)

Two other commercials for the Republicans proved especially powerful. One showed a car driven by a dead-ringer for white-haired, overweight, jowly Tip O'Neill—Speaker of the House and the most recognizable of congressional Democrats. As his young companion repeatedly warns him that "we're running out of gas," the driver laughingly says, "No, no, no," while the announcer says that Democrats "actually passed laws that cut back energy explorations here at home and makes us dependent on foreign oil." The car jolts to a stop, the driver moans, "We're out of gas!" and the announcer uses a shopworn but effective slogan, appealing to Democrats to alter their habits in order to alter policy: "Vote Republican—For a Change."

In another ad, a moustached, long-haired factory worked named James Wilders of Baltimore walks through an abandoned factory. He recounts his days of past employment, and the fact that his job was lost when the plant shut down. "I've got just one question for the Democrats," he says. "If you're so good for the working people, how come so many people aren't working?"

This campaign, the best of any 1980 effort, did not attempt to refight the New Deal or to preach the values of hard work and open shops. It spoke directly to the shaky base of the Democratic Party, using concerns that were troubling this base, and issues on which the Democrats and President Carter were vulnerable. It was a media campaign stripped down to the simplest of all political appeals—"throw the rascals out!"—and in November, when Reagan took the blue-collar vote and almost split the union vote evenly with Carter, and when Republicans made enormous congressional gains, this media campaign was shown to be speaking to some of the root causes of the collapse of the Democratic coalition.

ix The Republican Convention: The Networks Hoist by Their Own Petard

Politicians and journalists often demonstrate a common habit by using a specific moment from the past as a touchstone for their present behavior. Hubert Humphrey's public life was played out in Washington; yet he frequently harkened back to his days as mayor of Minneapolis in the 1940s in talking about his policies and deeds. For Richard Nixon, the Hiss case was the shaping moment of his life; all through the Watergate tapes Nixon constantly referred back to the battles and crises of his first important public deed. Lyndon Johnson's passion for great public programs was rooted in his memory of rural Texas poverty; Jimmy Carter was sure that the United States Congress was simply a better-paid version of the Georgia legislature.

For the press—and especially for the news divisions of the major television networks—the most important political events were the 1952 national nominating conventions. These were the first conventions at which television was really a functioning presence—TV cameras were in place in 1948, but almost nobody had home television then—and its presence was a revolutionary event. In celebrating the coming of TV to the conventions, RCA ran a postconventions *New York Times* ad which proclaimed:

> With the aid of television, we had what amounted to the biggest town meeting ever held . . . 60 million people had front-row seats and got a better picture of what was going on than any delegate or any reporter on the convention floor. . . . Because of television, American citizens will be better informed than they ever were before. . . . They will be able to vote for men and principles and not for party labels.

What the 1952 television coverage brought the American viewer were two dramatic, hotly contested battles for the Presidential nomination, in which the outcome was a product of convention delibera-

152

tions themselves. At the Republican convention, Senator Robert A. Taft came to the gathering with more votes than Dwight Eisenhower. But a crucial battle over contested credentials—the so-called "fair play" fight—produced a change in several big-state delegations and swung the convention to Eisenhower. Television viewers saw political wheeling and dealing, impassioned speeches to the convention (Taft supporter Everett Dirksen pointed an accusing finger at Thomas Dewey's New York delegation and thundered, "We followed you before, and you took us down the road to defeat!"), and a struggle of great consequence played out live on national television. At the Democratic convention, it took three ballots before a reluctant Illinois governor, Adlai E. Stevenson, was "drafted" for the Presidential nomination.

Out of this first experience emerged the pattern of television coverage of national conventions: deploy as many reporters as possible throughout the convention and the hotels in an effort to find out what deals were being cut, what disputes were emerging, what new rumors were sweeping the halls, what different delegations were planning to do with their votes. It was a reasonably sensible way to cover a divided, contentious, brokered convention. The only problem was that conventions, partially because of television, more because of the changing nature of Presidential politics, were becoming less and less the kind of forum television had first encountered in Chicago in 1952.

That was the last year that both Presidential conventions convened with any suspense over the identity of the Presidential nominee, the last year either party took more than one ballot to choose its candidate. There were still tense moments at conventions; it wasn't until the balloting started that John F. Kennedy knew he would have a first ballot victory in 1960, and Richard Nixon's 1968 nomination was by no means a sure thing. But as the primary system grew, especially after 1968, the nature of conventions changed dramatically. The formula of big-state delegations coming to a gathering prepared to exchange endorsements for commitments, platform planks, or jobs was more and more replaced by conventions dominated by blocs of delegates committed to a candidate, rather than to a party organization. The wheeling and dealing of 1952 had been transformed.

Just as important, the political parties and the press began recognizing that television's presence at the conventions could well be the single most important element in the entire proceedings. If a convention was bitterly divided, as were the Republicans in 1964 or the Democrats in 1968, television would bring those divisions right into the homes of voters. The spectacle of New York's Governor Nelson Rockefeller being heckled in San Francisco, the sight of antiwar demonstrators fighting with police in the streets of Chicago, would speak more powerfully than a dozen keynote speeches. A united convention, in contrast, could produce a week's worth of prime-time advertising—

for free—about the virtues of a party's candidates and traditions. Films could be run in the middle of a slow convention night, celebrating departed leaders or this year's standard bearer; and by dimming the lights in the hall, television networks could not do any live interviews with convention participants. Any unseemly diversions over disputed platform planks could be relegated to daytime sessions, which networks were loath to cover for fear of offending soap opera audiences.

The networks, for their part, saw in the conventions the most critical showcase for their news operations, "a chance to show your people off," as CBS vice-president Ernest Leiser put it. The team of Chet Huntley and David Brinkley had first been put together for the 1956 Democratic convention. It had grown to dominate network evening news until Huntley retired in 1969. Had CBS found gold instead of dross in the pairing of Roger Mudd and Robert Trout in 1964, Walter Cronkite would never have survived as the dominant figure in broadcast journalism until his 1981 retirement. Moreover, as television grew more and more competitive and profitable, as prime-time hours became so valuable that news programs became strapped for time, the national conventions remained as events that promised network news divisions unequaled prime-time hours, with budgets inflated considerably beyond nonelection year constraints; by 1980, each network would spend more than $10 million apiece for each convention. Even without counting the pre- and postconvention specials and the extra efforts made on the evening and morning news broadcasts, the conventions meant between them more than forty prime-time hours of exposure: more prime-time coverage for the Presidential campaign in those two weeks than *in the rest of the year put together*.

The omnipresence of network television had, by 1980, produced a kind of schizophrenia among the press, including network television. On the one hand, the intensity of the coverage validated the convention as a major league news event, even beyond the political importance it had always had. To be a big-league journalist meant you were at the conventions, even if you were at the conventions to write or air pieces mocking the importance paid to the convention. The clearest indication of this desire to be "in the hall" was the huge increase in the number of *local* television stations that sent reporters, producers, and crews to "get the local angle." Because of the birth of satellite technology and the relative easing of costs, any local station with an earth station back home could dispatch a news team and receive live and taped reports direct from the convention floor. In 1980, more than 150 local stations sent crews to Detroit for the noneventful Republican convention; a tenfold increase over 1976. (This had an unanticipated but important consequence; it greatly increased the congestion on the floor. Each network had a ring of cameras circling the hall, so the floor reporters worked with a headset and a floor microphone, enabling them to be dispatched to delegations by producers who talked to them through the headsets. Local crews, however, had to move about the floor with producers, camera operators, and sound technicians in their wake.)

On the other hand, the lack of suspense combined with the crush of press and the enormous expense in time and effort and money of televising the conventions produced in 1980 something of a revolt within the press at its own apparent excesses. Report after report expressed astonishment at the fact that 15,000 members of the press were in attendance at a convention where only 1,998 delegates would show up. This count, inflated because it included every technician and engineer, is less shocking than it seems, given the fact that 2,000 journalists showed up in Ottawa in the summer of 1981 to cover an economic summit with seven participants, or the fact that a few thousand press people cover a heavyweight championship fight with *two* principals, but it served to dramatize the consensus belief—among the press—that the press in general, and television in particular, had come to take over the conventions and wrest them from the political parties themselves. Anyone walking into Detroit's Joe Louis Arena or New York's Madison Square Garden would have received symbolic confirmation of this impression. High atop each arena, dominating the floor, were the three skybooths of the major networks, each with its own symbol, each painted a different color, with huge glass walls behind which anchor reporters and analysts sat, much like captains on the bridge of an ocean liner. (NBC and CBS engaged in a brief but intense squabble over NBC's desire to run Christmas tree lights across its booth in Detroit. In a last-minute compromise, NBC was allowed to keep its lights, but was forbidden to turn them on.)

The numbers alone suggested wretched excess. The three networks dispatched a total of some 2,000 people to the Detroit convention; moved their morning and evening news programs to the convention sites; in effect transferred their entire news operation 1,000 miles for the better part of two weeks. Each of them occupied thousands of square feet in Cobo Hall, adjacent to the Joe Louis Arena, in which they established temporary offices: 28 trailers in the case of CBS and ABC, splendid modular offices with dramatic graphics and blown-up sketches of its major journalistic celebrities in the case of NBC. Public relations staffers coordinated requests for interviews with star correspondents and cranked out press releases about the nature of the enterprise. CBS noted it would have 14 cameras, 5 minicam crews, 4 mobile units, 5 control rooms, 204 television monitors, 750 telephones. Unmentioned in any network's press release was the astonishing number of young "pages"—to fetch coffee, pick up reporters' laundry, and perform other "gofer" functions—whose last names bore a curious similarity to those of important producers, executives, and correspondents. ("Once every four years," CBS President Bill Leonard said cheerfully, "we say 'the hell with the nepotism rules.' ")

In another sense, however, these numbers were misleading reflecting another example of that curious growth in a species of media analysis that attributes to the medium power that it either does not have or possesses only passively. This can best be understood by examining the logistics and the political factors that govern how a convention is covered.

The three networks began planning their convention coverage at the beginning of 1979, fully eighteen months before the conventions were to take place, at a time when only the broadest outlines of the contest could be grasped. The technological complexity of establishing such coverage is so immense that a decision *not* to commit resources that far in advance means the networks must decide—a year and a half before the conventions—to forgo even the possibility of live coverage. Are the networks supposed to know that a convention will be a routine coronation that far in advance? It requires a belief that television somehow dictates what will happen to assume that. And even when the apparent outcome is known months in advance—as it was with Jimmy Carter in 1976 and Ronald Reagan in 1980—there is no way of knowing whether or not fate will intervene to remove the apparent nominee from the scene—through death or disabling accident or illness—in which case the conventions would, in fact, become events worthy of continuous coverage. Thus, ABC, CBS, and NBC came to Detroit and New York, each having committed roughly $10 million per convention, hundreds of bodies, hundreds of miles of cables and telephone lines, months in advance of the event. For *Newsweek,* the decision to send ten fewer bodies to Detroit was a matter of cancelling a few airplane tickets and hotel rooms. The *New York Times* could pull back on its planned coverage by 40 percent with the same lack of impact. For the networks, a decision to cancel live coverage on the ground that the convention turned out to be cut-and-dried would have meant an economic loss of staggering proportions.

News executives fully recognized that neither convention—especially the Reagan coronation in Detroit—was a paradigm of suspense. "There's nothing here so newsworthy that it couldn't be televised in a single day—perhaps a single hour—rather than taking up four nights of prime time," CBS News president Bill Leonard remarked. "We've built this elephant gun, and we have aimed it squarely at a gnat"— although as it turned out, at least one night demonstrated the promises and pitfalls of aiming an elephant gun at a suspected elephant mating ritual. It may well have been a mistake to think that a national nominating convention should be covered with gavel-to-gavel thoroughness, even without the certainty of a coronation. Roone Arledge, supervising ABC's convention coverage for the first time as that network's news president, said, "If I were to operate strictly on the basis of news judgment, I couldn't justify four nights of prime time." (Ironically, in its past incarnation as the poor man's news network, ABC had always refrained from gavel-to-gavel coverage, providing wrapups and summaries in the midst of entertainment programs. Now, a full equal of CBS and NBC, it was proudly going gavel-to-gavel when the conventions would produce comparatively little news.) Whatever logic and news judgment might have recommended about reduced coverage, logistics demanded that the original game plan be followed.

Nor were other alternatives as easy as they may have seemed on the surface. Should the networks have rotated coverage of the convention, one each night, as the three commercial networks did during the 1973 Senate Watergate hearings? Then which network would have agreed to cover which night? The Republican convention on Monday was a night of stultifying boredom, broken by a Las Vegas-style presentation of stars with clear appeal to Republican convention delegates: Donny and Marie Osmond, Glen Campbell and Tanya Tucker, Wayne Newton, Chad Everett, Robert Conrad, and Michael Landon (it is a measure of Republican estrangement from black America that a convention taking place in Detroit—"Motown, U.S.A."—could not produce a single performer in that tradition), and a well-received speech by former President Gerald Ford. The Democratic convention on its Monday night was supposedly the most dramatic of nights, when the debate over an "open convention" rule would decide if Jimmy Carter could possibly be denied a first ballot nomination.

No news organization could possibly agree in advance to telecast live coverage of a convention only on a night on which nothing at all was supposed to happen. And no news organization would possibly refrain from going on the air when a potentially historic event, such as the possible agreement of a former President to run with his one-time rival as Vice-Presidential candidate, was unfolding, live, on a competing network.

Television network news organizations understood that they were being given an enormous chunk of time to cover an event whose intrinsic news worth had been steadily diminishing over the years. They were determined to use that time to tell as many different political stories as they could. Walter Cronkite may have meant it when he said, "I still feel this is one of the great national civics lessons; conventions represent grass-roots democracy at work." And John Chancellor may have been sincere when he said, "What audiences get, or what they ought to get, is a civics lesson; these conventions give us time to raise and discuss the most important issues of the day." But the civics lesson the viewers got from the conventions had very little to do with the conventions themselves. For by 1980, television had decided to provide gavel-to-gavel television *in name only*. Given the fact that so little of importance was happening at the conventions, at least as defined by television news, the networks used the conventions as a staging area, from which expeditions of various sorts—history, interviews, humorous sidebars, commentary and analysis—could be provided, in order to try to make sense of the unfolding political story.* Since public television offered no convention coverage because of a shortage of funds, this meant that there was no way for a devoted political follower to have actually watched the conventions unfolding. This may have been a great blessing in the main; but it also meant, for example, that intense platform debates over the Equal Rights Amendment, the MX missile system, and abortion, all of which took place at the Democratic convention, went unheard by the American people. Despite the catchphrase, there was no gavel-to-gavel coverage of either convention by any network.

More fundamentally, the very lack of passion at the Republican convention may well have been, in a political sense, the most significant story of the convention. Precisely those events that are most "static," the least susceptible to the drama of television coverage, are the ones that, in 1980, told us some critically important things about what had happened to the Republican Party, and what its intention was for the general election. All three networks reported these factors from their anchor booths, from the floor, from taped pieces, and in their analyses. Yet it was not the kind of dramatic, political confrontation of which exciting television—such as the 1952 convention coverage—is made.

What, for example, were the Republicans doing in Detroit—a city of blacks and ethnic blue-collar Democrats, a city with a black Democratic mayor, Coleman Young, loyally supporting Jimmy Carter, a city buffeted by unemployment, high crime, and racial tension? The same thing the Republicans were doing in their political advertising and in their political organizing. They were trying less to convince black voters to switch parties than they were signaling their devotion to blue-collar concerns by holding their convention in the symbolic city of the labor movement; the city where Democrats from FDR to JFK had traditionally begun their campaigns for the White House with a Labor Day rally at Cadillac—now John F. Kennedy—Square. And by gathering, however nervously, in the midst of a black-run city, the Repub-

---

* Since I served as one of CBS's resident analysts during the conventions, along with James J. Kilpatrick and Bill Moyers, I am hardly arguing that commentary and analysis—or interviews or floor reports—are out of place at conventions. The fact, however, that not a single American viewer could have actually seen the conventions, even if he had wanted to, surely says something about the debate over "gavel-to-gavel" coverage.

licans were sending a soothing message to the more liberal of their members, a message that conservative Republicanism was not to be confused with racism.

What did the party unity tell us about the Republicans? It strongly suggested, as all of the commentators on all of the networks noted at one time or another, that the Democrats would find it extremely difficult to realize their hope of turning Ronald Reagan into another Barry Goldwater. Both because of style and because of the growing distrust of and disillusion with government, the conservative gospel no longer sounded like a slightly daffy suggestion to rush backward into the nineteenth century. The 1964 analogy, so hoped-for by the Carter campaign, was totally missing in the Reagan coronation. When Henry Kissinger, archenemy internationalist to the traditional Taft-Goldwater conservatives, addressed the convention Tuesday night, his speech was met, not with heckling or booing, but with indifference. When NAACP Executive Director Benjamin Hooks arrived to meet with the 2.8 percent of delegates who were black, convention organizers altered the schedule to permit him to speak to the convention, and his praise for a laundry list of social spending programs was met with polite indifference.

There was, as it turned out, only one genuinely divisive area in which true-believing conservatives acted to reaffirm their beliefs at the expense of inclusion: the area of women's issues. In a break with a forty-year tradition, the Republican platform did not endorse the Equal Rights Amendment, preferring instead to acknowledge the sincere beliefs of both sides. This failure resulted in a preconvention march of 5,000 people, including liberal Republicans such as Senator Jacob Javits and Governor William Milliken; but pro-ERA forces could not muster the support of six delegations in order to bring the fight to the floor. Further, the platform flatly endorsed a right-to-life amendment to the Constitution to outlaw abortion and urged the appointment of federal judges who would "honor the sanctity of innocent unborn life"—a litmus test on a single issue that stirred the public opposition of notables such as former President Gerald Ford.

Fundamentally, however, the entire structure and rhetoric of the Republican convention was a signal to the traditional Democratic voter that their party, the party of prosperity, jobs, and economic growth, had lost sight of the fundamental interests of millions of working-class voters. This line was drummed home repeatedly by Republicans of every stripe, who took full and fair use of the free media afforded by massive convention coverage.

Thus, Congressman Jack Kemp appeared on the "Today" show on Tuesday morning to say "it's really a contradiction in terms to call this a conservative platform, because conservative, in the status quo sense, means no change. . . . It's now the other party that is passive in the face of a depressing economy, and all the news this morning is that inflation is going to be 12 percent this year, and unemployment up to over 9 percent.'' That same morning, on CBS ''Morning,'' viewers saw excerpts from speeches by former Defense Secretary Donald Rumsfeld (''the best argument I know against the six-year term is sitting in the White House tonight''); former Treasury Secretary William Simon (''President Carter has produced larger deficits than any other President in our history. . . . Sometimes, my friends, I think that Mr. Carter has the Midas touch in reverse. Everything he touches turns to mush''); and Gerald Ford, who declared, ''You've all heard the Carter alibis: inflation cannot be controlled; the world has changed; we can no longer protect our diplomats in foreign capitals nor our working men on Detroit's assembly lines; we must prudently retreat. Ba-loney!''

The point is not that the networks failed to cover the new Republican offensive aimed at pulling blue-collar America away from the Democrats: from Bill Moyers, on loan to CBS, who went to a Detroit unemployment office, to David Brinkley's essays on ''Nightly News'' for NBC, they did. The point, rather, is that the essential premise of televised coverage of conventions is to find the breaking story and turn loose all of the enormous resources of a broadcast network to find and report—*first*—every nugget of information. There was no such story at the Republican National Convention of 1980—until Wednesday, July 16, at 7:05 P.M. For the next five and a half hours, viewers across the United States would witness an astonishing example of the powerful influence of the presence of live television; as well as an equally astonishing confusion between a real political event and what has come to be known among students of modern politics as a ''media event.''

The idea that former President Gerald Ford might be a strong candidate to run as Vice-President had been intriguing some Republican politicians, and some journalists, for months. As early as February 11, *New York Times* columnist William Safire, in a column mourning the declining chances of Ronald Reagan, had suggested that Ford would make a good running mate for George Bush or Howard Baker. George Will raised the possibility in a *Newsweek* column of March 31. And interest at the convention was sparked by Ford's Monday night speech, in which he promised, ''This Republican is going to do everything in his power to elect our nominee to the Presidency of the United States. . . . This country means too much for me to comfortably park on the park bench. So, when this convention fields the team for Governor Reagan, count me in.''

This line in a speech may have been only a spark, but it was a spark that flickered in a tinderbox of speculation, since no other news whatever was going to be made at the convention. In a ''60 Minutes'' interview with Ronald Reagan, broadcast the night the convention opened, Mike Wallace seemed to be prosecuting the prospective nominee for his failure to disclose his choice. "Everybody says it's the most important decision that you've got to make between now and November. And here we are, less than a week before you've got to make the choice. You mean to say you haven't got your mind made up?"

And in that kind of atmosphere, Ford's availability for the Vice-Presidency was a common thread of speculation. A brief review of some television news coverage before the Wednesday night firestorm demonstrates the point.

• Sunday night, on a CBS preconvention special, Bill Plante ran down a list of possible choices—Bush, Baker, Kemp, Senator Richard Lugar, Rumsfeld, Congressman Guy Vander Jagt, William Simon, Senator Paul Laxalt—and then said, ". . . everyone does agree, though, around here, that the dream ticket would have been Ronald Reagan and Gerald Ford. And that rumor surfaced again today, until Mr. Ford had a chance to deny it on television, and said that under no circumstances would he be a candidate. . . . [Polls show] Gerald Ford's the only one who does him any good."

• On Monday night, Bill Moyers offered a whimsical essay on the "CBS Evening News," wondering what would happen if "Ronald Reagan called up Gerald Ford after the session tonight" and importuned him with promises of real power as Vice-President. "So suppose Ronald Reagan then went before the delegates, made the same case for Ford, and asked them to draft him. What do you think would happen, Walter?"

"I think Jesse Helms would faint," said Cronkite.

• On Tuesday, Ford and Reagan met for an hour and ten minutes. Reagan denied that he had offered Ford the Vice-Presidential nomination, saying, "No, I just wanted his consultation in the decisions I have to make." NBC's Judy Woodruff said on the "NBC Nightly News" that "some of Reagan's aides had told reporters that he would offer Ford the Vice-Presidential slot—expecting him to turn it down. But later Reagan said he hadn't made the offer."

• On the Wednesday "Today" show—the day Ronald Reagan would be nominated for President—Ford was interviewed by Tom Brokaw, who asked, "Are there any conditions under which you would accept . . . ?"

"Let me put it this way," Ford said. "Nothing has changed from the statements that I've been making for the last year. . . . There is a constitutional problem . . ." (as residents of the same state, Ford and Reagan could not both receive the votes of California electors). And Ford added, "I think Governor Reagan can get a better person to do the job for the next four years than myself."

"I know it must be very hard, once you've been President, to be Vice-President of the United States," Brokaw said.

"The pride problem would not bother me at all," Ford replied. "If I thought the situation would work, if I thought all the other questions could be resolved, the problem of pride and so forth would not bother me in any way whatsoever." And later in the interview, Ford denied several times that he had been asked to run with Reagan. In their analysis segment, "Today" guest columnist Jack Germond said of the Ford rumor, "It has no solid substance that I could discover. . . . I don't think it's serious at all."

• On Wednesday's CBS "Morning," Bob Schieffer reported on "a draft-Ford movement that seemed to sputter by night's end. . . . Friends of the former President put out word that he was becoming annoyed by the effort."

By the time the network evening broadcasts hit the air at 6:30 P.M.,* the Ford story had taken on new strength. NBC's John Chancellor reported that "a mighty effort is underway tonight to get former President Gerald R. Ford to run for Vice-President on a ticket headed by Ronald Reagan. Ford has so far refused. . . . The former President is still listening, but his position is that he doesn't want to run." Judy Woodruff reported that "politicians and advisors close to Ford were . . . dropping hints that they were trying to talk Ford into accepting Reagan's offer . . . Reagan aides say Ford agreed to reconsider the number two spot on the ticket, on the condition that he be given more authority once in office as Vice-President."

On the "CBS Evening News," Dan Rather reported that Ford and Reagan "just a short while ago, held their second meeting in the past twenty-four hours to discuss the possibility of Ford becoming Reagan's Vice-Presidential running mate. All day long, Ford has been under pressure to agree." Rather recounted meetings between Ford, Kissinger, and former White House chief economist Alan Greenspan, and quoted an anonymous congressman who said, "I'd still be amazed if Ford did it. I personally think it's going to be Bush, but Reagan isn't kidding. He really wants Ford . . ." At the end of the broadcast, Rather reported that a Ford-Reagan meeting had in fact taken place at about 5 P.M., and reported that a top Ford aide had said, "There is no final answer from Ford."

Because the Gerald Ford interview with Walter Cronkite occurred just after the end of the evening newscasts, and because it has been cited as a prime example of a media event, it is critical to recognize both the setting in which the interview took place and the clear distinction between the generally accurate reporting that had taken place

* All times are Eastern Daylight Time, since Detroit is in the Eastern time zone.

before the Ford interview and what the viewers saw in the hours after the interview.

Did Ronald Reagan want Gerald Ford as his running-mate? Postconvention stories, by *Time, Newsweek,* and a host of political reporters, clearly show the answer was yes. The Reagan camp interpreted Ford's Monday night speech to the convention as a signal of potential willingness, and by Tuesday, Reagan was asking groups of his own supporters how they would react to a Reagan-Ford ticket. By Wednesday negotiations were well underway between the Ford and Reagan camps to try and reach some understanding about what kind of Vice-Presidency Gerald Ford would find acceptable. Television reporters, in other words, were not popping up on network newscasts to offer idle speculation gathered in the halls of the Detroit Plaza Hotel. They were reporting hard, specific information, which was, in retrospect, unquestionably correct.

What happened between 7:00 and 7:30 P.M., however, was that television news switched over into its most troublesome area: the merging of news gathering and news reporting.

Gerald and Betty Ford came to the CBS anchor booth at 7 P.M. to participate in one of a series of network interviews: NBC and ABC had already had their turns with Ford, but they had taken place earlier in the convention, before the Ford-Reagan negotiations had begun. (A more prudent Gerald Ford might have cancelled the interview, but as one CBS correspondent remarked later, "Ford had to decide whether to tick off Reagan or Cronkite, and he knew who had more power.") Just before the interview, Dan Rather was back on the air from the Detroit Plaza, reporting that the story was "certainly more than rumor," and offering details about the people and the pieces of the "unofficial negotiations . . . [about] exactly what would Ford's duties be." Rather's sources were saying, "We don't think, in the end, Gerald Ford is going to say yes, but this is for real, until he doesn't say a final no, that Ronald Reagan isn't going to consider anybody else."

Whereupon Cronkite turned to the former President and said, "Can you verify that Dan's reporting is accurate today? Now, you're not going to go back on Dan?"

Ford began with admirable caution. "I'm not at liberty, of course, to make any comment on what transpired today. I am interested in what Dan reported, but I better stop there."

After a few more noncommittal words by Ford, Cronkite asked the former President, "What would happen if [Republicans] got out there on the floor tonight or tomorrow and said, 'It's got to be Gerald Ford'?"

Now was the time for a circumspect politician to repeat his noncommittal words and let Cronkite move on to a less charged point. Instead, Ford said, "If there is any change, it has to be predicated on the arrangements that I would expect as a Vice-President in a relationship with the President. I would not go to Washington, Walter, and be a figurehead Vice-President. If I go to Washington—and I'm not saying that I'm accepting—I have to go there with the belief that I will play a meaningful role across the board in the basic and the crucial and the important decisions that have to be made . . ."

Well, said Cronkite, what about the matter of pride for a Presidential candidate accepting a running mate "who, as in your case, has said, 'it's got to be something like a co-Presidency'?"

The word "co-Presidency" was, to be sure, Cronkite's. But Ford never blinked. "That's something that Governor Reagan really ought to consider," Ford said. ". . . For him not to understand the realities of some of the things that might happen in Washington is being oblivious to reality."

The conversation turned to Betty Ford and her feelings—she offered no objection; to the age question ("We'd be a pretty healthy team," said Ford. "But don't jump to the wrong conclusion now." "Well," said Cronkite prophetically, "we're going to jump to conclusions all over the place tonight"), to the constitutional issue of two candidates from the same state, to Ford's dissent from the platform planks on the ERA, abortion, and the appointment of prolife family judges. But by the time the interview ended, at 7:28 P.M., those earlier statements by the former President had already sent shock waves through Joe Louis Arena.

As soon as the interview ended, Ford tried to leave the CBS anchor booth and found a wall of reporters awaiting him—including ABC's Barbara Walters who, close to tears, begged Ford for several minutes, in near-hysterical terms, to grant her an immediate interview. Ford agreed, and ABC aired her interview with Ford shortly before 8 P.M., in which the former President said—somewhat more circumspectly—the same things he had told Cronkite. By now, however, all three networks went into action; all of the massive resources which had seemed so out of place at a coronation-style convention were to be put into play. There were, however, two problems. The first was that the actual negotiations and decisions were taking place on two floors of the Detroit Plaza Hotel, away from the reach of television cameras and reporters. Second, the cameras and reporters were deployed to speak with people who had little or no idea what was happening.

The consequences were inevitable. Once the decision was made to go to instant news reporting, the audience became the equal of the reporters, producers, and news executives. Earlier reports on the evening news were the products of news gathering, filtered through judgment, the checking of facts, the squelching of rumors. By the time Rather, Woodruff, and company went on the air, they had the story in accurate, presentable form. Now, however, the audience was being taken inside the news-gathering operation, as reporters were put on the air with opinions, facts, rumors, guesses, and anything else that came from "sources" who had no firsthand knowledge of what was taking place.

NBC, the network which, by luck of the draw and the absence of a reporter with Barbara Walters's willingness to prostrate herself for an interview did not have Ford on camera this night, began moving around the floor, talking with Republican National Committee deputy chairman Drew Lewis ("Ford and Bush are both attractive to me"), Senator Jesse Helms ("Ford would make a super ticket"), party official Mary Louise Smith ("I don't think a Ford acceptance is realistic"), and Robert Dole ("I'd divide the Oval Office to get him"), Illinois Governor James Thompson ("Ford told me I haven't changed my position"). At 8:02 P.M., diplomatic correspondent Marvin Kalb was reporting that a "knowledgeable source" had told him "there's now a 50–50 chance" of Ford accepting.

ABC's Sam Donaldson talked with former Michigan Senator Robert Griffin ("I'm a bit more optimistic today than I was yesterday"), Senator Dole ("I believe they can work out any arrangement that President Ford may want"), and former Michigan Governor George Romney, who said a draft-Ford resolution would be offered on the convention floor ("He can always say no, but I think he would respond yes"). Romney, Drew Lewis, and Helms were also interviewed by CBS. In the CBS analysis booth, Bill Moyers, James Kilpatrick, and I expressed both political and substantive doubts about the "dream ticket," with Moyers waving "a red flag" in the face of the euphoria, and Kilpatrick expressing dissent from the idea of dividing up a Constitutional office.*

From 8:25 until 9 P.M., the on-air rumor flood was stilled by the keynote speech of Guy Vander Jagt, a Michigan congressman reputed to be a spellbinding orator and a possible Vice-Presidential choice. His "spellbinding oratory," consisting of the densest packing of cliches in years ("Republican ends in I-CAN; AMERICAN ends in I-CAN"), provided only temporary relief from the wave of speculation, which had by now totally captured the networks, although it, too, reflected

---

* Kilpatrick, whose rhetorical gruffness conceals a warmhearted personality, is a gentleman of an earlier age; modern technology offends him. Just as we went on the air, Kilpatrick's earpiece dislodged, and he began gesturing with frustration. This was interpreted by some sharp-eyed media analysts as a measure of Kilpatrick's outrage over the idea of a Reagan-Ford ticket. My own view was that the spectacle of a Presidential candidate in his first moment in the public eye with the mantle of nominee negotiating away his office would reflect a sense of weakness and self-doubt that would have hurt Reagan badly in the fall.

the Republican determination to reach out to blue-collar America. Ronald Reagan, Vander Jagt said, "did not have the support of the country clubs, the boardrooms, the media, the Washington establishment, or the Republican establishment. The only thing Ronald Reagan had was the support and loyalty and love of the people."

Once the keynote speech ended, the Ford story took over. Columnist George Will, serving as an ABC commentator, reported that "the negotiations were about an enhanced Vice-Presidential office . . . that might include a formalized understanding that would give Gerald Ford unprecedented responsibility for at least coordinating—and of course it remains to be seen what all that would involve—the national security apparatus." And Will, Frank Reynolds, and Ted Koppel speculated about how Reagan or Ford could stop the deal if either wanted to. "If this fish gets away," Will said, "then the convention will suffer a tremendous letdown . . . [Ford] is going to find it very hard, logically or psychologically, to pull back."

James Wooten, reporting from the podium, talked with George Bush and quoted Bush as saying of the Ford-Reagan deal "it looks like it's all set." Said Wooten, "He seemed rather shaken by it, as a matter of fact, rather bitter." Sander Vanocur interviewed Senator Laxalt, one of Reagan's closest advisors, who said, "So far as I know, nothing is settled at this time. But I have been gone for the last couple of hours, so I am a little out of touch." Howard Baker seemed to confirm George Will's accounts of the proceedings by noting that "The Vice-President, by statute, is chairman of the National Security Council. I can't think of anything that would be better served than a former President, with his wealth of experience, in that role."

Beginning at 9:05 P.M., just as George Bush was ascending the podium to begin his speech, the rumors began hardening. ABC's Frank Reynolds reported, "We now have reports that a deal has been made between Governor Reagan and former President Ford and that it has been accepted and agreed to, and that former President Ford will be Governor Reagan's choice to be the number-two man on the ticket to run for Vice-President. That is historic. It is unique. It is unprecedented, and we don't know it for sure, but there are reports confirming what our correspondent Jim Wooten told us some time ago, that the deal was underway."

NBC, which was the most cautious of the three networks throughout the night, either because of better judgment or because it was the one network not to have interviewed Ford that evening, reported via Tom Pettit that some consideration was being given to giving the Vice-Presidential nominee a cabinet post in addition to the ceremonial office. As part of its ongoing "Democratic responses," Carter campaign Chairman Robert Strauss said that he didn't think a Reagan-Ford ticket would be harder to beat than any other. At 9:40, however,

Garrick Utley interviewed Robert Griffin, who said that "it looks good" for the deal. Utley commented, "This is practically a confirmation of Ford's nomination as Vice-President."

CBS, which had launched the story with the Ford interview, now went the farthest out on the speculative limb. At 9:10, Rather had reported that "the number of sources on the floor who say that a deal has been cut is increasing," although whether these sources were doing anything more than watching TV news reports is intriguing. By 10:10 P.M., Cronkite reported, "CBS News has learned that there is a definite plan for Ronald Reagan and the former President of the United States, Gerald Ford, who will be his selection as running mate, an unparalleled, unprecedented situation in American politics . . . to come to this convention hall tonight to appear together on the platform for Ronald Reagan to announce that Gerald Ford would run with him."

There was no room for maneuver in this declaration, in contrast to ABC's anchor, Frank Reynolds, who reported that the rumors "are more than rumors," but then added, "We are obliged to report that this has not been confirmed by either Mr. Ford or Governor Reagan. So the question is still open, and it is entirely possible that this Ford business . . . may prove as ephemeral and as short-lived as the Bush move that swept here earlier this week . . ." (ABC did then cut to Iowa Governor Robert Ray, who said the story of the deal "comes from a very good source . . . it seems to have some substance to it.")

And Ted Koppel mused aloud, "The only thought that keeps flitting through my mind is, I hope we're not all feeding off each other, you know. The delegates feeding off the television reports and the television reporters feeding off the delegates. But those reports seem to be becoming more and more pervasive. There seems to be more and more substance to them."

Similarly, when Sam Donaldson reported the story about Ford and Reagan coming to Joe Louis Arena, he phrased it this way, "I have a report from a source whom I cannot name, . . . that Governor Reagan and former President Ford will come to this hall and appear before the convention together, which of course would mean that the announcement that Mr. Ford is in fact going to be on the ticket will have been made tonight. I am told that Mr. Ford is already in the building here . . . but I cannot tell you for a fact that it will happen."

NBC's coverage, as with ABC's, followed the rumor and reported the growing certainty of its truth, but never committed to the kind of flat declaration Cronkite had made. Robert Ray told the network, "My understanding is a deal has been made." Tom Brokaw, reporting that a Ford advance team had been spotted on the floor, said, "We'll have to wait and see" if Reagan persuaded Ford to take the second spot on the ticket. Governor Milliken told the network, "I understand a Ford-Reagan arrangement has been set, that they are on their way here."

Former cabinet member Caspar Weinberger said, "I think a deal will be set by morning." At 10:38 P.M., Senator Laxalt told Jessica Savitch, "I understand there's still no deal."

CBS itself began moving away from the certainty of Cronkite's declaration; by 10:44, Republican convention official Tully Plesser was saying to Dan Rather, "I still believe the deal can be cut," but Rather was cautioning viewers that "no deal has been finally reached."

The print press, meanwhile, was pursuing the same rumors with the same feverishness, but outside the pressure cooker of live reporting. Associated Press and United Press International were reporting flatly that agreement had been reached. The *Chicago Sun-Times,* with a 10:30 P.M. deadline, ran off tens of thousands of first editions with the front-page headline, "It's Reagan and Ford." The *Wall Street Journal,* which was highly critical of television reporting, carried the same story as fact in its first editions. With these exceptions (and a handful of others, such as the *Cleveland Plain Dealer,* the *Charlotte (N.C.) Observer,* and the *Raleigh (N.C.) News and Observer*), the print press could let the developments unfold. Live on-scene television, however, carried the story into tens of millions of homes—in effect, turning every viewer into a newsroom eavesdropper, watching reports flow into their homes at the same instant the report was being discovered by the journalist. The ultimate absurdity was that interviews were being held by network news reporters with sources who were telling reporters what the television reporters had told *them.* At 11:15, for example, Governor William Milliken told CBS's Bob Schieffer, "The reports I'm getting from the networks and radio is that the deal hasn't been done."

By 11:30, Ronald Reagan had been nominated all but unanimously for the Presidency, and the speculation was still based on the certainty that Ford would take second place on the ticket. ABC's analysts were explaining, in the words of Elizabeth Drew, that "he couldn't say no," that Ford would be, as *Washington Post* writer Haynes Johnson noted, part of "a very strong ticket for the Republican Party."

At 11:54 P.M., the final bizarre twist in the story broke, which again demonstrated the obsessive nature of the get-it-on-first competition that had characterized the entire evening. The convention had been in suspension for some moments, with the post-Reagan nomination demonstration extended to permit the nominee to come to the hall —presumably with Ford at his side. As it happened, Ford had been offered and had already turned down the job; and Reagan and his aides recognized that something had to be done to bring the delegates back up from what was sure to be a letdown, to reestablish Reagan's dominance over the convention atmosphere, and at all costs to avoid letting rumors and counterrumors play on network television through the night and into the morning. In order not to have Reagan's appearance disappoint the crowd, Reagan lieutenants rushed onto the convention floor to begin spreading the word that Bush, not Ford, would be the Vice-Presidential candidate.

At 11:54 P.M., correspondent Chris Wallace, with Reagan Midwest coordinator Dan Totten by his side, burst into NBC's audio to announce that "Governor Reagan is coming to make a speech, and the nominee will be George Bush!"

Perhaps thirty seconds later, as Cronkite was reviewing the motorcade, Lesley Stahl appeared on CBS in a state of high excitement to report, "Walter, a top lieutenant just came and said it's not Ford! They're coming all around me to tell me it's not Ford! Someone told me it was Bush! They said it's absolutely definite! They're all yelling Bush all around me! Everybody's yelling Bush, Walter!" She turned her head to ask another operative. "Bush? They're all telling me Bush, Walter. Reagan lieutenants, men with colored hats all around telling me, Bush!" And with that, Stahl pushed her face into a "who-the-hell-knows-what?" grin and threw it back to Cronkite, who buried his head in his hands and shook his head in mock bewilderment. "Did somebody write the script?" he said. "It's hard to believe."

Even harder to believe was the idea that anyone could treat the story as a scoop. ABC may have been derelict in reporting the story several minutes later than NBC or CBS, but the story was "broken" not by reportorial skill, but by a mob of men in red hats racing onto the floor screaming "Bush! Bush!" Nonetheless, NBC's anchors heaped praise on Chris Wallace for "being the first to break the story," and Garrick Utley put his arm on the correspondent's shoulders toward the end of the evening and said, "the kid did it." CBS took out advertisements praising Stahl for breaking the story, and noted that her report was the first *on-camera* report.

The post-convention reports were severely critical of the television networks for what *Newsweek* called "TV's Rush to Judgment," and what *Time* described as "A Convention Hall of Mirrors." The *Wall Street Journal* described it as "The Night the TV News Dam Broke," arguing that "we saw the mighty organ [of modern media] take control." (The *Journal* also managed to misreport the "scoop" story, reporting that CBS finished last—demonstrating that the perspective of print did not insure protection against mistakes in reporting.) The *New York Times* "News of the Week in Review" pointed to the "relentless speculation and pursuit of the rumors by network 'floor reporters.' . . . Television once again focused attention on itself as perhaps the nation's most important shaper of political agendas." John J. O'Connor, the *Times*'s television critic, warned of the competitive focus on being first, suggesting that "perhaps accuracy and not speed should be made the ultimate criterion."

One of the clearest consequences of the "video melodrama," as

Washington Post reporter Lou Cannon described Wednesday night, was to inflate to vast proportions the political consequences of the night of decision, suggesting that the *procedure* Reagan used to select his running mate was a matter of major electoral weight. Mark Shields, *Washington Post* columnist, argued that "the whole Ford fiasco provided proof, if any was needed, that the Reagan team is not ready for the World Series." Evans and Novak wrote that "Reagan emerged looking disorganized and careless of the prerogatives of the office he seeks." The *Post*'s Lou Cannon, who had covered Reagan for fourteen years in California, said the episode provided "a quick education on how Ronald Reagan might operate as President," and suggested the hesitant decision making would "heighten" the "lingering doubts" about Reagan's fitness for the Presidency. The Democrats sought to make instant political capital out of the affair; President Carter called the indecision a "debacle," saying "the Oval Office is not something to be traded in a hurried fashion in the middle of the night," and Robert Strauss, appearing on CBS "Morning," charitably suggested that "the Republicans messed one up last night." (Reagan's more ideological supporters were much kinder to the nominee. George Will wrote that "if Moscow calls President Reagan, they will speak to a man who, one testing day in July, passed the test. Under intense pressure, and in circumstances of extreme fluidity, he showed that he could imaginatively attempt a moderate departure from tradition; that he could modulate the pursuit of his objectives and forestall immoderate departures; and that he could decisively tidy up a ragged situation." William Buckley called it "brilliant political maneuvering"; Reagan, he said, had tried to spare the Republican Right the specter of George Bush, and then had turned to the logical, inclusive running mate.)

In fact, the entire Ford-Bush decision almost immediately dropped from the political spotlight, never to be seen or heard of again for the rest of the campaign. In part, this happened because Vice-Presidents rarely make news in a general election campaign, unless their statements move beyond the pale of normal political rhetoric, as happened with Spiro Agnew in 1968, or unless some shocking fact about their past emerges, as happened with Senator Tom Eagleton in 1972. (It is a matter of intriguing speculation to wonder whether a Gerald Ford on the ticket might not have kept a spotlight on the second spot, both because of his role as former President, and because the question of a negotiated "co-Presidency" might have persisted throughout the campaign.) In this sense, the *New York Times*'s reference to television as the "most important shaper of political agendas" was clearly true. Since the Vice-Presidential decision was (a) the only real news out of the convention, and (b) the event that threw the convention into an evening of high drama, a good deal of the press coverage of the event assumed that it would be a matter of enduring interest to the electorate. On this matter, NBC's "Today" show analysts, Germond, Pettit, and Broder, and CBS's James Kilpatrick were correct in dismissing the notion of the Ford-Bush story as one of major campaign significance.

In contrast, the acceptance speech of Ronald Reagan was almost surely the political event of lasting significance to emerge from the convention—a fact that offers some ironic insights into the nature of campaign coverage. There are indeed times when events beyond the formal convention dominate the politics of a national nominating convention. Examples such as the Chicago riots of 1968 and the chaos of a party forced to drop its Vice-Presidential nominee, as in 1972, are examples. But as a general proposition, the acceptance speech of a party's Presidential nominee is the singular event of a convention. Why? For one thing, it will be one of the first—and one of the last—times in an election when a candidate is permitted to speak to the voters in his own terms, in words, phrases, and paragraphs that are not then placed at the mercy of the editing process. In compressing a speech into a thirty-second sound bite, perhaps taken from two or three different parts of a speech, all surrounded by a reporter's interpretation of the strategic meaning of the remarks, it is very difficult for a voter to get a coherent sense of how a candidate's ideas fit together —or if they fit together at all. An acceptance speech provides a candidate with that forum.

For another, no matter how often a candidate for President has been on television, the acceptance speech is the nation's first chance to judge him as an honest-to-God potential President: one of the two (or three) individuals in the entire country who might soon be holding life-and-death power over the world. The careless errors of fact, the excesses of rhetoric, are judged by a much harsher standard now; this is why Senator Goldwater's famous line in his 1964 acceptance speech —"extremism in the defense of liberty is no vice; and moderation in the pursuit of justice is no virtue"—had such a devastating impact on his electoral fortunes. He was not now speaking to the Tucson Elks Club; he was speaking to the world, and the bravado of the words took on a chilling quality as the listener realized that the man speaking those words might soon have the power to send nuclear missiles "in the defense of liberty" or "the pursuit of justice."

Ronald Reagan was determined not to make that mistake. The clue to his intentions had been the rhetoric used by all of the speechmakers, both to the convention and on the national news shows. It had been signaled again in Senator Laxalt's nominating speech, a speech that had gone totally unexamined, in which the spear carrier for conservative Republicans had been described as something of a modern-day Hubert Humphrey, increasing aid to the "truly" needy by 43 percent as California governor; increasing aid to higher education;

protecting the environment; improving California's mental health facilities. If Reagan was the candidate who was going to dismantle the welfare state apparatus of government, it certainly was not apparent from Laxalt's speech.

Nor was it any part of the Reagan biography, which ran just before the acceptance speech. The film emphasized the nominee's "strong, basic Midwestern ethic," in the words of Reagan media chief Peter Dailey. It panned still photos of Reagan's early life, talked about the "thrifty, hardworking, closeknit family," and avoided the entire Communist infiltration-blacklisting issue which had surrounded Reagan's tenure as President of the Screen Actors Guild. Instead, it referred to Reagan's unique position as a former union president now running for chief executive, and talked of how Reagan "prevented a takeover of the film industry by organized crime."

The speech itself was a rhetorical gem. In this media age, what voters were seeing was a candidate, unadorned by any visual tricks save the networks cutting between candidate and audience, making out his case for the right to assume power. It began with a typically self-deprecating remark—Reagan talked about how pleased he was "to find myself, for the first time in a long time, in a movie in prime time." Then he moved on to the case for his cause.

Recognizing that the abandonment of the Equal Rights Amendment had hurt him badly among moderate Republicans and independent women, Reagan said, "We've had a quarrel or two, but it was only as to the method of attaining a goal. There was no argument about the goal. As President, I will establish a liaison with the fifty governors to encourage them to eliminate, wherever it exists, discrimination against women. I will monitor federal laws to insure their implementation, and to add statutes, if they are needed."

To remind the social conservatives—the "New Right" amalgam of causes committed to "traditional family values" and against the "secular humanism" that had produced abortion rights, sex clinics, an end to prayer in public schools, and other scourges of the modern age, Reagan offered his promise to "build a national consensus with all those across the land who share a community of values embodied in these words: family, work, neighborhood, peace, freedom."

His appeal to disillusioned Democrats was aimed directly at their pocketbooks, and at the general consensus that Jimmy Carter had not been up to the job.

"We must," he said, "overcome something the present Administration has cooked up: a new and altogether indigestible economic stew—one part inflation, one part high unemployment, one part recession, one part runaway taxes, one part deficit spending, seasoned with an energy crisis. It's an economic stew that has turned the national stomach."

And in what turned out to be a preview of his closing summation in the Cleveland debate, Reagan gave the delegates their chance to work up enthusiasm with a "responsive reading":

"Can anyone look at the record of this Administration and say, 'well done'?"

"No!" roared the delegates.

"Can anyone compare the state of our economy when the Carter Administration took office with where we are today and say, 'Keep up the good work'?"

"No!"

"Can anyone look at our reduced standing in the world today and say, 'let's have four more years of this'?"

"No!"

"I believe the American people are going to answer these questions as you've answered them in the first week of November, and their answer will be, 'No, we've had enough!' "

The true measure of the speech, however, was Reagan's effort to give it weight, *gravitas,* a sense of Presidential timbre. In contrast to the personal center of Jimmy Carter's language ("I will never lie to you"), Reagan cast his rhetoric outward, to the traditional sources of American thought. Much as John Kennedy sought to overcome the impression of his youth by constantly quoting the Founding Fathers, Reagan referred again and again to historical figures and mileposts as a method of giving more heft to his own policies. He talked of the Mayflower Compact of the Pilgrims, quoted the Declaration of Independence's authors who "pledged their lives, their fortunes, and their sacred honor to found this nation," quoted Lincoln's Gettysburg Address. Reagan tried to give his own words a tone of grandeur, as when he said, "I pledge to restore to the federal government the capacity to do the people's work without dominating their lives," or when he declared, "The United States has an obligation to its citizens and to the people of the world never to let those who would destroy freedom dictate the future of human life on this planet"—a sentence shaped very much like the Sorensonian declamations of John F. Kennedy.

At the end of his speech, Reagan had two surprises for the delegates and one for the press. At the end of his speech, Reagan offered a long quotation attacking excessive government spending and size; the author of those remarks, Reagan said, was Franklin Delano Roosevelt, accepting the 1932 Democratic Presidential nomination. It marked the second time in the speech Reagan had quoted FDR—the other being the more familiar "rendezvous with destiny" line—and it was a neat device, since it appeared to embrace the godhead of the Democratic Party while implicitly criticizing the party itself, and FDR, for abandoning those words.

Then, at the close of his prepared speech, Reagan declared that he had something else to say. Referring to the American hostages, to refugees from tyranny around the world who sought to come to America, he said, in a voice bordering on tears, "I'll confess that I've been a little afraid to suggest what I'm going to suggest. I'm more afraid not to. Can we begin our crusade together in a moment of silent prayer?" The hall fell totally silent. Then Reagan looked up and said in a breaking voice, "God bless America."

Here, out in public, was the story that the thousands of journalists at the Detroit convention were trying to ferret out—the strategy of the Republican campaign. The irony of the enterprise was that a campaign *cannot conceal its strategy*. It must reveal it in the language of candidate speeches, advertising, in the whole range of methods used to convince voters of how their votes should be cast. In front of the entire country, Ronald Reagan was mapping out the central story of the 1980 Presidential campaign: the Republicans were out to steal Democratic turf by claiming the mantle of growth and economic well-being, by abandoning the party's role of nay-sayer to argue that the Democrats had become the reactionary party of no growth, and pessimism, and fear.

So accustomed had television been, however, to getting "behind" the story that this most traditional of convention activities was all but eclipsed by the Wednesday night furor over the possible nomination of Gerald Ford for Vice-President. With the massive technology and manpower in place, the news-gathering behemoth waited only for the breaking of a real story to move into action. The point is *not* that television made up the story; it did not. All through the evening, reporters were getting information from the principals involved in the negotiations, and the stories turned out to be almost all true: Ford *was* considering the offer, his people *were* negotiating with Reagan's people for a formal agreement about power sharing. But so powerful was the television machinery that the live coverage changed from hard-nosed reporting into something of a frenzy, with sources confirming what the inquirer (TV news) had, in fact, reported earlier to the source. In this sense, television had been "hoist by its own petard"—jolted into excess by the overwhelming power of its own weaponry. In the process, the most memorable aspect of the convention turned out to have almost no political significance at all, while the window dressing of the Presidential acceptance speech presaged a campaign—and an Administration—very likely to change the course of American politics fundamentally and permanently.

X   The Democratic Convention: Reality Triumphant

The Republican Convention demonstrated that the more heavily television covers an event, the more tempting it is to treat the event itself as a creature of television. With all three networks providing hours of live, prime-time coverage of political conventions, it is not surprising that the conventions have at times come to be judged as TV programs, praised or damned depending on the drama they provide.

When the Democratic National Convention of 1980 adopted a rule binding delegates to vote for the candidate they had favored during the primary balloting, it guaranteed the renomination of President Carter and ended whatever small possibility had remained that an "open" convention might turn to Senator Kennedy, or to an alternative to both Kennedy and Carter. As a television show, the convention immediately forfeited much of its dramatic tension, leading the *Washington Post*'s first-rate television critic, Tom Shales, to write, ". . . just like that, the Democratic National Convention from New York [was] over, and another TV talk show had begun." "Even convention diehards should prepare for some leaden moments ahead," wrote *Rochester Times-Union* critic Lee Krenis. *New York Times* television writer Tony Schwartz noted, ". . . there were about 20 minutes of genuine drama on the first night. . . . Undeterred, the three major television networks devoted more than five hours each to covering the proceedings. The result was soporific television, a show without suspense . . ."

As in Detroit, the sheer presence of the three television networks and the press corps of some 11,500 people came to be seen as a deplorable example of massive media overkill.

"We're smothering the story, we're choking it," said Theodore H. White, whose *Making of the President* series had helped send waves of journalists tracking down the "behind the scenes" campaign stories. "Younger reporters are chasing older reporters who are chasing politicians. There's press congestion." Reporters swapped tales of waiting on line for two hours for floor passes, of being forced to *stay* on the convention floor because they lacked the credentials to leave it, of being denied access to lavatories, of security rules that seemed to have come straight out of Kafka. On Monday, the perforated bottoms of press passes were torn off; to leave the convention and return, a reporter had to obtain a perforated strip from a guard. On Tuesday the strips were ripped off, but reporters could come and go without getting a strip back. By Wednesday, the press passes remained intact. Throughout the convention, every reporter carrying so much as a briefcase had to clear it through an airport X-ray device, while passing through a metal detector. At times, the line of reporters waiting outside Madison Square Garden's 31st Street entrance stretched half a block.

Just as clearly, much of the convention coverage could best be understood as an example of overkill. What nuggets of hard news—in the sense in which that term is generally understood—were present after the rules fight were examined so intensely that they seemed to take on cosmic significance. For seventy-two hours, for example, the key question dominating interviews with Kennedy and Carter partisans was "would Teddy come to the podium Thursday night?" As a symbol of Democratic Party unity, it was a significant question; as the keystone of dozens of interviews with people who could not possibly know the answer, it was absurd.

In another sense, however, the coverage of the Democratic Convention was a kind of triumph. Clearly present throughout the four-day convention, on all three networks, was a story that was, *in fact,* the most significant political story at the convention: the deep-seated divisions and dispirit within the Democratic Party, the loss of ideological optimism, the recognition that neither the party's incumbent President nor its central assumptions were trusted by the core of its constituency. It was a story that emerged despite the continuing attempt by the Carter campaign to put into practice the lessons learned about politics in the age of mass media. No apparatus at a political convention worked more carefully to shape the coverage of its own efforts; none more shrewdly understood the demands of live network coverage; none more faithfully executed a "game plan" to dominate media coverage than did the Carter campaign. And it did not matter. The story of the Democratic Party was played out on national television and in the press because of the unique capacity of a convention to reflect the mood of a political party. The weakness of the incumbent President broke through the efforts to disguise it because the press clearly recognized that weakness, and because the President's inherent inability to rouse the constituencies within his party would throw into bold relief the comparative efforts of Carter and Ted Kennedy to speak to the faithful from the podium.

Whatever the excesses of live, gavel-to-gavel coverage by the television networks—and they were legion—the coverage of the 1980 Democratic Convention demonstrates the weakness of a prevalent assumption about the national nominating conventions: they may be *planned* as carefully scripted television shows, but they have a way of taking on a life of their own, as when Ronald Reagan felt compelled to answer the entreaties of important Republican figures to put Gerald Ford on the ticket, or as when feminist delegates pushed through the "Support-the-ERA-or-no-support-for-your-campaign" platform plank. Conventions in a primary age may lack inherent dramatic appeal, but they always convey important messages about the state of a political movement (as in Detroit, when the very presence of unity around Reagan's nomination demonstrated the futility of attempting to cast Reagan as another Goldwater). They tell the electorate and the press what strategies the candidates will employ (Reagan's attempt to paint the Democrats as the enemy of growth, Carter's attempt to paint Reagan as an enemy of peace). To assume that they are nothing *but* media circuses misses the crucial distinction between what politicians *attempt* to do with organs of mass communications and what they are *able* to do. And to assume that conventions are nothing but anachronistic legacies of a preprimary age misses their capacity to throw into sharp relief deep-seated shiftings of the political tide.

For President Carter, the ten weeks between the end of the primaries and the start of the Democratic Convention was a time of uneasiness. He had ended the primaries—to drift into the beloved sports analogy—as a fighter who has piled up a huge point lead in the early rounds, only to find his opponent pressing for a knockout in the late going. On May 29, only five days before the end of the primaries, Carter finally emerged from the Rose Garden to stage an unimpressive one-day swing through Columbus, Ohio, where he declared "America is turning the tide." It was a theme that opened and closed that day. On June 3, in what had come to be called "Super Tuesday," Kennedy defeated the President in five of the eight primaries, winning a 59–41 margin in New Jersey and a narrower seven-point victory in California.

As he had done in 1976 when he had lost both of those primaries, Carter rode home on Ohio, winning that state's primary by a comfortable twelve points, and appearing live on national television at 9:15 P.M. Eastern time to proclaim victory—and, not so incidentally, to diminish the damage of his New Jersey and California losses.

Despite the near-certainty of his renomination, however, the press coverage of Carter reflected the dilemma his campaign would face. There were, of course, the polls, which had shown a steady decline in Carter's popularity from March right through the summer. By the end of June, Ronald Reagan had overtaken the President in national public opinion polls—Gallup had it 45 percent to 42 percent. An AP-NBC poll, taken among voters leaving the polls in New Jersey and California on June 3, reported that only a *third* of the Democrats voting in those two states were prepared to vote for the President. Encouraged by his late showing and by these expressions of discontent with the President, Kennedy declared his intention to remain in the contest ("Today is the first day of the rest of the campaign," he said after winning in California). The weapon at hand was a move to prevent the adoption of a proposed convention rule—F(3)(c)—that would bind the delegates to vote for the candidate they were committed to on the first ballot, and that would authorize a campaign to remove a recalcitrant delegate from the floor.

Weeks before the convention, the competing forces began their attempts to shape the debate to suit their causes. On the July 7 "MacNeil-Lehrer Report," Kennedy aide Jim Flug called the rule "a radical change from the whole history of the Democratic Party . . . a reversal of all the reform efforts that have been made to open the processes and open up the convention. . . . It is not the time to be reversing 140 years of history of the Democratic Party." Carter aide Richard Moe argued that the Kennedy move was "one of the oldest tricks in politics, and that's an attempt by a defeated candidate to try to change the rules after the game's over . . . [The rule] really represents a continuation and perhaps even a culmination of reform efforts which have taken place in the Democratic Party for the last 12 years." However impossible it was to separate good convention rules from the self-interest of the candidates, the debate helped to insure that Kennedy's efforts would continue to plague the President right up until the convention.

A more serious threat to Carter—and one that provided problems for the President and second thoughts for the press—was the revelation in mid-July, in the midst of the Republican Convention, that the President's brother Billy had signed a consent agreement with the Justice Department acknowledging that he had received $220,000 in gifts and "loans" from the government of Libya to act as an agent on that government's behalf.

Because the story broke in the middle of the Republican Convention, it was at first swamped by the news, or nonnews, coming out of Detroit. In the weeks between the two conventions, however, there was no "hard" political news to cover, and the affair began to achieve front-page and nightly network news status. For one thing, Billy Carter had long been an attractive magnet for press coverage. As a gas station owner in Plains, he had buttressed the Carter image as a "good ole' boy." As a colorful, beer-drinking, profane figure, he had been a source of laughs. As a man determined to cash in on his brother's preeminence with paid endorsements for everything from Billy Beer to auto race attendance to an appearance on "Hee Haw," he had become something of a raffish nether side of the pious, born-again Jimmy. Other escapades of his—relieving himself on an airport runway, telling Jewish groups that objected to his trips to the Middle East to "kiss my ass"—had kept him in the gossip columns and *People* magazine.

The Libyan connection, however, was more sinister—especially for the President. Libya, under the dictatorship of Muammar el-Qaddafi, was considered something close to an outlaw government: publicly celebrating and privately funding groups from the Palestine Liberation Organization to Black September to the Provisional Irish Republican Army, proudly standing as Israel's most virulent enemy. The concept of the President's brother being promised as much as $500,000 for unspecified services suggested an attempt by a hostile foreign government to buy its way into influence with the First Family.

Moreover, a White House statement of July 22, which became a lead or prominent item on all three network evening newscasts, raised other disturbing questions. National Security Advisor Zbigniew Brzezinski's statement that the White House had tried to use Billy to enlist Libyan aide in freeing the American hostages in Iran raised questions about whether the White House, in the words of CBS's Fred Graham, "seemed to bolster Billy's image" in Libya. Further, since Billy had registered as a foreign agent just after the Justice Department had learned of his loan, the question of possible cover-ups and favoritism arose. Inevitably, the press almost instantly seized on the term "Billygate" to label the affair.* On the same day as the release of the White House statement, the Senate Judiciary Subcommittee appointed a special subcommittee to investigate the affair.

Facing this political threat, the White House demonstrated how well they had learned the lessons of Watergate. It had become a cliche in the years after Watergate to observe that it was the Presidential cover-up, more than the break-in itself, that had doomed Nixon. The original decision to lie about White House and campaign involvement had poisoned the press and the country, leaving Nixon helpless when the extent of his dishonesty had become clear.

To make the distinction between Nixon and Carter compelling, the President held a nationally televised news conference on August 4, in prime time, in which he skillfully diffused the impact of "Billygate." Two key questions were facing the President: his brother's alliance with the Libyans, and Attorney General Benjamin Civiletti's

---

* One of the enduring consequences of the Watergate scandal, which drove Richard Nixon from the White House, was to make the suffix "gate" a shorthand term for any scandal. The freespending ways of Korean lobbyist Tongsun Park became "Koreagate"; the vagaries of Bert Lance, Carter's original director of the Office of Management and Budget, who was forced from his post in the summer of 1977, became "Lancegate."

belated admission—after first denying he had mentioned the affair at all to the President—that he had held a "brief, informal" exchange with the President in which he had observed that it had been "foolish" for Billy not to register. This last admission was especially worrisome, because it raised at least the possibility that the President had somehow tipped off brother Billy to register quickly because the Justice Department was closing in.

The President, proclaiming that "integrity has been and will continue to be a cornerstone of my administration," flatly asserted that "neither I nor any member of my administration has violated the law." He acknowledged the possibility of "bad judgment" in involving Billy with attempts to get Libyan help in freeing the hostages, but generally moved to divorce his brother from any hint of White House influence.

"He is a colorful personality," the President said with a small smile. "We are personally close. I love him and he loves me. Billy is extremely independent. On occasion, he has said, 'I don't tell Jimmy how to run the country, and he doesn't tell me how to run my life.' " The President then announced a new rule, which would forbid anyone in the Executive Branch from dealing with the President's family "under any circumstances that create either the reality or the appearance of improper favor or influence."

The press response to Carter's prime-time defense was highly favorable. *Time* magazine reflected the media consensus when it reported that the press conference "did persuade millions of television viewers that there was nothing illegal or unethical in the way he had handled the affair of Billy and his Libyan friends." "NBC Nightly News" reported the next evening (August 5) that White House and Carter campaign aides received an "overwhelmingly favorable reaction to the President's explanation," and surveyed delegates who reported similar responses. "I think he turned the corner tonight on the whole issue of Billy," said Iowa State Chairman Ed Campbell. And within the press, there was a sense that the rush to judgment (as *Newsweek* called it) had not been fair to the President. James J. Kilpatrick, no friend of Carter's politically, had written even before Carter's televised explanation that "the catamounts of the press are after Brother Jimmy, and their self-righteous rectitude is showing. There is a conscious or subconscious desire to demonstrate that the press can be just as rough on Democrat Jimmy Carter as it was rough on Republican Richard Nixon [but] the equation will not compute."

The success of the White House strategy in the affair of the First Brother, however, was only a small hint of what was planned for the Democratic Convention. And here it is instructive—if repetitive—to look again at how the political realities of 1980 limited even so powerful a figure as an incumbent President of the United States in plotting the media strategy at a convention.

The defusing of "Billygate" had taken much of the steam out of the push toward an "open convention." Without a devastating scandal clouding the fall campaign, Carter had a comfortable margin of delegates committed to him on the first ballot; this despite the endorsement of the "open convention" by prominent Democrats such as New York Governor Hugh Carey, Senate Majority Leader Robert Byrd, and Washington lawyer Edward Bennett Williams, and despite polls showing that most Democrats favored such a rule (*Newsweek*'s Gallup poll reported a 55–38 majority among Democratic voters against the binding rule F(3)(c)). In this fight, as he had been throughout the primaries, Carter's strongest "ally" was his opponent, Ted Kennedy. As long as Kennedy remained in the race, the "open convention" gambit looked like a Kennedy ploy. Since his own willingness to release his delegates was a political maneuver by a trailing candidate, the push lacked that sense of detached principle that might have beckoned Carter delegates to such a call.

Thus, the renomination of Carter was *not* the critical goal for the Carter campaign. It was, rather, to use the convention to begin making the strongest possible case for the President against Ronald Reagan in the fall. That case would be, not the right of President Carter to a second term based on his record, but the necessity of his reelection to avoid turning the country over to a dangerously unfit opponent. The convention, then, was a staging area to argue over and over that 1980 would present Americans with "stark differences" between Carter and Reagan; and that those differences placed Reagan beyond the pale of acceptability.

Even before the convention opened, representatives of the President issued a joint statement with Kennedy negotiators declaring that "whatever differences we may have, they pale in comparison to our common differences with the Republicans and their nominee." And as delegates gathered in New York City, Carter's campaign began an intense effort to promote this theme by using its supporters to flood the three television networks. Carter media chief Gerald Rafshoon and his aides, camped in a trailer under the Madison Square Garden rotunda, began watching all three networks continuously; each time a pro-Kennedy or anti-Carter spokesman got air time, a figure friendly to the President was dispatched onto the floor or into a network anchor booth. Jody Powell, Walter Mondale, Robert Strauss, Anne Wexler, Chip Carter, First Mother Lillian were part of some 300 Carter surrogates who would be made available to the networks to insure that the "stark differences" theme would win the biggest possible exposure. As one Carter aide told *New Yorker* correspondent Elizabeth Drew, "More time and energy have gone into the massive scheduling and press operation than into the floor fights. We haven't talked about it much—but we're going to take the networks for a ride."

The intentions of the Carter campaign became clearer as the week progressed. Looking at what the President's allies were saying—on network news shows and during the convention—demonstrates how convinced the White House was that the convention could be used to lay out the case against Reagan, even in the midst of a divided convention about to renominate a clearly unpopular incumbent.

On Monday, August 11, the opening day of the convention, Vice-President Mondale appeared on the NBC "Today" show. Asked about the persistence of Senator Kennedy, Mondale replied, "I think what really counts is whether we come out of this convention united, or we're united as soon as possible. [Kennedy] knows that Reagan's policies would repeal everything that we've stood for all of these years . . ." On the same day's CBS "Morning" program, Mondale said, "There's no disagreement between us and Senator Kennedy about the objectives we want in this society. . . . On the other hand, Mr. Reagan classically collides with everything that the senator and the rest of us have believed in and fought for all of our lives. . . ."

On Tuesday, after Carter's forces won the rules fight and Kennedy officially withdrew from the race, White House Chief of Staff Jack Watson, appearing on the "Today" show, offered his version of the "stark differences" theme.

"We have," he said, "to contrast what the President's positions are, and the actions he's taken, and his decisions, his position, his vision for the next four years with that of Mr. Reagan and the Republicans. The differences between those two visions and the positions of the two men and the two parties are profound. I think they are as profound as any differences between the two major political party candidates for the President in your and my lifetime."

A few moments later, Watson was joined by Hamilton Jordan, Carter's key political strategist, who argued that "once this party and its candidates present to the American people a vision of this country's future and where this party would take our country, I think the differences between the parties, their platforms, and the candidates will be sharp. . . ."

One could almost see Pat Caddell's poll results in the similarity of the responses ("People say the President has no vision for the future . . . we must remind them, as we did with Kennedy, that it's not a choice between Carter and perfection but between Carter and somebody else . . . remind people that Reagan is a Republican, and we're the Democrats"). And Tuesday night, the insistence on the "stark differences" theme grew even greater as Kennedy demonstrated once again how the "anachronistic" national convention and the "anachronistic," pretelevision device of the speech can still combine to produce a political explosion.

The excuse for Tuesday night's appearance at the convention by

Kennedy was the debate on four unresolved economic planks in the Democratic Party platform: endorsement of wage-price controls, a $12 billion jobs program, and two pledges never to make unemployment the price of controlling inflation or federal spending. Kennedy had decided to appear while still a candidate—it would have been the first such appearance since William Jennings Bryan had done it in 1896—but his appearance now, having withdrawn his name from consideration, was neither a plea for votes nor a part of any specific debate. It was a chance for Kennedy to demonstrate that he was something more than the incoherent stumbler who had careened his way into a Presidential campaign nine months earlier, a chance to demonstrate a sense of class. It was also a chance to reaffirm the old-time gospel of the Democratic Party. Jimmy Carter had come onto the national stage four years earlier as the consummate outsider, pledging reluctant fealty to the Democratic tradition, attacking the bureaucracy, red tape, and spending excesses of Washington with the fervor of a Young Republican. Now, Kennedy was preparing to demonstrate that the full-throated liberalism, which had come under such attack in the last decade, still had the power to electrify at least the party that had given it birth. In so doing, he posed a major political dilemma for Carter's media strategy at the convention.

The speech was instantly recognized as the best Kennedy had ever given; one of the best speeches in recent convention history. It touched on the specific platform debate only casually, calling "the commitment of the Democratic Party to economic justice" the "cause that brought me into the campaign and that sustained me for nine months across a hundred thousand miles . . ." and asking the party to "pledge that there will be jobs for all who are out of work . . . we will not compromise on the issue of jobs."

The main thrust of the speech combined a skillful political attack on Ronald Reagan with a ringing defense of idealistic liberalism. The attack on Reagan wove old statements by the Republican nominee into a litany that derided Reagan's attempt to appeal to the Democratic Party's constituency (". . . that nominee is no friend of labor . . . that nominee is no friend of this city and our great urban centers . . . that nominee is no friend of the senior citizens of this nation," and finally, ". . . that nominee, whose name is Ronald Reagan, has no right to quote Franklin Delano Roosevelt!"). The defense of the party's efforts sought to blend recognition of political reality with a reassertion of old truths. ("It is surely correct that we cannot solve problems by throwing money at them. But it is also correct that we dare not throw out our national problems on a scrapheap of indifference. The poor may be out of political fashion, but they are not without human needs. The middle class may be angry, but they have not lost the dream that all Americans can advance together.")

After taking the audience through a list of causes, from the Equal Rights Amendment to national health insurance to full employment, Kennedy ended his speech with a moving, if not entirely accurate, recollection of his campaign journeys. "I have listened," he said, "to Kenny DeBois, a glass blower in Charleston, West Virginia, who had ten children to support but has lost his job after 35 years . . . [he had gotten a new and better-paying job] . . . I have listened to the Tractor family, who farm in Iowa, and who wonder whether they can pass the good life and the good earth on to their children [the Tractors were in fact doing quite well] . . ."

"For me," Kennedy concluded, "a few hours ago, this campaign came to an end. For all those whose cares have been our concern, the work goes on, the cause endures, the hope still lives, and the dream shall never die."

Effective as the speech was, it was given added power by the way television covered the speech; indeed, as they cover every important political speech. The television camera (which is to say, the people in the control rooms who call up the pictures to be seen) is impatient with "talking heads." To give visual variety to the speech, those in the control rooms move their cameras through the hall, calling up shots of delegates, celebrities, and other members of the audience. Often, this can produce a devastating indictment of the power of a speaker, as it did Monday night when Congressman Morris Udall, giving an unenthusiastic keynote speech to a hall emptying after the open convention rules fight, was seen addressing a crowd of chatting, yawning, and sleeping delegates. Kennedy's speech, in contrast, *did* grab the audience, and the searching cameras found dozens of moving scenes: a plump black woman staring at her fallen hero, a Kennedy hat on her head and a single tear rolling down her cheek; a young man and woman tearfully embracing each other, both clutching Kennedy posters in their hands; the explosion of cheers, tears, waving fists, and the chants of "We Want Ted!"

The networks clearly recognized what had taken place.

"Wasn't that the best speech you ever heard from Edward Kennedy?" asked NBC's David Brinkley. "What would have happened," he asked, "after this speech if the delegates had been released? No other Democrat could have turned on this hall like Kennedy did tonight."

ABC's Ted Koppel said it "may have been the most forceful, and perhaps even the best speech in his long and distinguished career in the U.S. Senate." And George Will agreed that "it was a good speech for Edward Kennedy," but added "it was a great speech for Ronald Reagan . . . the Los Angeles grandmother who lost her telephone because of inflation didn't lose it under President *Reagan*'s inflation." CBS's Bill Moyers, speaking of the "Kennedy magic," said, "there's no magic to it. It's the power to move people with the human language. It's an old art; it's an honorable art; and it's a neglected art, and a necessary art if you're ever going to bring people into your cause.''

The emotional outpouring left the Carter people with a dilemma. What were all those surrogates lined up by Gerald Rafshoon supposed to say? The answer was to define the frontal attack on the Carter Administration's economic philosophy as a unity speech, and return to the theme that the differences dividing Carter and Kennedy were insignificant compared to the differences between Democrats and Ronald Reagan. A look at the comments by Carter's surrogates throughout Tuesday night illustrates how carefully that campaign sought to send out a single line of commentary.

On ABC, Robert Strauss said Kennedy "made a good Democratic speech, and he took on Governor Reagan, he said the right things. We were pleased with the endorsement of the statement of reunification of the party"—actually, Kennedy had congratulated Carter on his victory and talked of "marching toward a Democratic victory" in 1980— and said Kennedy had made a "positive contribution" toward unity. Richard Moe, Mondale's top aide, said Kennedy "obviously brought a degree of unity to this convention that we haven't had before . . . the mood he's created out there is a very positive one in terms of the message that we, as Democrats together, are sending the country.''

On NBC, Jody Powell called it "a burn-burner of a speech, one everyone could feel good about." Detroit Mayor Coleman Young, one of the President's consistent supporters, said "there's a narrow hair of difference between Kennedy and Carter." On CBS, Pat Caddell said, "It was a great unifying speech to the convention, and [he] called for the party to rally around. And I don't think anybody's holding back for anything that I can see. . . . What I think the speech showed is whatever differences exist inside the Democratic Party, they're minuscule compared to the gulf that exists between the things that all Democrats believe in and Ronald Reagan and the Republican Party." House Majority Leader Jim Wright said, "You know, the choice is Jimmy Carter and the Democrats on the one hand, or Ronald Reagan and the Republicans on the other." The President's mother, Lillian Carter, told Walter Cronkite, "I thought it was an excellent speech. I don't see how he could have lost . . .''

The attempt to cast Kennedy's triumph as a *Democratic* triumph had a more practical impact, one that was captured fully on network television. The Carter forces realized that the emotional fervor sweeping the hall, combined with a more deeply seated conviction among most Democrats for job-creating federal programs and other forms of government intervention, might sweep all of the contested platform planks to victory. Instead, while the cheers for Kennedy continued on and on, Carter and Kennedy forces negotiated a platform agreement.

Tip O'Neill, House Speaker and chairman of the convention, called for a voice vote on the four contested planks: a ludicrous method of taking a vote, since 80 percent of the people in the hall were alternates, guests, reporters, and other people with no right to vote. Within a minute, O'Neill announced that the Kennedy positions on a $12 billion jobs program and the jobs pledges had won, while the wage-price control plank had been defeated.

' "Four hours' work in two minutes," John Chancellor noted wryly. ABC's Ted Koppel noted that "it takes an extraordinary ear" to distinguish the voice votes, but since the arrangement had been agreed to by Carter and Kennedy negotiators, the actual results in terms of decibel level were irrelevant.*

Did the kind words for Kennedy and the platform accommodation on the part of Carter's forces in fact move the convention to a more unified stance? In large measure, no; and the continued coverage of the convention as a dispirited affair demonstrated that when an army of journalists descend on an event, it is not necessarily true that they will miss the point. A strong feminist contingent, for example, pushed through a platform plank—sought by neither Carter nor Kennedy—that cut off Democratic National Committee funds to any candidate who did not support the Equal Rights Amendment. Nothing more clearly illustrated the dangers of a convention dominated by causes rather than party-loyal delegates. For the feminists, the possible injury to Democrats in the South and West—forced to choose between campaign funds and taking on a highly unpopular cause—was irrelevant. The litmus test of what it meant to be a Democrat, which had never been imposed in past elections with respect to such issues as civil rights, the Vietnam War, or any other single issue, was now to be applied to an issue that deeply divided regions of the country. The adoption of this plank was covered extensively on all three networks on Tuesday and Wednesday. Although the platform debates were scheduled out of prime time, and did not receive live coverage (except for the economic planks, which Kennedy and Carter forces agreed would receive prime-time coverage), the meaning of the ERA-or-else plank was spelled out clearly.

More dramatic was the question that gained in force after Tuesday night's triumph by Kennedy: would he come to the podium Thursday night? Would he give Jimmy Carter the picture he wanted in tens of

---

* This agreement also illustrates a dramatic change in convention behavior. No state ever gained recognition from the floor at either convention; so elaborate had the staging requirements of the convention become that unless a chairman knew who was scheduled to speak or to make a motion, he could not possibly pick out floor seekers from the convention floor. The parliamentary process in this sense had become an empty shell.

millions of living rooms Thursday night and on front pages across the country Friday morning? For the Carter campaign, this was a literal concern, one that helped explain the concessions on so many of the platform planks. The press, however, was quite properly using the "will-Teddy-show-up?" question as the starting point for a much broader discussion of what was ailing the Democratic Party.*

This probing went beyond the exposure given, during live convention coverage and during the morning and evening news programs, to the deep divisions over candidate and program—although Carter's campaign could hardly be happy with delegates on the CBS "Morning" program saying of Kennedy "that was a true Democrat we heard tonight," and "we're just waiting for 1984." The probing included CBS analyst Bill Moyers noting that 500 teachers were delegates to the convention and saying that the Democratic Party had become a "federation of constituencies and interest groups." It included columnist Jack Germond saying on Thursday's "Today" show that "I have never seen a convention that had less enthusiasm at the point of nomination than that one"; and NBC's Tom Pettit saying, "There was no joy in Mudville. It was not a joyous occasion"; and columnist David Broder pointing out that "what they seem to think they can do as a substitute [for enthusiasm] is to develop a kind of anti-Reagan posture."

What the television coverage of the Democratic Convention illustrated, then, was the other side of the argument about the pervasive intrusion of the medium of television into the national conventions. Clearly, the extent and the nature of coverage raised serious questions: Why cover an event as if drama would break out at any moment, as if momentous decisions were in the making, when, in fact, there was no drama, and the decisions had been made by primary voters months before the conventions began? Why flood the floor with reporters attempting to ferret out developing news, when there was no news to ferret out, and when the consequence of network TV on the floor was the disruption of the floor itself and the loss of control over the convention by what remained of the national party structure? Why cover a session of a convention when the convention was turning its session into a free film commercial to be broadcast over television? If a na-

---

* In a fine demonstration of the dangers to politicians of ongoing live coverage, CBS and NBC gleefully used on their evening newscasts on Wednesday an exchange between Tip O'Neill and party chairman John White, which had been picked up by live microphones at the rostrum.

"It's my understanding," said White, "that Kennedy . . . will not come unless the President invites him himself."

"Hey, listen," O'Neill said a moment later. "He's going to be here . . . [but] the President's got to call him personally."

tional political campaign was expending most of its energy moving surrogates around the hall in an effort to dominate television coverage, then what was television doing there in the first place?

All reasonable questions. And yet, the very enormity of the time given over by the networks to the convention forced them into other kinds of coverage. Beyond the brief historical snippets, there were essays comparing President Carter's record—on the economy, national defense, and other issues—with his 1976 promises; there were Republican responses on NBC, and a mixture of conservative and liberal analysts on CBS and ABC, and, above all, there was a filter between the rhetoric of the convention and the audience. To aficionados of conventions, this filter was undoubtedly intrusive; but it was also a limit on the ability of a campaign to force media coverage into a preset mold. The sins of network television may be many, but they do not include passivity or credulity. Jimmy Carter had a record; it had not convinced most American voters yet that he had earned a second term; his own party was divided over whether he should be its nominee and what it should offer to the electorate. And these liabilities were laid out—in interviews, reporting, and analysis—despite the most earnest attempt by the Carter campaign to paint the convention as the start of a unified crusade to save the nation from Ronald Reagan.

The most telling illustration of the interplay between the campaign, the coverage, and reality came Thursday night, when Carter and Mondale gave their acceptance speeches. The Carter campaign fully understood that Kennedy's triumphant speech Tuesday night had posed an enormous challenge to Carter, whose ability to move a large crowd with rhetoric had never been his strong suit as President or as candidate—the one exception being a speech he delivered at the dedication of the Kennedy library in October of 1979, when he bested the soon-to-declare Ted Kennedy on his own home ground. In a version of the traditional move by primary candidates to lower expectations about the speech, Carter aides briefed network correspondents and reporters *not* to expect an emotionally compelling acceptance speech by Carter—while doing everything possible to insure a rousing reception. The effort was captured well by ABC's Sam Donaldson, reporting from the floor just before Thursday night's session.

". . . the White House speaker will say that the President does not intend to draw a lot of applause," Donaldson said. "He wants people to think, not applaud. But . . . look at this credential . . . at one time the convention might have gone five days, so they printed up a fifth day credential. You find them all over the floor tonight. How did they get here? Well, the Carter people have given out these fifth day credentials like there's no tomorrow. And they have sent people on this floor. Perhaps they sent them here to think, but I bet they sent them here to applaud."

NBC's Garrick Utley and CBS's Bob Schieffer both described the convention floor as "gridlocked"—stealing a phrase from urban traffic administrators to describe the ultimate traffic jam—and Schieffer noted that "the only way anyone's going to walk out of here is if someone greases 'em up"—this last a reference to public announcements by such anti-Carter delegates as machinist president William Wimpisinger that he would lead a walkout when the President rose to speak. In part, then, the papering of the house was designed to avoid any embarrassing TV shots of a not-quite-full arena, and to make it impossible for any dissident to stage a dramatic walkout. As we shall see, the ploy may have backfired.

The acceptance speeches were divided up between raw meat and Presidential solemnity. Vice-President Mondale, who remained reasonably popular with Kennedy partisans, served up the red meat by taking a clue from his mentor, the late Vice-President Hubert Humphrey, who had ridiculed Senator Barry Goldwater in his 1964 Vice-Presidential acceptance speech by listing cause after cause endorsed by "most Democrats and most Republicans," and then adding after each one "but not Senator Goldwater!" By the end of his speech, delegates to that convention were shouting right along with him. In his 1980 version, Mondale declared that "most Americans, indeed most Republicans, believe that the Constitution of the United States should incorporate an Equal Rights Amendment. . . . but not Ronald Reagan. . . . Most Americans believe that workers' health and safety should be protected on the job by federal law. But not Ronald Reagan. . . . Most Americans believe we need energy conservation to cut our dependence on foreign oil. But not Ronald Reagan!" By this time the audience, most of it, was joining in, shouting, "but not Ronald Reagan!"

Then, borrowing some of the quotes of Reagan that Ted Kennedy had used two nights earlier, Mondale asked, "What kind of person would try to wipe out every program since Roosevelt? Well, he'd have to be a person who believes, and I quote, 'fascism was really the basis for the New Deal.' Now who would say something like that? Ronald Reagan would." A litany of Reagan's woollier statements followed, with the crowd chanting each time, "Ronald Reagan would," when asked, "Who would say such a thing?"

Then the hall went dark, and Gerald Rafshoon's film about Carter was shown. The film was a mixture of Democratic Party figures, such as San Francisco Mayor Dianne Feinstein, former Secretary of State Cyrus Vance, House Speaker Tip O'Neill, and others, praising Carter, along with an attempt to link Carter to other Presidents who had been maligned in their lifetimes.

". . . No President has been entirely beloved in his own time," the narrator said. "Putting them down is one of the favorite pastimes of American politics. Of Franklin D. Roosevelt, it was said he is a liar, a thief, a man given to bursts of maniacal laughter. . . . Of Lincoln's Gettysburg Address, it was written, 'This is a flat, dishwatery utterance.' " The film ended with a montage of great Presidents, as the announcer explained that a perfect President "would have the military genius of George Washington, the common touch of Andrew Jackson . . . the zest and shrewdness of FDR, the rich humor of Jack Kennedy, the feistiness of Truman, and the solidity of Ike." While the words explained that no mortal could achieve such greatness, the visual images of past leaders were all designed to link Carter with his more distinguished predecessors. Then the narrator said, "Ladies and gentlemen, the President of the United States," and the lights came up on Jimmy Carter. Four years earlier, in a dramatic demonstration of his populist roots, he had entered the hall and strode the length of the floor. Now he appeared behind the Presidential seal.

This was without question the most important speech of Jimmy Carter's career. Here there was no way to manipulate the medium of television, no way to convey with images or gestures or symbols such as an empty garment bag or a peanut a host of personal characteristics. It was Jimmy Carter, his record, his intentions, face-to-face with America. He began by invoking the legacy of the party, glancing briefly over to his right as a Communist Workers' Party member set off a string of firecrackers that threw a brief but chilling scare into the hall. Perhaps it was this distraction that caused his first problem, or perhaps it was an improperly functioning TelePrompTer; whatever the cause, as Carter got to the last departed leader, he said that Democrats were "the party of a great man who should have been President, who would have been one of the greatest Presidents in history, Hubert Horatio Hornblower—Humphrey!" So crowded was the hall, so difficult to hear were Carter's words, that many delegates, and many members of the press covering the speech from the print press section hard by the rotunda, did not hear the slip. On television, it was unmistakable.

After pleading for Ted Kennedy's support and proclaiming that "my thoughts and my prayers for our hostages in Iran are as though they were my own sons and daughters," Carter began laying out the first of the themes that were to dominate his fall campaign: the burden of the Oval Office. Designed to establish the point that the Presidency was no place for a seventy-year-old simpleton, Carter's message was that "the life of every human being on earth can depend on the experience and judgment and vigilance of the person in the Oval Office . . . and the power is greatest exactly where the stakes are highest, in matters of war and peace."

Carter then moved to the "stark differences" theme which had already been in the air throughout the convention. The election, he said, is "a stark choice between two men, two parties, two sharply different pictures of what America is and what the world is. But it's more than that. It's a choice between two futures." Reagan, Carter said, represented a "fantasy America [where] inner-city people and farm workers and laborers do not exist. Women, like children, ought to be seen but not heard. . . . It's a make-believe world, a world of good guys and bad guys, where some politicians shoot first and ask questions later. No hard choices, no sacrifices, no tough decisions. It sounds too good to be true. And it is."

The attack gave way to a defense of Carter's own record, and here the speech began to unravel. Carter talked about strengthening America's defense, reversing the spending cuts of the Republicans, and then said of his response to the Soviet invasion of Afghanistan, "I suspended some grain sales to the Soviet Union. I called for draft registration. . . ." And boos were heard loudly and clearly through the hall, though Carter partisans quickly overcame them with cheers. For what seemed like endless moments, Carter delved into the kind of language that had haunted him throughout his term of office: an engineer's language, flat, often complex ("with our new energy policy now in place . . . we will use American resources, American technology"; "our economic renewal program will . . . lower inflation, better productivity, revitalize American industry, [provide] energy security and jobs"; "industry will provide the convenience of futuristic computer technology and communications to serve millions of American homes and offices and factories"). It was the language of an industrial public relations film strip for a high school, not a summons to a party in distress.

The speech was not only too long and too prolix, but it was delivered to a hall filled to more than capacity in an effort to provide a rip-roaring response to the President. Instead, the heat, the noise, and the bodies made it almost impossible for delegates and guests to hear the speech or to respond with any enthusiasm. Carter finished his speech with what was supposed to be uplifting rhetoric ("The choice between the two futures could not be more clear. If we succumb to a dream world, then we'll wake up to a nightmare. But if we start with reality and fight to make our dreams a reality, then Americans will have a good life, a life of meaning and purpose and a nation that's strong and secure"), then waited for the balloons to fall and for Kennedy to show up.

The balloons did not fall. As delegates—and more important, the television commentators, from their perches near the Garden roof—began to point and note the embarrassment, workers climbed into the rigging trying to shake the balloons free. They simply would not fall, dribbling down to the floor in unhappy clusters of two and three. (The next morning, David Hartman would free the balloons on "Good Morning, America.")

More important to the Carter campaign and the commentators, Kennedy was nowhere to be seen. The demonstration began running out of steam within minutes, and at the podium, more and more Democrats with fewer and fewer credentials were being introduced—one of them, National Security Advisor Brzezinski, drawing a huge round of boos.

What happened was another instance of media wizards outsmarting themselves. The Kennedy and Carter camps agreed that the senator should not leave his hotel for the convention in the middle of Carter's acceptance speech because the networks would have cut to that picture, thus distracting from the President's remarks. Nor did the Carter camp want Kennedy to leave during the film, since they wanted this free commercial carried without interruption on the networks. Since Kennedy was unwilling to sit in a holding room for two hours, the decision was made to have Kennedy leave his hotel as soon as Carter's speech ended; surely the demonstration for the President would last ten minutes. The problem was that there was no demonstration for Carter that lasted anywhere near that length of time, and Kennedy's motorcade was stuck in traffic. Thus, as Robert Strauss kept dispatching cabinet members, White House staff members, and various mayors, Kennedy's entourage was still making its way to the arena.

When Kennedy finally did arrive and mount the podium, the "celebration" appeared more like the first meeting of two heavyweight fighters. Kennedy, his face grim, shook hands briefly with Carter (he was studiously ignored by Rosalynn), then stood to one side of the rostrum and flashed a clenched fist at the audience, while Carter strode after him for another handshake.

"What we're still lacking," said ABC's Ted Koppel, "is that classical political photograph of the two men, arm in arm, holding their hands up together."

"I think, Ted," said Frank Reynolds, "we have seen broader smiles on the face of Ted Kennedy."

"Kennedy didn't look happy to me," said NBC's John Chancellor. Commentator Theodore White said, "Kennedy appeared for the minimum amount of time that would be courteous, and then disappeared with a seigneurial wave of his hand like a grand lord tossing a tip to the coachman."

"Senator Kennedy leaves the stand, seems quite sober, unsmiling," reported CBS's Walter Cronkite. "There will be no pictures in tomorrow morning's paper, and none for posterity of Ted Kennedy holding Jimmy Carter's hand aloft in the usual unity and victory salute.

. . . One has to say that it was a fairly cold reception on the stand, and a cold one by Teddy Kennedy. There was no embracing, and no arms around each other's shoulders; a handshake and that was just about it."

Thus, in their all-out effort to plan a minute-by-minute scenario that would provide television and the national press with a symbol of unity, the Carter campaign managed to produce a moment of media drama that had all of the commentators pointedly noting the lack of enthusiasm. Indeed, there was more enthusiasm for the celebration of Walter Cronkite's valedictory as convention anchor, after twenty-eight years, than for the President of the United States. On the convention floor stood a knot of delegates waving "Goodbye, Walter" signs, and Charles Kuralt, unbeknownst to Cronkite, prepared a tribute to the anchorman that included the presentation of Cronkite's first microphone. On ABC, the unlikely image of the CBS anchor booth was televised, as Frank Reynolds tipped his hat to "Walter Cronkite of CBS, who has been an ornament to our profession for a long time . . . we're just happy to have him on our screen and wish him very, very good luck."

For Carter and his campaign, the Democratic Convention was an opportunity to flood the media with their own spokesmen, so that the campaign might be redefined as the President and his aides saw it. For the television networks, the clash between Carter and Kennedy opened the door to a focus which, at least in part, remained fixed on the political liability of a party at war with itself. That reality was captured and transmitted in impressive measure by the networks. Whether it justifies live coverage of such an event for so long is another question. But the fact is that by the time the conventions were over, the media had a clear focus on the campaign, in which an eloquent spokesman for a united party was facing an unpopular and not very prepossessing President of a divided and confused party. It is a measure of the resources of contemporary journalism that this story managed to become so confused and unclear the longer the general election campaign lasted.

xi   Anderson
and the Media, II:
...And No Farther

For a time in the spring of 1980, the possibility of a precedent-shattering election seemed to be in the making. Aided by a growing national mood of dissatisfaction with the apparent nominations of President Carter and Ronald Reagan, Congressman John Anderson's move toward an independent candidacy was winning the approval of remarkably high numbers of Americans. If the polls were right, and if they, in fact, were measuring the future intentions of likely voters, Anderson —without benefit of political party, ideological cause, or regional base —was in a position to affect materially the outcome of the Presidential election, and perhaps even win the Presidency.

A Gallup Poll taken at the end of April showed Anderson with 19 percent of the vote against 38 percent for Carter and 35 percent for Reagan. A California survey by the *Los Angeles Times* gave Anderson 27 percent of the vote, only one point less than Carter's level (Reagan had 40 percent). The ABC-Lou Harris poll had it Reagan 39, Carter 33, and Anderson 23. But when Harris asked, "Now suppose the polls showed that John Anderson had a real chance of winning the Presidential election in November," the numbers produced a genuine three-way race: Reagan 35, Carter 31, Anderson 29. The question stirred criticism from other pollsters, who argued that the question created an artificial bandwagon effect, but the level of Anderson's support was clearly high, already approaching the 1912 showing of Theodore Roosevelt, whose Progressive "Bull Moose" campaign produced 27 percent of the popular vote—and Teddy Roosevelt had been a former President. By mid-May, Anderson was running at 21 percent in the Gallup poll, 23 percent in the Yankelovich-*Time* magazine poll, and— when the "chance to win the election" question was asked—28 percent in a Roger Seasonwein poll, only one point behind Carter and two points behind Reagan.

Whatever the numbers, pollsters and the press alike were taking Anderson seriously. In retrospect, perhaps the high-water mark of

1980 for the Illinois congressman came on June 22, when a front page *Washington Post* story reported, "Anderson Could Win, Pollsters Agree." The pollsters interviewed agreed that Anderson's success "revealed a high level of discontent with the likely Democratic and Republican nominees," and would fade "unless Anderson can develop strong, positive support for his candidacy." But in a year universally described as reflecting "volatile" voting behavior, Republican pollster Robert Teeter pointed to a possibility, "He's a tinderbox, and if someone should drop a match on him . . ." Further, some well-known big guns were lining up behind Anderson. He had media advisor David Garth to plan commercials and media strategy;* he had lawyer Mitchell Rogovin to help him fight the problems of ballot access; he had had access to the "Malibu Mafia," a collection of affluent California liberals such as television producer Norman Lear and philanthropist Stanley Scheinbaum, to help in the fund-raising efforts.

What, then, accounts for John Anderson's almost unbroken slide from potential President to possible "spoiler" to a candidate who did not carry a single state, won seven percent of the popular vote—barely half the level reached by George Wallace in 1968—and who all but disappeared as a factor in the outcome of the election? Specifically, if the media attention given to John Anderson during the Republican primaries elevated him to national recognition—which it almost certainly did—then was Anderson's fall the result of the media? Or did it lie in more fundamental factors over which the political press had little sway? Although it is clear that a more critical, skeptical view of John Anderson became a regular part of press coverage, it was no more critical or skeptical than that afforded any contender moving into a general election. Much more significant was the failure of the Anderson campaign to overcome 120 years worth of political custom, and the structural, financial, and institutional odds against any independent candidacy. John Anderson's run for the Presidency was made in the face of the overwhelming conventional wisdom that argues that there are simply too many hurdles between a man without a party and the White House. In this case, the conventional wisdom turned out to be right.

In the press coverage of any Presidential candidate who emerges from relative obscurity, there is a consistent pattern of stories from "who's he?" to "he can't win" to "hey, look at him go!" to "hold on a minute." George McGovern had gone through those stages in 1972; so had Jimmy Carter in 1976. Although Anderson's "winner phase" had, in fact, only lasted through the afterglow of his strong March 4

* In the British parliamentary tradition of "declaring my interest," it should be noted that I worked for seven years for David Garth and remain a good friend.

showings in New England, the move toward an independent run in the spring had kept a kind of "momentum" coverage building. Some conservative writers had zeroed in on the emerging liberal hero early—Evans and Novak and George Will had taken sharply critical shots at him in March—and had begun to raise questions about his retreat from past commitments to nuclear power and Kemp-Roth tax cuts. Now the media—particularly the writing press, with the time and space to explore a candidate's past—began to raise these same questions.

As early as April 27, the *Washington Post* gave national circulation to a report, first broached in the *Detroit News,* that the Congressman had three times sponsored a constitutional amendment recognizing "the authority and law of Jesus Christ, savior and ruler of nations, through whom are bestowed the blessings of almighty God." Other parts of the amendment would have prohibited the establishment of a state religion and protected non-Christians from an oath of allegiance, but it was the first genuine embarrassment to Anderson—particularly given his levels of support among academics, Jews, and the more secularly inclined of voters. All Anderson could say was "it was a dumb thing to do" and repudiate it.

There was no way, however, for Anderson to remain a self-created candidate for the Presidency. With the Carter campaign regarding him as a potentially fatal threat to preserving the Democratic base, and with the natural, healthy determination of the press to put the harshest possible spotlight on a potential chief executive, other contradictions began to emerge.

The *New York Times* noted on April 28 that Anderson had shifted dramatically from "orthodox conservatism," citing the "Jesus Christ" constitutional amendment, as well as his opposition to food stamps, Medicare, antipoverty programs, and federal aid to education. Although the piece was a generally sympathetic account of Anderson's claim that "I have matured, I have evolved, I have seen the world change," it also quoted critics who claimed that Anderson simply played to the national press. A June 6 *Wall Street Journal* column pointed to some difficult days ahead in Anderson's attempt to break into the blue-collar vote; he had in the past voted to deny food stamps to strikers, against increases in the minimum wage, against labor law reforms making union organizing easier. And it pointed to his past support for nuclear power as a trouble spot in his appeal to environmentalists. More significantly, as it turned out, was writer Dennis Farney's criticism that Anderson had not "outlined a political philosophy, a grand approach to government, that integrates the many individual positions he has taken and helps him to defend them."

Moreover, the press had by 1980 come to look critically on its most recent performance in evaluating suddenly prominent political unknowns—specifically, Jimmy Carter, whose 1976 role had been something of an empty vessel into which journalists could pour whatever brew they wished, from rural populist to evangelical Christian to hard-headed engineer. There was no predisposition to accept another version of the Unknown Candidate; so it was no compliment when *Newsweek,* in a June 9 cover story characterizing Anderson as a "wild card," wrote, "he strikes some as Jimmy Carter without the smile; they share a certitude about their own convictions, an air of higher morality expressing them and a manifest unease at the lower arts of coalition-building, horse-trading, and flesh-pressing."

Eventually, the skepticism in print found its way into television. In a long take-out on the "NBC Nightly News" of July 3, Bob Jamieson took a hard look at Anderson's changes of heart, with a piece that began, "The more you know about John B. Anderson, the more confused you become about just what he is." The piece began by contrasting Anderson's warm reception from "the liberal smart set" with the past record of "the man who voted against Medicare, food stamps, the war on poverty, and national health insurance," and showed college students applauding "the same John B. Anderson who in the past voted for the neutron bomb, the B–1 bomber, who helped fund the Vietnam War until 1974." Anderson acknowledged his changes of heart, but the piece concluded on a skeptical note, with Jamieson asking "whether Anderson's constituency, attracted by his current position, put off by the choice between Ronald Reagan and President Carter, will be satisfied with the record of Anderson's past."

This kind of scrutiny might serve to shake up some liberals, but it was hardly the stuff of which mass desertions are made, especially given the growing gulf between the liberal wing of the Democratic Party, still welded to the lost cause of Edward Kennedy's campaign. Further, Anderson's long-shot hope for the White House could not hinge on emerging as the pure white hope of liberalism, since that cause was hardly the trendy mainstream of 1980. Rather, Anderson's appeal was broad and thin: he was *not* Reagan, he was *not* Carter, and he was willing to level with the American people. It was this impression that was damaged in July by three separate decisions—all of which were aimed primarily at keeping his candidacy alive in the media, all of which brought down heavy criticism aimed at his most valuable asset: his candor and straightforwardness.

Summer would pose a dangerous eight weeks for Anderson. Apart from the struggle to get on fifty-one state and district ballots, apart from the struggle to raise money without any public financing, Anderson had to maintain a presence during the national nominating conventions. Even with little or no suspense in the outcome, each convention turned the focus of political attention toward one political party for ten days to two weeks (counting preconvention coverage). And as surely as nominated candidates usually benefit from this coverage, so a candidate without a party or a convention would be likely to slip in the polls. And this would produce a Catch–22 nightmare for Anderson. Already, in the spring, the argument against his campaign was that he couldn't win. Unless he could maintain visibility and push his standings in the polls to the mid-twenties by August, there would be no flood of money, no flow of support from politically powerful people from either party, no chance to overcome the inevitable movement back to the two parties as summer turned to fall. The scenario for a winning Anderson campaign was clear: a weak President Carter stumbles his way to renomination; collapses further in the polls against Reagan as Anderson takes second place; and Anderson's independent campaign becomes the only alternative to Reagan, without any of the vulnerability of a weak incumbent tied to big-spending liberalism. To make it work, Anderson would have to survive the summer.

The first key decision to maintain the candidate's visibility in the press was to launch an eleven-day trip to Europe and the Middle East in an effort to strengthen Anderson's foreign policy credentials. The trip coincided with the Republican National Convention, on the theory that viewers watching so much news about so unsuspenseful an event would find Anderson a welcome alternative. But the candidate's staff coupled this trip with a second decision: to get Anderson free television time by providing political commentary for NBC's "Today" show. It was a remarkably foolish idea, since prospective Presidents of the United States do not cut deals with one network's morning news show. Furthermore, it threw an unsavory light on the entire foreign trip, and television's coverage was decidedly chilly, focusing not on what Anderson did or said, but on the political motive for the trip.

On July 10, on the "CBS Evening News," Bob McNamara offered this account of Anderson's trip to a settlement on Israel's West Bank:

"This is the image John Anderson's media strategists are trying to project: Anderson with a top Israeli general on a West Bank mountain; the candidate getting foreign policy schooling through his own eyes. . . . Portrayed as a fact-finding mission, Anderson's foreign trip is still an image-building campaign tour, designed to show him with famous faces and orchestrated to sell credibility, particularly to Jewish voters, who might see Anderson visiting Israel's memorial to the victims of the holocaust, a sight he has seen before without cameras. A strong supporter of Israel and its defense policies, Anderson has told Israelis what they like to hear about the PLO joining the peace process."

In one news report, viewers had seen "Mr. Integrity" as a media manipulator, who poses for pictures to gain votes, and who—in direct contradiction of his earlier stance—tells an interest group what they like to hear.

That same kind of cynicism greeted Anderson at the end of his trip, on a July 20 piece on the "NBC Nightly News." Bob Jamieson offered these comments:

"They took the pictures on this trip that John Anderson wanted the papers back home to see [meetings with world leaders]; images gathered in the hope they would add credibility to Anderson's independent campaign and get him attention during the Republican convention. . . .

"The meetings . . . took up only five hours of his eleven-day trip. Anderson filled out the rest of his schedule with sightseeing . . . .

"Egyptian newspapers called him a meddler. Newspapers at home accused him of shameless ethnic politicking. Anderson has been on the defensive ever since."

Whatever the trip accomplished in the way of visibility was more than offset by the impression that Anderson had become just another politician. In the words of a second Bob McNamara piece on CBS on July 12, "More and more it's become clear Anderson's new politics look a lot like the old, and the political courage he claimed to have a few months ago has largely been abandoned in favor of saying whatever suits the occasion and the audience wherever he happens to go."

This notion that Anderson was "just another politician" was reinforced by a third media-based decision by the Anderson campaign. By the end of July, Ted Kennedy had regained much of the luster he had lost in the early days of the primary. Perhaps because the electorate knew he was not going to be nominated, perhaps because President Carter's popularity had again slipped to disastrous levels, it was clear that Kennedy had won the respect, if not the support, of a huge chunk of the Democratic Party constituency; one that Anderson would have to get to have any chance of building a winning coalition. So on July 31, Anderson met with Kennedy in his office on Capitol Hill—and came out with Kennedy to face a huge press corps with what sounded like a promise to pull out of the race if Kennedy could somehow gain the Democratic nomination.

"The majority of the American people are dissatisfied with being limited to a choice between Jimmy Carter and Ronald Reagan in November of this year. Should a different decision emerge out of the Democratic convention in August, it would only be prudent for one like myself, who believes very much in the two-party system, to perhaps consider what my position then would be."

Both Kennedy and Anderson flatly denied any promises of mutual support or of a combined ticket. In fact, the purpose of the meeting, other than to associate Anderson with Kennedy, wasn't very clear at all. On "NBC Nightly News" that evening, John Chancellor called Kennedy and Anderson "the political odd couple of the year." And resident cynic Tom Pettit noted, "We may be seeing something here of political importance. But then again we may only be seeing two candidates trying to use each other on television." The meeting was a severe shock to those moderate Republicans and independents who liked Anderson's candor early in the campaign, but who were in no mood to support a liberal big-spending Democrat. It took Anderson six days of backing and filling before finally stating flatly that he would remain in the race whether or not Kennedy won the nomination.

The impact of these maneuvers was well captured in a *Washington Post* piece on August 9 by Robert Kaiser, who was covering the media and the broader rhythms of the Presidential campaign. "Saint's Halo Slips," was the headline. "Anderson Turns Expedient, Lusts for Bloodbath Among Democrats." Wrote Kaiser, "He spends his time with corporate executives, politicians, special-interest groups, and television interviewers, not college students. . . . He speaks from carefully crafted—and emotionless—prepared texts. He is whisked away from reporters to secret fund-raising efforts and meetings."

It was, in other words, very much like the schedules most Presidential contenders follow, but in Anderson's case, the very drift of his campaign toward conventionality was a desertion of the images that made him an exceptional face in the crowd.

The summer of Anderson's discontent had taken its toll in the poll numbers as well. In most major polls, Anderson's 20 percent—the base from which he had to advance in order to be taken seriously—had been whittled away. A mid-July NBC-AP poll had Anderson at 15 percent; the ABC-Harris poll gave him 18 percent (down from 24 percent in early June); a CBS-*New York Times* poll had Anderson at 13 percent (down from 17 percent a month earlier). *Newsweek*'s poll had Anderson at 17 percent.

Was this decline caused by the media? In part, yes—but the major factor was the dominance of the Republican National Convention in mid-July. The unity, the shower of praise for Ronald Reagan, the impact of a powerful acceptance speech, and the slide of Jimmy Carter had combined to make Reagan—for the moment, at least—a respectable alternative to Carter. His lead in the polls, temporary though it had to be, was enormous: 20 points in the CBS-*Times* poll, 18 points in the *Newsweek* poll, 27 points in the ABC-Harris poll, 31 points in the NBC-AP poll. In a period of unbroken positive coverage of Reagan, there was no room for Anderson to move up. For Anderson to have gained political support, something very different had to have happened at the Republican Convention in Detroit: *a substantial sense of disaffection with the party's nominee.*

In recent political history, three conventions have failed to produce a surge of support for the party's nominee: the Republican convention of 1964 and the Democratic conventions of 1968 and 1972. In both cases, substantial elements within the party demonstrated a refusal to abide by the choice of the party; in both cases a sense of turmoil and confusion clouded the sense of celebration and confidence a nominating convention usually produces. At the Republican Convention in Detroit, however, no such turmoil, no such division was apparent. Except for the forced resignation of Vice-Chairman Mary Crisp, who bolted the convention over the Equal Rights Amendment and abortion issues, the party stayed together, even though the nominee emerged from the ideologically committed conservative wing of the party. No moderate or liberal Republican of any stature at all appeared to denounce the choice as unacceptable. There were no walkouts, no "statements of conscience" by William Milliken or Jacob Javits or Mark Hatfield or Charles Mathias or Lowell Weicker. If John Anderson's intention was to build a "National Unity" campaign from the discontent of the major parties, the Republicans were providing no fuel at all for an Anderson bandwagon.

It is easy to forget the still-critical role of political parties in Presidential elections, because so much has been written and said about the decline of party strength over the last twenty years. This decline is a fact, measured by party identification among the citizenry, or measured by the power of party organizations to deliver votes at national conventions or in primaries and general elections, or measured by the declining strength of political machines to control the machinery of government (excepting Chicago's Democrats, Nassau County's [N.Y.] Republicans, and the state apparatus in Indiana). It is not, however, true to argue that political parties have no role in the process of choosing a President. The electorate, after all, still expects to choose from one of two candidates for the highest office in the land: one Democrat, one Republican. It tends to take very seriously the substantial objections within a party that a nominee may really not be up to the job. If an independent candidate were to be seriously regarded as a potential President, that candidate would need substantial support from within the two-party structure to validate that candidacy. The unified, optimistic Republican Convention certainly provided no support for Anderson.

Among Democrats, the summer provided a similar lack of support, but for a very different reason. As the Democratic Convention approached, those party members disaffected with the President were still battling for a chance to nominate someone other than Carter. Ted Kennedy had more than a third of the delegates in his corner; some substantial figures within the party were calling for an "open convention" to permit delegates to vote as they chose for a candidate, rather than being bound to the primary victors. This had an important adverse consequence for Anderson, since it froze any potential movement toward the independent candidate. By the time Carter's renomination was made official, less than eighty days remained until the general election—and Anderson's inability to mount a serious campaign over the summer, in part because of the Democratic Party's maneuvering, became a reason for anti-Carter Democrats to decide, in the main, to stick with the President rather than rally to the side of John Anderson.

There was one substantial favor done to Anderson by at least one Democrat: President Jimmy Carter. So worried was the White House by Anderson's candidacy, so heavy-handed were its attempts to fight the independent, and so conscious was the press of White House attempts to play fast and loose with the political process, that Carter probably helped Anderson achieve a kind of rehabilitation in the press during the late summer and early fall by switching the focus from Anderson's own campaign manipulations to a "fair play" issue.

As early as June, President Carter had declared flatly that he would not debate John Anderson in the fall, because Anderson was a creation of the press, because the prospect of his election was a "fantasy," and because it would force him, the President, to "debate two Republicans." But this was not the only opposition that the White House was throwing up to Anderson's candidacy. In addition, there were clear indications that on matters such as ballot access and financial support, Anderson would face a fight from the President's campaign.

Access to the Presidential ballot is one of federalism's lasting legacies. Each state has different requirements: signatures on a petition; the holding of a convention attended by a certain number of people. In addition, several states have "sore loser" laws, banning someone who has lost in a primary from running in a general election. By the time John Anderson announced his move toward independence, five states—including the major state of Ohio—had deadlines that had passed for getting on the ballot. In June, reports began surfacing that the Democratic National Committee was prepared to spend almost a quarter of a million dollars to keep Anderson off state ballots. Bob Strauss put the best possible spin on the fight from Carter's point of view, telling the "Today" show on June 23 that "obviously, in these states we feel that the law could be violated, or at least some bizarre interpretation of the law to place Congressman Anderson on the ballot, our regular lawyers for the committee will take a look at it." What this meant was that in states where Anderson looked vulnerable, lawyers hired by state Democratic organizations would attempt to knock the candidate off the ballot. And since the press knew full well that the Carter campaign was heavily involved in such maneuvering, it gave some credibility to a "Fair Play for Anderson" committee, launched in late June, to argue against Democratic attempts to force him off the ballot.

Senator Tom Eagleton called it "bonehead politics. It's going to turn people off." Sixteen other members of Congress, including Senators George McGovern and Adlai Stevenson III joined the effort. Even Senate Majority Leader Robert Byrd was skeptical of the National Committee drive to get Anderson off state ballots, on the theory that Anderson would help increase voter turnout, which, in turn, would help liberal Democrats, many of whom were believed to be in political trouble. The fact that "fair play for Anderson" was a political as much as a moral judgment was obvious; especially since some state Republican officials were as eager to drag Anderson onto the ballot—and thus help Reagan by draining votes away from Carter—as Democrats were to keep him off.*

The perception of political manipulation, however, was very different. Juggling the rules to put a candidate *on* a ballot did not seem nearly so sinister as mobilizing money and lawyers to force a candidate *off* a ballot. The struggle to put Anderson on the ballot in the fifty-one states and districts was probably the story that best helped Anderson retain his "struggling underdog" image during a time when press treatment of the candidate was turning chilly. And by achieving the goal of getting on ballot after ballot—the Anderson campaign would ultimately succeed in all fifty-one fights—a certain sense of momentum was retained throughout the campaign.

The other major favor dealt Anderson by Carter was the President's determination to keep the independent out of the debates; first, by refusing to debate him at all, then by agreeing to debate him only *after* a one-on-one debate with Reagan. As with the ballot fight, but in a much more visible way because of press coverage, it made Anderson's campaign a question of fair treatment for the underdog; more than two-thirds of those asked in September believed that Anderson should be included in the debates. And while Carter succeeded in keeping Anderson out of a three-way debate, and thus helped to reduce the audience by tens of millions for the Baltimore confrontation between Reagan and Anderson, the President paid for his position heavily.

The most intriguing question about the Reagan-Anderson debate —and one that explains much about the power and limits of the media —is why did Anderson's campaign begin to collapse almost as soon as the debate was over? All of the predebate analysis argued, with a good deal of logic, that Anderson would "win" the debate simply by showing up, since a huge prime-time audience would be watching the independent in a "Presidential" setting. Further, the debate came when Anderson seemed to be returning to a level of plausibility as a candidate after the summer of his discontent. On August 24, Anderson

* In Texas, where a "sore loser" law prevents voters in a Presidential primary from signing an independent's ballot petition, the Republican secretary of state ruled that Democrats *could* sign Anderson's petitions, since the Democratic primary was a "straw poll."

named Patrick Lucey as his Vice-Presidential running mate. If not a major-league Democrat, Lucey—two-term governor of Wisconsin, ambassador to Mexico, and a high-ranking supporter of Ted Kennedy —was a respectable candidate, and one whose close ties to labor in the Midwest might help ease the pain of Anderson's antilabor voting record.

On August 30, the National Unity ticket released a 317-page platform, which was widely praised and largely unexamined (Anderson himself said it seemed to bore his audiences), but which helped bolster the sense that Anderson was, in fact, a candidate of ideas. In early September, the Federal Election Commission ruled that, even though Anderson had not formally launched a new party, the National Unity campaign would be treated as a third party for purposes of the campaign finance law: a critical ruling, because it meant that if Anderson got 5 percent of the vote on November 4, he would receive postelection public campaign financing. This meant that large loans could be floated on the near-certainty of repayment. In mid-September, New York State's Liberal Party refused to endorse the Democratic candidate for President for the first time since its founding in 1944, and gave Anderson its Presidential line. Finally, Anderson's showing of 15 percent, taken as an average of four national polls, got him the League of Women Voters' invitation to Baltimore, and a prime-time audience of at least 55 million viewers. The consensus immediately after the debate, among the press and among those polled, was that Anderson had performed well, perhaps a bit better than Reagan.

Yet within a week after the debate, the "Anderson is dead" stories emerged all over again. Reporters noted that the day after the debate, Anderson had received a large and friendly reception from a lunchtime Chicago Loop crowd, but had scheduled a nighttime rally in Philadelphia when the National Football League Eagles were playing at home in a nationally televised game, while a Tuesday rally in Pittsburgh was moved indoors to lessen the appearance of indifference. In a September 27 "CBS Evening News" report, Bob Faw laid heavy emphasis on these portents, "Campus crowds . . . are still large and enthusiastic. Most aren't. The day after the debate, one hall was half empty, and it would have seemed that way the next day, too, if the audience hadn't been moved inside to cramped quarters."

More chilling were findings of pollsters that Anderson had begun to decline again in their standings. Another CBS-*Times* poll, taken after the debate, showed that from a 14 percent level a week before the debate, Anderson had slipped to 9 percent in the days just after the poll.

Why did this happen? Why was the single biggest triumph of Anderson's bid for credibility—his inclusion in a major-league prime-time Presidential confrontation—the beginning of a decline in which more than half of Anderson's support melted away in the forty-four days between the debate and the election?

The first explanation requires an amendment to the idea that debates are nothing but attempts at image crafting. Of course candidates seek to leave a favorable impression with the viewers in a debate; of course they practice thrusts and parries with their campaign aides, in an effort to anticipate questions and frame the answers in a manner most favorable to their cause. It is a first principle of any campaign advisor to remind a candidate that in a political debate, answer the question you want to answer, and make the points you want to make, regardless of what question is being asked.* And reporters and politicians ceaselessly remind each other of the 1960 postdebate finding that among radio listeners, Nixon beat Kennedy, but among those who watched television, the calm and tanned Kennedy beat the haggard, sweating Nixon. (This last point has always sounded much more impressive than it actually is. First, who were the people in 1960 listening to, rather than watching, the debate. Were they disproportionately older than the general populace? More conservative? People in their cars, hence more affluent, hence more Republican? Moreover, important information is often conveyed by what the law calls "demeanor" evidence: how someone looks, acts, moves, uses body language— which is why the rules of legal evidence always require a witness to be produced in person wherever possible. A voter who can see a candidate appearing nervous, shifty-eyed, hesitant, may well have a *better* sense of a candidate than a voter simply listening.)

The voter of 1980, however, was different from his 1960 counterpart. Political debates were nothing new; apart from the Presidential level, they had become commonplace events over the last twenty years in senatorial, gubernatorial, congressional, and municipal elections. The sheer wonder of watching candidates argue in our living rooms was no more dazzling in 1980 than roller derby telecasts would have been. They were exciting when a viewer could be impressed by anything that moved on his television screen. But by 1980 we had become thoroughly used to images that moved. Similarly, by 1980, viewers had discounted the "gee whiz" factor in debates. It is just possible that they were listening to what Reagan and Anderson had to say, and liked Reagan's optimism and antigovernment philosophy more than they liked Anderson's "share-the-sacrifice" arguments. Whether they were *right* to prefer that approach is a very different question. Their opinion seems to have been captured by Bruce Morton's summary of the CBS-*Times* findings:

"As for Anderson, the debate gave him exposure. Fewer people

* An exhaustive account of this technique appears in *Playing to Win; An Insider's Guide to Politics*.

said afterward that they didn't know where he stood on this issue or that. . . . Our sample had learned more about Anderson, but it didn't like what it had learned."

Even beyond the question of what Anderson was saying was the frame of reference in which he was making his case. We have already looked at the enormous handicap under which his campaign was laboring: the lack of support by important figures from mainstream politics whose presence might have encouraged voters to see Anderson as a figure with genuine Presidential weight. A running mate of the stature of a Senator Henry Jackson or Daniel Patrick Moynihan or Governor Hugh Carey, support from a dozen United States senators and fifty congressmen, would have been clear signals that John Anderson, independent though he was, was taken seriously by practicing politicians. Anderson never achieved this level of support (one of his few "prestigious" supporters, former Undersecretary of State George Ball, bolted the campaign in October to endorse Jimmy Carter), and this failure to impress the establishmentarians was a major blow to his candidacy.

Anderson also was missing another essential ingredient of contemporary politics: money. The post-Watergate reforms had sought to end the influence of huge campaign contributions in Presidential campaigns by establishing a public financing mechanism: federal funds collected from voluntary taxpayer tax check-offs would be supplied to the two major party candidates, and no private funds could be collected. For 1980—since the amount was subject to an inflation index —the Carter and Reagan campaigns received $29.4 million each, from which campaign travel, office expenses, salaries, and advertising would be paid. Third-party and independent candidacies received no public financing in advance; but under the law, they would be eligible for postelection subsidies, provided they won five percent of the popular vote. To raise funds *before* the election, Anderson had to rely on private campaign contributors who were limited to $1,000 contributions. (Had Anderson chosen to establish an official "third party," he could have raised $20,000 contributions, but the campaign felt this was politically unwise.) Since 1976, thanks to inflation, even this thousand-dollar limit had lost more than a third of its value; and in some areas, increases in campaign costs had far outstripped even the steep rise in inflation. For instance, the cost of an average prime-time television spot had gone up 76 percent since 1976.

The search for money was a constant struggle within the Anderson campaign, which made for some of the more bizarre legal and political manipulations in 1980. After the Federal Election Commission ruled in September that Anderson would get postelection funding if he achieved 5 percent of the vote, the campaign sought to borrow a minimum of $3 million from a consortium of banks. In effect, Anderson's standing in the public-opinion polls was offered as collateral for the banks, one of the most dramatic demonstrations yet seen that poll results had a tangible as well as psychological value in modern-day politics. Even a $3 million figure would have made it impossible for the campaign to raise its voice on a level comparable with that of Carter and Reagan, who would each spend between $16 and $18 million on radio and television alone. (The original Anderson campaign budget was projected at $15 million.) At best, it would have provided something of a "miniblitz" on television for the last three weeks of the campaign.

The Carter campaign, however, was determined to reduce Anderson's presence to invisibility in the last month. An "internal" memorandum from the Carter-Mondale reelection committee, leaked to ABC and therefore given wide circulation, argued that a loan to a political campaign based on public opinion poll standings would raise serious legal questions about potential violations of campaign contribution laws, at the least subjecting such banks to substantial legal fees.

"In such uncharted waters," the memo said, "the prudent lender should proceed with caution before making any unsecured political loans." Even after the Federal Election Commission ruled in early October that such borrowing would not violate campaign financing laws, banks shied away from such loans, leaving Anderson to finance his "blitz" from incoming contributions, and by borrowing from individual supporters. It turned out to be less than $2 million, and the campaign did become invisible. (No doubt coincidentally, a major argument against permitting such loans was made to the FEC by Timothy S. Perry, a partner in an Atlanta law firm that worked for the Citizens and Southern Bank. This bank lent the Carter campaign more than $1 million in 1976 against anticipated public financing funds. Without this money, the Carter campaign could not have survived into the primaries.)

In the last month of the general election, Anderson returned to the role he had occupied back in the spring; the classy candidate with no chance to win. As it had done with Kennedy, the press began to rediscover the independent's virtues as soon as it had become convinced that his victory was an impossibility; or, to put it in a more neutral manner, as soon as Anderson became resigned to his fate and returned to a less manipulative, more free-wheeling style.

Both *Time* and *Newsweek,* in their October 13 editions, filed Anderson away as an also-ran. "Finally Caught by Catch-22," *Time* wrote. "With no chance of winning, Anderson vows to fight on." Pointing to the CBS-*New York Times* postdebate poll, which pegged his support at 9 percent, *Time* wrote, "To his credit, [Anderson] has shunned much of his image-shapers' advice to win votes by artificially changing his platform behavior. Instead, Anderson has remained true to himself: erratically ebullient, enthused, inspiring, as well as dour, bored, cranky and preachy.'' In an interview in which the "why stay in the race?" question emerged—as it would throughout the last month—Anderson said, "One of the things that all those people come up to me and say [is] 'Thank you, John, for giving me a choice.' "

Newsweek described him as "playing for posterity," and was more critical than *Time,* pointing to "mounting evidence that he can do little more than tip the election to Ronald Reagan." But the weekly gave a fair amount of space to Anderson aides, who argued that the campaign "could purify the Democratic Party and leave it open to a whole new wave."

A more positive—and typical—account of Anderson's last month appeared in the *New York Times* of October 17.

"Anderson's Campaign Style Gains as He Loses Ground," the headline read, and the piece began, "The further John B. Anderson falls behind his Presidential rivals, the more vigorous and effective his campaign performance seems to become. [he] has lost the election to President Carter and Ronald Reagan and has thereby achieved a liberating relaxation."

The final blow to Anderson came when the League of Women Voters excluded him from the October 28 confrontation with President Carter and Ronald Reagan, on the ground that he had failed to meet the 15 percent poll limit. (In fact, the League had offered to Carter and Reagan the prospect of a one-on-one debate, followed by a three-way contest, a deal that Carter and Anderson had both accepted, but that Reagan had rejected on the ground that no one could insure Carter's attendance at the later debate. It was a good illustration of the political motivation that underlay most of the "debate debates," since Anderson was, by October, desperate for any visibility, whereas Reagan was still checking his bets. But after the League found that Anderson no longer met the criteria, Reagan decided to accept the one-on-one.) In a last-ditch effort for some presence, Anderson accepted the invitation of the Cable News Network to stage an unusual kind of "debate." With Anderson in Washington's Constitution Hall, Cable News started live by airing the answers of Carter and Reagan to the first question. Then Anderson's answers were inserted in the programming; Carter and Reagan then were "joined" by Anderson through a tape-delay mechanism. It was a fascinating demonstration of video technology, but not much more than that. Although in the fall of 1980 there were roughly 3 million households receiving Cable News Network, the actual number of viewers was certainly less than that, especially since a series of technical glitches kept holding up the "three-way" debate.

Anderson did appear on the postdebate shows of CBS and ABC (he boycotted NBC's wrap-up because the network had failed, for technical reasons, to run a five-minute Anderson commercial just before the debate), and on the next day's news shows. In addition, all three networks, which were conducting multipart interviews with Carter and Reagan, gave John Anderson one interview each on the evening news programs, although most of the time was spent asking why the independent was still in the race.

The questions asked by Walter Cronkite on the October 30 "CBS Evening News" were typical:

"How can you be a realist and look at the figures that all the polls come in with, and still say that you're likely to win on Tuesday?"

"How are you going to feel if [you] know that the votes that you garnered have made, say, Governor Reagan the next President of the United States?"

"If you're not elected, do you think you've still had an impact that will have importance to the future of the parties?"

To say that John Anderson was doomed by his press coverage is simply wrongheaded. The press's skepticism about the power of a third-party or independent candidate is well grounded in history. When the polls in the spring were reflecting broad, if thin, support for Anderson, that was the story being reported in the media. When the fall campaign was launched, with Anderson beginning to slide in the polls, the networks and the print press tried to balance the likely contest between the two major parties with the possibility of an independent surge. When the Carter campaign began arguing, as key Carter media and press aide Greg Schneiders did on the September 10 "MacNeil-Lehrer Report," that the media were "keeping alive by their coverage of a candidate, a candidacy that would not otherwise be a significant one," it was a political, rather than factual, analysis.

On the same program, CBS News vice-president Ernest Leiser noted that, between January and Labor Day, the "CBS Evening News" had given six hours and ten minutes of coverage to President Carter, three hours and nine minutes to Ronald Reagan, and one hour and forty-six minutes to John Anderson. "We think it reflects his value as a newsmaker in this country," Leiser said. Robert Kaiser of the *Washington Post* pointed to his paper's Labor Day coverage, when the fall campaign "officially" began. There was, he said, ". . . the top block with a picture, Carter and his first day. Under that, exactly the same size picture and story, Reagan and his day. And then under that at the bottom, no picture and a smaller block, Anderson and his day. . . . It was a deliberate decision that . . . Anderson deserved to be on the front page, but not quite in the same proportion."

The press, in other words, was making daily or weekly instinctive decisions about how to cover John Anderson, not following some predetermined plan either to inflate or ignore his candidacy. They were perfectly prepared to treat the "darling of the media" with the same hostility as they treated every other candidate who demonstrated a notable level of support. They were prepared to reveal every attempt at media manipulation, such as his foreign trip, every apparent trimming of his principled sails, such as his mysterious visit to Ted Kennedy at the end of July. They were prepared to chart with great detail his steady decline in the polls.

In the end, however, the press treatment of Anderson was a consequence, not a cause, of his 7 percent showing, and his failure to gain more than 10 percent of the vote in any state in the union. Clearly, the coverage of Anderson in the spring had brought a new face into national recognition, and Anderson's astonishing rise in the polls to apparent comparability with Carter and Reagan reflects a basic truism about politics in a mass-media age: that it is possible to become known, quickly and widely, without using any of the "mediating" forces that once governed politics, such as local and state party organizations. But just as clearly, there was no underlying structure to a campaign, and a movement, launched barely six months before the November election. It is one thing for an unknown such as George McGovern or Jimmy Carter to emerge out of nowhere, achieve enormous media exposure, and then capture a *party* nomination. Generally, the party, even in its contemporary weakened state, can provide a sense of stability and reassurance to the electorate (unless the candidate himself undermines it, as McGovern did in 1972).

To emerge on the national scene with a self-created movement, however, without the trappings of former high office (Theodore Roosevelt), strong regional identification (George Wallace), or the money and credibility to wage an equal battle with the parties (a $15 million war chest and prominent political backing) was simply battling against odds that were too high. What the press saw in John Anderson's 1980 campaign was another demonstration of the limits of media-based campaigning. The Anderson campaign floundered for lack of a pre-established political structure, money, and the willingness of major elements within the two parties to join the independent campaign. The press may well have helped in bringing Anderson to the threshold of plausibility. But forces far more important than the press prevented the independent from crossing that threshold.

xii   The Reagan-Anderson Debate: A Clear Case of Impact

The 1980 campaign for the Presidency offered compelling evidence that the role of the media is a vastly exaggerated factor in the outcome. We witnessed sudden bursts of momentum that led nowhere, press coverage of candidates that twisted and turned so frequently as to be self-nullifying, elaborate and expensive advertising campaigns that had nothing to do with the success of the candidates.

One element of modern media politics, however, *did* have a consistent impact on the outcome of the nominations and the election; ironically, it was the element least affected by attempts at manipulation, least under the control of the candidates and the advisors, and most in keeping with the passive, though still important, role of the media as distributors of the candidates' messages. That element was the political debate. In the primary and general elections, the clash of candidates before national television audiences clearly affected the fortunes of the Presidential hopefuls. Moreover, despite the belief that the interpretation of the debates by the media is the critical part of a debate, the evidence suggests that the debates *themselves* had a clear impact on the voters. As a general proposition, the press treated the debates as they treated every other public part of the battle for the Presidency: as a wholly tactical process in which candidates sought to shape images, in which every statement, every answer to a question, was to be understood as nothing but an appeal to votes. What the debates' impact suggested, however, is that, at least in 1980, the public was examining the debates for something more than tactical clues: they were attempting, in some measure, to get a sense of who these contenders for the Presidency were, and in what broad direction they intended to take the American people. Of course political strategy and tactics played a major role in the structuring of the debates, and in what the candidates said; only a fool would argue otherwise. But the debates also had another side, all but ignored by the press's coverage:

211

they offered the best opportunity in 1980 for the public to make a relatively informed judgment about who was worth voting for.

The most important point to make about the debate among Democratic primary contenders was that no debate took place. In late 1979, the *Des Moines Register and Tribune* invited Ted Kennedy and Jimmy Carter to participate in a January 7 debate, two weeks before the Iowa precinct caucuses. Both men accepted the invitation. California Governor Jerry Brown was denied an invitation, on the ground that he was not a candidate in Iowa. Recognizing the national attention that would be paid to the debate, and anticipating that his formidable debating skills might overcome his underdog political status at a single blow, Brown promptly decided to enter the contest for Iowa's votes and opened up headquarters opposite the newspaper plant; he was invited in.

But after the Iran and Afghanistan crises erupted, after Kennedy sank in the political polls, after Carter had announced his refusal to leave the White House for any campaigning, he withdrew from the debate in a decision crafted to make it appear as if he had accepted a political setback for patriotic reasons. The cancellation of that debate in itself insured that Jerry Brown, the late-starting whiz of 1976 who beat Carter in five of six contested primaries, would be nothing but an afterthought in 1980. The Iowa debate was Brown's one chance to use television to become an instant equal of the incumbent President and the famous last Kennedy. It did not happen, and neither did his campaign. Throughout the remainder of the campaign, Carter persisted in his refusal to debate Kennedy, refusing even when Kennedy, in a postprimary, preconvention desperation move, promised to release his delegates to vote their consciences provided a debate was held. But Carter had the delegates needed for his renomination. There was no apparent benefit to his campaign, especially given the no-holds-barred attack on his record by Kennedy.

In contrast, the Republican candidates for the nomination debated throughout the early primaries, until the nomination of Reagan was a certainty. Each of these early debates produced a measurable impact on the outcome of the campaign, and an impact on the Republican Party as well.

The absence of Ronald Reagan from the January 5 Iowa debate emphasized his "nonincumbent-incumbent stance" and materially contributed to his two-point defeat at the hands of George Bush. John Anderson's blunt answers to questions about economics and his acknowledgment of his past "mistake" in voting for the Gulf of Tonkin resolution made him an instant hero to liberals and gave "the Anderson difference" its first national exposure. At the Manchester debate in New Hampshire on February 20, Reagan's presence reminded Republicans of why they held him in esteem, and he began to open up a lead over George Bush from that moment on. At the Nashua debate, Reagan's one-upmanship in demanding the inclusion of other Republicans, and Bush's inability to respond to Reagan's indignation, was an important element in Reagan's landslide. In Illinois in March, the combination of Republican attacks on John Anderson and Reagan's easygoing charm, helped Reagan to a double-digit victory over Anderson and propelled the liberal Congressman into abandoning the contest for the GOP nomination and contemplating an independent run for the Presidency.

Moreover, with the single exception of Nashua, there was no bad blood among the Republican contenders; the general adherence to Reagan's famous "eleventh commandment" made the debates a polite series of discussions about indexing taxes, restricting government regulation of business, increasing defense spending, and promoting economic growth. From the very first Republican debate, press coverage was overwhelmingly favorable; the Republicans, it turned out, had fielded a group of attractive, articulate candidates, whose broad agreement on the issues presaged a united convention and a united party.

It was when the nominations of Carter and Reagan, and the independent candidacy of John Anderson, became certainties that the issue of debates took on a new cast; and even before the first of the two fall debates, one candidate had suffered seriously as a result of the controversy over the structure of the debate. In a curious irony of 1980, it was the Carter campaign's fondest hope that the entire matter would be seen as a battle over political self-interest; and it was the press's insistence that some form of principle was involved that cost Carter heavily in the first month of the fall election campaign.

A bit of background is necessary. Because of the "equal-time" rule written into broadcasting's basic legislation—Section 315 of the Federal Communications Acts—broadcasting outlets are not permitted to stage political debates, except under very limited circumstances. A television station or network can invite some, and not all, candidates onto a regularly scheduled public affairs show, such as "Meet the Press" or local equivalents. In local elections, this is, in fact, how most debates are presented. But in the context of a general election for President of the United States, it would be ludicrous for major party nominees to debate on only one network, and other networks could not carry such a program, because it is not part of *their* regular schedules. Thus, the only time in American political history that television networks were permitted to carry Presidential debates on their own was in 1960, when Congress temporarily suspended the equal-time rule.

What networks *are* permitted to do, however, is to cover, as a legitimate news event, a political debate sponsored by some other organization. In 1976, and in some of the 1980 Republican debates, the sponsor was the League of Women Voters. The legal fiction was that candidates were debating before an audience of a few thousand people, and television and radio just happened to decide to cover the event as part of their news coverage. (The fiction was neatly exposed during the first Carter-Ford debate when the broadcast audio failed, and for twenty-six painful minutes the two potential future Presidents of the United States stood in absolute silence.)

Early in 1980, President Carter had agreed to participate in League-sponsored debates, and so had Ronald Reagan. But by May, John Anderson was embarked on an independent run for the White House, with polls suggesting that he would win 20 percent of the popular vote, with a chance of taking some of the major industrial states. Although the polls differed, they were in general agreement that Anderson, with his liberal message and his appeal to students, intellectuals, and upper-middle-class suburbanites, would hurt Carter much more than Reagan. And the Carter campaign began a determined campaign to keep John Anderson out of the debates.

At the end of May, White House Press Secretary Jody Powell declared flatly that President Carter would refuse to debate Anderson on the ground that it was a "fantasy" to pretend that Anderson could actually be elected President. As a matter of political prognostication, Carter's press secretary may have been right, and the spring polls a kind of reflection of voter discontent that traditionally fades when the leaves fall. But the combination of Anderson's remarkable popularity at the time—he was, for example, running only two points behind the President in a California poll—and the press cynicism that had come to characterize Carter's use of the White House had begun to make Carter's political tactics a matter for skeptical press treatment. In addition, Anderson's political appeal was that of a courageous, thoughtful, urbane liberal—a species not unknown to the universe of political columnists. Carter was shutting *their* fair-haired boy out of the debates, and the response was angry.

The *Washington Post*'s Mark Shields called Powell's "fantasy" argument "patently fatuous . . . oatmeal logic," pointing to public opinion polls as a way of distinguishing Anderson from other minor party candidates. *New York Times* columnist Tom Wicker said, "The only fantasy in sight . . . is Mr. Carter's apparent belief that he can get away with refusing to debate Mr. Anderson, when Ronald Reagan, the uncrowned Republican nominee, has already agreed to do so." It was fear of Anderson's strength, not objection to his weakness, that was keeping Carter from debating him, Wicker argued. James Reston noted at the end of May that the decision "could hurt Mr. Carter by drawing attention to the contrast between the President's moralistic lectures and his hard-ball political tactics."

The League of Women Voters, for its part, put off any decision about whether anyone other than Carter or Reagan would be invited; but League President Ruth Hinerfeld understood how to play a kind of "hard-ball" politics of her own. Noting that a twenty-four-person advisory board of Democrats and Republicans had been established to set up criteria for the fall debates, Hinerfeld said in mid-July, "The one thing there's a national consensus on in this country is a sense of fair play, and we won't ignore that," she said. "I don't think we'll be cowed by the possibility someone won't show up."

Thus, by the time Reagan and Carter had won their parties' nominations formally, the lines seemed to be clearly drawn. Reagan had expressed his willingness to debate with Carter and Anderson; Carter had ruled Anderson out. Everyone understood the political calculations at stake. Since Anderson appeared to be drawing more votes from Carter than from Reagan, the last thing the Democratic nominee wanted was to put the independent on an equal footing with the major party nominees—especially since, in the summer, the principal objection to Anderson appeared to be that he could not win. For Reagan—at least according to the polls—any boost given to Anderson's candidacy would come at the expense of Carter, so boosting the independent would actually help the Republican.

Given its obsession with pointing out the political calculations underlying candidates' decisions, the press might have been expected to treat the entire controversy as an exercise in public relations. After all, debates themselves were a subject of ambiguous press attention, given the candidates' desire to manipulate public opinion. Tom Wicker said in 1976 and again in June of 1980 that "televised debates afforded the two candidates opportunity to make more misrepresentations, false claims, calculated appeals and empty promises than probably ever were offered to a long-suffering electorate." And in 1964, 1968, and 1972, candidates had avoided debates with very little effective press criticism; in fact, in 1968, Richard Nixon used independent George Wallace as the *reason* for his refusal to debate Hubert Humphrey.

In the first weeks of the general election campaign, however, President Carter began to come under heavy attack for his posture on the debates. In August, the League of Women Voters announced a schedule of four nationally televised debates, three among the Presidential candidates, one for the Vice-Presidential candidates, and set a standard for inclusion: any candidate with 15 percent support averaged among four public opinion polls would be invited to the first debate. The President insisted that the first debate be a one-on-one with Reagan; and to avoid the accusation that he was the candidate unwilling to debate—never a politically helpful posture—Carter accepted invitations for a one-on-one from the *Ladies' Home Journal,* the National Press Club, and "Face the Nation." But it did not work. The overwhelming opinion, both in the press and among the populace at large, was that John Anderson ought to be included in the debate.

A *New York Times* editorial of August 31, after noting that such debates "are neither mandatory nor time-honored," argued that whatever political calculation was at stake "citizen attention" arising from debates "is an immense asset for democracy," and "to limit participation unreasonably to the two major parties is to eviscerate independents, mavericks, and new parties." The Gallup, Roper, and ABC-Harris polls showed that between 60 and 70 percent of Americans thought Anderson should be included in the debate. It was a "fair play" question—a political term that was used as far back as the 1952 Republican Convention, when Eisenhower's supporters got their delegates seated in critical contested states by adopting a "fair play" credentials resolution. And it was, in substantial consequence, a product of Jimmy Carter's very success in the primary season of avoiding any political combat with his rivals. Reagan, after all, had debated his opponents, including John Anderson, five times. Carter had not ventured from the White House from November to April. Politically, Carter had left behind from his primary battle plausible evidence that he was not willing to debate; Reagan had, after Iowa, demonstrated a kind of openness to meet his rivals. This disparity clearly left Carter vulnerable to charges of manipulation.

There was, indeed, a case to be made that Ronald Reagan's position was at least as politically motivated as Carter's. In addition to the Anderson question, Reagan's advisors were pushing for only two debates, on the ground that a challenger needed more campaign time than an incumbent. "We don't want to run around the country to win the debates but lose the election," Reagan aide James Baker said. There was a hint that the Reagan campaign was also concerned that more debates meant more chances for the candidate to make a major tactical error. But because Reagan was in the position of insisting that "fair play" apply to an underdog, he reaped two substantial benefits: he was seen as the fair-minded, let's-let-everyone-play candidate— just as he had been at the Republican debate in Nashua in February— and it projected a sense of confidence that helped make up for the slips that were troubling his general election campaign in the first weeks.

For its part, the Carter campaign sought to define the issue as more political than anything else. In a break with the tradition that demands each side in a "debate debate" claim the high moral ground, Carter campaign chief Robert Strauss repeatedly made the point that these skirmishes were to be regarded principally as battles for political advantage.

On the September 3 "MacNeil-Lehrer Report," Strauss said that "the American public is a pretty wise body out there, and they understand what goes on. . . . There are very logical reasons for each of our positions . . . obviously, we think our political fortunes are better served if we have Governor Reagan one-on-one first, and then get to the other candidates. . . . Do we have a selfish reason? Yes. Overriding that, of course, there is a public interest." On the NBC "Today" show on September 10, Strauss said, "There is a lot of political hocus-pocus in this thing. We have our selfish political reasons. Of course we do, and Ronald Reagan has his. Of course he does, and so does John Anderson. They're all good, but we're no villain in this thing." And he added later, "We believe the American people understand this issue, that it's a critical issue being politicized, and also it's a great press issue, and Anderson is a creation of the press." (This last point became the general White House line during the controversy over the Anderson debate factor. Carter himself had said a few days earlier, "I see Anderson as primarily a creation of the press. . . . He and his wife handpicked the Vice-Presidential nominee." This brought mocking commentary by Tom Wicker and other journalists, who noted acidly that Carter's 1976 campaign was aimed at press credibility, and that he and Rosalynn had chosen Walter Mondale as Carter's running mate in 1976.)

When the League announced on September 10 that Anderson had indeed met the 15 percent poll standard, and Carter rejected the invitation to appear in Baltimore on September 21, the press reaction was highly negative. "By refusing to admit Mr. Anderson," the *Times* said on September 11, "President Carter makes himself a target for two big [attacks]; that he is afraid of Anderson, and "that it is not just debates he wants to avoid, but having to defend his record as President." Syndicated cartoonist Mike Peters showed Abraham Lincoln being turned away from a debate as a reporter said, "After all, you're only a Congressman from Illinois." Wright of the *Miami News* showed Anderson, accompanied by a figure labeled "Issues" being turned away by a League official saying, "You and your friend will have to bug off! We've got a debate going here." "Mr. Carter comes out looking frightened," The *Washington Post* commented.

In his weekly review of media coverage, the *Post*'s Robert Kaiser noted that the debate controversy had kept Anderson on the network newscasts at the very time he was beginning to fade in the polls, and "overwhelmingly, editorialists perceived a question of fairness, or a challenge to the openness of the American political system."

Two other events set the stage for the Anderson-Reagan debate— in one case, literally. Initially, the League had announced that there would be no "empty chair" on the Baltimore stage if Carter chose to skip the debate—the classic symbol of the candidate afraid to meet his rivals.* But on September 15, League President Hinerfeld announced there "probably would be an empty chair" in Carter's place; a chair depicted by *Washington Star* cartoonist Oliphant as a baby's high chair —a stinging reference to a sense of Presidential petulance. But the chair was scrapped when nervous League officials—after "guidance" from the White House—concluded that such a step might be interpreted as a partisan attack, jeopardizing the League's standing and its tax exemption.

And three days before the Sunday debate, the American Broadcasting Company announced that—unlike NBC and CBS—it would not carry the debate live, but would instead show the movie *Midnight Express,* in accordance with its original schedule. Cynics argued that this was an attempt to rack up huge prime-time ratings by "counterprogramming" a blockbuster movie against public affairs programming. In fact, according to ABC executives, the news division was given complete power to make the decision on its own. And the decision, two high-ranking news executives insisted, was a *news* judgment; without the President's appearance, the debate was not of sufficient importance to warrant live coverage, as opposed to extended news coverage later that night.

It was a close call, clouded by the fact that any decision by the network had obvious political implications. To carry the debate would have been, one executive argued, to inflict a political cost on the Carter campaign for its decision, even though the "pure" news judgment was that this event was not worth live prime-time coverage. Not covering the debate meant that the Carter campaign would be aided in its strategy by having ABC offer tens of millions of viewers an alternative to the debate, inevitably diminishing the audience. It is also apparent that ABC was determined to flex its muscles as a network now fully equal in news coverage to its seniors, after more than two decades of second-class journalistic citizenship.

"This is *our* decision," one executive said, "and I'll be damned if we'll cover the debate just because the other guys are. If CBS announced its decision the day the League invited Anderson, fine; that's their decision. But it isn't ours." (It is also true that most of the political reporters and producers at ABC strongly dissented from the executive decision.)

As it turned out, the American viewer appeared more interested in the Reagan-Anderson debate than predictions indicated. Across the country, about 55 million viewers watched the debate, slightly more than viewed *Midnight Express.* (It was still a clear ratings victory for

---

* Johnny Carson drew laughter and applause from his audience by asking one night, "What if the chair wins the debate?"

ABC, since the debate audience was split between CBS and NBC.) What they saw was a one-hour exchange of views in which both Reagan and Anderson acquitted themselves handily—and from which Reagan gained an enormous advantage, whereas Anderson began a rapid descent in the polls. Although the initial views of the debate did not gauge this outcome, the benefit of hindsight makes it clear why the September 21 debate was one of the most important events in the entire fall campaign. ·

The format was a rigidly structured affair, the outcome of lengthy negotiations between the League and the candidates. The moderator was PBS's Bill Moyers; the questions were posed by a panel of six journalists, all from the print press, to avoid alienating the commercial networks.* Each journalist had to pose the same question to each candidate, for a two-and-a-half-minute answer from each, followed by a one-minute, fifteen-second response. There was no chance for follow-up questions, no opportunity to correct the candidates for the kind of clear misstatement of fact that, for example, had Gerald Ford spinning Poland out of the Soviet orbit during the second 1976 debate. It made the presence of the journalists more a question of set design than utility; except for the variation in dress and voice, the questions might as well have been read aloud by moderator Moyers. The absence of follow-up questions proved especially disconcerting to Ms. Quinn. When she asked the candidates to detail the impact of their defense, energy, and urban programs on inflation, Reagan said, "I've done it. . . . we have a backup paper to my economics speech a couple of weeks ago in Chicago that gives all of those figures." Ms. Quinn said after the debate, "If anyone can find an inflation forecast in Reagan's economic fact sheet, send it to me and I'll eat it on toast. It's just not there." Lacking the chance to follow up her question, there was no chance for Ms. Quinn, or for any other panelist, to note inaccuracies or confusions in the answer. To understand the significance of this kind of limitation, it was a follow-up question by *New York Times* editor Max Frankel in 1976 that led President Ford into his famous, perhaps fatal, Poland-is-not-dominated-by-the-Soviet-Union answer.

Even given these limits, both the questions and the answers produced an impressive exchange of ideas; what the *Wall Street Journal* called a "surprisingly good show." The questions touched on some of the most important issues in the 1980 campaign: what specific, unpopular measures might be necessary to reduce inflation; what changes in American living habits might be necessary to cope with energy short-

* They were: Carol Loomis of *Fortune* magazine; Daniel Greenberg, a syndicated science columnist; Charles Corddry of the *Baltimore Sun;* Lee May of the *Los Angeles Times;* Jane Bryant Quinn, *Newsweek*'s economic columnist; and Soma Golden of the *New York Times* editorial board. It was the first time in memory that white males formed a minority on so visible a panel.

ages; how to get American military forces up to combat strength without the draft; how to aid the cities of the United States in the context of fiscal restraint; how would the candidates' spending and tax policies affect inflation; and whether organized religion should guide candidates' views on abortion or equal rights or defense spending.

The questioners, it must be said, tended to pose more difficult questions for Reagan than for Anderson; an understandable fact, given that Reagan was obviously more likely to be elected President than John Anderson. Anderson had long since advocated politically unpopular measures to control inflation, such as his opposition to a deep and permanent tax cut; Reagan had embraced the "pain-free" supply-side view that tax cuts would produce so much *additional* revenue that no sacrifice would be necessary. Anderson was a wholesale advocate of energy conservation and reduced reliance on the automobile; Reagan had argued for years that an end to regulation would produce a bonanza of new energy sources within America. Reagan's links to politically active, conservative evangelical groups had become a campaign issue; Anderson had repudiated his early congressional support for a constitutional amendment recognizing Jesus Christ as Savior, and had become a strict church-state separationist. Clearly, the questions were probing for weaknesses in Reagan's campaign positions much more so than in Anderson's.

In their answers, both Anderson and Reagan reflected their stylistic and substantive essences. In the most familiar cliche in postdebate analysis, uttered by reporters who have heard the candidates hundreds of times to a television audience that may well be hearing them for the first time, there was "nothing new." That is, Ronald Reagan did not declare that he had misunderstood the nature of the Soviet threat for the last twenty years, or announce his conversion to the principle of public ownership of basic industry. John Anderson did not choose the debate forum to repudiate his proposal for a fifty-cent-a-gallon gasoline tax. What the contestants did provide the national television audience was an hour of reasonably informed discourse on some of the country's most vexing problems. And in contrast to the disconnected, random snippets of arguments heard on the nightly newscasts, viewers got some sense of the way these two public men actually viewed the world.

The substantive clash could not have been more fundamental; as Anderson said at the close of the debate, rebutting President Carter's argument that he should not be forced into a debate with two Republicans, ". . . Governor Reagan and I have agreed on exactly one thing; we are both against the imposition of a peacetime draft. We have disagreed, I believe, on virtually every other issue."

Specifically:

• Anderson opposed an election year tax cut on the ground that it would "result in a higher rate of inflation"; and proposed adjusting the civil service retirement index to lessen automatic pension increases. Reagan specifically denied that sacrifice was needed to control inflation, arguing that what was needed "would be unpopular with government, and with some special interest groups who are closely tied to the government." A tax cut, he argued, would increase productivity and thereby cut inflation. Anderson called again for a fifty-cent-a-gallon gasoline tax, recycled back to taxpayers through Social Security tax cuts; Reagan opposed the idea.

• Reagan called for stepped-up energy exploration, including nuclear power, off-shore oil drilling, and use of coal, and relegated conservation to a secondary role; Anderson called for "a new conservation ethic," and support for alternatives to the automobile.

• Anderson opposed the MX missile; Reagan supported it, while expressing opposition to the elaborate, land-based Carter proposal to use thousands of square miles in Utah and Nevada to shuttle the missiles about.

• Reagan called for state, local, and private initiatives to rebuild inner cities, including "urban enterprise zones," which would be tax havens for businesses employing inner-city residents. Anderson called for a $4 billion, federally funded community trust fund, and asked, "where has the private sector been, Governor Reagan, during the years that our cities have been deteriorating?"

• Anderson denounced attempts by churches "to tell the parishioners of any church, of any denomination, how they should vote," and argued that abortion was "a moral issue that ought to be left to the freedom of conscience of the individual." Reagan argued that "too many of our churches have been too reluctant to speak up in behalf of what they believe is proper in government." And he said of abortion, "I've noticed that everybody who is for abortion has already been born."

As important as the issues on which they disagreed was the way they made their cases. Anderson, whose intense speaking manner had earned him the nicknames "Parson John" and "St. John the Righteous," spoke as if in a congressional debate. He warned of "the monetization of debt," called for "the retrofitting in the design of our homes," pointed to "a shortage of about 104,000 in the ranks between E4 and E9." Reagan, in contrast, used language far more accessible to the voter, resorting over and over to the concrete, homey words that had characterized his long career as a master political rhetorician.

When Anderson accused Reagan of increasing spending during his term as California's governor, Reagan chuckled and said, "Well, some people look up figures and some people make up figures. And John has just made up some very interesting figures." "I don't see," Reagan said at another point, "where it is inflationary to have people keep more of their earnings and spend it, and it isn't inflationary for government to take that money away from them and spend it on the things it wants to spend it on." In arguing that lower taxes would lower government spending, Reagan said, "If you've got a kid that's extravagant, you can lecture him all you want to about his extravagance, or you can cut his allowance."

To a panel of experts in public policy, Anderson's points were more tightly reasoned; to a voter of ordinary intelligence, Reagan's answers were far more comprehensible, far easier to understand in the context of a general election campaign still in its initial phases.

In addition, both candidates treated the absent Carter with care, recognizing that a wholesale assault on the President might have been regarded as dirty pool. Instead, there were flicks, jabs, quick references to the President on the way to a substantive point.

For example, in answer to a question about inflation, Anderson said, "Governor Reagan is not responsible for what has happened over the last four years, nor am I. The man who should be here tonight to respond to those charges chose not to attend." When faced with a question about increasing America's combat readiness, Reagan said, "It's a shame now that there are only two of us here debating, because the two that are here are in more agreement than disagreement . . . and the only one who would be disagreeing with us is the President, if he were present."

At the end of the debate, before launching into his closing speech, Reagan covered this question of unfairness to the President.

"We have criticized the failures of the Carter policy rather considerably, both of us, this evening, and there might be some feeling of unfairness about this because he was not here to respond. But I believe it would have been much more unfair to have had John Anderson denied the right to participate in this debate."

In his final comments, Reagan changed his tone of voice dramatically. As he had in his acceptance speech, as he was to do in the debate with Carter and in his election eve speech to the nation, the Republican candidate slipped out of his informal, easygoing approach —he had called Anderson "John" throughout the evening—and into a more formal, inspirational tone. It was all familiar to the press; but to the country, it was, for most of them, the first time they had heard the Republican candidate as the spokesman for growth, optimism, the future—precisely the vision that Carter's pollster Pat Caddell had said a year earlier America had been missing. The comments are worth noting at length:

After expressing his belief that "this land was placed here between two great oceans by some divine plan," Reagan said:

Today, we're confronted with the horrendous problems that we've discussed here tonight, and some people in high positions of leadership tell us that the answer is to retreat, that the best is over, that we must cut back, that we must share in an ever-increasing scarcity; that we must, in the failure to be able to protect our national security, as it is today, we must not be provocative to any possible adversary.

Well we, the living Americans, have gone through four wars. We've gone through a Great Depression in our lifetime that literally was worldwide and almost brought us to our knees. But we came through all of these things, and we achieved even new heights and new greatness. The living Americans today have fought harder, paid a higher price for freedom, and done more to advance the dignity of man than any people who ever lived on this earth. For 200 years we've lived in the future, believing that tomorrow would be better than today, and today would be better than yesterday. I still believe that. I'm not running for the Presidency because I believe that I can solve the problems we've discussed here tonight. I believe the people of this country can. And together, we can begin the world over again. We can meet our destiny. And that destiny—to build a land here that will be for all mankind a shining city on a hill. I think we ought to get at it.

The postdebate analysis, on television and in print, focused almost not at all on what the candidates said; instead, as has become customary in press coverage, it was confined almost exclusively to a strategic assessment.

CBS's Bruce Morton, echoing the comments of every other commentator, noted that Anderson was helped because "he's up here with Governor Reagan as an equal, one of the big boys, certified and all that." Bill Plante noted that "not one syllable from Ronald Reagan was different from anything we've heard in the last several months . . . Reagan was reassuring. That's what his handlers wanted him to be; Presidential if you will." Walter Cronkite noted that "our reporters heard no gaffes of the Ford proportion tonight."

NBC's Tom Brokaw, in that network's coverage, called the debate "a dead heat." "A rather emotionless debate," ABC's Ted Koppel observed.

Both UPI's and AP's political writers concluded that President Carter had not been hurt by his nonparticipation, while columnist Jack Germond said on the next morning's "Today" show that "the one thing that is clear is that President Carter lost." "An undramatic and controlled confrontation," was the New York Times review. Eric Engberg, who covered Anderson for CBS, said on Monday's "Morning" show that "Anderson's purposes in the debate were accomplished the

224 • JEFF GREENFIELD

minute the television lights went on and he was seen on the same stage as Reagan . . . the key for him in this debate was just being seen.''

Anderson might have taken heart from two other initial findings: an AP panel of debate experts rated him the winner over Reagan on formal debating rules by a 6–1 margin. And an ABC-Harris survey found that likely voters who watched the debate thought Anderson had beaten Reagan 36–30. Since this poll obviously included both Carter and Anderson voters, it may have been skewed. But what makes the finding so remarkable in view of the flow of the campaign was that, within a matter of days, Anderson lost more than 30 percent of his supporters, whereas—depending on which poll measured the impact —Reagan either held his support or gained five points against the President. Thus, while *Newsweek* called the debate "a boost for the stay-at-home"—in their Gallup poll Reagan maintained, but did not increase, his four-point lead over Carter—the facts suggest that Reagan gained enormously from the debate.

Why? In the first place, the debate followed several weeks of press coverage in which Reagan had been portrayed as a blunder-prone candidate, committing gaffe after gaffe, raising doubts in his own campaign about how adept he was on his feet. While this coverage may have exaggerated the political impact of these blunders—in part because the press was examining the weight of its own comments—the Sunday confrontation with Anderson showed the Republican nominee on his feet for an hour, wading through the complexity of military, tax, inflation, and energy questions. And whether he was right or wrong, he was clearly in command of his own arguments. To a public expecting a befuddled candidate, the debate showed Reagan to great advantage.

Second, the vaunted "stylistic" skills of Reagan were less acting skills and more a basic political skill that has stood candidates in good stead for hundreds of years: the ability to speak naturally, in ways voters can understand. Whether because of hostility to Reagan's views or to his former career, observers persisted in mocking Reagan's skill with words, his sense of humor, his easygoing presence. In fact, these were the same skills that John Kennedy had displayed in the later 1960 debates with Richard Nixon and during his Presidential press conferences, the same skills FDR had displayed in using homey metaphors during his fireside chats. Reagan, far from being the candidate of the television age, was unprogrammed, in command, willing to listen to questions and to his opponent's answers. In contrast, Anderson was an intelligent, well-informed, well-briefed candidate who spoke in the language of congressional committee reports and legal briefs.

Third, Reagan demonstrated in this debate, as he had throughout the campaign, that he and the Republicans seized the high ground from the Democrats. Traditionally, the Republicans had been the party of chilly restraint, cautioning against boldness and risk. When the Kennedys used to quote Emerson talking about "the party of hope versus the party of memory," it was clear that the Republicans were the party of memory.

But in this debate, it was Reagan who was warning against timidity, promising that new action could indeed solve America's problems. The candidate of conservative gospel, the oldest nominee in history, was espousing rhetoric much more suited to 1960 and to John Kennedy. And if we are willing to entertain the heretical notion that viewers were actually *listening to what the candidates were saying,* then the debate helped turn Reagan from a stumbling candidate into (in James Baker's words) a "reasonable, competent candidate." The ogre already being portrayed by the Democrats wasn't there.

In contrast, Anderson—for whom this debate was his great chance—began to fade, not because he performed badly, but because the case for an independent campaign had to be something extraordinary. The conventional wisdom about third-party campaigns turned out to be quite right; voters always tend to desert these campaigns as the general election draws near, even when an independent candidate has a clear ideological or regional base. In Anderson's case, his campaign was that of a moderate-liberal, running on the premise that he was not one of two unacceptable men. The more the major party nominees looked acceptable, the weaker the case for Anderson grew. And given his lack of money, base, or credible political support, the visibility of the debate simply was not sufficient to overcome these overriding political liabilities.

Once the Carter-Reagan debate became a reality, with the consequent press hoopla about the "single roll of the dice," the Anderson-Reagan debate faded from memory. It was a footnote to campaign '80. For Ronald Reagan, however, the Anderson debate may have been to his fall campaign what the Manchester, New Hampshire, debate was to his primary campaign: overshadowed by a later, more dramatic confrontation, dismissed by the press for its lack of theatrical drama, it nonetheless may well have been the place where Reagan scored one of his major triumphs of the campaign: because 50 million Americans had the chance to see a consummate political animal arguing a cause that had come to seem more hopeful and more convincing to a majority of the American electorate.

xiii The Carter-Reagan Debate: Beyond the Metaphors

No other event of the 1980 campaign so sharply revealed the nature of the coverage of the Presidential election as the single debate between President Carter and Ronald Reagan on October 28 in Cleveland. Almost without exception, the question of what the two potential future Presidents of the United States had to say to the American people was shunted aside in favor of an orgy of strategic and tactical speculation: What would the "showdown one-on-one" produce in the way of a winner; who would appear more "Presidential"; how would President Carter force Ronald Reagan onto "the defensive"? How would Governor Reagan appear "reassuring"? Who would make the key gaffe that would affect the press interpretation of the debate and thereby decide the winner?

One way to measure the limits of the tactical obsession of the press with political events is to look at the Carter-Reagan debate in slightly different terms. For example:

• As the campaign approached its end, the battle was seen as a contest between Carter's weakness on economic questions and Reagan's weakness on foreign policy matters—the so-called "Tolstoy" issue of war and peace. The debate was fought out preponderantly on President Carter's preferred grounds of foreign policy and war and peace. Yet the debate hurt him badly.

• Debates are supposed to be won by the candidate who keeps his opponent on the defensive. In spite of the fact that Jimmy Carter was the incumbent, Ronald Reagan was on the "defensive" for most of the evening, defending himself against a steady barrage of charges that he was proposing "disturbing," "dangerous," and "irresponsible" ideas that could jeopardize world peace. Yet Reagan profited greatly from the debate.

• President Carter's great challenge, predebate analysis said, was to summon the traditional elements of the Democratic Party coalition back to the cause—a challenge that polls at the time of the debate suggested was being met in many key industrial states vital to Carter's chances. In the debate, the President managed skillfully to weave appeals to the different aspects of the coalition into his statements and answers, and to remind his audience that Reagan had broken step with past Republican Presidents on a number of important issues. Yet, on Election Day, the Democratic Party coalition suffered its worse collapse since it first took shape during Franklin D. Roosevelt's New Deal.

• The debate was generally regarded as the overriding event of the Presidential election: "a single showdown hand with the Presidency very possibly at stake," *Newsweek* called it; "make or break," *Time* said; it "could be decisive in the tight race for the White House," the *New York Times* reported; "the Super Bowl, the World Series, and a heavyweight fight, a title, all rolled into one," NBC's Tom Brokaw called it on the "Today" show. Without questioning the importance of a nationally televised debate between the major party candidates for President, it is highly arguable that the voters of the United States were not really asking the questions that the polls and the press suggested they were asking. Rather, the events of the last four years, and the arguments of the candidates over the campaign season, had already led the voters to a judgment that they wanted a new President in the White House; and that the only question Ronald Reagan really had to answer on the night of October 28 was whether there was any compelling reason for voters to ignore their desires. Further, in an ironic rebuttal to the "substance-doesn't-count" attitude toward campaigns, the final tactical battle had been defined by the burden imposed on the incumbent President by his own record, and by the domestic and international conditions that were in front of the electorate when the campaign first began. The President, for all the power of the office, the capacity to set the agenda, the control of the media, had been forced into the *tactical* posture by the *substance* of the campaign.

As we have seen, the Carter campaign had from the beginning understood the impossibility of asking for another term on the record of the first term. One of the most damaging comments from the White House had come from Press Secretary Jody Powell early in 1980; when asked what the second Carter Administration would be like, he replied, "pretty much like the first." That was the first and last time such a comment was heard from any Carter official. Except for a brief appearance on the day of his acceptance speech at a morning rally of the faithful in New York, President Carter never heard the chant "four more years!" at any time in the campaign. Fairly or not, the climate among the American electorate was such that the slogan of Carter's 1976 campaign—"Why Not the Best?"—had a distinctly sarcastic ring to it.

The campaign, then, had to be waged on the proposition that if

Carter was not the best, then Reagan was much worse: that Ronald Reagan represented a clear and present danger to the interests of millions of Americans and a possible threat to the survival of the world. This, in its most elegant formulation, was what Carter's bid for a second term came down to: *I may not be so hot, but the other guy's a disaster.*

This strategy, however, has one basic problem: *it cannot be executed without the active cooperation of the opposition.* Voters looking at a campaign cannot be persuaded that one candidate has repudiated the principles of his party unless substantial, visible figures within that party make the case. This is exactly what happened to Barry Goldwater in 1964, and to George McGovern in 1972, when major figures within the nominees' parties refused to endorse their candidacies, or even endorsed their opponents. In this sense, at least, party labels mean a great deal, because voters tend to be swayed by a rule which is also powerful in childhood ballgames: "Your own man says so." In a close play at first base, arguments are always settled when one conscience-stricken member of the team says grimly, "Yeah, they're right. He was out." The other team screams joyfully, "See? Your own man says so!" and the argument ends.

In 1964, moderate and liberal Republican figures were, in effect, agreeing with Democrats that Senator Goldwater was out of the mainstream of his political party, and such venerable Republican institutions as the *New York Herald-Tribune* and the *Saturday Evening Post* endorsed Lyndon Johnson. In 1972, conservative and moderate Democrats refused to support George McGovern, and such traditional Democratic bulwarks as the AFL-CIO refused to back the Democratic nominee. In 1980, this had not happened; the Republican Party was united behind Ronald Reagan from Jesse Helms to Jacob Javits, from William Loeb to Mark Hatfield. There were no visible Republicans of any magnitude saying, in effect, "Yeah, you're right; the guy's too far out."

The second essential element to the "unfit" strategy is for a candidate to wound himself with statements and actions that appear uninformed, ludicrous, dangerous, or simply beyond the limits of mainstream politics. Goldwater had done it in 1964 with notions about making Social Security voluntary, sawing the Eastern Seaboard off the American continent, "lobbing one into the men's room of the Kremlin," and seeming to defend political extremism. George McGovern had committed hara-kiri with casually formulated income redistribution schemes, an apparent embrace of fringe elements on the far left shore of the Democratic Party, his selection of a running mate with a history of mental illness, and a general sense of incompetence at controlling his own campaign, which raised substantial doubts about his competence to run the Executive Branch of government.

Here Ronald Reagan, with an assist from the press, had made the Carter strategy more credible. A series of comments and actions early in the general election campaign had helped to create the impression most feared by the Reagan campaign; an impression of carelessness and ignorance that would make it dangerous to entrust the life-or-death power of the White House to such a nominee. The fear of continued slipups had persuaded the Reagan campaign to tighten control over its candidate and diminish the changes for ad-lib, face-to-face exchanges between Reagan and the traveling press. In retrospect, these slips may have been less damaging than they first appeared, since some of them —"Vietnam is a noble cause," the debate over evolution—were matters of belief rather than flat factual errors.

The most significant aspect of Reagan's hesitant general election start may well have been the false signal it gave to the Carter campaign that the anti-Reagan premise was a correct one. Neither in its primary battle against Senator Kennedy, nor in the positioning of Jimmy Carter at the Democratic National Convention, nor in its general election media had a coherent argument for the President's reelection been formulated. Why not? Because, in the context of the 1980 electorate, *it did not exist*. The argument for the President's reelection had to be based on the quality of the opposition. That argument had worked against Kennedy, who struggled under the weight of doubts about his character and (with his horrendous campaign beginning) about his competence. It had been buttressed, however, by the short-lived but powerful surge of support *for* the President in the wake of the twin foreign policy crises of Iran and Afghanistan. Now that support was a memory, tarnished by the continued holding of the hostages and Carter's own unpleasant campaign behavior. This meant that the case against Reagan had to stand or fall on its own weight. There was no longer an aura of competence and commanding presence around the White House. When Reagan began coming under fire in August and September, the Carter campaign may well have believed that the primary campaign was repeating itself; that under intense press scrutiny, their opponent would self-destruct.

Even though Reagan's performance in the debate against John Anderson had gone a long way toward dispelling that image of recklessness, the Carter campaign was officially pressing for a one-on-one debate with Reagan, on the premise that the President's command of the facts would contrast with the challenger's vagueness. The *New York Times* supported the demand this way on October 17: "Anyone who was exercised about Jimmy Carter's refusal to appear in a three-man televised Presidential debate last month should, in all fairness, be just as exercised about Mr. Reagan's continuing unwillingness to engage in a two-way debate. He is now the candidate responsible for keeping the public from seeing the rivals slug it out, side by side."

That case against Reagan had a short run, however, for on the same day, October 17, both Reagan and Carter agreed to participate in a one-on-one debate sponsored by the League. Reagan could not resist one last jab at Carter for excluding Anderson, saying, "I will leave to his conscience and the judgment of the American people whether or not Mr. Carter should meet Mr. Anderson." Reports suggested a variety of reasons for the decision, which was debated vigorously within the Reagan camp: his lead was slipping, the campaign was dead in the water; a debate "froze" the campaign where it was, with Reagan still holding a slim lead, while preventing any momentum toward Carter; Reagan himself felt he should debate if he was asking voters to replace the incumbent President. An additional explanation actually had its roots in the 1976 election, when an unelected incumbent President, trailing badly in the polls, challenged his opponent to debate in his acceptance speech at the Republican Convention. When President Ford became the first sitting President to debate a rival major party nominee, it helped to institutionalize Presidential debates as an event the American voters had a right to see. No candidate wanted to be stigmatized as the one who killed the 1980 debates: not Ronald Reagan, who had made great political capital out of the President's refusal, and not President Carter, whose entire counterargument had been that Reagan was ducking a two-man debate. In fact, by mid-October, some of Carter's own advisors were having serious second thoughts about just how masterful the President would be.

They had seen Reagan treat John Anderson with indulgent good humor, and a perfectly competent command of the facts. Worse, the two major party candidates actually had met face-to-face, at New York's Al Smith dinner in mid-October. This white-tie gathering of the city's Catholic community tends to be unbalanced toward the more affluent, conservative Catholics, and Ronald Reagan's reception can be partially explained on grounds of political preference. The more important explanation, however, is that Reagan followed the spirit of the evening, which is one of jocular good-humor. (It was at the Al Smith dinner in 1960 that John Kennedy delivered a succession of one-liners that disarmed the largely Republican audience, reporting that after announcing that political contributions would not be a factor in picking nominees, "I have not heard one word from my father.") Reagan declared "there is no foundation to the rumor that I am the only one here who was at the original Al Smith dinner" (thirty-five years earlier), and mocking Carter's Southern drawl, he told of the President's asking him, "Ronneh, how com yew look younger every day when I see a new picture of yew ridin' horseback?" "Jimmeh," Reagan said he had replied, "I jes keep ridin' older hawses." Carter's speech included a lame crack that "the paint on Reagan's 'I Love New York' button is still wet,"—a reference to his change of heart about loan guarantees for the city—and an attack on a right-wing evangelical who had argued that "God does not hear the prayers of a Jew." It was after the Al Smith dinner that Reagan decided to accept the League's invitation to debate, and the Carter camp had firsthand evidence that their man was capable of being decisively beaten in a public forum. There was, however, no way for Carter to avoid the debate without suffering enormous political damage. There was no Situation Room to retreat to, no "commander-in-chief" aura to insulate him from the demands of politics. He had been out campaigning since the convention two months earlier; thus, a retreat back into "Presidentiality" would have been, literally, unbelievable.

The ten days between the mutual acceptance of the debate and the October 28 meeting in Cleveland was filled with the kind of predebate debate skirmishing that is a reflexive instinct of any campaign worker. The League had set Cleveland and October 28 as the place and time of the debate weeks earlier; in the Washington negotiations that began on Monday, October 20, the Carter campaign argued for an earlier debate, in the hope that the expected Reagan errors would have time to percolate through the electorate. In a whimsical moment, Reagan aide James Baker argued that the debate be held on November 3, the night before the election, "when most voters are making up their minds," and "after all the campaign advertising and hoopla has had its effect and is over." To that argument, Jody Powell, the White House Press Secretary, noted that such a debate "would leave no time for anybody to be called for misstatements, contradictions, or inaccuracies." (As it turned out, the last-minute movement on the hostages might have given Carter an excuse to cancel an Election Eve debate with at least a cover of plausibility.)

There was a short-lived argument over format; should journalists ask questions, or should the two candidates speak and rebut each other with only a moderator to control the proceedings? The Carter camp seemed for a time to be arguing for a wide-open format, to minimize the fact that Reagan "is a very polished performer," in the words of a Carter aide. Reagan argued for a replay of the 1976 format, with closing statements and reporters' questions, and in the end a compromise of sorts was reached: journalists would ask questions and receive answers for the first forty-five minutes of the debate, as well as in the second; but during the last forty-five minutes, there would be a chance for an extended colloquy of answers and responses. Other negotiations focused on the mechanics of the debate: the two podia would each be belt-buckle high (minimizing Reagan's height advantage); a hundred seats in the first rows of the Music Hall at Cleveland's Convention Center would be removed, so that audience reactions would be more difficult to pick up by the television cameras (no campaign wants a picture of sarcastic laughter to be seen following a slip of the tongue);

"cutaway" shots of the candidates would be held to a minimum (some-times a candidate relaxes while his opponent is speaking, or rubs his eyes or picks at his face. This makes for bad results when the camera picks up such a gesture).

Carter and Reagan were meeting at a time when the United States economy was in a perilous state: interest rates were beginning a rapid climb that would see them double within six months; Ford and General Motors would, in the days before the debate, announce the two worst quarterly losses in American industrial history; joblessness was spreading through the industrial Northeast; and in major cities, the lack of capital had reached the point where subways, buses, bridges, tunnels, and water systems were in peril of physical collapse, while the crime rate was rising to the point where New York City would approach 2,000 homicides a year. Internationally, the continuing hos-tage crisis was a small element in the American dilemma: Western European nations were expressing doubt about the will and determi-nation of the United States to shore up the Western alliance, while retrenching on their own commitments to bolster defenses (West Ger-man Chancellor Helmut Schmidt was openly contemptuous of the American President); the combined fears of nuclear proliferation and Soviet expansionism were confronting American policy makers with questions of the most complicated sort.

These questions deserve mention in the context of the debate because, in the days before the two major party candidates for Presi-dent met, the overwhelming weight of press coverage did not focus on these questions at all. So heavily was the tactical element of the con-frontation played up by newspapers and television that the average voter might have been forgiven for believing he needed a scorecard or a tout sheet, rather than an informed mind, to judge the debate. The sports-and-battle metaphors had routed the idea that questions of past deeds and future intentions were the questions at hand. It was, to be sure, hardly the sole responsibility of the press, since aides to the candidates openly talked about what images and impressions they in-tended to convey. For by 1980, the tactical calculations of politics had long since come out of the closet. Not only was there no pretense that politicians spoke only to matters of high principle, there was at times a suggestion that nothing else was at stake except tactics. It would probably have seemed the height of naivete for either the campaign organizations or the press to set down a group of major questions facing the country and say, "This is what the debate should be about."

If the American economy was in peril, then the question was how Reagan could capitalize on that Carter vulnerability; if the world was a dangerous place, then the question would be how Carter could gain points by painting Reagan as a reckless extremist.

As *Newsweek* summarized the prevailing view of the contest in its

October 27 issue, "Jimmy Carter will try to project himself as an experienced world leader, a calm man in a crisis, a thoughtful policy-maker with a firm grasp of complex issues. Ronald Reagan will seek to reassure the undecided voters that he is Presidential timber, not a rash extremist who will plunge the nation into war or dismantle the social-security system." The analysis was studded with hopes and fears about the impressions each candidate might leave.

A Carter aide warned that "he just can't get personal." "He had to re-prove the fact that he is President." He "should force Reagan into a mistake and jump on it." Reagan, said a political consultant, "has to have an uplifting, optimistic, can-do attitude." "I think appearance is much more important than a whole bunch of facts—how you look, how you act, and how you present yourself," said deputy campaign manager William Timmons. "Reagan will be calm, cool, and collected, and the President will be tense, just as he was at the Al Smith dinner."

The October 24 *New York Times* view of the debate was filled with much the same kind of focus. "For the Carter side," the *Times* said, "the ideal result would be for Mr. Reagan to make a gaffe that would put him on the defensive."

In a predebate view on CBS "Morning" on October 27, correspondent Jed Duvall noted that "You've heard the President say for several days now that this debate gives us the opportunity to show the sharp differences, the stark differences. And that's what he wants to do. He wants some distance between them. He wants to show that I'm the President, I'm distinguished and responsible, and this other fellow, he's an actor, he's shallow, he's frivolous, he's dangerous. That's the impression Carter wants to get across tomorrow night." On the next day, the morning of the debate, NBC's "Today" show had columnists Jack Germond and David Broder and NBC correspondent Tom Pettit previewing the candidates' "game plans."

David Broder, noting that Carter "has finally discovered once again, as he did in 1976, that it pays to emphasize the fact that he is a Democrat" warned that if Carter "tries to destroy [Reagan] in personal terms, . . . everything we've seen of Governor Reagan in the past shows that he is a master at protecting himself . . ." Pettit and Germond noted that Reagan would gain points just by standing on an equal footing with Carter. "For a great many voters," said Germond, "this is going to be essentially a first impression of Ronald Reagan, and if he does well, if he doesn't start talking about killer trees or whatever, he is going to profit from that."

The "Today" show also featured interviews with Carter campaign chief Robert Strauss and Reagan campaign director Ed Meese; both men demonstrated the way in which campaigns attempt to frame the question before the actual event.

As Carter had done in his acceptance speech, Strauss attempted to cast Reagan as a candidate outside the mainstream of responsible thinking. The President, he said, using the key catchphrase of Carter's campaign, would "hammer away not so much at one issue as trying to structure the *stark differences* between himself on the one hand, and Governor Reagan on the other." (Later in the program, Rosalynn Carter told Richard Valeriani that the debate "will point out the *stark differences* between my husband and Mr. Reagan.") In an effort to lower expectations—particularly within the press corps—about the stylistic confrontation, Strauss said, "I suspect that Governor Reagan has more style, more performing talent on the one hand, and I really think the President has a bit more substance, a good deal more, on the other . . . [the people] will ignore the style if you will, and oratorical, theatrical ability, and get down to substance."

Meese argued that "there's no question that the failures of this administration in the economic issue will stand out probably as the highlights of the debate. . . . The key issue is whether we need a change, and I think the governor's feelings is that the President's record, his failures, constitute the main issue and illustrate why we need a change."

It is certainly wrong to argue that either television or the press was pushing policy debate completely off the stage. The nightly network newscasts were all using interviews and speeches of the candidates to stage "minidebates" over the last weeks of the campaign, and the "Today" show put together what Tom Brokaw called a "primer on what you may hear in terms of the issues tonight," showing brief exchanges from Carter and Reagan speeches about SALT II, military preparedness, and defense. (The exchange lasted about two and a half minutes.) The point, rather, is that the great mass of information communicated to the public about the debate focused on one critical aspect of the confrontation—who would win the strategic battle—and chose not to cast the debate as a battle over ideas, the records of the two men, the problems with the policies each was advocating. When 120 million Americans sat down in front of their sets at 9:30 P.M. Eastern time, they were watching a debate whose substantive dimension had gone largely unexamined. They had been splendidly prepared to watch a boxing match or a football game; they had been left largely to their own devices in judging the discourse. That does *not* mean, however, that the public ignored that part of the debate; it means, rather, that the press had largely failed to help set out the agenda on which the arguments could be judged.

Unlike the Reagan-Anderson debate, the rules of the Carter-Reagan confrontation permitted follow-up questions for the first forty-five minutes of the debate. In addition, as panel member Barbara Walters said after the event's conclusion, "We had met last night. We decided that we would not try to ask trick questions, or even those that might make the headlines, but to really try to ask the issues that we thought were most important to the public at large, even if we might know some of the answers. And we divided the areas and knew what each of us was going to ask." Marvin Stone, editor of *U.S. News and World Report,* said, "We chose not to play an adversarial role, not to needle the candidates." Instead, Walters, Stone, *Portland Oregonian* editor William Hilliard, and *Christian Science Monitor* reporter Harry Ellis framed their questions for breadth and specificity. For all of the legitimate concerns about the presence of journalists and the wistful longing for a Presidential debate with direct confrontation, the reporters played a valuable role in turning attention toward some of the hard questions on the national agenda.

For the audience of 750 in the hall, one of the most dramatic moments came just before airtime, when President Carter entered from stage left and Ronald Reagan from stage right to take their places at the podia. Carter went right to his podium, and began jotting down notes to himself. Reagan, perhaps remembering that he and Anderson had moved toward center stage and shaken hands at the start of their debate, walked across the stage, stopped in front of Carter, and extended his hand to the startled President. Intended or not, the gesture had the impact of a psychological ploy just before the start of a heavyweight fight, when one combatant forces the other to look away. Given the emphasis on style that characterized the predebate analysis, it is fortunate the television cameras did not capture the confrontation, or Carter might have been declared the loser by a prefirst round TKO.

The very first question, posed by Marvin Stone to Ronald Reagan, demonstrated two aspects that would dominate the ninety-minute exchange: the journalists' determination to pose relevant, specific questions, and the candidates' determination to follow the first rule of political debating: to answer the question *you* want to answer, making the points most important to your campaign, no matter what is asked.

What, Stone wanted to know, are the differences between the two of you on the uses of American military power?

Reagan began clumsily, saying, "I don't know what the differences might be, because I don't know what Mr. Carter's policies are" —a silly remark given Reagan's four-year attack on those policies. But then, trying to fulfill his advisors' desires that he be reassuring on the war and peace issue that was supposedly his biggest vulnerability, Reagan said, "I'm only here to tell you that I believe with all my heart that our first priority must be world peace, and that use of force is always and only a last resort when everything else has failed." He ended his first answer by repeating the theme.

"I have seen four wars in my lifetime; I'm a father of sons; I have a grandson. I don't ever want to see another generation of young

Americans bleed their lives into sandy beachheads in the Pacific or rice paddies and jungles in Asia or the muddy, bloody fields—battlefields of Europe.''

When the same question was posed to Carter, the President immediately wrapped himself in the mantle of the White House, from which he would hold forth for the entire debate.

"I've had to make thousands of decisions since I've been President, serving in the Oval Office. . . . There are decisions that are made in the Oval Office by every President which are profound in nature. There are always trouble spots in the world. And how those trouble spots are addressed by a President, alone in the Oval Office, affects our nation directly. [Military force] is a basic decision that has to be made so frequently by every president who serves.''

It might have been a Carter campaign commercial featuring Carter poring over secret papers at his desk, reminding us of his burden. It was the first of many answers all designed to stress the key distinction between the two contenders in the frame of the Carter campaign: that Jimmy Carter was in fact the President, familiar with burdens and complexities beyond the ken of this aging, not very bright ex-actor. In addition, Carter raised the question of Reagan's "seriousness" at the first opportunity, arguing that Reagan "has advocated the injection of military forces into troubled areas when I and my predecessors—both Democrats and Republicans—have advocated resolving these troubles and those difficult areas of the world peacefully . . .'' Thus the attempt to read Reagan out of the Presidential mainstream.

Harry Ellis's question shifted the ground to Reagan's turf, to the area of the troubled economy. The President pointed to OPEC price increases as the key villain in the inflation scenario, cited third-quarter inflation figures showing inflation dropping to 7 percent a year—ludicrously misleading numbers, it turned out—and then attacked Reagan's tax-cutting plan by quoting his running mate, George Bush ("Voodoo economics"), and *Business Week* ("would result in inflationary pressures which would destroy this nation"). Carter pointed to economic prosperity ahead. "The new economic revitalization program that we have in mind, which will be implemented next year, would result in tax credits which would let business invest in new tools and new factories to create even more new jobs. . . . And we also have planned a youth employment program which would encompass 600,000 jobs for young people.''

Reagan took full advantage of the chance to lay waste Carter's record. He cited inflation figures—proof that he was not speaking in generalities—but then moved to his rhetorical strength, the encapsulation of an argument in a memorable, if frequently used phrase.

Carter, said Reagan, has blamed "OPEC; he has blamed the Federal Reserve System; he has blamed the lack of productivity of the

American people; he has then accused the people of living too well, and that we must share in scarcity, we must sacrifice and get used to doing with less. We don't have inflation because the people are living too well. We have inflation because the government is living too well."

Reagan dodged the question about lessening government spending by arguing for the elimination of those old standbys, "fraud and waste," but when he cited his record in California, it resulted in the first effective exchange of the night. Carter, as had John Anderson a month earlier, pointed to "the three largest tax increases in the history of [California]; he more than doubled state spending while he was governor." In his reply, Reagan said with a broad smile that "while I was governor of California our spending in California increased less per capita than the spending in Georgia while Mr. Carter was governor. . . . The size of government increased only one-sixth in California of what it increased in proportion to population in Georgia."

Carter had his first opening during the next exchange on conditions in the inner cities. Reagan offered his proposal for "development zones" in poor neighborhoods, where business development and job creation would be spurred by tax abatements (a similar idea had been proposed in 1967 by Senator Robert Kennedy, and such a citation might have partially disarmed critics who saw him as antiblack; but either Reagan did not know of Kennedy's idea or did not want to alienate his own more conservative supporters). When questioner Hilliard asked Reagan for his view of the future of a multiracial society, Reagan said, "I happen to believe that we've made great progress from the days when I was young and when this country didn't even know it had a racial problem."

Carter answered the same question with a stream of facts about job creation under his Administration.

"Of the 9 million people put back to work in new jobs since I've been in office," Carter said, "1.3 million of those have been among black Americans, and another million among those who speak Spanish. We're now planning to continue the revitalization program with increased commitments of rapid transit, mass transit. Under the windfall profits tax, we expect to spend about $43 billion in the next ten years to rebuild the transportation systems of our country. We're also pursuing housing programs. We've had a 73 percent increase in the allotment of federal funds for improved education."

Then, shaking himself out of the fog of overpreparation, the President said, "I notice that Governor Reagan said that when he was a younger man, that there was no knowledge of a racial problem in this country. Those who suffered from discrimination because of race or sex certainly knew we had a racial problem." It was an effective rejoinder, accurately reflecting Reagan's roots in a small town of long ago, where blacks were simply invisible. But it also demonstrated

Carter's intention to appeal to his constituencies: the question had had nothing at all to do with *sex* discrimination; but Carter was running far better among women than among men, and part of the reason was Reagan's opposition to the Equal Rights Amendment. Carter's reference to victims of "sex discrimination" who certainly knew we had a *racial* problem was a non sequitur, but a politically clever one.

Similarly, Carter was engaged throughout the last weeks of the campaign in a desperate effort to patch up the Democratic coalition. So in talking about racial justice, Carter broadened the focus.

"There's no doubt in my mind," he said, "that the commitment to unemployment compensation, the minimum wage, welfare, national health insurance, those kinds of commitments that have typified the Democratic Party since ancient history in this country's political life, are a very important element of the future. In all those elements, Governor Reagan has repeatedly spoken out against them."

That same effective tactic was used by Carter to deflect Barbara Walters's question about terrorism—potentially the most sensitive question, since it approached the issue of how a President should deal with a future Iranian crisis. Carter, however, wanted to shift the ground to the area of Reagan's greatest vulnerability: the war and peace issue in a nuclear age. Supposedly answering Walters's questions about what America learned from the Iranian seizure, Carter offered a few sentences about terrorism. Then he abruptly changed course:

"Ultimately," he said, "the most serious terrorist threat is if one of those radical nationals who believe in terrorism as a policy should have atomic weapons. Both I and all my predecessors have had a deep commitment to controlling the proliferation of nuclear weapons in countries like Libya or Iraq. . . . When Governor Reagan has been asked about that, he makes a very disturbing comment that nonproliferation, or the control of nuclear weapons, is none of our business."

Reagan tried to note the shift by saying, "Barbara, you've asked that question twice. I think you ought to have at least one answer to it." But at the end of his rebuttal, Reagan appeared to recognize the danger of ignoring the issue, so he said, "I have never made the statement that he suggested about nuclear proliferation." It was a flat-out mistake. Reagan had said exactly that the policy of other nations was not a matter of American concern. "I just don't think it's any of our business," he told a press conference in Jacksonville, Florida, on January 30. Not only did the Carter campaign know it, they had a video tape of it, and a Carter commercial attacking the contradiction was on the air within forty-eight hours.

The debate was now entering the most treacherous ground for Reagan: the question of nuclear arms control. In this area, any incumbent starts off at a double advantage: first, he is deemed to know facts no one else, even a major party nominee for the Presidency, could know; second, because the world has not been blown up in an incumbent's first term, he has already answered the question, "Can this man be trusted with the button?" Reagan recognized the danger; Carter the opportunity. Perhaps fittingly, the exchange would end with the President tossing away a clear advantage by resorting to a compulsion to personalize that had plagued his entire public life.

Reagan's response was protective; after charging the President with blocking or delaying important weapons systems, he wrapped his own opposition to the SALT II treaty on nuclear arms reduction in a bipartisan mantle.

"I have not blocked the SALT II treaty," he said. "It has been blocked by a Senate in which there is a Democratic majority. Indeed, the Senate Armed Services Committee voted ten to zero, with seven abstentions, against the SALT II treaty . . ."

Now it was Carter's turn. For months, the President and his aides had been talking about the "stark differences" between the two candidates, a curious term that conjures up fear and trembling. Reagan, the Carter campaign had been arguing, was a frightening figure to contemplate controlling nuclear power. Now Carter's answer showed —perhaps too obviously, but still effectively—what the essence of their campaign against Reagan was all about:

"There is a *disturbing* pattern in the attitude of Governor Reagan," Carter said. "When a man who hopes to be President says take this treaty, discard it . . . that is a very dangerous and disturbing thing." And a moment later, Carter went on in the same vein. "Governor Reagan is making some very misleading and *disturbing* statements. [Resumption of the arms race] would be very *disturbing* to the American people . . . and would also be very *disturbing* to our allies . . . This attitude is extremely *dangerous* and *belligerent* in tone— although it's said with a quiet voice." Reagan tried a quip to defuse the Carter attack—saying that Carter's attack was "like the witch doctor that gets mad when a good doctor comes along with a cure that'll work"—but Carter was making his argument with real force. Every past President had indeed sought nuclear arms limitations with the Russians, and Reagan was, *in fact,* advocating a policy that was different in substance and in tone from this history. Further, foreign policy was an area in which Reagan was, *in fact,* comparatively unsure of himself, comparatively inexperienced. His inept handling of the status of Taiwan in August had demonstrated that. And in warning the voters of this inexperience, Carter was ploughing fertile soil.

Then, in the final comment on this issue, Carter dropped this bombshell—on himself.

"I had a discussion with Amy the other day before I came here to ask her what the most important issue was," the President said. "She thought nuclear weaponry and the control of nuclear arms." He compared the power of a fifty-megaton bomb to "a trainload of TNT stretching across the country," and again said that Reagan was pursuing "a very *dangerous* approach." Inside the Music Hall, however, a faint snicker rippled through the crowd. Carter had once again cast a critical public policy matter into personal, familial terms; a political character trait that was something of a compulsion. He had first run for the Presidency on the basis of his character, on the promise that "I will never lie to you," claiming a "close, personal, intimate relationship with the American voter." He had argued in the primaries that the role of good family man was "inseparable" from that of good President. Now, in an attempt to put a personal perspective on the question of war and peace—and, as CBS's Dan Rather noted, to evoke memories of Lyndon Johnson's 1964 "Daisy" girl being obliterated in a holocaust—he had trivialized the issue and made himself faintly ridiculous. In the postdebate analysis and comments, this single moment was the most memorable of anything Carter had said; and it was powerfully "unpresidential" and foolish.

Perhaps encouraged by this moment, Reagan seemed to relax as the debate progressed. The television cameras showed him listening to his rival, occasionally jotting down notes, occasionally smiling. Carter, by contrast, seemed to grow more formal, stiff, frozen-eyed. The two men sparred with facts and figures over energy and conservation, government regulations to protect the environment and to encourage exploration and oil drilling. Carter tried to link Ronald Reagan with the idea of making Social Security voluntary, and Reagan insisted that "I am pledged to a Social Security program that will reassure these senior citizens of ours they're going to continue to get their money." Still pursuing the "fear and trembling" approach, Carter said, "These constant suggestions that the basic Social Security system should be changed does cause concern and consternation among the aged of our country," and concluded by arguing that Reagan had opposed Medicare.

Reagan smiled, shook his head, chuckled, and said, "There you go again." His answer was an explanation of the alternative to Medicare he had favored sixteen years earlier, but here style clearly did count over substance. Reagan was, it appeared, enjoying the combat by now, willing to address a personal observation directly to his rival.

When Walters asked the last question—an open-ended invitation to contrast the records of the candidates—Carter offered something of a checklist of the elements of the Democratic coalition he sought to retain.

He was, he said, "a Democrat in the mainstream of my party" as opposed to Reagan, who was radically departing from the positions of Eisenhower and others. He pointed to Reagan's advocacy of military force, and—after Reagan listed President Carter's own "misery index of inflation and unemployment to show how it had grown under Carter —the President turned to the Equal Rights Amendment as proof of "the radical departure from the principles or ideals or historic perspective of his own party." When Reagan sought to defend his opposition to the ERA by promising to attack discriminatory regulations, it triggered an appeal by Carter to yet another wavering part of the Democratic coalition.

"I'm a Southerner," Carter said, "and I share the basic beliefs of my region about an excessive government intrusion into the private affairs of American citizens, and also into the private affairs of the free enterprise system. . . . My heritage as a Southerner, my experience in the Oval Office, convinces me that what I've just described is a proper course for the future." Here the viewer could almost see the stitches of the advisors at work. Carter was coming to the end of the debate and had not yet made any appeal to his Southern constituency, without which reelection would be hopeless. Reagan's reference to "regulations"—in the context of discrimination—somehow reminded Carter of this group.

Now it was time for the closing statement. Carter had won the coin toss, but had chosen to let Reagan speak first; his advisors had seen early nervousness on Reagan's part in the Anderson debate and had hoped to capitalize on that fact. By letting Reagan speak first, however, they were also required under the rules to let Reagan have the last word. This turned out to be a disastrous miscalculation.

A nervous Jimmy Carter began his closing statement by thanking the League of Women Voters and "the people of Cleveland and Ohio for being such hospitable hosts during this last few hours of my life—" a remark which suggested impending death. He then tried again to remind the voters of the majesty of his office. "In each case" of danger abroad, he said, "I alone have had to determine the interest of my country . . . the final judgment about the future of a nation, war, peace, involvement, reticence, thoughtfulness, care, consideration, concern has to be made by the man in the Oval Office. It's a lonely job, but with the involvement of the American people in the process, with an open government, the job is a very gratifying one." He reminded his audience that a small number of votes can make a difference, and concluded, "I ask the American people to join me in this partnership."

Now it was Reagan's turn. After thanking the League, and expressing regret that John Anderson had not been included in a three-way debate, Reagan looked directly into the camera and delivered what commentators later—much later—agreed was a knockout punch.

"Next Tuesday," he said, "all of you will go to the polls, you'll stand there in the polling place and make a decision. I think, when you make that decision it might be well if you would ask yourself: Are you better off than you were four years ago? Is it easier for you to go and buy things in the stores than it was four years ago? Is there more or less unemployment in the country than there was four years ago? Is America as respected throughout the world as it was? Do you feel our security is as safe, that we're as strong as we were four years ago? And if you answer all of those questions yes, why then I think your choice is very obvious as to who you'll vote for. If you don't agree, if you don't think that this course that we've been on for the last four years is what you would like to see us follow for the next four, then I could suggest another choice that you have. This country doesn't have to be in the shape it is in.'' He briefly defended his record as governor of California, and ended by promising a crusade ''to take government off the back of the great people of this country and turn you loose again to do those things that I know you can do so well, because you did them and made this country great.''

In that closing statement, Reagan had done to Carter much of what Carter had done to Kennedy in the primaries; he had forced the voters to face the fact that on November 4 they would be choosing a President. It was a perfect example of what I have elsewhere called ''political judo.'' Carter had tried to stress his ''Presidentiality,'' to remind voters of the burdens of the Oval Office. Reagan, in effect, had said—''You're absolutely right, Jimmy. You *have* been in that Oval Office for the last four years, and the question is—what have you been doing and do the American people want you to keep doing it?'' That had been the single most damaging question for Carter since 1978, when he had begun to sink in the polls; it was the question for which there was no effective political answer, and in raising it, Reagan had said, in effect, ''Now that I have proven that I can duel with the President on more-or-less equal footing, why not go back to the choice you have been wanting to make for months? Let's get a new President.''

The postdebate analysis on the part of the networks and the next day's print press paid comparatively little attention to these closing remarks, probably because the press is so cynical about the power of political speech. There was no clear declaration of a ''winner,'' since the press had learned over and over again that its interpretation of the winner tends to influence public opinion more than the debate itself. Instead, the networks hustled about the hall, grabbing political partisans, going to remote locations where ''typical Americans'' were watching the debate, and otherwise attempting to assess the impact.

CBS's Dan Rather reported that ''The general impression was that neither had scored a particularly large advantage over the other, that neither had made any kind of error that would hurt greatly in the campaign." Vice-President Mondale said Carter had won; Vice-Presidential candidate George Bush said Reagan had won. Republican Senator John Tower said Reagan had won, and recognized one of Carter's unhappier moments, quipping "I think Jimmy Carter made a very interesting revelation, and that is that Amy is now his National Security Advisor." Jesse Jackson picked up on one of Reagan's unhappier moments, attacking Reagan's lack of knowledge of a racial problem in his youth as "gross insensitivity." Bruce Morton and Walter Cronkite thought Reagan had come off more relaxed; Morton observed, "Reagan is the only one who seemed to have any fun with it. I thought Mr. Carter looked stiff, not ill at ease, but formal and no warmth." Reagan, said Cronkite, "was a little more at home tonight with the audience." Lesley Stahl argued that Carter "accomplished most of what he set out to do. He tried very hard to reach out to the traditional Democrats. . . . I was surprised that he was as relaxed and composed as he was." Stahl also said that "I think he'll regret having mentioned Amy as a person who talks to him about nuclear policy." Bill Plante, who covered Reagan throughout the campaign, noted that "Reagan wanted to present himself as a competent man of peace. I thought he was a little bit more nervous . . . but nonetheless I think he got his major point across."

ABC used liberal columnist Tom Wicker and conservative columnist George Will as commentators, with Will providing an unusual insight since he had helped brief the Republican candidate for the debate. Both made the point that, in Wicker's words, "the fact that there's no clear winner probably—and I say this with great caution— probably gives an edge to Governor Reagan," since Reagan did not appear "as ill-informed, as unfit to be the President, as unpresidential, as being sort of a mad bomber." This, in Will's phrase, was Reagan's "virtually guaranteed plus." The network also aired the views of two debate coaches, who were divided in their view of the victor. ABC scored something of a coup by having Barbara Walters chat with her fellow panelists, none of whom expressed an opinion about a clear victor. But Walters reflected her recognition of the single most memorable event of the evening when she said "I think Amy won. And I'm going home to my child, who's the same age as Amy, and if she doesn't tell me that nuclear proliferation is the major concern on her mind she's going to hear it from her mother."

It was also ABC that provided the most notable—and criticized —postdebate analysis in an attempt to offer some objective sort of measurement to indicate who won the debate. The network set up, in its words, "a massive computerized telephone poll, nationwide," to enable callers to register their views on who won by calling one of two numbers, after which their votes would automatically be recorded. From the moment ABC's Ted Koppel began the postdebate show, until the end, ABC announced, at least a dozen times, that the poll was "not scientific," "No scientifically selected sample." This was so for obvious reasons. Callers could dial the numbers as often as they wished. In some locations, the telephone lines were busier than others. The fifty-cent-per-call charge skewed the poll away from poorer, and presumably more heavily Democratic viewers.

Most important, however, was the manner in which the poll was covered. Correspondent Ron Miller sat in the Bell Systems' Network Operations Center in Bedminster, New Jersey, in a room stuffed with maps, computers, and other space age gadgetry. A map of the United States dominated the background; flashing lights and lists of locations were frequently panned by the camera. And every time a new figure was announced, it flashed on the screen with graphics that looked exactly like Election Night returns. The words of the correspondents were meant to explain—repeatedly—that there was no scientific validity to the straw poll, but the pictures totally belied that. As for the numbers, they remained constant throughout the evening: by the end of the broadcast, more than 700,000 people had called in to vote, and Reagan was judged the winner by an almost precisely 2–1 margin.

The poll was denounced by most professional polltakers the next day in strong terms.

"No credence at all should be given to the figures," said George Gallup, Sr., dean of the pollsters. He compared it to the infamous 1936 *Literary Digest* poll, predicting victory for Alf Landon over Franklin Roosevelt because of its income bias. Albert Cantril, president of a polling association, said, "Disavowing it as vigorously as they did raises the question of why they did it at all." An executive of Lou Harris and Associates, which did the election polling for ABC, said, "I think it was a terrible disservice and very misleading." * But for all of the questions—about income bias, about the fact that in some cities people who dialed the numbers for Carter and Reagan were told they had voted for the other candidate, the fact that more people in the pro-Reagan West may have stayed up longer after the debate—the numbers were reported on the wires and in most newspapers and broadcast reports the next day. And at least some political observers suggested that the poll, if nothing else, measured the intensity factor, the degree to which supporters felt sufficiently engaged in the campaign to participate in a straw poll. True or not, the poll did confirm the intuitions of most reporters that Ronald Reagan had a much stronger core of true believers than did Jimmy Carter.

The initial press responses tended to produce the same analysis as did the networks: no clear winner, pretty much of a draw, which

---

* After the 1980 election was over, the Harris organization and ABC dissolved their association.

favored Ronald Reagan by making him appear "Presidential." John Stacks of *Time* magazine, who thought Carter had effectively hurt Reagan on the war and peace issue, and whose summation he judged "slightly better and more coherent than Reagan's" felt Reagan had come off well by simply being "on the same stage as the President of the United States." Other participants on PBS's "MacNeil-Lehrer Report," local newspaper editors and political consultants, were cautious and divided. "No Clear Winner Apparent," the *New York Times* put it the next morning. Polling data suggested an edge for Reagan— the CBS poll had it 44–36 with 4 percent calling it a tie—but that poll still showed Carter ahead of Reagan in the vote for President. It also showed, however, that the undecided voters were moving toward Reagan by a 2–1 margin.

News programs on television the next day were filled with partisans of the candidates proclaiming victory in a kind of coverage that had become a parody of itself. To hear Governor Reagan's chief debate negotiator or the job-seeking Henry Kissinger extolling Reagan's performance, or to see Carter's campaign chief and press secretary proclaiming victory for the President was ritual and nothing more. Perhaps in 1960 a campaign aide might have confessed to unhappiness with Richard Nixon's makeup, but by 1980 the players knew their parts well—to the point where, at breakfast the next day, Jody Powell was telling reporters of a Pat Caddell survey showing that Carter had helped his cause in the debate, while Caddell was explaining—at almost the same time—that Reagan would gain a small "bump-up" from the debate which would not affect the outcome.

Newspapers did attempt to assess the factual claims in the debate, finding flaws on both sides. A *New York Times* piece discovered that Ronald Reagan had indeed said that nuclear proliferation is none of the United States's business, that President Carter had indeed played loose with the facts in condemning Republican defense cutbacks while praising his own increases, that Carter's citation of a 7 percent inflation figure was misleading, that Reagan had indeed advocated something close to a voluntary Social Security system.

What appeared irrelevant, to judge by the press reaction to the debate, was what the two candidates were trying to tell the viewers— the voters—about what they had done and what they had intended to do. Even accepting the fact that candidates themselves are seeking to leave behind images rather than a packet of substantive points when they debate, the fact is that the tools they must use are descriptions of beliefs and deeds. This exercise was left behind in the rush to fill in the demands of th debate metaphor: Was there a knockout? If not, who won on points? Who landed the deepest hits? Who parried better? It was, remarkably enough, not until after the election that Reagan's closing peroration—"Are you better off than you were four years ago?''—became recognized as something of a classic in American political rhetoric.

The press, in other words, had become so sophisticated about imagery and impressions, the candidates' aides had become so fixated on the manipulative aspects of their own jobs, that no one was left to consider the prospect that large numbers of undecided Americans *might be listening to the arguments the candidates were making*. Thus, it was not just that Reagan could look good-natured and reassuring that may have dampened the war and peace doubts, but the fact that he could demonstrate that he was indeed well within the mainstream of respectable thinking about nuclear arms. If Senator Henry Jackson and Henry Kissinger agreed with him, how could he be an extremist?

Thus, if President Carter was defending his record on providing 9 million new jobs, the blue-collar workers across the industrial Northeast and Midwest, looking at closed plants and neighbors out of work, might have heard a Democratic president, in effect, refusing to recognize the depths of joblessness among members of one of the key constituent groups within the Democratic Party—and in listening to the Republican candidate talking about growth and jobs and productivity, they might well have concluded that party loyalty had been stretched to the breaking point.

And perhaps most important, if we make the daring assumption that voters are not dim-witted fools, we might even imagine them gathering about their television sets to consider this basic question: "I know I am dissatisfied with Jimmy Carter's stewardship. I know I want to change Presidents. But I have been told that the alternative is a candidate so extreme, so unstable, as to risk our very survival. I want to see if Ronald Reagan can pass the test of acceptability. If he can, I know what I want to do, not from what will be said for the next ninety minutes, but from what has been happening for the last four years.''

The Carter campaign from its inception had been forced into the negative campaign by the limits of political credibility that are usually operative in elections. Carter's record, as it had come to be understood by most Americans, did not entitle him to a second term. Everything in the fundamental strategy of Carter's reelection bid reflected that reality and turned back to the familiar assault on the challenger that had worked in the spring. The debate was, we had been told, Ronald Reagan's Waterloo where his campaign would meet the impregnable forces of fact and reasonableness. But laboring under the perception of his record, Carter could not convince the voters that he was to be rewarded with a second term by virtue of his opponent's unfitness for the job.

The debate, then, was not a prize fight or football game or horse-race or crap shoot. It was a political exchange in which both candidates made their appeals with reasonable effectiveness. The problem for Jimmy Carter was that his arguments had been rejected perhaps a year earlier by most Americans. *Restating* them did not mean that they were *convincing*. We *knew* he had been alone in the Oval Office making decisions, but they were, most Americans felt, the wrong decisions. We *knew* he was working for a comprehensive energy policy, but gasoline was $1.40 a gallon, and inflation was out of control, and people were out of work, and the hostages were still in Iran. Ronald Reagan had a remarkably small test to pass, which he not only passed, but in which he defined the choice so clearly that the "stark differences" of which Carter and his aides had spoken so often became a *Reagan* advantage: the difference was that Ronald Reagan had not been leading America down the path it had been following for the last four years.

Of course television communicates personal qualities better than it does abstractions; it is the very essence of the medium. Of course Ronald Reagan's personal charm and humor worked to his advantage; it is what lawyers call "demeanor evidence," the way a witness holds his body, gestures, looks jurors in the eye or evades their glances. It is not only clear that people make political judgments from such data, it is probably quite sensible to do so, since gestures and facial expressions can be an effective guide to clues about character and even ability. This does *not* mean, however, that Ronald Reagan won the debate on acting ability (in fact, he was far less sure of his "lines," far more likely to invert a word every now and then, than the tightly programmed Carter). If anything, it was Carter who was the media creation, and Reagan who was speaking more naturally, more artlessly, using the arguments he had been using in the political and public arenas for the last three decades. In the end, the debate simply enabled him to contrast his beliefs with the record of Jimmy Carter's Presidency. That argument was powerful and influential in the outcome of the 1980 campaign.

xiv Advertising in the Fall Campaign: The Message Is the Message

In 1976, two academics named Thomas E. Patterson and Robert D. McClure offered a radically heretical view of the role of advertising in Presidential campaigns. In their book, *The Unseeing Eye,* Patterson and McClure argued that "amidst all of the elite concern, even horror, that some voters might pick a candidate in the same way that they buy a brand of soap, one aspect of televised political advertising has been ignored almost completely. Political commercials contain substantial information. Spots contain many appeals designed to give voters solid reasons why they should support one candidate instead of the other." In fact, they argued, given the superficial coverage of campaign substance by major organs of the press, television advertising may *better* inform the voter than news coverage of the campaign.

The race for the White House in 1980 offered dramatic confirmation of this revisionist thesis. For the voter trying to decide between Jimmy Carter and Ronald Reagan, the political advertising provided much clearer arguments about the nature of the choice than did the overall coverage of the campaign on television and in the mainstream press. Moreover, the advertising run by the major party candidates was—judged as a whole—less manipulative, less visually elaborate, and generally less dishonest than in any past campaign since the development of modern political advertising.

Several qualifications must be stated at the outset of the argument:

• Were there exaggerations, some distortions, omissions of fact in the commercials of Carter and Reagan? Absolutely; but they were well within the boundaries of acceptable political rhetoric. There was nothing approaching a personal smear, a dirty trick, or an outright lie.

• Were the commercials relatively restrained and straightforward because the campaigns and their media advisors were suddenly stricken with an attack of nobility? Not at all; the nature of the advertising was itself dictated by clear political realities. The public had

248

been exposed to political ads, and to their gimmicks, ever since the Eisenhower campaign of 1952 used spot advertising. They had grown in sophistication along with the medium. The techniques that might have been dazzling in 1964 or 1968 were by now shopworn and obvious. More important, the press itself was so conscious of campaign advertising that political commercials had ceased to be isolated from the scrutiny given to speeches, position papers, and charges and countercharges. As the primary coverage had shown, any attempt by a campaign to play with images brought the countervailing power of journalism to bear on the "offender"—whether it was George Bush stepping off an airplane he hadn't actually flown on, or Howard Baker receiving an out-of-context standing ovation, or Ronald Reagan failing to remember his own words in an ad. In the far more intense spotlight of a general election campaign, corner-cutting political packaging brought with it costs no campaign wished to bear.

• Were the political commercials swift-moving, thirty second contentless compilations of sentence fragments and pretty pictures? Far less so than in earlier campaigns. Both Carter and Reagan employed far more five-minute commercials than did their Presidential predecessors, and in the case of Ronald Reagan, some of the most important advertising he used was advertising only in the technical sense that the campaign had paid for the time. They were, in fact, half-hour speeches, put on television with little or no "production values." In the case of the Carter campaign, the commercials were designed to look as simple as possible; and while the ads were more elaborate than those of Reagan, they were, in the main, straightforward presentations of an argument.

• Perhaps most important, even granted that political advertising was designed to leave a favorable impression on the viewer, the tools used by the campaigns to leave those impressions were arguments about the nature of the choices facing the electorate. Was Ronald Reagan more than an effective television performer? To prove that, the Reagan campaign had to present its argument that Reagan had provided effective stewardship of the state of California. Was Jimmy Carter the legitimate heir to the Democratic Party tradition? Then Carter had to be seen juxtaposed with FDR, Truman, and John Kennedy, and perhaps risk the wrath of voters who did not accept the comparison. Was the President's campaign against Reagan as a threat to peace working? Then the Republican had to rebut that with a half-hour speech on national television in which his foreign policy beliefs were set down in some detail. Was Carter seen as an unworthy chief executive? Then the record of the Carter Administration had to be set down with some specificity.

To a substantial degree, political advertising—especially in a general Presidential election where information flows in something of a torrent across television, radio, the print press, and the general public —is emphatically *not* a creation of a campaign or its "high-priced media wizards" who spin fantasies out of thin air. It is indeed possible to do this in less visible elections, with candidates who come before the public as relative unknowns. The campaigns of major-party Presidential candidates, however, do not have this luxury. An incumbent President of the United States has a record and a political past that is unavoidable. His principal challenger will, by the time of his nomination, have been the subject of relentless examination. The very sophistication of modern-day campaigns further limits their advertising strategies. The combination of polling and press attention makes it very clear to a candidate's entourage that some claims and charges will not pass the credibility test. Thus, a better-organized Kennedy campaign would have recognized the futility of arguing about Chappaquiddick or painting the candidate as a devoted family man. Thus, the Reagan campaign would never have considered ads that showed Reagan and his wife riding horses and clearing brush at their Santa Monica retreat, *even though they did ride horses and clear brush most weekends,* because it would have been too obvious an attempt to manipulate the age issue. Thus, Carter commercials could not have shown a grateful America celebrating the rebirth of national pride and spirit, because those feelings about President Carter's term did not exist.

The choices made by the media advisors for Reagan (Peter Dailey, working off data from pollster Richard Wirthlin) and Carter (Gerald Rafshoon, working off data from pollster Pat Caddell) were limited. And they cannot be judged by the outcome of the campaign. The fact that Jimmy Carter went down to crushing defeat does not mean that an alternative media campaign could have saved him, unless it is assumed that there is always *some* advertising campaign that will convince passive voters to change their minds. Until the very end of the campaign, Reagan supporters and some sympathetic commentators were assailing Peter Dailey's decision to avoid sharply negative commercials attacking President Carter and his record (Evans and Novak, writing only days before the election, summarized their distaste for the Reagan strategy with the headline, "It Could Have Been a Landslide"). Conversely, the "people in the street" commercials attacking Ronald Reagan's judgment and stability were acknowledged by the Reagan campaign to have been effective in raising doubts about their candidate and in making the so-called "war-and-peace" issue the most difficult question for Reagan to answer. The best way to think about political advertising is to remember the words of Chief Dan George in *Little Big Man,* after he lies down and waits for the Great Spirit to take him up to the heavens. When nothing happens, the chief shakes his head, gets up, and says, "Sometimes the magic works, and sometimes it doesn't."

If there was one major disadvantage facing either of the candidates in planning advertising for the fall campaign, it was that President Carter had to redirect his message fundamentally, whereas Ronald Reagan could build on his primary campaign. Even though the agency was different, with Reagan's California-based organization favoring Californian and long-time associate Pete Dailey over Philadelphian Elliott Curson, there was no difference in what the candidate would be saying. Reagan's stripped-down primary campaign had talked about what he believed and why: the need for a strong defense, the need for tax cuts, his achievements as governor of California in cutting welfare fraud while helping the "truly needy," his conviction that a freer economy would also help the poor. This was the same Reagan who would be appearing in commercials during the fall.

For the Carter campaign, however, one of the major elements of the primary campaign was now irrelevant: the issue of character. Edward Kennedy's reputation as an adulterer, his strained marriage, and Chappaquiddick had given Carter a chance to exploit the asset that had been at the center of his public life: his personality, his strong family life. With a happily married exponent of traditional family values as his fall opponent, however, this message no longer made sense. Viewers seeing the President of the United States helping his daughter with her homework might well wonder why the chief executive was doing long division when Cuban troops and Soviet advisors were burrowing through Africa. The challenge for Rafshoon was not to convince Americans that the President was a good guy, but that he was up to the job; and since the record was clearly not sufficient to warrant a second term, the advertising had to suggest—first subtly, then explicitly—that electing Ronald Reagan posed an unacceptable risk to the United States.

A small element in the first phase of the advertising campaign did try to remind voters that the President was still one of them, a nonimperial President who would listen to ordinary citizens. In August, Carter slipped out of the White House to tape discussions with senior citizens, construction workers, and housewives. Ads crafted from the discussions showed ordinary citizens raising troublesome questions—"Why isn't America respected in the world anymore? Why is inflation so high?—and showed Carter talking about the great strength of the United States as the listeners nodded their heads in agreement.

"Everyone used to talk about how great and powerful the United States used to be," a black worker said. "Well, we're not so powerful anymore. It seems like we're second." No, Carter answered ". . . the

United States comes first. In almost every kind of new weapon, the United States comes first.''

Other commercials showed Carter at town meetings, which had been held around the country over the last three years, as an announcer said, ''Over the past three and a half years, in nineteen American communities, the quiet rhythm of everyday life was exploded by the same memorable event—the President came to town.'' What at first seemed a particularly effective commercial showed the wife of a small coal mine operator in Steubenville, Ohio, complaining about red tape that threatened the family business. Carter turned to an aide, and told him to personally invite Mrs. Mary Downend to a meeting in Washington; the audience burst into applause, and Mrs. Downend burst into tears and blew a kiss to the President. ''Thank you, I love you,'' she said. In mid-September, however, Mrs. Downend appeared on the networks, and in the press, to explain bitterly that at the meeting she attended nothing was settled. ''The realization hit me,'' she said, ''this isn't accomplishing anything. I'm going to walk out of here and go back . . . and probably have to shut down the mine.'' She announced her support for Ronald Reagan, and the commercial was pulled off the air.

The dominant portrait of the first phase of Carter ads, however, was not Carter the man, but Carter the President; a rediscovery of the theme, first portrayed in Bob Squier's half-hour documentary at the end of 1979, that Carter had to be shown competently filling the job of chief executive. The commercials showed the different roles of President—''Commander-in-Chief,'' ''Chief of State,'' ''Planner of the Nation's Future,'' and the visual symbols were far from subtle. In the ''planner of the nation's future'' commercial, cameras panned statues of great presidents, and in one remarkable cut, the face of Thomas Jefferson dissolved into the face of Jimmy Carter riding in the back of a car, poring over papers. In the ''commander-in-chief'' commercial, the announcer said, ''when President Carter sits down at the White House with the Secretary of Defense, he brings a hard, military professionalism to the meeting. The President is an Annapolis graduate. He spent eleven years in the Navy. And he knows what he's talking about.''

As the announcer spoke, the pictures suggested that President Carter was a modern-day Patton. We saw Carter reviewing military exercises, field glasses in hand, as explosions tore the earth and soldiers charged up a hill; tanks rumbled across some imaginary battlefield; missiles tore up from their submarines; the sun glinted off aircraft carriers. The ad ended with film of the Camp David peace accord, and the announcer saying that ''President Carter knows our final security lies not only in having a strong defense but in being willing to sit down and negotiate for peace," but the pictorial thrust of the commercial was designed to rebut Republican charges that Carter had weakened America's defense posture. How, the ad seemed to ask, could any President surrounded by this much hardware be considered a softy?

What voters saw principally about Carter the President was perhaps the most unchallengeable claim of the campaign: his capacity for hard work. Commercial after commercial showed Carter in the Oval Office, working far into the night, his once-familiar grin replaced by a somber expression and a furrowed brow. "There's nothing nine-to-five about it," an announcer said, reminding voters that Reagan was described as a "nine-to-five" governor. And in a backhanded reference to the challenges that would face a seventy-year-old President, another ad showed Carter climbing the stairs from his office to his study as the announcer said, "Even at the end of a long working day, there is usually another cable addressed to the Chief of State from the other side of the world where the sun is shining and something is happening." Then the light switched on in the study.

Ronald Reagan's initial advertising strategy could employ none of these pictorial techniques; as Dailey explained after the election, "in California, Reagan was known as a national political figure, then as a governor, then as a former actor. But outside of California, he was known as a political figure, then as an actor." Even the traditional techniques of campaign advertising would have raised suspicions about the depth of the onetime host of "General Electric Theater" and "Death Valley Days." So the first flight of Reagan ads were totally "unproduced"; they were simply film clips (film being kinder to a wrinkled face than tape) of Reagan, sitting in a distinguished-study set, talking.

He talked, most importantly, of peace.

"Nancy and I have four children, and a grandchild; hopefully, we'll be blessed with many more . . . we've traveled this great land of ours many times over the years, and we've found that Americans everywhere yearn for peace just as we do. It's impossible to capture in words the feelings we have about peace in the world, and how desperately we want it for our four children and our children's children." In short, he was saying, I don't plan to risk nuclear holocaust just because I've already lived threescore years and ten. Other commercials showed him talking in general terms about inflation ("We do not have inflation because, as President Carter says, the people are living too well. We have inflation in great measure because the federal government has lived too well") and economic growth.

The most critical ad during the entire fall campaign, however, was the attempt to shift the national impression of Reagan more toward the California impression: to make his eight-year governorship a more important factor than his career as an actor, and to demonstrate that Reagan had the kind of major executive experience that qualified him for the job. The five-minute commercial, which Dailey promised would play "until everybody was sick of it," looked very much like an old-fashioned newsreel, in part because it used a good deal of fourteen-year-old film from Reagan's first days as governor.

When Reagan was elected, the announcer said, "what he inherited was a state in crisis." The footage showed a motorcade flanked by motorcycles pulling up to the state capitol in Sacramento; Reagan, flanked by aides, strode into a room as flashbulbs went off; bills were signed; hands were shaken. The entire montage looked very "man in charge." When the announcer quoted from a San Francisco newspaper editorial which said, "We exaggerate very little when we say Governor Reagan has saved the state from bankruptcy," the screen was filled with the words crawling up next to the state capitol building. As with all of Reagan's ads, the slogan, read by actor Robert Stack, followed: "The Time is Now for Reagan—Reagan for President."

Predictably, the Reagan governorship record drew careful attention both from the press and from the Carter campaign. A detailed *New York Times* examination of the commercial, late in the campaign, noted (among other things) that the newspaper was originally said to be the *Chronicle* when it had, in fact, appeared in the *San Francisco Examiner;* that a state legislative analyst disputed the contention that the state was near bankruptcy; that the Democratic legislature had initiated many of the tax rebates; and, most significantly, that the commercial "forgot" to mention two huge tax increases that helped create the surplus, and ignored the fact that state spending rose substantially.

The Carter campaign ran its own commercial in the last days of the campaign, showing the Seal of California, and remarking "[Reagan increased] state spending by 120 percent. He added 34,000 employees to the state payroll. The Reagan campaign is reluctant to acknowledge these facts today, but can we trust the nation's future to a man who refuses to remember his own past?"

The point, of course, was that the details were largely irrelevant to the purpose of the commercial, which was less to argue that Reagan had turned California into Utopia, and more to show that this "actor" had in fact run the biggest state in the country for eight years in a reasonably respectable manner. Every voter who began thinking less of Reagan as an actor, and more of Reagan as ex-governor was moving toward a willingness to entrust Reagan with the reins of power.

For the Carter campaign, this effort to make Ronald Reagan more "Presidential" was exactly what had to be combated. They had seen from the primaries that when Carter himself was made the issue, voters consistently rejected him; he won when put alongside an unaccept-

THE REAL CAMPAIGN • 255

able alternative. Thus, the goal was to make people aware of a "clear choice" among "starkly different" men and futures. Just as the Carter campaign had defeated Kennedy in good measure by forcing Democrats to really consider whether they wanted him as President, the idea of the next phase of commercials was to force undecided voters to really consider the notion of Ronald Reagan in the Oval Office. And the technique used by Rafshoon was simplicity itself: the camera moved in on the desk in an empty Oval Office.

"When you come right down to it," the announcer asked, "what kind of person should occupy the Oval Office." Then the ads summarized different Reagan beliefs. For example, "should it be someone who, like Ronald Reagan, has a fractured view of America, who speaks disdainfully about millions of us as he attacks the minimum wage and calls unemployment insurance a 'prepaid vacation'? Or should another kind of man sit here, an experienced man who knows how to be responsive to all Americans, all 240 million of us? Figure it out for yourself." Another one asked whether the next President should be "someone like Ronald Reagan, who has proposed an economic plan that *Business Week* magazine called a completely irresponsible approach that would touch off an inflationary explosion that would wreck the country? . . . Or should a more prudent, realistic, and experienced man sit here? Figure it out for yourself." Nowhere in the copy was Jimmy Carter's name mentioned, since the whole point was to build up anxiety over Reagan, thus making Carter the "not-Reagan" choice for the Oval Office.

The first clear attack on Carter crafted by the Reagan forces did not flow from a long-established game plan, but was triggered by Carter's refusal to join the League of Women Voters' debate in Baltimore with Reagan and John Anderson. The commercial simply showed an empty podium, with a woman's voice reading the copy. (Since this was the only commercial aired by Reagan's campaign with a woman's voice as announcer, it is a fair assumption that the commercial was trying to leave the impression that the League of Women Voters had something to do with the ad.)

"The League of Women Voters invited President Carter to join the 1980 debates. He refused the invitation. Maybe it's because, during his Administration, inflation has gone as high as 18 percent, the number of Americans out of work has reached eight million . . ." Well into October, however, the Reagan campaign kept reinforcing the positive view of the candidate, running short clips of Reagan talking and different versions of the Reagan-as-governor documentary. But by October, the Carter campaign turned sharply negative—and with an advertising approach that was by now becoming a familiar aspect of a Jimmy Carter Presidential campaign.

Four years earlier, at the end of the 1976 campaign, Gerald Ford's media advisors unveiled a series of "man-in-the-street" interviews, in which Georgians talked critically about their former governor; the men and women talked about budget increases, Carter's failures to keep his promises, and, in one case, welcomed the idea of a Southerner as President, but not Carter. The commercials were an effective way of undercutting Jimmy Carter's argument that he had been an outstanding, much-admired governor of Georgia, and the Carter people had thought highly enough of the technique to imitate it in the Pennsylvania primary, taping voters commenting in sharply critical terms about Kennedy's trustworthiness and reliability.

Now, in the last month of the 1980 campaign, the Carter camp began a heavy schedule of "man (and woman)-in-the-street ads featuring Californians commenting critically on their former governor. They are decidedly heavy-handed. One ad had four or five Californians saying, in quick cuts, "he shoots from the hip," "Reagan shoots from the hip." Another commercial pieced together comments on Reagan's lack of compassion, attacking him specifically for his indifference to the plight of the mentally ill. The most hard-hitting of all, however, was a direct echo of the "war-and-peace" theme that the Carter campaign was hitting at every opportunity. Whether it was releasing memoranda about areas of the world where Reagan had suggested the use of American military might, or the President himself arguing that the election could decide "whether we have peace or war," the Carter camp was determined to paint Reagan as a threat to the stability of international relations and as a threat to world peace. Although heavy press criticism had forced the President to abandon this mode of attack in his own comments, the Carter commercials clearly did not. In one "man-in-the-street" ad, Californians were used to send a chill up the spine of the American voter:

"As governor," one said, "it didn't make much difference because California doesn't have a foreign policy, but as President, it's scary." "I think he would have gotten us into a war by now," another said, "I think it's a big risk to have Reagan as President," came the clincher. "Reagan scares me, he really scares me."

For its part, the most sharply negative Reagan commercial didn't show anyone at all; it was a simple bar graph with 1976 price levels for food, transportation, housing, and other necessities. As the announcer said that "in the last four years, every American has been staggered by the Carter economic record," the bars shot up to the accompaniment of a slide whistle. "Food prices *up* over 35 percent; auto prices *up* over 31 percent. . . . The Carter record speaks for itself. The time is now for Reagan."

There were much nastier commercials on the air attacking Carter; but these were *not* the product of the Reagan campaign. A series of independent political committees, acting under the freedom provided by the Supreme Court,* spent more than $6 million to support candidates in the Presidential campaign, virtually every penny of it on behalf of Ronald Reagan or against Jimmy Carter. These efforts ranged from efforts by well-known consultants, such as John Deardourff, to narrowly based organizations, such as Christian Voice, which attacked Carter for accepting the Democratic Party platform endorsing gay rights, to clumsy, dime-store commercials showing Uncle Sam being used as a punching bag by leering Communists, Arab sheikhs, and swarthy Iranians. They were often targeted regionally: the National Conservative Political Action Coalition pumped more than a million dollars into advertising aimed exclusively at the South, showing a clip from a Carter-Ford debate, in which Carter said, "And if I'm elected President—" The picture froze, Carter's words echoed over and over again in an echo chamber, and an announcer detailed how Carter had wrecked the national economy or weakened America's defenses. Although both Reagan and official Republican spokesmen complained about the advertising, worrying over its potential to confuse messages and to create a backlash of sympathy, it did put the Reagan media in an enviable position: running essentially uplifting and positive commercials, while knowing that the negative messages were also being heard.

Similarly, the $5 million spring effort of the advertising by the Republican National Committee, which had won widespread attention for its effective appeal to younger, blue-collar Democrats, was brought back for a $4 million fall replay. Once again, viewers saw a Tip O'Neill look-alike ignoring warnings that he was running out of gas as he drove his huge guzzler, only to run out of gas after all as an announcer attacked the Democrats for failing to encourage new sources of energy. Once again viewers saw "the Democrat commemorative dollar" shrinking to thirty-six cents after a quarter-century of Democratic control of the Congress; once again viewers saw James Wilders walking through an abandoned factory asking, "If the Democrats are so good for working people, how come so many of us are looking for work?"

These Republican ads were, I think, extremely effective and influential; they help account in part for the shocking events of November 4, when the Republicans won control of the Senate for the first time since 1952 and gained thirty-three seats in the House of Representatives. Why? To begin with, they were unopposed. Except for a

* In the wake of the post-Watergate reforms establishing the Federal Election Commission and setting down campaign spending limits, a suit challenging the constitutionality of the reforms came before the Court in *Buckley v. Valeo* (1975). While upholding most of the law, the Court said that independent expenditures on behalf of or against candidates were legal, provided there was no collusion between the candidate's campaign and the independent entrepreneurs.

last-minute surge of Carter ads which attempted to embrace the Democratic Party heritage, there was *no* Democratic Party media campaign; and it is a generally fair proposition that when a heavy political media campaign has no opposition facing it, that message will get across convincingly. Second, the Republicans had a specific message to get across. Unlike the Democrats, divided over whom they wanted to nominate and what they wanted to run on, the Republicans had a clear, consistent argument to make: *if you're suffering from conditions as they are, remember who has controlled the Congress for the last twenty-five years.* It was quite similar to the 1946 Republican slogan in the congressional campaign, which saw the biggest gain for the GOP since the dawn of the New Deal and consisted of the following slogan: "Had Enough?" In adopting the slogan, "Vote Republican—For a Change," the ads were arguing that the way to change conditions was to change the way you usually voted. For these ads were unmistakably talking to traditional Democrats. There was no reference to the Republican tradition, no assault on creeping socialism, no denunciation of social programs or greedy labor unions or the providential nature of trust funds. These were commercials that took a legitimate grievance of people who felt deserted by their party and suggested a specific step that could be taken to punish those responsible for the conditions. It was political advertising at its best: fair, tough, clear, and very effective. It was even healthy, for it helped to turn voters away from personalized Presidential politics into a realization that political parties and congressional power, rather than charismatic figures with magnetic personalities, just might have something to do with politics.

Among the minor candidates for the Presidency, advertising was a matter of small consideration, because the money just wasn't there. For John Anderson, faced with a constant struggle to get on the ballots of the fifty states and to find some mechanism for financing his campaign, the airwaves were out of reach. It was a supreme irony that David Garth, one of the best-known "media wizards" of contemporary politics, wound up running a Presidential campaign for which there was no media worth speaking of. An early network television buy featured a "bio" spot, showing John Anderson from his childhood days through World War II and congressional service. Its best line was a quote from former President Ford, praising Anderson's intelligence and concluding "his trouble is, he insists on voting his conscience." The only other campaign spot was a single "talking head"—cut in one-minute and five-minute versions—in which Anderson, sitting in his own version of a distinguished study, quickly ran down a laundry list of the independent candidate's courageous stands, and attacked Carter and Reagan for refusing "to face up to the issues."

Primarily, Anderson's commercial tried to remind voters of what they had found so appealing in May and June, when he seemed to pose the possibility of making a serious run for the White House: candor and specificity.

"I start with some hard facts," Anderson said. "The solutions to our problems are going to be difficult. That shouldn't come as a surprise to anyone. But if saying so jeopardizes my election, so be it. . . .

"We must reject proposals that feel good, but fail to get at the root of our difficulties. Multibillion dollar tax cuts sound good. I can't support them. A hundred-billion dollar MX missile system sounds tough. I am against it. Aid to our cities? We can't survive without it." Included was a strong pledge of support for the Equal Rights Amendment and opposition to a constitutional amendment to ban abortion. He concluded with an appeal to vote for "not a lesser evil, but a greater good."

Anderson's appeal demonstrated the other side of the lesson of the Republican National Committee ads: if unchallenged media can be powerful, virtually unheard media cannot be. In the entire fall campaign, Anderson spent less than $2 million on television advertising. Reagan and Carter each spent eight times that much. There is no way that so low-key an advertising campaign could make an impact in a Presidential race . . . almost no way. Another minor party candidate did demonstrate the fascination with sensationalism that is the soft underbelly of journalism.

A coalition of left-wing groups had formed a new political organization, the Citizens' Party, and had chosen prominent environmentalist Barry Commoner as its Presidential candidate. LaDonna Harris, an active feminist and wife of former Oklahoma Senator Fred Harris, was chosen as his running mate. The party offered a radical platform, calling for nationalization of the railroads, sharp controls and public representation on the boards of major corporations, and huge slashes in the defense budget. And except for the occasional whimsical piece on the evening news, or public television programs such as the "MacNeil-Lehrer Report" and "Bill Moyers Journal," no one was listening. So in mid-October, the Commoner campaign delivered this *radio* commercial to the national networks:

"Bullshit!" says a man.

"What?" says a shocked woman.

"Carter, Reagan, and Anderson—it's all bullshit," he says, explaining that only Barry Commoner is talking about what really needs to be done. The $5,000 media buy aroused hundreds of complaints and wails of anguish from local stations, but FCC rules are clear—as long as a candidate's face or voice is on a commercial absolutely no censorship is permitted. (In fact, most NBC local stations that previewed the commercial before it was broadcast chose not to run the ad.) In an irony to which Commoner himself pointed throughout the rest of the campaign, this single radio commercial earned the Citizens' Party more free media than all of the months of campaigning, speeches, and position papers put together. (It also revealed the differing standards of the mainstream press about colorful language. *Time* magazine used the word "bullshit"; the *New York Times* called it a "barnyard expletive"; CBS bleeped out the last half of the word, and one radio station called the term "bovine excreta.")

If an observer was looking for a single element of the fall campaign that encompassed the different approaches of Jimmy Carter and Ronald Reagan, and of their campaigns, he could not do much better than to look toward the last weeks' worth of paid media. In organization, in form, in content, it speaks volumes about what the Carter and Reagan camps were attempting to say to America, consciously and otherwise.

Both sides used a variety of different commercials, depending on time of day, region, and interest group involved. One of the Carter campaign's most-noted ads featured actress Mary Tyler Moore, who —after "inviting" the men in front of the set to leave the room— explained how much better Carter was on women's issues than Ronald Reagan. (The commercial was pulled off the air when Ms. Moore's son killed himself while toying with a loaded gun.) The Reagan campaign used Nancy Reagan in a commercial that spoke of her personal outrage over the campaign of personal assault and innuendo being waged against her husband. Both sides continued to mix positive appeals with attacks on the opposition. But the key difference could be measured by the scattershot approach of the Carter campaign—seeking to appeal to as diverse a set of emotions as is imaginable in the closing days of a national election—and the Reagan media effort, which relied overwhelmingly on the personal capacity of the candidate himself to talk directly, and largely unadorned, to the public.

On occasion, the President did speak directly to the American people—something consistently avoided in the overwhelming preponderance of Rafshoon's ads, either because Carter was ineffective as a speechmaker, or because his face and voice interfered with the attempt to inflate his Presidency and attack the opposition. On October 19, for example, Carter gave a nationally broadcast radio address assailing Reagan's opposition to the SALT II treaty, declaring that "this would be a very risky gamble. I do not propose to turn away from the duty to bring the terrible weapons of nuclear annihilation under some kind of rational control." There was also an Oval Office speech in which the President—perhaps smarting under the long-standing accusation that he had no "vision" of the country—invited Americans to "share with me my vision of the future."

More often, however, the Carter media pitch was aimed at a broad sweep of possible audiences. For those who still cared about Carter's link with "typical Americans," there were typical Americans speaking warmly of the President—a wheat farmer praising him for his courage on the grain embargo, a working mother endorsing his support of the ERA, a Maine Yankee praising Carter for being just plain folks. For Democrats there was a newsreel-looking montage of FDR, JFK, Hubert Humphrey, and Harry Truman, especially Harry Truman, inexplicably intercut with Democratic office-holders such as House Speaker Tip O'Neill, San Francisco Mayor Dianne Feinstein, Congressman Mo Udall, and other worthies, all talking admiringly about the President . . . as though undecided voters would be persuaded in their choice by politicians on the receiving end of Presidential patronage. There was a first-rate, quickly produced television spot capitalizing on Reagan's flatly wrong comment during the Cleveland debate that he had never brushed aside fears over nuclear proliferation as "none of our business."

Fundamentally, however, the most striking aspect of the late Carter ads was that *there was no theme to them at all; and there was no theme to the ads because there was no theme to the campaign.* The commercials could not effectively argue the case for Jimmy Carter because Jimmy Carter had never figured out what the case was. Were we supposed to vote for Carter to keep the Democratic Party legacy alive? Carter had won the Presidency by attacking that legacy, explicitly positioning himself away from the "establishment," bragging during his 1976 campaign that he had never *met* a Democratic President, promising to cut the bloated federal budget much as Ronald Reagan was now doing. Were we supposed to vote for him because ordinary Americans thought he was a nice guy? That was never the problem voters had with Carter—at least, not until the press began tagging him as a mean-spirited campaigner with a tradition of assaulting his opponents; the problem was he didn't seem to be doing a very good job. Were we supposed to vote for the President because the only reasonable alternative was too reckless, too extreme? The problem with that argument is that it put power in the hands of the opposition to dispel that fear: and that is, by and large, what Reagan did—personally and politically.

It is by now a commonplace that Ronald Reagan is the foremost rhetorician—"communicator" to use the cliché—of our day. His career was launched by a speech for Barry Goldwater in 1964; his 1976 Presidential primary campaign was saved by a speech in North Carolina on foreign policy; his "concession" speech at that convention kept the faithful faithful; his acceptance speech at the Republican National Convention laid out the clear pattern of a committed ideological conservative determined to make deep inroads into the traditional Democratic coalition. Now, in the last two and a half weeks of the Presidential campaign, the media campaign increasingly turned to its most powerful weapon: Reagan as speechmaker.

On October 19, just after the President's radio address about foreign policy, Ronald Reagan went on network television to deliver his own thirty-minute speech about foreign policy and the question of defense and war and peace. It was the issue that the polls showed was clearly cutting against Reagan, freezing voters in a pattern of indecision between an incumbent they did not admire and a challenger they had reason to doubt and fear. It was a cautious speech, beginning with the complaint that "my own views have been distorted in an effort to scare people through innuendos and misstatements of my positions." There was no brandishing of threats, no echo of the famous 1976 Panama Canal policy ("we bought it; we paid for it; it's ours; and we're going to keep it"), no endorsements of the war in Vietnam as a noble cause. Instead, Reagan talked about conducting a "bipartisan foreign policy"—a red flag to some of his most conservative supporters who saw bipartisan internationalism as a sellout of American strength—and pledged to "immediately open negotiations on a SALT III treaty." However, he warned "the way to avoid an arms race is not simply to let the Soviets race ahead, [but] to remove their incentives to race ahead by making it clear that we can and will compete if need be."

Five days later, Reagan returned to the half-hour format on the economy. He read a letter from a young girl who kept saving money for a pair of skates . . . but every time she went to the store, the price had gone up again. Is this fair, she wanted to know? "No," Reagan said. "It isn't fair." In what was to be a test run of a major theme in his face-to-face debate with Carter, Reagan said, "The symbol of this Administration is a finger pointing at someone else." And he posed a "simple question in economics" to the President: "Why is it inflationary if you keep more of your earnings and spend them the way you want to, but it isn't inflationary if he takes them and spends them the way he wants to?"

With $6 million to spend in the last ten days—the Reagan camp had deliberately husbanded its funds and was now able to outspend Carter by more than 2-1 on television advertising—Reagan commercials still included the bar graph attack on Carter's economic policy, a new ad very much in the pattern of the anti-George McGovern "weathervane" ad of 1972, showing Carter breaking promise after promise as photos switched from grins to frowns, and general patriotic appeals to Reagan true believers. The climax, however, the centerpiece of the media campaign of the challenger was played out on Monday, November 3—the night before the election. While the press was chasing across the country following Carter and Reagan in their last minute East-to-West race, examining the latest polls and wondering about the hostages, Ronald Reagan was scoring a knockout blow against the President on national television.

The President appeared early in the evening on ABC, before the "Monday Night Football" telecast, in a stitched-together twenty-minute presentation narrated by Henry Fonda, using clips from the Democratic legacy film, a brief Carter talk from the White House, and endorsements from prominent Democrats. John Anderson went on NBC and CBS with a fifteen-minute version of his straight-from-the-shoulder talk. Ronald Reagan had a half hour of time on both NBC and CBS during the telecast of the football game. If you were an American voter watching television on Election Eve, and you did not want to watch football, it meant you were almost certainly watching Reagan giving one of the finer political orations in recent years—a speech as well-crafted as Ted Kennedy's "concession" speech at the Democratic National Convention. The national press may not have been watching the speech—but tens of millions of Americans, especially American women, who may fairly be said to have a less than compelling affection for professional football, were watching the speech. And if pollsters are still looking to explain the gap between the last-minute numbers and the size of the Reagan victory, the Election Eve speech may hold an answer.

Reagan was seated with George Bush at his side, and Bush spoke briefly about his confidence in Reagan. Then Reagan, in twenty-five minutes, offered a sense of optimism and faith that many viewers had never heard before—because, other than during the debates, they had been afforded no chance to hear the candidates spell out their sense— or lack of it—of what the campaign was all about.

Reagan talked of "a vision of a better America." He asked, "Does history still have a place for America? For her people and her great ideals? There are some who answer no—our energy is spent, our days of greatness at an end. . . . Last year I lost a friend who was more than a symbol of the Hollywood dream industry. To millions he was a symbol of our country itself." John Wayne, he said, would have rejected the headline calling him "the last American hero. Duke Wayne did not believe our country was ready for the dustbin of history. Just before his death, he said in his own blunt way, 'just give the American people a good cause and there's nothing they can't lick.' "

Had this been a speech in front of the press corps, it would have been called routine, even corn-ball. But now there was no journalistic community standing between Reagan and his audience, and his capacity to evoke specific feelings of time and place, and specific emotions, was never being put to better use.

"It is autumn now in Washington," he concluded. "Residents there say that more than ever the last few years, Americans are coming to visit their capital. In a time when our place in history is so seriously questioned, they say Americans want their sons and daughters to see what is still for them, and for so many millions of others around the world, a city offering the last best hope of man on earth. . . .

"Let us resolve tonight that young Americans will always see those Potomac lights, that they will always find there a city of hope in a country that is free. And let us resolve they will say of our day and of our generation, we did keep the faith with our God, that we did act worthy of ourselves, that we did protect and pass on lovingly that shining city on a hill."

There were no pictures in this half-hour commercial; there was no music; there were no graphics save for the compulsory disclaimers before and after the address that this was a paid political announcement. It would never have passed muster as a demonstration of how the new generation of media wizards and technocrats were poisoning the minds of the voters of the United States. And it certainly did not look or sound like someone was "selling soap." Instead, it was a classic political demonstration of a prospective leader summarizing the mood of the people he hopes to lead. If there were undecided voters watching television that Monday, hoping for a clue as to the stature and gravity of the two candidates, the single contrast of last-minute commercials would have told them more than the combined efforts of the three networks to preview the election. The journalists—all of us —were still mired in revealing clues about the campaign and how to watch the votes from Connecticut and Pennsylvania. Reagan, Carter, and Anderson were each trying, through this most discredited and scorned of political tools, to explain what was at stake for the 85 million people who would vote on the next day.

xv The Chase and the Call: The Media and the General Election

On August 5, Republican Presidential nominee Ronald Reagan spoke to the annual convention of the National Urban League in New York City. For this conservative Republican, who had opposed the Civil Rights Act of 1964, who had assailed affirmative action programs, who attacked domestic spending programs, federal supervision of the hiring practices of private businesses contracting with the federal government, and the whole range of antipoverty efforts on the part of Washington, the appearance was a difficult one; something like the 1960 speech by John F. Kennedy to a Baptist ministers' conference in Houston. Reagan himself compared his speech with that of Kennedy, who "was facing an audience of Protestant ministers who wanted to know whether his religious beliefs would in some way affect his conduct in our nation's highest office."

His speech bluntly recognized that many in his audience of black professionals, civil rights veterans, and other committed allies of vigorous federal programs would "question whether a conservative really feels sympathy and compassion for the victims of social and economic misfortune, and of racial discrimination." After hammering away at statistic after statistic of black economic hardship, Reagan cited his California record as proof that tough-minded controls over welfare spending actually benefited the neediest and helped create more jobs for blacks, both in and out of state government. He argued for a specific program of jobs through tax breaks for ghetto-based enterprises, and through a national program of economic revitalization.

"We must get the economy moving again," Reagan said. "Instead of fighting over who gets the last piece of a shrinking economic pie, let's help American produce a bigger pie so that everyone will have a chance to be better off."

As a speech, it was one of Reagan's best of the campaign: a serious effort to meld conservative, tax-cutting, antiwelfare rhetoric with a sense of compassion, social justice, and economic health. It

265

reflected many elements: a dedication to the faith of supply-side economics, which insisted that lowering tax rates would create an era of prosperity in which all would benefit; a shrewd political calculation that an appeal to black Americans would soothe moderate and liberal Republicans, as well as "Establishment" members concerned with the possible polarizing effects of Reagan's nomination; a frontal assault on the governmental liberalism embraced by President Carter on the ground it simply did not work. It was a serious political speech: the kind that could be debated, supported, refuted, but which flatly contradicted the view that "candidates never talk about the issues."

The speech, however, was *not* the centerpiece of Reagan's day in New York. In order to dramatize the alleged failure of the Carter Administration to help minorities, Reagan journeyed to the South Bronx—perhaps the best-known symbol of urban decay—and stood on the spot where Carter had stood in 1977, promising a restoration. As the press watched and the cameras rolled, Reagan began talking to the members of the media, while the crowd chanted "speak to the people, not the press!"

"What are you going to do for us?" a woman shouted.

"If you will listen for a minute," Reagan shouted back, "what I'm trying to tell you is that I can't do a damn thing for you if I don't get elected!"

That night, on the "CBS Evening News," Reagan was seen delivering three lines from his Urban League speech; the visit to the South Bronx was the dominant visual event of the story. On "NBC Nightly News," viewers saw two lines of the Urban League speech, and the confrontation in the South Bronx. CBS's Jerry Bowen concluded his report by noting "Reagan's strategists hope the governor's speech and his symbolic appearance here will finally lay to rest the idea that he's insensitive to the problems of blacks. They also hope that translates into much-needed black votes in November." NBC's Heidi Schulman said, "It was Reagan's first major attempt to get through to black voters who four years ago cast 90 percent of their ballots for Jimmy Carter."

In this single event can be found, in microcosm, the coverage of the 1980 Presidential campaign. The candidates, convinced that visually dramatic settings are necessary for effective media coverage, gather up scores of reporters, correspondents, cameramen, sound technicians, and an army of logistical support for a two-month chase back and forth across the United States. The press, carried along as a captive audience for this traveling road show, simultaneously chronicles the travel while reporting the efforts of the candidate to manipulate the voter. The prime target of this meandering, the network evening news shows—which must compress stories into "minidramas" generally lasting less than two minutes—emphasize the visually compelling footage, even though producers, correspondents, and news executives alike fully realize the efforts of the politicians to force attractive settings into the coverage of their campaigns.

More fundamentally, the fall campaign—the chase—is over-whelmingly the chase after a single story: "Who is going to win the election?" While this is, in fact, a perfectly sensible view of the campaign, it produces a severe and dangerous distortion of it. Because the press is pursuing two or three campaigns across the country, the story is, in general, presumed to be whatever is happening where the candidates happen to be—especially if the candidate happens to say or do something that is "different" or "new" from what he has said or done before. Thus, a slip of the tongue, or a colorful turn of a sentence becomes the story on the evening news. And since the political press, no less than the candidates and their aides, has become convinced that what happens on the network news *is* the campaign, a controversial or clumsy statement on the news becomes the grist for analysis, commentary, and focus.

No one would seriously argue that the press should not be cover-ing the daily movement of the major candidates for the Presidency of the United States. If nothing else, the depressingly familiar practice of shooting at public officials would require any large-scale news organi-zation to maintain what is chillingly called a "body watch." The larger question is: does the campaign really *happen* on the campaign trail? Is this chase what the choice for President really involves? Is this daily barrage of images, charges and countercharges, clever visual back-drops, what is causing the electorate to decide for whom to vote?

Even if we put aside the broader questions about the political process; even if we ignore the possibility that there is a "social good" to be obtained by a radically different method of looking at Presidential politics; even if we deny for a moment that the electorate "deserves" to hear candidates, their supporters, their opponents, and a range of other voices examining the records and intentions of the candidates—we still must look at the 1980 general election with this question in mind: is "the chase" going to tell us very much about the dominant question the political press asks: who is going to win? The Reagan-Carter-Anderson race was accompanied by the most intensive polling in the history of politics; all three networks, major newspapers, news magazines, and wire services, state-based organizations in virtually every state, all put the electorate through the scientific polling process almost from the moment Jimmy Carter was inaugurated in 1977. By the time the fall campaign began, polls were flooding the press almost every day, and from Labor Day until Election Day, the central mes-sage of the polls was that the race was "going right down to the wire," in the words of Walter Cronkite's preelection promotional message broadcast almost continuously on CBS.

Instead, Ronald Reagan and the Republicans won a victory of historic dimensions, not only turning an incumbent Democratic President out of office for the first time since 1888,* but sweeping the Democrats out of control of the United States Senate for the first time since 1952, and winning an electoral vote victory that left the sitting President with only 49 electoral votes, the worst showing by an incumbent of either party since William Howard Taft won only eight electoral votes in 1912. Not one of the preelection polls by any of the news organizations came close to divining the size and nature of Ronald Reagan's triumph.

Instead, something else happened; by and large the press devoted the overwhelming preponderance of its money and manpower to an attempt to do what no journalistic enterprise can do: to predict the future, to tell the American people what was going to happen. In contrast, it spent a relatively minor effort in communicating the most accessible sort of information: the performance, proposals, intentions, and assumptions of the candidates. To be sure, television—especially NBC News—sought on Election Night to communicate the Reagan sweep as swiftly as possible: so much so that the 1980 campaign ended with a number of politicians and voters on the West Coast demanding legal sanctions against the networks to prevent any future projections of results while millions of Americans were still in the process of voting. But that triumph of computer technology happened *after* the votes had been cast, and was based on what was, after all, an extension of some very old-fashioned journalism: by interviewing thousands of voters leaving the polling places, and by factoring in facts about age, race, income, party affiliation, religion, and job description, all three networks were able to turn their exit polls into an instant, detailed mosaic of how Americans voted. What that mosaic demonstrated, however, was that none of the press's attempts to predict how that vote would be cast were successful. In essence, the $150 million spent by the three commercial television networks to cover the 1980 campaign, and the countless tens of millions of dollars spent by other news organizations were aimed at a target that was probably the wrong target, and was, in any event, missed and missed badly.

This failure was not, in the main, a function of political bias on the part of the press. During the course of the campaign, both partisans and observers of the media argued, at various times, that Ronald Reagan was getting a free ride, that Reagan was being savaged by the press, that Jimmy Carter was brilliantly eluding tough press coverage

* In that campaign, President Grover Cleveland won the popular vote by about 96,000 votes, but lost the electoral vote to Benjamin Harrison, 168–233. Cleveland regained the White House four years later. In addition, it is arguable that Harry Truman in 1952 and Lyndon Johnson in 1968 chose to retire rather than face the clear probability of electoral defeat.

because of the power of the Presidency, that Carter was being brutally attacked by a press that was personally hostile to him, that John Anderson was being borne into the fall campaign by a sympathetic press; that Anderson was being ignored by the press. There may well have been specific examples when the press was unfair to the candidates, or when certain cultural assumptions and personal views did affect the coverage of the candidates. On an overall basis, however, the press was "fair" in a specific political sense.

Nor was the media's failure due to candidates "buying" their way to the Presidency, or to the nomination, with a massive purchase of broadcast time. In the general election, both majority party candidates are provided with the same amount of public funds—$29.4 million in 1980—and however the independent expenditures of political action groups benefited Ronald Reagan in his campaign, there is no logical reason why the Democratic candidate cannot benefit from the same kind of expenditures in 1984. Moreover, Dr. Herbert Alexander, our foremost expert on campaign financing, noted after the primaries that money was no guide to success in the primaries. John Connally's $12 million campaign, including a $2 million media buy, produced *one* delegate. Howard Baker spent $325,000 on media in New England, but withdrew from the campaign after discovering that he had no political base. And, says Alexander, "President Carter far outspent Senator Edward Kennedy in the March 25 New York primary, but Kennedy scored an upset victory by a wide margin." Figures from the Federal Election Commission show that George Bush outspent Ronald Reagan in Illinois $1.3 million to $563,000, and Reagan won big. Only in Pennsylvania, where Bush outspent Reagan massively, did his huge media campaign produce a victory.

In two other ways, though, the press was decidedly *unfair;* and this unfairness had unhappy consequences for the 1980 campaign. First, the press was unfair to the process itself. Throughout the fall campaign—indeed, almost from the start of the primary campaign—the determination of the press not to be manipulated by candidates and campaign staffs led to a disparagement of the entire process of choosing the President that cast a cloud of cynicism on the election. While the stagecraft of politics, the attempt to manipulate press leverage is legitimate news, the media covered every statement, every move, by a candidate in those terms *and in no other terms.* Thus, Reagan's speech to the Urban League was properly examined as an appeal for votes from a generally hostile quarter (although the more subtle political pitch—calming fears of white moderates and liberals—went unexamined). As an argument in support of conservative economic paths to social justice, it went totally unexamined. The very idea that a candidate for President might actually be advancing an argument he deeply believed would have been treated as naive or simplistic by most of the political reporters. Similarly, President Carter's attacks on Ronald Reagan's policies on strategic arms and nuclear proliferation were analyzed solely in terms of the Democrat's attempt to paint Reagan as a warmonger. Again, this was a valid enough element in the mix; the entire Carter campaign was based on convincing the voters that Reagan was not to be trusted with the life-and-death power of the Presidency. But it is also true that Reagan's defense policies, and his foreign policy assumptions in general, represented a fundamental shift in the premises of the last four Presidents. Yet the fact that Carter had a political motivation behind his attacks made a more detached examination of Reagan's views somehow irrelevant.

The entire campaign rhetoric was treated with skepticism bordering on cynicism, if not with outright contempt. Combined with the drumbeat of pieces about the length, the carnival atmosphere, and the manipulative aspects which indeed accompany political campaigns, the result was to paint a picture of an unseemly, tedious, almost disreputable enterprise.

This skepticism flowed, in part, from the press's unwillingness to become part of the "conspiracies of silence" that had governed past campaigns, when the press had never run photographs showing Franklin D. Roosevelt in a wheelchair, or never revealed their knowledge of John F. Kennedy's philandering. In 1980, the media were looking for phoniness and manipulation at every turn. In a preprimary report from New Hampshire on February 25, for example, NBC's Tom Pettit observed that "it is important to keep New Hampshire in perspective—as with this handsome, bucolic waterfall, which really is part of the landscaping at a high-priced local motel."

It flowed also from the media's own weariness with the length of the campaign—a length imposed by the constant search for the first clue to the emerging front-runners—which had moved from New Hampshire in late February to the Iowa caucuses in late January to straw votes extending back into the autumn of 1979. As early as January 28, *Time* magazine was reporting—*a month before the first primary*—that "there is a growing uneasiness over the kind of candidate who ultimately emerges" (from the long process). By April, *Time* was telling us "How We Got to Hobson's Choice"—a misnomer, since a Hobson's choice is in fact no choice at all—and noting "it is enough to make many politicians, and ordinary citizens, yearn for the old smoke-filled room." On June 4, David Broder was reporting that "there is more widespread dissatisfaction being expressed with the choices for the general election than this report has heard in 25 years covering the political beat." CBS the next night aired a late-night special entitled, "Is This Any Way to Nominate a President?" *Newsweek* asked the same week "Is There A Better Way?"

This same despair characterized the approach to the general election—about the campaign, and about the press. Tom Wicker wrote a lengthy piece for the August 18 *New York Review of Books* titled "Why the System Has Failed." Columnist Richard Reeves summed up the choice facing America this way in his syndicated column on August 18:

"Two years, millions and millions of dollars, and incalculable human energy were spent for . . . for what? To renominate a failed President, to nominate an actor who has routinely performed as an extremist, and to allow the press to select its own candidate, a losing politician who couldn't win a single primary election." On September 21, *Washington Post* writer Haynes Johnson wrote that "the irony is that citizens now view the press with far more appreciation for its vital role in society than in the recent past. But, they say, at a time when they're looking toward the press for more serious information, the press is letting them down. And they are right. They expect better. They deserve it—and they're not getting it." On November 3, the day before the election, the *New York Times* editorial was headlined starkly, "The Campaign has bad breath."

One prominent journalist, and former campaign tactician, even came up with a striking, if controversial, explanation for this cynicism: women reporters on television. Said William Safire in the October 9 *New York Times,*

". . . some female reporters believed that their own youth and appearance damaged their credibility as journalists. How to gain that credibility? . . . emulate only those older male reporters known for their combativeness, outspokenness, and skepticism. . . . Politicians were no longer subjects to be listened to and reported upon, but targets whose deceits and unsupported assertions had to be interpreted on the spot."

More reasonably, Safire asked, "Would it kill the three networks to devote 60 or 90 seconds to each candidate's speech, provided he is saying something not said before? Can't we hear and see them speak with their own voices, out of their own faces, and not through the strainers of reporters campaigning for White House correspondent?"

Veteran *Wall Street Journal* editor Vermont Royster touched on the same point on October 29, drawing a key distinction between coverage of past campaigns and that of 1980.

"It was the custom, once, for the candidates to devote at least one formal speech to each of the major questions of the day, foreign policy, the domestic economy, and the like. These would frequently be carried by the radio networks and always reported in the press . . . their views would be set forth so that those inclined could hear or read them. . . . [Now] what we get is paragraph after paragraph scattered with a few of the speaker's phrases surrounded by the reporters' versions of what they think the speaker meant."

The concept that politics always mixes elements of the absurd and the serious, the idea that beneath the trappings there is a serious debate about the conduct of public policy, was relegated in the main to brief attempts to define "the issues" in the closing days of the campaign, generally through brief, excerpted interviews with the candidates. Praiseworthy as these efforts were on the part of all three networks, they did not begin to counter the dominant tone of Presidential campaign coverage, which suggested that no sensible citizen could participate in the election with any emotion other than disgust.

Second, the press coverage was, in the main, unfair to the voter. By 1980, it had become a commonplace among politicians and journalists alike to describe press coverage of campaigns as a "spectator sport," by focusing so intensely on who's ahead, who's behind, who's got momentum, who's faltering at the fifth furlong. The dominance of television, the decline of the traditional public fervor through torchlight parades, encampments, and other devices of another time, has tended to enhance the notion that politics is something to be watched rather than something in which to participate. The polls made that coverage of the election appear more like a fever chart than like a contest among competing philosophies of government. So prevalent was the "spectator sport" analysis of the campaign that when the "issues" were covered, through the device of excerpted interviews with the candidates in the last weeks of the campaign, they almost seemed an afterthought, something divorced from the real election, which was, of course, solely a question of who would win what votes.

Implicit in this sort of coverage was the premise that issues, the past records of the candidates, their intentions about the economy or social issues of foreign affairs were pure tinsel, the necessary but irrelevant trappings of a struggle for great power. For the voter, this view of politics carried with it a clear corollary: that the fight for the Presidency was a struggle fought far beyond the boundaries of home, family, job, neighborhood, community; a struggle about which a citizen had almost nothing to say. Convince a citizen that politics is indeed a spectator sport, and that citizen is left with nothing to do save cast a vote and stand on the sidelines cheering and booing. But even this becomes difficult when a campaign is covered only tactically and strategically. A Pittsburgh resident knows which teams to root for: the Pirates, the Steelers, and the Penguins. It goes with the territory. But who does a citizen cheer for in a campaign if he has no idea which candidate is speaking to his interests? How does a citizen know what the stakes are in a contest for political power if the link between citizen and presumptive President are never spelled out?

However, voters, being more or less rational, almost certainly do not sit passively letting campaign coverage pour over them. In fact, an analysis of the 1980 election that ignored campaign coverage and advertising and listed only purely "rational" voting factors could explain the unexpected Reagan Republican landslide as well, if not better, than any convoluted look at the specific content of major newspapers and network television news and public affairs programs. The persistence of double-digit inflation explains the desertion of Democratic blue-collar voters better than a raised eyebrow by Walter Cronkite does; layoffs in the auto plants of Michigan, the steel mills of Pennsylvania and Indiana, the auto-related industries of Ohio and Illinois account for the loss of the heartland states better than clever ads. Ronald Reagan's martial posture toward the Soviet Union, and his opposition to the Equal Rights Amendment and freedom of choice on the abortion question, provide perfectly adequate explanations for the remarkable split between the sexes in 1980: according to the CBS News exit poll, men gave Ronald Reagan an eighteen-point spread over President Carter; among women, the election was a virtual tie.

Thus, superficial television coverage of a Presidential campaign cannot be said to prevent citizens from exercising an intelligent choice about their vote. What it *does* do is force the choice into a private realm to create an environment in which each voter tends to grope for answers in the dark, unable to find a common forum for debate and discussion in which he might join with fellow voters. In an age of mass media, television is, in theory, an ideal arena for such a debate. It reaches "everyone" (except those who deliberately choose to avoid informing themselves about public policy) in more or less the same language at more or less the same time. It is free, instantly accessible, bridging barriers of class, education, and infirmity. It is, in theory, the *agora* of classic Greek democracy, the "open market" in which a public discourse can take place before the eyes and ears of the entire nation.

That television chose a different course—that it chose to narrow its focus to the "horse race" question—meant that voters were denied this kind of *agora*. This did not happen out of any malicious intent or political ignorance. It happened for the reasons this book has analyzed; television's instinctive preference for the visual images to make the highly competitive network news programs more attractive to a mass audience; the pressures of time that force all of the network news into a twenty-two minute format; the conviction that the campaign happens where the candidates and their enormous journalistic entourages happen to be; the belief that daily statements and movements of the candidates constitute the campaign; the financial consideration of networks that shut the campaign—except for paid advertising, the conventions, and the debates—out of prime time altogether.

But it happened. And because it happened, the voters were cheated out of the possibility of an election battle that might involve more choices than the identity of the next President.

The general election's first focus was on challenger Ronald Reagan's propensity for those infamous "slips of the tongue" that have become a staple of Presidential campaigns. Although the primary campaign had seen Reagan frequently misstate facts and twist his words, these "gaffes" had no appreciable impact on his march toward the nomination, a march best explained by the general adoption of the Republican Party of views Reagan had been espousing on the national political stage since 1964. With his nomination, however, Reagan was on a national stage with a relentless spotlight; so much so that opinions he had long held, and long expressed, were being treated as new, and, in some cases, clear proof of ignorance.

The first such case was Reagan's address to the Veterans of Foreign Wars on August 18. Speaking to the enthusiastic group in Chicago —a group that abandoned its traditional political neutrality to endorse his candidacy—Reagan attacked the "Vietnam syndrome," the idea that the war in Vietnam had been immoral.

"Well," Reagan said, "it's time that we recognized ours was, in truth, a noble cause. . . . Let us tell those who fought in that war that we will never again ask young men to fight and possibly die in a war our government is afraid to let them win."

This was, in fact, a position Reagan had held for years. Indeed, a 1976 campaign collection of Reagan's speeches and statements quoted Reagan as having said, "I think we were right to be involved in Vietnam. . . . The plain truth of the matter is that we were there to counter the master plan of the communists for world conquest." But in the spotlight of the 1980 campaign, this single line was given a prominent place on all three network newscasts. And within days, given the print press's focus on television coverage as a principal source of campaign news, the "noble cause" statement became embedded as a campaign goof. An August 27 analysis by the *New York Times*'s Howell Raines described the phrase as "perhaps the turn in Ronald Reagan's luck and in the momentum of the campaign," and cited "apparently shaky staff work" for letting Reagan "plung[e] ahead on instinct, making strong statements that provided ammunition for his critics." The *Washington Post*'s Haynes Johnson referred to the remark in an August 22 column on "Reagan's Combative Rhetoric." Thus, a statement that four American Presidents once held as a matter of faith—a statement highly debatable, to be sure, but something far different from a palpable misstatement of fact or sign of mental deficiency—almost instantly found its way into a pantheon of famous candidate blunders.

Less than a week after his "noble cause" statement, Reagan found himself under attack for another remark, this one in answer to a press conference question. Here the criticism—for one of the few times in the campaign—reflected something more of the cultural assumptions of the journalists, and in so doing, managed to misread the political weight of the remark, while turning attention away from what was potentially a genuinely serious threat to Reagan's general election coalition. On August 22, Reagan traveled to Dallas, Texas, for a speech at a Public Affairs Briefing of the Religious Roundtable. At this event, more than 15,000 followers of the so-called "religious Right" gathered to mark the full-fledged participation of the evangelical Christian movement in electoral politics. Fueled by the high visibility of the electronic church, whose television ministries reached across the country through satellite and cable technology, the religious Right was encouraging its followers to register, vote, and organize to bring "Christian values" into the political sphere: specifically, an antiabortion amendment to the Constitution, opposition to the Equal Rights Amendment, and a host of other social values. As a longtime partisan of traditional values, Reagan was a hero of this movement and journeyed to Dallas to make a speech in which he said, "I know you can't endorse me, but I want you to know that I endorse you."

During his visit to Dallas, Reagan was asked, at a press conference, about the religious Right's effort to fight for the teaching of the creationist theory of man in public schools alongside the theory of evolution.

In a remark that, once again, made all three network newscasts over the next two days, Reagan said of evolution:

"Well, it is a theory. It is a scientific theory only, and it has in recent years been challenged in the world of science and is not believed in the scientific community to be as infallible as it once was believed."

This remark, too, was instantly seized upon as evidence that the Republican Presidential nominee was somewhat addled in the head, one of those goofs that columnist Joseph Kraft would describe in early September as "the hallmark of his campaign." As a matter of fact, Reagan had a point; the scientific community had long regarded Darwin's theory as something less than revealed truth. More important, however, was the assumption that this remark was a clear political liability. For the press, evolution was a question that had been settled in the Scopes trial more than half a century earlier, when Clarence Darrow had taken William Jennings Bryan to the cleaners in a debate over the literal truth of the Book of Genesis. Expressing a doubt over so "modern" a theory, they seemed to suggest, must be a position with which no sensible person could agree.

Judged purely in terms of political effect, however, the remark could just as easily have cut the other way, convincing millions of deeply committed Christians that Reagan was, indeed, the exemplar of their deepest beliefs. Given the strength of this movement in Carter's South—a region absolutely critical to the President's electoral success—one might have thought that the press would have been less hasty in assigning this remark to the list of Reagan's "goofs." But it did not happen. Nor was the public exposed in any serious way to the context of Reagan's remark—at least, not that part of the public that relied on the network news for its information. More than a month after Reagan's appearance, however, on "Bill Moyers' Journal," the relative handful of viewers who watched this weekly examination of the Presidential campaign received a far fuller picture of the public affairs briefing.

On September 26, the "Journal" devoted an hour to the Dallas briefing. With time to produce the piece, and time to devote to a single subject, the "Journal" showed in detail what the commercial networks had barely touched on. Viewers saw Reagan on stage as Reverend James Robison delivered a thundering attack on liberals and secular humanists, proclaiming that "God might raise up a tyrant" to restore America to Christian principles. Viewers saw Reverend Bailey Smith, President of the Southern Baptist Convention, arguing that "God Almighty does not hear the prayer of a Jew, for how in the world can God hear the prayer of a man who says that Jesus Christ is not the true Messiah. It is blasphemous!" The portrait of politically energized zealots drawing up voting lists based on a candidate's moral positions drove liberal columnist Anthony Lewis to write in the *New York Times* that the "Journal" was "the scariest piece of television I have seen in a lifetime." It could, had it been seen in homes across America, have seriously undermined Reagan's attempt to appeal to the moderates among Republicans and independents, and its impact on the Jewish vote—clearly disenchanted with Carter and attracted by Reagan's strong support of Israel—can only be imagined.

In fact, however, this tableau went largely unseen. It was the candidate's gaffe, and not the context, that was featured on the evening news programs.

A more serious mistake, and one that haunted Reagan's footsteps throughout the first weeks of his campaign, came when the Republican nominee sought to paint himself as a reassuring performer in the area where his experience was weakest: that of foreign affairs. On August 16, Reagan dispatched running mate George Bush to Japan and China in an effort to shore up his foreign policy credentials. Reagan had long advocated strong ties with the Nationalist Chinese regime on Taiwan; he had, in fact, attacked Richard Nixon's opening to mainland China in 1971, and now reporters wanted to know where Reagan stood on the issue. What would Bush tell the Chinese?

"I don't know," Reagan said, with his running mate—one-time envoy to China—at his side. "I hope I haven't put you on a spot, George."

CBS's Bill Plante reported at the close of the August 16 story that

"Reagan's foreign policy advisor insisted that the candidate had not advocated official government-to-government relations with Taiwan, though it seemed quite clear that he had."

Over the next several days, the networks had a field day with the dispute—one that was clearly the candidate's own fault. On August 19, CBS's Richard Roth reported from Tokyo that "reporters (accompanying Bush) were more interested in the controversy over running mate Ronald Reagan's policy on Taiwan than in talk about trade or defense matters affecting Japan." The piece quoted Reagan foreign policy advisor Richard Allen denying any intention of "jeopardizing" U.S.-Chinese relations. And George Bush, reverting to his primary campaign habit of focusing on the press perceptions of the campaign, said, "I'm just not going to get off into that, trying to buy into trouble, or think that 'oh, my gosh, here's a great big major flap.' "

On August 21, NBC's Bernard Kalb concluded a piece on the China flap by reporting, "with the Chinese Communists sounding almost as if they were in President Carter's political corner, attacking the views of the Republican Presidential candidate . . . Administration officials [were] laughing in their teacups." When Bush returned from his Asian visit, the controversy continued, as the Chinese ambassador visited the State Department on August 25, with Secretary of State Muskie "nonpolitically" hoping that "problems that Mr. Reagan and Mr. Bush have on the question don't disturb the relationship." American ambassador to China Leonard Woodcock attacked the Reagan position, and Vice-President Mondale argued that Reagan's position "could seriously damage our national strength and give cheer to only one nation on earth—the Soviet Union." As CBS's Lem Tucker noted, "every time Governor Reagan or George Bush seem to make a mistake, Vice-President Mondale will be waiting, eager to make sure the public doesn't forget about it."

With these three incidents—the "noble cause," "evolution," and "China," as the political press would soon shorthand them—the Reagan campaign quickly became vulnerable to the same tendency in political journalism that had afflicted Ted Kennedy in the primaries: the desire of all parts of the media to cover themselves on the "major" political theme. If Roger Mudd showed Kennedy to be a fumbler, every reporter had to find his own example of the fumble. If Ronald Reagan was now beginning to commit a steady series of gaffes, then every journalist had to find a new Reagan gaffe. Moreover, the campaign aides, so responsive—if not obsessive—to press coverage as the key to a successful campaign, would now be under the temptation to treat these "gaffes" as an enormous liability to the campaign—because they had come to accept the predominant view that the perception of a campaign in trouble by the press is indistinguishable from a campaign which is, in fact, in trouble.

Thus, on August 27, on "NBC Nightly News," anchor John Chancellor introduced a Reagan speech on the economy this way: "Ronald Reagan today accused the President of taking the country into a depression, in his words, 'a Carter depression.' Economists agree that the country's in a recession, but one expert told us today that it's an exaggeration to call it a depression, and one of Reagan's senior economic advisors said later that depression is the wrong term."

Correspondent Heidi Schulman, reporting from Columbus, Ohio, showed Reagan describing "a severe depression," and then said, "But Reagan was again forced to explain himself when economic advisor Alan Greenspan disagreed the country is in a depression," although Reagan later issued a statement "saying depression should not be judged just in economic terms, but in human terms."

Later in the same broadcast, correspondent Ken Bode reviewed all of Reagan's gaffes, and wound up his piece, "With his remarks on Vietnam, his backpedaling on China policies, and the association with a whole bunch of filibuster conservative causes, Ronald Reagan probably made it somewhat easier for the Democrats to portray him as a right-winger."

In fairness, Reagan's description of the economy as a depression, rather than a recession, was hardly an outrageous breach of the standards of political rhetoric. Putting the declamations of candidates up to the standards of detached scholarship would almost certainly breathe much of what life remains out of our public life. No journalistic enterprise brought a social philosopher in to test Jimmy Carter's 1976 proposition that the American tax code was "a disgrace to the human race," or a historian to judge Richard Nixon's 1969 exclamation that the moon landing was "the greatest event since the Creation." But Reagan was now the candidate making mistakes—and the reinforcement of that perception built steadily.

Two days after NBC's "gaffe" roundup, CBS's Bill Plante offered the same view as had NBC's Bode; with clips from the "noble cause," "China," and "evolution" flaps. Said Plante, "No one in the campaign regards Reagan's mistakes as fatal—not yet. But the senior staff is anxious to get things back under control. One advisor put it this way: 'As long as we can keep the focus on Carter's record,' he said, 'we should be all right. But if Reagan becomes the issue, then we could have problems.' "

These problems flared again when the campaign "officially" began on Labor Day. Both campaigns carefully chose symbolic backdrops for their campaigns. President Carter went to his Southern base, without which reelection would be impossible, and appeared at a huge Labor Day picnic in Tuscumbia, Alabama. Standing in front of a stageful of Southern symbols—liberals such as Jim Folsom of Alabama and

Albert Gore of Tennessee, racists such as George Wallace of Alabama and James Eastland of Mississippi—Carter attacked a small group of Klansmen, charging that "these people in white sheets do not understand our problems. . . . We must go forward in the South and we will."

Reagan, striking at the heart of the traditional Democratic constituency, the "BCEC's" (Blue-Collar Ethnic Catholics), appeared in Liberty Park, New Jersey, across from the Statue of Liberty at Liberty Island, which he gestured to in the course of his speech ("The Lady standing there in the harbor has never betrayed us once," he said, "but this Administration has betrayed the working men and women of this country"). The *Washington Post* and other press reports, reflecting the growing tendency of the media to note attempts at image manipulation, gleefully noted that "it was the backside of the State of Liberty that actually overshadowed the Liberty Park picnic."

After this appearance, Reagan flew to Detroit for an appearance at the Michigan state fair and, in a single ad-lib, kindled again the perception of a candidate eager to do grievous injury to himself. In an attempt to score regional points with his Michigan audience, Reagan said: "I'm happy to be here where you're dealing at firsthand with the economic policies that have been committed, and he's opening his campaign down in the city that gave birth to and is the parent body of the Ku Klux Klan."

As a matter of accuracy, Reagan was wrong: Tuscumbia was the headquarters of a branch of the modern-day Klan. As a matter of political fairness, Reagan was, to put it charitably, out-of-bounds. While Carter's political career had, in its Georgia days, involved complicity with racism,* and while he was willing to embrace symbols of the region's segregationist past, there was nothing in his Presidency to suggest the slightest sympathy with the Klan. Indeed, Reagan may well have been trying to combat his own unwanted support at the hands of the Klan, and the statement by a Klan leader that the Republican platform "reads as if it had been written by a Klansman"—factors that had prodded Carter's Health and Human Service Secretary, Patricia Roberts Harris, to say—unfairly—that "Reagan's nomination raises the specter of white sheets."

Most significantly, Reagan's remarks reflected an ignorance of mass-media politics which belies the notion that this ex-actor was a finely tuned product of the television age. In an earlier time, politicians could indeed make regional appeals without the risk of being called to account in other regions. In 1980, of course, the national press and network television traveled constantly with the major candidates; any

* The best account is to be found in Betty Glad's remarkable book, *Jimmy Carter—In Search of the Great White House* (1980).

remarks made anywhere in the country were transmitted, by wire service and by network news, to the whole country. Thus, on September 2, Reagan's Labor Day remarks were splashed across the network news shows—and the Carter campaign jumped on them with both feet.

Carter, managing to work the words "South" and "Southerner" three times into a twenty-second answer, said, "it was something that all Southerners will resent. As an American, and a Southerner I regret it." "NBC Nightly News" quoted Alabama Governor Bob James demanding that Reagan apologize, and quoted Southerners to the effect that Reagan was "sort of a bozo" . . . "I would go somewhere, go crawl in a hole . . ." Chris Wallace concluded that the Klan remark "has once again put him on the defensive. Reagan aides say that the bloopers, as one called them, are now beginning to add up."

By this time, even Reagan insiders were appearing in the press with apprehensive statements. Senator Paul Laxalt said on CBS on September 3 that "I think, in terms of the reaction that's been received during the last several days, that he'd be the first to recognize that hereafter he'd have to be a bit more careful in the characterization of these statements." By the end of the first week of the campaign, longtime Republican strategist Stu Spencer—whose consulting firm had launched Reagan into the California governorship in 1966 and then helped defeat him in 1976 on behalf of President Ford—had been assigned to travel with Reagan to insure that what the *New York Times* called "the ragged edge" of the campaign would be smoothed over by rigid adherence to the prepared speech texts, and almost no opportunities for jerry-built press conferences on airport tarmacs. It was a recognition that Reagan's "self-inflicted embarrassments on the stump," in the *Times*'s words, could pose a major threat to his election.

For President Carter's campaign, the early Reagan slips suggested that their long-held hope that they might have Reagan as an opponent was well founded. By his comments, the Republican nominee seemed to be painting himself as the Goldwater of 1980, sure to raise unanswerable doubts about his Presidential capacity. As champions of a candidate for whom media perceptions were the key to political success, they saw the contest as purely a battle of media-dictated images about the candidates. Build up enough doubts about the challenger, and President Carter would be turned to by a reluctant electorate, much as the Democratic voters had renominated Carter out of disillusion with the alternative of Senator Kennedy.

The idea that the general election campaign might be something else, might be about the validity of the ideas advocated by Jimmy Carter over four years, seems never to have troubled the campaign; not if we are to judge by the efforts of Jimmy Carter and his supporters. To illustrate by way of contrast, on September 17, Reagan, Bush, and virtually every Republican candidate for the House and Senate gathered on Capitol Hill to promise fealty to the Republican platform, most specifically on tax and budget cuts. As the *Washington Post*'s David Broder noted, "the implicit message of Monday's ceremony is that there can be only one government at a time and that if voters want Reagan to lead it effectively, they have to go all the way with the GOP"—a message few other journalists picked up at the time, but which may explain much of Reagan's astonishing success in holding the Republicans all but unanimous behind his tax and budget proposals.

The Carter campaign, however, chose to keep focusing on Ronald Reagan's unsuitability for the job. In part, this kind of campaign was endemic to the political character of Jimmy Carter. As Betty Glad demonstrated in her book *Jimmy Carter: The Search for the Great White House,* the candidate of love and morality had always had a hard edge to his politics. From his first campaign for the Georgia state senate in 1962, Carter had tended to regard his opponents not as rivals for power or advocates of competing philosophies, but as candidates somehow beyond the bounds of morality; it was almost as if, by challenging the candidate of goodness and decency, the opponent of Jimmy Carter was, by definition, the candidate of darkness. Further, throughout Carter's public life, the personal and political were inseparable. Whether it was sending his family to state funerals or talking of great public events in highly personal terms,* it was often difficult to determine where Carter thought his personal interests stopped and the national interest began.

In 1980, Carter's instincts and the demands of politics seemed to coincide perfectly. As pollster Pat Caddell had been contending for more than a year, Carter was suffering from a lack of opposition. When the voters were asked whether they wanted Carter to be reelected, the answer was overwhelmingly no. When forced to measure Carter against an alternative, the President had a fighting chance, since the alternative often did not seem any better. In Caddell's terminology, this was the "moving-van" argument: the unlikelihood of anyone doing much better than Carter did not justify the moving expenses involved in changing Presidents. To make the "moving-van" argument, however, required that Ronald Reagan be discredited as an alternative; and Reagan was helping this process by rhetorical carelessness in an arena where the press focused on such carelessness minutely. A more popular, or less combative, incumbent, might have remembered Napoleon's dictum: "Never interfere with the enemy when he is in the

---

* Even during one of Carter's best speeches—when he bested Senator Kennedy at the October, 1979, dedication of the John Kennedy library in Boston —Carter talked of John Kennedy by recalling where he, Carter, had been when he heard of the President's death.

process of destroying himself.'' By ignoring this advice, Carter helped to do exactly what his campaign wanted *not* to do: turn the focus of a critical, skeptical press on the President rather than on his challenger. Within hours, literally, of the formal Labor Day opening of the campaign, the press had made the ''Is Reagan Dumb?'' question a prominent aspect of the campaign. Within a fortnight, a second question had achieved equal prominence: ''Is Carter Mean?''

Carter's killer instinct was hardly new to the press. In 1976, he had openly regretted Hubert Humphrey's failure to enter the campaign, wanting the pleasure of defeating this ''loser.'' In early 1980, he had used a prime-time press conference to imply a lack of patriotism in Senator Kennedy. When Cyrus Vance resigned as Secretary of State after the Iranian rescue attempt, Carter went out of his way to note that the new Secretary of State, Senator Edmund Muskie, would be a much more influential and effective cabinet officer. Now, as Carter began his general election campaign, his first counterpunch gave hints of what was to come. Speaking in Missouri at Harry Truman High School, Carter said, ''The Republican Party now is sharply different under Reagan from what it was under Gerald Ford and presidents all the way back to Eisenhower. I believe in the rights of working people of this country. I believe in looking forward and not backward. I don't believe the nation ought to be divided one region from another. In all these respects, Governor Reagan is different from me.''

Since the President's speech came in the wake of a Reagan gaffe, the possible implications of this remark went without comment, although Reagan's ideological allies were quick to note that Carter might face the charge of taking the low road. The *Wall Street Journal* noted editorially on September 4, ''. . . here it is just past Labor Day and the President is already getting mad. . . . On foreign affairs, Mr. Carter has already moved to calling his opponent an outright warmonger. This may be meant as Trumanesque, but it is not very Presidential. The Reagan campaign may look somewhat inept at the moment, but the Carter campaign may soon begin to look low.''

Over the next week, press reports began to drift away from the Reagan blunders story, largely because the Republican candidate was placed under highly restrictive wraps by his staff. This fact was duly noted—NBC's Heidi Schulman devoted most of her story on the September 13 ''NBC Nightly News'' to showing how ''Reagan was carefully shielded from explaining his own [economic proposals]'' and how ''Reagan advance men threatened to throw [a reporter] out if he tried to ask a question''—as was Reagan's success in charging that the Carter Administration had deliberately leaked news of a radar-immune ''Stealth'' aircraft for political purposes, despite the threat to national security. The President, who remained in the Oval Office signing a military pay bill he had originally proposed, and awarding a long-delayed Medal of Honor to an Italian-American war hero, nonetheless kept up a barrage of rhetorical attacks on Reagan, speaking of "an absolutely false and ridiculous allegation" his challenger had made "without one shred of supporting evidence." Here again, the political reporters made sure that their readers and viewers were let in on what Jack Germond called "the daily media events in the White House," with NBC's Judy Woodruff pointedly noting that "aides [are denying] any deliberate Rose Garden strategy." This kind of intensely skeptical reporting suggested another reason why Carter may have felt that a "high-road Presidential" campaign would not work. Apart from his lack of success at making an advantage of incumbency, Carter's blatant use of the White House during the primary season had made the press, and eventually the public, acutely aware of the political uses to which Carter was putting the Presidency.

Finally, the "morning line" in the battle for the White House was less than encouraging. While the CBS-*New York Times,* ABC-Harris and Gallup polls all showed the election very close in popular vote terms, Reagan's electoral base was clearly stronger than Carter's. The *New York Times* on September 13 summed up the view, reporting that "in the big battleground states, where Mr. Reagan has been concentrating the opening phase of his campaign, both Democratic and Republican politicians now agree he has an edge despite recent Carter gains." David Broder, reporting a day later in the *Washington Post,* said that his informal polling revealed that "voters under 45—particularly men—are turning away from Carter in droves, because of unemployment, inflation, the hostages in Iran, and the pervasive sense they expressed that America has been diminished—not enhanced—in the eyes of the world during his Presidency." And in the coming week, criticism over the President's refusal to debate Reagan and John Anderson would mount.

With less than two months before the vote, then, the essential element of the Carter strategy had yet to take hold. By September of 1964, Barry Goldwater was a beaten candidate; by September of 1972, the only question facing George McGovern was whether he would lose by a bigger margin than Goldwater. But from the perspective of the Carter campaign, the discrediting of Reagan had not yet worked. So, on September 16, Carter turned the rhetorical heat up, and in so doing, turned the political press into an adversary.

It happened in the Ebenezer Baptist Church in Atlanta, Georgia, where Martin Luther King, Sr., and Martin Luther King, Jr., had preached, and where the early moral impetus of the civil rights movement had been generated. With his habit of telling the particular audience in front of him what they wanted to hear, Carter strongly implied that the Reagan campaign was rooted in racism:

"You've seen in this campaign the stirrings of hate and the rebirth of code words like 'states' rights' in a speech in Mississippi, and a campaign reference to the Ku Klux Klan relating to the South. That is a message that creates a cloud on the political horizon. Hatred has no place in this country. Racism has no place in this country."

The "states' rights" point was fairly taken; Reagan had indeed used this long-standing code word for segregation and racial oppression in Neshoba County, Mississippi, where three civil rights workers had been killed with the complicity of a law-enforcement official in 1964. As an opponent of the 1964 Civil Rights Act, Reagan was fair game for an antagonist who wanted to remind blacks and civil rights sympathizers that Reagan had been on the opposite side of a major constitutional fight.

But the rest of Carter's charge was indefensible. If anything, Reagan had tried to attack the Klan and, by implication, Carter. The oily phrase, "a campaign reference to the Ku Klux Klan relating to the South," uttered in front of a black audience and linked to warnings against hate and racism, could only be read as suggesting that Reagan had somehow *embraced* the Klan. The press, which had grown wary of Carter's rhetorical devices, jumped on the President with both feet. Both NBC and CBS noted, in Leslie Stahl's phrase, that press secretary "Jody Powell was pursued by reporters asking if Mr. Carter was calling Reagan a racist." Both quoted a more-in-sorrow-than-in-anger Reagan; NBC showing Reagan calling Carter's charges "shameful, because whether we're on the opposite sides or not, we ought to be trying to pull the country together, not tear it apart." CBS showed the Republican nominee noting that "I just don't know how much farther he'll go to try and divert attention from the fact that he could say all these things to a nationwide audience in a debate if he just wanted to debate."

Editorialists and columnists across the political spectrum weighed in on Carter. The conservative *Washington Star* called Carter's performance, "a squalid exercise in church," charging that the President "was trading in tarnished coin at Dr. King's church." The liberal *Washington Post* called it "running mean," arguing that "Mr. Carter, as a candidate, tends to convey a mean and frantic nature. . . . Jimmy Carter seems to have few limits beyond which he will not go in the abuse of opponents and reconstruction of history." The *New York Times*'s James Reston, asking "what ails Carter?" warned the President that "many of his supporters—even many members of his own Administration—are deeply disappointed by the mean and cunning antics of his campaign."

The impact on the President was not confined to columns and editorials. Indeed, what happened next to Jimmy Carter provides a lesson for those who casually refer to "media manipulation" as the unchallengeable weapon of an incumbent President.

Carter made his remarks on September 16, a Tuesday. Two days later, on the 18th, Carter called an afternoon White House press conference, and all three networks, with some misgivings, agreed to carry it live. The Reagan campaign filed a complaint with the Federal Communications Commission, demanding equal time, as every candidate does when an incumbent President takes to the airwaves. The press conference, it was clear, was another powerful advantage of the Presidency, able to command hundreds of thousands of dollars worth of air time and newspaper coverage.

The flaw in this assumption, of course, is the belief that publicity in a campaign is like the old press agent rule, "I don't care what you say about my client as long as you spell his name right." Marshall McLuhan to the contrary, the medium is not the message. The President's press conference demonstrated that the message can blow apart the efforts at media manipulation.

As soon as Carter had finished his prepared statement—a five-minute pat on the back about his accomplishments—the hostile questions began. Did the President really think Reagan was running a campaign of racism and hatred? ("No, I do not think he's running a campaign of racism or hatred, and I think my campaign is very moderate in its tone.") Don't you attack all of your opponents in a mean fashion? ("I do not indulge in attacking personally the integrity of my opponents, and I hope that I never shall.") Why, then, had Carter used words such as "racism" and "hatred" before a black audience?

"My message," Carter said, "was that the Presidential election is no place for the reviving of the issue of racism under any circumstances."

Then Lisa Myers, of the *Washington Star,* stood up and faced the President.

"It was your own cabinet secretary, Patricia Harris, who first interjected the KKK in the Presidential race," she said. "She said in Los Angeles recently that Governor Reagan was running with the endorsement of the Ku Klux Klan and raised the specter of white sheets. So then how can you blame Governor Reagan—?"

"I am not blaming Governor Reagan," Carter interjected. "That's just exactly the point. The press seems to be obsessed with this issue. I am not blaming Governor Reagan."

"You accused him of interjecting the Ku Klux Klan into the campaign."

There was a moment of silence. Sitting several rows behind Ms. Myers, I saw Carter's eyes fixed on Myers, as though trying to stare her down. Finally, he said, "The only thing I said Governor Reagan interjected into the campaign was the use of the words 'states' rights' in a speech in Mississippi." And he then concluded by praising Reagan for rejecting the Klan endorsement.

The coverage of the conference, on the network news shows and in the print press, was overwhelmingly critical. ABC's Sam Donaldson, pointing to Carter's denial that he had interjected the Klan into his remarks, said flatly, "The President's recollection was wrong," and showed the tape of what Carter had actually said. Donaldson wrapped up his report saying, "The President says issues, not personalities, will decide the election, but his own campaign personality may now have become an issue." The President, noted NBC's Judy Woodruff, "did not look comfortable as he answered" the critical questions about his tone. *Time*'s Hugh Sidey wrote that "the past few days have revealed a man capable of far more petty vituperation than most Americans thought possible even in a dank political season." Mark Shields, writing in the *Washington Post,* said that "to hear the apostle of love and compassion talking about 'hatred' and 'racism' with the practiced and knowing wink, is for some of us too much like finding Carrie Nation under the influence of cheap whiskey. It leaves us more uncomfortable than amused."

With Reagan performing well in the September 21 debate with John Anderson, looking "Presidential" as he jousted with the independent in the absence of the President, Carter went to the attack again; in large measure, according to his aides, because the campaign believed the press would raise the issue of Reagan's "unacceptability" only if the charges were made by the President himself. On Tuesday, September 23, campaigning in California, Carter said:

"Six weeks from now the American people will make a very profound choice—a choice not just between two men and two parties, but between two philosophies. And what you decide on that date—you and those who listen to your voice—will determine what kind of life you and your families will have, whether this nation will make progress or go backward, and whether we have peace or war."

The reasonable meaning of that statement was that a choice for Reagan meant a choice for war; and even Presidential press secretary Jody Powell conceded that the President had "overstated" the case. For his part, Reagan continued the more-in-sorrow response, saying "to accuse that anyone would deliberately want a war is beneath decency."

This statement, coming on the heels of the criticism leveled at Carter, at first looked like a mistake. But—in a move that revealed how publicly the strategy game was being played out—high Carter aides told reporters that the attack had indeed been deliberate, and that it was working.

Speaking not-for-attribution—but clearly understanding that their remarks would be quoted—Carter aides told *New York Times* reporter Steven Weisman that "a campaign can help reinforce the perceptions the public already has. We are trying to reinforce certain perceptions the public already has about Reagan." The attacks on Reagan, they said, had "put Mr. Reagan on the defensive on a series of issues and had pushed aside discussion of the economy, which is the most vulnerable issue for Mr. Carter himself."

For his part, Jody Powell maintained—at least in public—that the problem was the mean-spirited view of the press itself toward the candidates. Appearing on the September 29 "MacNeil-Lehrer Report," Powell said, "I've never seen a political campaign where the invective was any worse than what is directed toward men and women that hold public office or who seek public office, by some of the people who now seem to be so upset." And he also defended Carter's statement, made on the day of the broadcast, that Reagan had "repeatedly" advocated the use of American military force around the world. Indeed, on the campaign plane, Powell produced a list of Reagan statements, going back to 1966, advocating the use or presence of American military might in crisis areas. In Powell's view, as stated on the "MacNeil-Lehrer Report," ". . . the statement that he had repeatedly advocated the use of American military force in places like Cyprus or in the Lebanese civil war, or on a peacekeeping mission in Zimbabwe, those are also true."

Here the distinction between print and broadcast journalism becomes crucial. Whatever its other limitations, and however much the political writers in print tend to be seduced by the narrow focus of how a candidate is doing among regional or ethnic groups, the fact remains that there is room in newspapers and magazines for an extensive examination of so critical a question as a potential President's view of the use of force in the world. Even before his formal nomination, Reagan's foreign policy and defense views were subjected to lengthy examination in the print press. *Time* magazine, for example, devoted a long article in its June 9 issue to a look at Reagan's view of the world, examining his opposition to the SALT II treaty, and his advocacy of military assistance to the anti-Marxist guerrillas in Afghanistan and Angola. In the *Wall Street Journal* on June 2, diplomatic correspondent Karen Elliott House wrote a detailed piece on Reagan's views, quoting the candidate's flat assertion that "the Soviet Union underlies all of the unrest that is going on. If they weren't engaged in this game of dominoes, there wouldn't be any hot spots in the world."

Given the time to examine more than a decade of speeches and proposals, and the years of an incumbent President's policies and pronouncements, the print press could—and frequently did, in the 1980 campaign—enable a reader to make some sense of the distinctions between the candidates. Television did not have this time: or, rather, chose not to devote its scarce time to the lengthy discussion of how a candidate proposed to avoid war and protect American security. With local stations opposed to an expanded network newscast for fear of diluting profits, with networks unwilling to extend such a newscast into prime time, with equal-time laws ostensibly blocking special network broadcasts where major—but not minor—candidates would be examined at length, the debate was confined to an exchange of charges and countercharges in forty-five-second sound bites on the evening news.

As a highly skilled rhetorician, Ronald Reagan had long demonstrated the capacity to arouse support with shorthand arguments. Now, President Carter was using a "war-and-peace" argument—the "Tolstoy" argument—to spread doubts about Reagan's ability to keep the world from being blown up. Given the reliance on this scare tactic in political advertising aimed at Reagan, there is no question that the Carter strategy was deliberate: use the press, specifically the television news shows, to reinforce doubts about Reagan by forcing the programs to carry the charges of an incumbent President. The intention was to take advantage of the simplicity television imposed on itself to paint the picture of a candidate bent on war.

As a political strategy, the tactic ultimately backfired, since it ignored the other side of the coin: a candidate attacked simplistically could reply simplistically. A televised speech on foreign policy, a calm, credible showing in the debates could dissipate the picture of a monster as effectively as broad charges could enhance a picture. There were, indeed, bothersome questions about Ronald Reagan's foreign policy. Is it, in fact, true that there would be *no* "hot spots" in the world without Soviet mischief? Does that view of the world explain *fully* the tension in the Middle East, the rise of Moslem fundamentalism, the upheavals in Latin America? If strategic arms talks are to be, in effect, abandoned for a search for superiority, and if the Soviets respond with a new burst of arms expenditures, then what has the United States accomplished, other than to impose enormous burdens on its own economy?

In the view of the Carter campaign, "the press never picked up on these questions," in the words of one high aide. Carter's rhetorical excesses, he explained, were made necessary by the failure of television news to put Reagan's views under a microscope. For their part, Reagan's adherents might have pointed to the analogous questions about Carter's foreign policy. Where, apart from Olympic boycotts and grain embargoes, was the coherent response to Soviet adventurism? How could allies rely on the word of the United States if longtime supporters, such as the Shah and Somoza, were publicly abandoned to anti-American forces, and others were hectored and threatened with arms cutoffs for their human rights policies?

This debate had been raging for more than a decade, especially within the Democratic Party. It had led those opposed to the war in Vietnam to challenge the assumptions of containment and massive defense spending. It had led others within the party—Henry Jackson and Pat Moynihan, the "neoconservative" intellectuals grouped around *Commentary* magazine—to repudiate the policies of George McGovern and what they viewed as the accommodationist policies of the Carter Administration. It was, in fact, the context within which the "war-and-peace" charge of Carter and the "vacillation" charge of Reagan gained meaning. That meaning was, as a general proposition, never provided on the network evening news.

Instead, what the public heard was a shrill exchange between the two major-party candidates; and that shrillness, in turn, enabled the press to characterize the campaign as a "low-road" affair (the *New York Times,* September 21), filled with "dirty rhetoric" (UPI, October 16), "trench fighting" (Walter Cronkite, October 7).

To be sure, both candidates provided more grist for the mills with comments during the remainder of the campaign. On October 6, President Carter told a Chicago fund-raiser that "you'll determine whether or not this America will be unified, or, if I lose the election, whether Americans might be separated, black from white, Jew from Christian, North from South, rural from urban." ("I think he owes the country an apology," Reagan replied.) Publicly, the Carter campaign seemed to be saying that the President might have gone too far; that in the words of CBS's Lesley Stahl, "there is an acknowledgment and growing concern in the White House that the President's increasing stridency is beginning to look like desperation." In an attempt to cauterize that wound, Carter—at the White House's initiation—replied to a long-standing interview request by ABC's Barbara Walters to offer a backhanded "mea culpa" for the tone of the campaign.

"No more name calling?" Walters asked.

"I'll do my best," Carter smiled, adding, "sometimes human nature comes through. And when I feel extremely deeply about a subject as I do the subject of arms control and peace and a strong defense and see the crucial nature of it to the American people, it's incumbent on me, I believe, to express it. But I will try to do it with more reticence in the future and stick exclusively to the issue itself." The answer reflected a decision to raise the doubts about Reagan in paid advertising, while avoiding the danger raised by a *Boston Globe* editorial that charged that "the President seems bent on discarding his last ace, his reputation as a decent and compassionate man." (Carter had some problems with his supporters. In mid-October reports from a campus newspaper surfaced, revealing that former UN Ambassador Andrew Young had told an Ohio State University audience that Reagan's "states' rights" advocacy in Mississippi "looks like a code word to me that it's going to be all right to kill niggers when he's President." The White House swiftly disavowed that remark.)

For his part, Reagan's sometimes whimsical approach to the facts caused him some further problems, none of them rising to the level of Carter's discomfiture over his "meanness." On October 7, attacking federal regulations for causing joblessness in the steel mills of Youngstown, Ohio, Reagan raised the question of what really caused most of our pollution. Noting the eruption earlier in 1980 of Mount St. Helens, Reagan said, "I just have a suspicion that one little mountain out there in these last several months has probably released more sulphur dioxide into the atmosphere of the world than has been released in the last ten years of automobile driving or things of that kind that people are so concerned about." As Carter's Environmental Protection Agency quickly pointed out, automobiles emit carbon monoxide, not sulphur dioxide, and that one major power plant over the course of a year emitted as much sulphur dioxide as the volcano did. Further, said Reagan, the haze of the Great Smoky Mountains is caused by decaying vegetation and might actually benefit tuberculosis victims. The first part of that statement was true, experts said, the second totally unsupported.

Reagan's views, including his statement, just before arriving in smog-ravaged Los Angeles, that the air-pollution problem had been largely solved, did not endear him to the environmentalists either. Campaigning at a Los Angeles university, he was greeted with a sign draped around a tree that read, "Chop me down before I kill again." But as with his frequent factual slips during the primary campaign, these comments seemed to do him little harm, compared with the doubts about his peace-keeping capacity, which emerged as the central obstacle between Reagan and the White House.

In attempt to explain this fascination with the news-grabbing remark, CBS devoted a segment of one of its weekly late-night "Campaign Countdown" reports to the question. Reagan aide Lyn Nofziger, noting the tendency of the press to pick out a specific off-the-cuff line to highlight a day's campaign activity, noted that "one of the reasons is the insatiable demand of television for a hook each night on the six o'clock news, for something different, because each television network is competing with the other one."

Correspondent Bill Plante noted that candidates "have an agenda which they want to follow. We are more interested, many times, in getting the candidate to react to the day's news, to the world events that are going on, than we are in hearing what he has to say for the twenty-seventh time . . . out of his standard speech. So our interests and theirs diverge."

And veteran CBS correspondent Charles Collingwood added, "It's not to make trouble for a candidate that reporters listen so closely for his impromptu remarks. It's because they represent rare clues to his real thinking, real character—important when he is as isolated from intimate contact with the reporters as Ronald Reagan."

Thus, the conundrum. In an effort to keep a candidate to the themes established by campaign strategists the campaign keeps the candidate relatively isolated. Thus frustrated, the press treats any deviation from the theme of the day as a major news event. And time is further limited, thus making a coherent examination of the themes— which may, in fact, give a stronger clue to the "real thinking" and "real character" of a potential President—even harder to accomplish on the evening newscasts.

In the effort to predict who the winner of the election would be, the media demonstrated, at the least, a minimal level of sophistication by moving away from a national perspective and devoting a consistently heavy part of evening newscasts and print articles to a focus on the "battleground" states: California, New York, New Jersey, Illinois, Ohio, Pennsylvania, Texas, Michigan, and Florida, which would provide 245 of the 270 electoral votes needed to win the Presidency. A look at how the networks covered the horserace in these battleground states during the month of October suggests that the networks did attempt to blend the question of issues into the horserace question; it also suggests the limits inherent in such an approach.

As CBS's Bruce Morton noted on October 2, "the action is focused on these nine states. Once upon a time, it would have been Democratic machines in the big cities versus Republicans on the farms, in the small towns, the suburbs. No longer. The big-city machines, even Chicago's, are rusting or broken. The farms don't hold as many people as they used to. And the suburbs are no longer always Republican, as traditional inner-city Democrats grew up and moved out of the old neighborhoods. The suburbs of these nine big states are likely to be where this election is won or lost."

On NBC's "Today" show that same day, David Broder observed of the big Midwest states, "if you think [they're] sinking under the campaigns now, wait 'til you see what it's like in the last ten days, because you're not going to be able to cross the street in Cleveland or Columbus or Chicago without having your hand shaken by Ronald Reagan or Jimmy Carter."

In pursuing the story of the major states, the networks and their associates polled the states repeatedly. A major network correspondent, armed with the poll, would leaven the statistics with interviews and a brief sketch of the voting patterns of the state's constituent groups. Occasionally, the focus on these groups would reveal a concern over a specific issue; at other times, the focus was purely "political" in the narrower, electoral sense of that term.

On October 8, for example, CBS correspondent Bob Schieffer offered the "Evening News" audience a detailed look at the battle for Texas.

"The fight for Texas's 26 electoral votes is hotter than Houston in

July," Schieffer reported, quoting the CBS-*New York Times* poll showing the state "too close to call"—Carter at 40 percent, Reagan at 39 percent, Anderson at 3 percent, with 18 percent undecided. A Carter aide observed that "most of the vote that we're going to get in the state is an anti-Reagan vote," and a Reagan aide said that "the best thing we've got going for us is Carter's record," while another poll finding revealed that the "anti" feeling was more prevalent among Reagan voters than Carter's. Viewers saw a massive vote-pull operation within the Reagan campaign, Democratic emphasis on the black and Hispanic votes, and a Schieffer note that Republicans were making inroads in traditionally Democratic central Texas. Concluded Schieffer, "With the race now so close, victory may hinge on whether the Republicans lose narrowly or badly in these Democratic strongholds."

Why were Republicans making inroads in these traditionally Democratic strongholds? What were the political differences between blacks and Hispanics? What aspects of Reagan's program might cause him difficulties among what parts of the Texas Democratic Party? There was no time for such an analysis.

An attempt to fuse broader analysis with polls was made two days later, when CBS's Bruce Morton looked at Pennsylvania.

"Pennsylvania," Morton said. "Twenty-seven electoral votes. Third richest prize. Pennsylvania: old industry. More people than jobs."

Viewers saw the owner of United Foundries talking about losses and layoffs. Then, blended in with the poll results (Reagan had a two-point lead with Anderson at 10 percent and 22 percent undecided) was a brief mention of Carter's problems in the northeast of the state—a problem linked to a weak economy. Democrats, Morton said, had to have a 250,000 vote bulge coming out of Philadelphia. But Reagan was cutting into the ethnic Catholic vote because of inflation ("it's killing us," said an official of the Polish-American Congress). But, Morton concluded, with moderate Republicans doubting Reagan, "Pennsylvania is a prize still to be won."

In his analysis of Pennsylvania on ABC on October 18, correspondent Sander Vanocur covered much of the same ground; but his analysis went deeper, noting that "traditional Democrats have been moving away from the national party for more than a decade." Vanocur was one of the few network correspondents to note that the "social issues"—crime, permissiveness, and the like—had not disappeared, but had become a given in ethnic Catholic Democratic dissatisfaction with the liberal positions of party standard-bearers. For these voters, Reagan's position on abortion, prayer in public schools, and the more general appeal for "a return to traditional values" was a powerful factor eating away at their lifelong propensity to vote for the Democratic Party.

A more general attempt to analyze a region, rather than a state, was provided by NBC's Ken Bode on the October 8 "Today" show. Bode, a one-time Democratic activist and print journalist, had an acute sense of the political terrain in which this election was being fought. Given the time pressures of a network news report, Bode could only sketch a summary. The Reagan strategy, he noted, was to "force Carter to spend time and money defending his own base. . . . Carter's problem," Bode observed, "is that Ronald Reagan also has a base in the South. He won every Southern primary and caucus. Another problem for Carter is indifference."

Quoting a Carter operative who warned—accurately, as it turned out—that "a lot of people think they've got the hay in the barn, but he'll have some problems from the Southern states," Bode concluded by pointing to the Carter campaign's effort to turn out heavy black numbers. Here again, it was emphatically *not* the fault of the reporter that viewers got so mechanical a look at the battle for the South. Given the time, Bode could have pointed to Reagan's support among evangelicals, his strong stands on defense, his opposition to federal power which still resonated in the white South. But there was no time.

In looking at the last month's worth of press polling and state-by-state analyses, the most striking aspect of the coverage is the gap between most of the poll projections and the final result. A poll issued by *Time* magazine during the first week of the campaign showed Carter and Reagan tied at 39 percent each. By October 23, the CBS-*New York Times* poll gave Carter a 39–38 lead over Reagan. CBS's Bruce Morton noted that "what stands out is how little has happened in the last month. . . . President Carter was just a hair ahead [a month ago]; it was really a dead heat then. It's really a dead heat now." Said the *Times* a day later, ". . . President Carter and Ronald Reagan are perceived today very much the way they were perceived in early September. . . . The frozen composite of perceptions underlines the closeness of the Presidential race, as weakness in one area continues to balance strength in another."

On October 31, ABC's Lynn Sherr reported that an electoral survey showed "Reagan still leads 24 states with 197 electoral votes; President Carter is ahead in 15 states with 149 electoral votes; and 12 states with an enormous 192 electoral votes are still rated even, meaning that either man can still get the 270 votes needed to win." Sherr concluded that "Ronald Reagan has the advantage right now. He needs only a few breakthroughs, big ones, to win . . . President Carter needs to make everything work to win." That same day, looking at the

294 · JEFF GREENFIELD

Midwest, Dan Rather reported that it was "too close to call in Wisconsin, Missouri, Illinois. Michigan, and Ohio—breathtakingly close."

Even on the last days of the campaign, after the debate, and after the false hopes raised by the possible release of the hostages, the polls showed a very close race, although movement to Reagan was detected by NBC and ABC. On Monday, November 3, the CBS-*Times* poll had the national numbers at 44–43–8, in favor of Reagan, but with "a sizable lead" for Reagan in the state-by-state battle. NBC's "Today" show reported a close race, but with Reagan leading in states with 280 electoral votes, and Carter ahead in states with but 92 electoral votes, Lou Harris, reporting on election morning for ABC, showed Reagan with a five-point lead nationally, and reported that Reagan's lead was "beyond the margin for error." Walter Cronkite, reporting on election eve, said the "polls [were] showing it too close to call." No network, no news organization, came close to predicting anything like the ten-point, eight million vote spread for Reagan, much less the electoral landslide or the sweeping Republican gains in the Senate and the House.

Why not? One explanation, offered by Carter's pollster, Pat Caddell, was that the focus on the possible release of the American hostages over the last weekend of the campaign turned a nip-and-tuck race into a landslide by driving home all of the discontents of the past four years. "All year long," he said on Election Night, "we were trying to keep real events out of the campaign"—an unintentional indictment of the Carter strategy. The focus on the hostages, the one-year anniversary specials featured on the network news and in the press on Election Eve and Election Day, crystallized the disillusionment.

This explanation is challenged by Reagan's pollster, Richard Wirthlin, whose firm, Decision Marketing Information, showed a post-election gathering in Washington data that suggested that Reagan's ten-point lead was solid at least a week before Election Day and that Reagan's national plurality never dropped below five points in the last seventeen days of the campaign. It is further challenged by the self-interest of the Carter campaign in arguing that last-minute factors, rather than the inherent weakness of the candidate, accounts for the landslide. Other pollsters suggested that Reagan benefited from "closet" voters, who were unwilling to tell interviewers that they were going to vote for a man so frequently characterized as an amiable buffoon.

In a larger sense, however, the reasons for the gap between the polls and the results do not matter. If a Presidential election can swing nip-and-tuck battle to a landslide within forty-eight hours, then what is the point of the constant reporting of state and national polls weeks before the election, complete with the unwittingly arrogant disclaimer that the polls are "subject to a margin of error plus or minus 3 percent"? The victory margins for Reagan in state after state that were "too close to call"—380,000 in Illinois, 250,000 in Michigan, 450,000 in Ohio, 700,000 in Texas—made mincemeat out of the preelection forecasts, as did Reagan's capture of New York, a state put safely in Carter's column throughout the campaign. The pouring of resources into these predictive stories, resources that consumed not just money, but the time that networks complain is never available for longer analytical pieces, suggests the general futility of attempting to see into the future at the expense of examining the past and present of the candidates and their intentions.

If, in contrast, Reagan voters were unwilling to admit their preferences to pollsters, then what does that tell us of the capacity of these polls to offer a clue as to the behavior of the electorate? Pollsters always argue that a poll must be understood as a "snapshot" of the electorate at a given moment in time. But if the electorate is, in effect, hiding behind the furniture when the pollster comes to take his picture, then the snapshot is going to be misleading. To use the dreaded sports analogy, it is as if the snapshot showed us a picture of the Super Bowl when the players were deliberately wearing the wrong uniforms—or, if the "last-minute shift" explanation is correct, it would be like trying to guess the final score of the game from a "snapshot" taken half an hour before kickoff.

To be sure, the coverage of the hostage story on the last weekend is worth a look, because it demonstrates how conscious both camps—and the press—were about the possible influence of coverage on the outcome of the election. All through the general election, commentators hedged any guess as to the outcome of the election with the proviso, "of course, if the hostages are released before Election Day . . ." So conscious were Reagan's supporters of the possibility of Carter greeting returning Americans at a lavish White House ceremony that they had devoted months to conditioning the press to the possibility of media manipulation. As early as June of 1980, Senator Paul Laxalt, a key Reagan advisor, had warned Washington lobbyists to beware of "the October surprise"—a last-minute attempt by the Administration to create a shock wave through the political process.

This warning, repeated again and again throughout the campaign, found a receptive ear among members of the press who had seen Carter's Rose Garden strategy dominate the primaries, complete with White House receptions for the United States Olympic hockey team and early morning press conferences on the day of a critical primary to announce a hostage breakthrough that in fact never happened. It took on added importance when the Iran-Iraq war broke out in September. As the President said on September 22, "The signals coming out of Iran lately—and they have all been public signals—have indicated some new desire on the part of the Iranians to resolve the problems between ourselves and them." It gained in intensity when Iranian Prime Minister Mohammed Ali Raji visited the United Nations in mid-October and made conciliatory comments about the hostage issue—comments linked to Iran's need for billions of dollars in assets frozen in the United States with which to buy war materiel.

For Reagan, the challenge was to stake out high political ground without letting the Carter Administration escape liability for the seizure of the hostages in the first place. It was a challenge that tested Reagan, who moved from blaming Carter for permitting the seizure of the embassy in Teheran (September 9) to promising that "no one in America will rejoice more than I" when the hostages are released (October 18) to attacking Carter for permitting the "humiliation and disgrace" of the seizure (October 20). When Reagan even hinted at alternative policies—saying on October 25 that "I do have some ideas," Carter attacked him for employing a 1980 version of Richard Nixon's "secret plan" to end the war in Vietnam in 1968.

When the Iranian *majlis* began meeting on October 27 to consider what specific conditions it would demand for the release of the hostages, the issue loomed over the candidates. For the press, it posed a special dilemma. As *Washington Post* columnist Philip Geyelin said on October 27, the question of Carter having played "hostage politics" in the past was one many reporters and editors would have answered "yes." Pointing to the Rose Garden campaign, the Wisconsin primary press conference, and the postrescue operation campaigning, Geyelin said, "I call that hypocrisy. I call that expediency." However, Geyelin said, "I don't say how we could hope to control the government of Iran, if there is one, which is clearly not our ally." For at least one top news executive at CBS, the dilemma was how to cover such a hostage release without turning it into a campaign pitch for Jimmy Carter.

For weeks, technicians from all three networks had been encamped in Wiesbaden, West Germany, near an American Air Force base to which the hostages would be flown upon release for debriefing, medical attention, and recuperation. There was no question of not covering the event, should it happen, before the election. For this executive, the question was how to balance the coverage politically. One solution that CBS had under serious consideration was to bring Richard Queen on to talk about the conditions under which the hostages had been held—the occasional physical abuse, the constant mental torture, the threats of execution, culminating in a "mock" execution staged by militants. According to this executive, Queen's testimony would have taken some of the celebratory "edge" off the coverage.

As it happened, the contingency plan never happened. Instead, the Iranian Parliament announced, in the predawn hours of Sunday,

November 2, the conditions that the United States would have to meet
to win the release of the hostages: a pledge of nonintervention, release
of frozen assets, and a meaningless promise to investigate the charge
that the late Shah of Iran had illegally spirited national assets out of
Iran. Informed of this development, President Carter cut short his
campaigning in Chicago, gathered as much of the press corps as could
be roused out of bed at 3:30 A.M., and flew back to Washington, where
those watching television on Sunday morning saw President Carter
descend from the helicopter on the White House lawn, and walk back
to the White House accompanied by National Security Advisor Brzezinski.

The Republicans, however, had an ace up their sleeve. They
booked high-ranking politicians on all of the Sunday news shows, and
were able to send their message to television audiences all that Sunday
afternoon. Former Secretary of State Kissinger, on ABC's "Issues
and Answers," did not accuse the Carter Administration of knuckling
under to the Iranians, but he did insist that Iran was manipulating
events because they feared a Reagan Presidency.

Former President Gerald Ford, on NBC's "Meet the Press," argued that "the sale of arms to Iran or even the delivery of arms they
paid for would put us in the quagmire of the Middle East, and it would
be worse than the experience we had in Vietnam."

Vice-Presidential candidate George Bush, on CBS's "Face the
Nation," called the hostage experience "a year of shame, a year of
suffering as a country. . . . I think the American people don't want
these mullahs, the ayatollahs, to affect the election one way or another."

This presence helped prevent the Sunday before the election from
becoming an unchallenged presentation of the Carter Administration's
"success" in moving toward a resolution of the crisis. And as it turned
out, the deeply ingrained suspicion of the press kept the President
under severe wraps. When he went on national television at 6:25 P.M.
to announce a "positive step" toward resolution of the crisis, he did
so after his aides, according to a postelection comment by media advisor Gerald Rafshoon, had rejected the idea of attacking the Iranian
government. "It would have been demagogic," Rafshoon said—and,
it could be added, the press would have been quick to attack any
posturing on the part of Carter as another illegitimate use of the Oval
Office for political gain. Instead, Carter simply said that "the calendar" wouldn't affect his decisions on the crisis. Carter went back on
the campaign trail Sunday night, and the network newscasts over the
next day and a half—up to Election Day morning—were filled with
more images of the year of captivity. Any chance the President had to
manipulate the media at the close of the campaign had effectively been
foreclosed, both by Republican warnings of the "October surprise,"

and by the press's own determination not to permit such manipulation in the face of suspicion over incumbency politics in general, and Carter's use of the office in particular.

Determining the impact of this last weekend's events on the campaign is probably impossible; depending on one's biases, one can accept the Caddell conclusion that it destroyed Carter's reelection, or the Wirthlin projection that it had no effect on an already clear Reagan landslide. A final controversy about predictions and projections emerged when Election Day produced, not a cliff-hanger, but a landslide for Reagan and the Republicans.

All three networks spent Election Day conducting "exit polls": interviews with thousands of voters leaving the polling places, selected for a statistically valid sample of sex, age, race, income, party affiliation, and other characteristics. By early afternoon, the dimensions of the Reagan triumph were clear; and by 5 P.M. Eastern time—2 P.M. Pacific time—CBS, NBC, and ABC all went on the air with bulletins stating that a strong Reagan trend was developing. At 6:30 P.M. Eastern time John Chancellor was reporting on the "NBC Nightly News" that "based on information gathered today in our NBC-Associated Press Poll, in the key states all around the country, we believe Ronald Reagan will win a very substantial victory tonight—very substantial." ABC's "World News Tonight" reported, more circumspectly, that "throughout the day we have talked with voters after they cast their ballots and it appears Ronald Reagan is running very well." CBS's Walter Cronkite declared that "a strong national trend is running toward Ronald Reagan."

To put in context what happened next, a bit of history is required. The technology of computers, enabling massive exit poll data to be instantly digested and analyzed, had been growing all through the 1960s and 1970s. But the political outcome of the five elections before 1980 made the question of projections moot. In 1960, the Kennedy-Nixon race was a squeaker; only Wednesday morning did Kennedy's narrow, tainted win in Illinois insure him the White House. In 1964, the Johnson landslide was a certainty as early as July. In 1968, Nixon and Humphrey battled down to the wire in state after state; Nixon's win was not clear until 5 A.M. on Wednesday. In 1972, Nixon's landslide was clear as soon as Thomas Eagleton was forced off the Democratic ticket. In 1976, there was another close finish, with Carter waiting until Mississippi's votes broke his way at 3 A.M. until claiming victory. In all of these campaigns, there was no measurable surprise, no sudden revelation breaking on the East Coast, persuading West Coast voters to stay home.

In 1980, by contrast, all of the preelection predictions were shown to have been shockingly wrong. And the same networks that had characterized the Reagan-Carter race as a toss-up were reporting, in the midafternoon hours on the West Coast, that it was all over; that Reagan would win in a landslide.

Moreover, one network—NBC—scored a clear beat on election night by changing the rules of the game. Traditionally, projections of individual states were not made until sample precincts reported their *actual vote tabulations*. These sample precincts, selected for demographic qualities as well as historical voting patterns, have traditionally enabled networks to "call" a state hours before the total "raw" vote is counted. Using this method, NBC has, it says, never called a state wrong over six Presidential elections. In 1980, however, NBC—unlike ABC and CBS—decided to use exit poll results, not simply to analyze the national vote by income, age, sex, race, party affiliation, and occupation, but to *call specific states*. For example, in five states NBC projected Presidential winners at 8:01 P.M., just one minute after the polls closed. In Texas, NBC projected Reagan the winner at 8:02 P.M., two minutes after the polls closed. Although an NBC spokesman insisted publicly that key precincts were used in making these projections, all three networks, in fact, received tabulations from the News Election Service, and all three networks used key precincts to predict statewide voting patterns. Clearly, exit polls were the key to NBC's swift calls.

Partly because the spread in most states was so clear, partly because the Reagan sweep was so national, the NBC election analyst was confident—rightly, as it turned out—that these exit polls could be used to predict how individual states would go. Thus, long before its competitors were listing states in the Reagan column, NBC's effective wall-sized map was lighting up state after state in the swimming-pool-blue color indicating Reagan would take the state. And, by 8:15 P.M. Eastern standard time—5:15 P.M. Pacific standard time—NBC projected enough states in the Reagan column to call him the next President of the United States.

Added to this projection was the behavior of President Carter, who had been told late Monday night that he would lose by a landslide. Hoping to end the suffering, Carter went on national television at 9:50 P.M.—6:50 Pacific time—to concede the election. In a metaphor for his lack of links to the Democratic Party which had twice nominated him, Carter either did not think about the congressional candidates on the West Coast or else concluded that the networks had already carried the bad news (in fact, ABC did not project Reagan as elected until 6:52 Pacific time, and CBS, plagued by computer breakdowns, did not report until 7:32 Pacific time).

Whatever the cause, the apparent impact on West Coast voting was heavy. California Secretary of State March Fong Eu said, "Would-be voters suddenly became nonvoters after the media projections. Election volunteers did not show up, and voter information

phones stopped ringing during a time when they are usually tied up.''
A California poll in January, 1981, found that 10 percent of voters who
were asked specifically cited network projections for not voting. Two
West Coast congressional races were repeatedly cited as examples of
the influence of the early projections. California Democratic Representative James Corman lost his seat by 752 votes, and Oregon Democrat
Al Ullman lost his seat by 3,765 votes.

The facts about this impact are not conclusive. Who knows, asked
NBC analyst Scammon, whether the stay-at-homes were Republicans
who knew their man had won, or Democrats who knew their man had
lost? "It's a little like the rain, which falls impartially on Democrats
and Republicans." And what would have happened if President Carter
had urged West Coast Democrats to save the seats of their Congressmen? Morever, in aggregate terms, West Coast voters seem to have
voted in slightly *higher* numbers than their East Coast counterparts.
The total election turnout fell from 54.5 percent to 53.9 percent—a
lower falloff from 1976 than had been predicted in the days before the
election. In Oregon, the falloff was only .2 percent—from 62.1 percent
to 61.9 percent In California, the dropoff was .3 percent from 50.9
percent to 50.6 percent. In Washington, the falloff was much greater
—from 61.1 percent to 58.5 percent.

Whatever the reality, West Coast officials are convinced the networks did indeed have a clear impact on voting. Washington Democratic Congressman Al Swift has said, "A lot of people [in Congress]
feel the networks are wrong, and we hope this will push them to change
their guidelines." Bills in Congress include everything from prohibit-
ing networks from making projections—clearly unconstitutional if applied to exit polls—to creating a twenty-four-hour voting day, with
polls opening and closing at the same time, preferably on a Sunday or
a national holiday—a proposal made as long ago as 1968, when CBS
President Frank Stanton told the Republican National Convention's
resolutions committee that a "twenty-four-hour Election Day, with the
polls opening simultaneously everywhere, and closing twenty-four
hours later regardless of the local clock time . . . would end unsupported speculation as to whether results of reports from early-closing
polls in one state influence the voters in other states where polls close
hours later." * A more unsettling prospect in the future is that, driven
by the competitive urge to project the winner first, networks will begin
issuing exit poll projections in the early afternoon—midmorning in the
West—thus driving down the turnout all over the country, as voters
come to believe the election is over because the networks say it is

---

* I have suggested, semiseriously, that Sunday voting will produce maximum
turnout only if the National Football League takes the day off. Otherwise, the
women of America will elect our President each and every time.

over. The Constitution almost certainly prohibits controls on such projections, because it is unimaginable that a journalist can be forbidden to stand outside a polling place with a clipboard in hand. Perhaps the networks ought to look back on their own polls and decide, as a matter of restraint, that the best kind of political coverage would be to give the voter a chance to be heard *before* telling the voters what they have done.

Any look at the network performance in the general election campaign would be misleading if it did not note the attempt, during the last month of the election, to provide the citizenry with some understanding of the issues. Throughout the month of October, the three commercial networks all devoted time during their evening newscasts to examinations of the candidates and their positions on major issues. Each of them conducted lengthy interviews with Jimmy Carter and Ronald Reagan—and less lengthy interviews with John Anderson—and edited them to produce a series of "minidebates" on key issues.

Viewers could see Ronald Reagan, on NBC's "Nightly News" on October 8, talking at some length on the proper uses of American military power, suggesting that a greater show of force might have prevented the *Pueblo* from being seized by North Korea in 1968. They could see ABC economics correspondent Dan Cordtz examining the economic philosophies of Carter and Reagan, with Carter charging that Republicans opposed ". . . those very programs that are so dear to Americans who have suffered from poverty and alienation and discrimination," and Reagan pledging "to take the lead in taking government off your backs and out of your pockets." They could see CBS's Walter Cronkite closely examining the two men on the size of the projected defense buildups both had advocated, and on how they judged each other's respective strengths and weaknesses.

Over the last month, a reasonably steady viewer would have been able to hear the candidates, in interview excerpts, discuss how to get the economy back on track, how to preserve the peace, how to govern the country; and they would have seen surrogate supporters and opponents judge the credibility of the candidates' views.

This effort ought not to be ignored. But it ought not to be exaggerated, either. This last month came after a ten-month period during which the voter had been taught, in effect, that the race for office was nothing more than a struggle for power. The chance to hear the candidates at length, in their own words, the attempt to place the daily charges and countercharges in context, was postponed; and by the time it took place, it did so in an atmosphere unanimously described by the press as a disillusioned if not disgusted electorate.

As a general proposition, there was no "public discourse" except as a separate, late-emerging category that seemed almost out of place, given the context in which the campaign had been described. And what makes this so dispiriting is that 1980 was indeed an election in which there were clear choices; in which the candidates had, in Carter's incessant phrase, "stark differences." In the spring of 1981, rested from their unsuccessful labors at star-gazing, the press awoke to the fact that the Administration now in power really did mean to change fundamentally the relationship between citizens and the government. This was no secret; it was in the entire public life of Ronald Reagan, in the speeches he had been making for three decades.

Had this fact been made clear—early, often, and repeatedly—in 1980, the results may not have been any different. But those in favor of this change, and those opposed to it, would have understood how high the stakes were in 1980. Coverage that leavened the relentless "chase" with an attempt to spell out the stakes for the citizenry might have met a reception far different from the "who cares?" mood reported—and in some cases influenced by press coverage that treated the candidates as nothing but cynical combatants for power. By 1980, the contours of American politics had changed drastically: with working men and women cut loose from the moorings of the Democratic Party, with the New Deal exhausted, with the governing party of the United States no longer sure of what it stood for, with a united, ideological Republican Party offering the country a candidate and a philosophy radically at odds with what had gone before.

Perhaps it is asking too much of the media to provide a coherent frame of reference for this kind of political coverage. Professor Thomas Patterson, one of the most perceptive academic observers of politics, argues that in a process where political parties have been as severely weakened as ours, there is no effective way of presenting such a choice.

"A workable system," the Cornell political scientist has written, "must take into account what the people, the parties, and the press can and cannot do. However appealing the image of the omnicompetent public, and however attractive the idea of the press as the corrective for defective political institutions, these beliefs are not the basis for a sound electoral system."

It may be foolishly optimistic, but I believe otherwise. In my view, a mass media with the determination to spell out these facts, and the willingness to let the candidates present these alternatives in their own words, would have, I believe, produced a much more enthusiastic electorate—not because they would have embraced the candidates as God's noblemen, but because they would have understood what was at stake for *them* in the outcome. Either out of enthusiasm or opposition, they would have had a fairer chance to care about the choice.

This is no naive faith in the inherent Godlike quality of the American voter. People vote for all sorts of reasons: from those who despise a candidate's accent to those who believe him to be an agent of the devil, to those who pore over every position paper offered by the League of Women Voters. It is entirely possible that given the chance to learn more about the stakes in a Presidential election, the majority of voters would turn the set off or find a rerun of a game show. But in a sense, 1980 proved as no outside criticism can that voters *do* understand when a choice has to be made; that they are capable of defying polls and predictions and determining that it is time for a basic change in American life to an extent no expert could have imagined. From the surface of 1980—which is where the mass media positioned itself most of the time—the election was a disjointed, dispiriting contest. In the end, what appears to have decided the election was a series of fundamental changes in the beliefs of millions of Americans.

If the press attempts to explore the underlying political events of a campaign next time, it just may find itself better able to report on what is, in fact, happening in those places where the campaign is happening—not just on the campaign trail, but in the schools and supermarkets, the factories and the churches, the offices and homes of the Republic. In so doing, it also might find that—in the journalistic search for the "real" campaign—it had brought Americans closer to the process that shapes our country, and had given them a reason to care.

Index

ABOUT THE AUTHOR

Jeff Greenfield is an author, syndicated columnist, and television commentator. His commentary on politics and the media is featured on CBS "Morning" news program and on the highly acclaimed television news magazine "Sunday Morning." During the 1980 conventions, he provided political analysis along with Bill Moyers and James J. Kilpatrick.

A graduate of the University of Wisconsin and of the Yale Law School, Mr. Greenfield was a legislative aide to Senator Robert Kennedy, chief speechwriter for New York Mayor John Lindsay, and a consultant with the political media firm of Garth Associates, Inc. Mr. Greenfield is the author of eight books, including *Television: The First Fifty Years* and *Playing to Win: An Insider's Guide to Politics*. His syndicated political column appears in newspapers across the country. Mr. Greenfield lives in New York City with his wife and family.